VILLAGE D-tails

2nd Edition

Includes All Buildings and Accessories for All Department 56® Villages.

- The Original Snow Village® Series
- Dickens' Village Series®
- New England Village® Series
- Alpine Village Series®
- Christmas In The City® Series
- North Pole Series™
- Small Collections

  Historical Landmark Series®
  Meadowland
  Literary Classics® Collection
  Disney Parks Village™ Series
  North Pole Woods Collection
  Seasons Bay® Series
  American Pride™ Collection
  The Holy Land™ Collection

- And Other Related Series

Highlighting Historical Facts, Information, Secondary Market Values, and Trivia, all designed to enhance the hobby of collecting Department 56® Villages.

This Book Belongs To:

_____

VILLAGE D-TAILS

A Reference Source & Secondary Market Guide Serving
Department 56® Village Enthusiasts

To order books: 1-800-352-8039 (Toll-Free Inside the U.S. and Canada)

www.villaged-lights.com

Table Of Contents

On the Cover...
"Welcome to Windham Country Inn" 805528, from the New England Village® Series
by Department 56®, was released May 2009 and retired in December 2009. It is
one of the thousands of products documented in this edition. *(Photos courtesy of
Department 56®.)*

Village Timetable

1975: Christmas Holidays, The concept for a Christmas village was inspired by a Christmas Eve visit to the small town of Stillwater, MN on the banks of the St.Croix River. A group of friends from Bachman's Florists planned to enjoy a quiet dinner at the Lowell Inn, but none were aware of how it would change their lives and millions of others, too! As they rounded the bend in the road, they came upon a stunning site. This small turn-of-the-century river town was decked in full holiday decor. Christmas lights twinkled through the falling snowflakes, the colored lights refracted from icicles dangling from the eaves of the Victorian-styled buildings. Christmas wreaths and garland hung on and over the doors. Lampposts were wrapped in holly. Church bells were ringing. It brought back cherished memories of Christmas' long past, but not forgotten. Their mission from that point forward was to recreate that awesome scene for others to enjoy. Their plans were quickly put into motion.

1976: The set of six holiday hand-painted, ceramic houses was introduced by Bachman's Florists in Minneapolis. Although crudely made by today's standards, they were the beginnings of a hobby enjoyed by millions of collectors. The new products were inventoried into a new classification to distinguish them from other items offered at their stores. The division became known as Department 56 within the store. The buildings were known as The Original Snow Village. The following year, more building designs were offered to add to the tiny village.

1979: The original set of six buildings retired. Twelve new designs replaced them. The first accessories were issued to complement the village.

1984: Heritage Village Collections® were introduced, starting with The Dickens' Village Series® — seven original shops plus a church celebrating Christmas in Victorian England. The porcelain buildings featured a matte finish.

1986: New England Village® and Alpine Village Series® were added to the Heritage Village Collections. Snowbabies™ bisque figurines were introduced.

1987: Christmas in the City®, a Heritage Village, debuted representing New York City. The original Little Town of Bethlehem was issued.

1990: The cornerstone buildings of The North Pole Series™ became the fifth Heritage Village Collection.

• 1975 • 1976 • 1977 • 1978 • 1979 ⚊ 1984 • 1986 • 1987 • 1988 • 1989 • 1990 • 1992 • 1993 • 1994 •

1992: Department 56 was purchased by Forestmann Little, a New York Investment Firm. National Collector's Club (NCC) was formed.

1993: Department 56 was listed on NYSE under the symbol DFS. A Stock Exchange building commemorates the occasion in the CIC village.

1994: The Disney Parks Village™ Series and Snowbunnies® were introduced.

1996: First Profile Series® building — The Heinz® House — was produced. The Disney Parks Village™ Series became the first entire village to retire.

1997: The Tower of London became the premiere design in the Historical Landmark Series™.

1998: Season's Bay™ (the first year-around village) and Elfland™ (the residential suburb of North Pole) were introduced. The Haunted Mansion became the cornerstone piece of The Snow Village Halloween Village. Great Expectations became the first building in the Literary Classic® Collection.

1999: Detailed interiors added to select buildings within several villages. Little Town of Bethlehem Series® retired, and was replaced with The Holy Land™ series.

2000: North Pole Woods™ became an off-shoot of The North Pole Series™. Building animation became more prevalent in several villages.

2002: Entire Season's Bay Village retired.

2003: North Pole Woods retired.

2005: The Holy Land™ retired.

2008: *Village D-tails* — Reference resource and value guide for Department 56 Collectibles published its inaugural issue.

Active Villages:
The Original Snow Village®, Snow Village Halloween®, Dickens' Village Series®, New England Village®, Alpine Village Series®, Christmas in the City®, The North Pole Series™ and Elfland®. Literary Classic® Collection and The Historical Landmark Series®, as well as the Profiles Department 56® are on going, but may not have new introductions each year.

From Our Village To Yours...

Pioneer Communications, Inc. is pleased to publish this second issue of *Village D-tails*, made possible through the cooperation and resources of Department 56® — www.Department56.com, consumer services 952.943.4416.

The *Village D-tails* reference source and market guide has been designed to meet the needs of collectors, dealers, and insurance underwriters. Its purpose is to provide a photographic and written record for accurately identifying, dating, and pricing current and older lighted buildings and accessories produced by Department 56®, while also detailing the variations and rarities which contribute to collector value and enhance collecting and the "thrill of the hunt."

The organization of *Village D-tails* continues in the format proven successful by its predecessor. Each village has its own section, followed by its coordinating accessories. Listings are arranged chronologically, generally following the sequence used by Department 56 in its product literature and History List.

DATING NOTE
This second edition lists all product releases, including the first group of introductions in 2010 (released in December 2009). Since Department 56 has become part of Enesco LLC, their dating pattern has changed. The items previously released in December of 2009 are now considered 2010 releases and are noted as such in this guide. The diagram below explains the formatting for each listing.

The recent stated values in this issue are determined from actual secondary sales reported from around the country — representing auctions, brokers, and traditional retailers across the country. If more than one price was reported for an item, a range of the high and low values was stated. Of course, not every item listed has a reported sale during the last year. In these instances, the last reported price from the 2008 first edition was retained. Prices are affected by general economic conditions, regions of the country, rarity, condition, and even the type of sale. In most instances, it's unrealistic for sellers to expect to receive the top price in a range. Rather, the price ranges in this guide are provided as a reasonable guide of values. Be advised that, in the end, true worth is determined by what the buyer is willing to pay, and the seller is willing to accept.

If oversights are discovered in this edition, Pioneer asks that they be brought to the attention of our staff. Also, we invite anyone interested in participating as a contributing Secondary Market Dealer to contact our offices. We solicit your comments and suggestions. If we can be of more help in making your collecting more complete and enjoyable, or if you just want to say "hi," call 800.352.8039 or e-mail lkruger@pioneermagazines.com.

Linda Kruger, Executive Editor
Pioneer Communications, Inc., P.O. Box 306, Grundy Center, IA 50638
800.352.8039 • Fax 319.824.3414 • www.villaged-lights.com

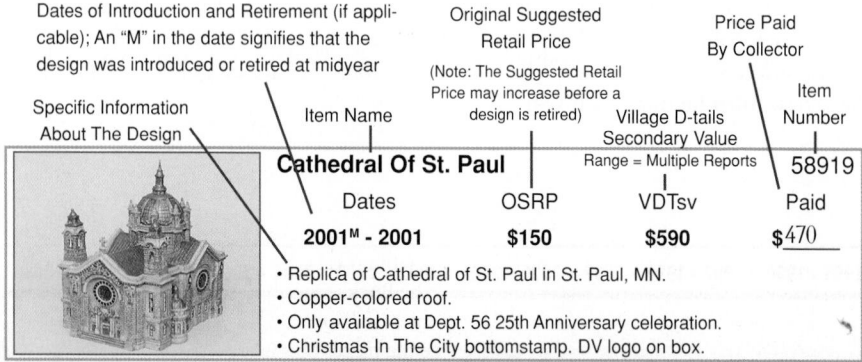

Dates of Introduction and Retirement (if applicable); An "M" in the date signifies that the design was introduced or retired at midyear

Original Suggested Retail Price
(Note: The Suggested Retail Price may increase before a design is retired)

Price Paid By Collector

Specific Information About The Design

Item Name

Village D-tails Secondary Value

Item Number

Cathedral Of St. Paul		Range = Multiple Reports	58919
Dates	OSRP	VDTsv	Paid
2001ᴹ - 2001	$150	$590	$470

- Replica of Cathedral of St. Paul in St. Paul, MN.
- Copper-colored roof.
- Only available at Dept. 56 25th Anniversary celebration.
- Christmas In The City bottomstamp. DV logo on box.

6

The Original Snow Village® Collection

"The first fall of snow is not only an event, it is a magical event. You go to bed in one kind of a world and wake up in another quite different, and if this is not enchantment then where is it to be found?" — J.B. Priestley (1894 – 1984)

Probably in Stillwater, Minnesota. The entire concept of developing a Christmas village began on one of those magical nights when huge snowflakes slowly fell from above. It was then that the inspiration of recreating that moment for others to enjoy was conceived. The year was 1976. Six crudely made hand-painted ceramic houses were inventoried into Department 56 of Bachman's Florists. The village became known as the The Original Snow Village® Collection. Snow Village and its spin-off, Snow Village Halloween, are the only two ceramic villages in the line. Most of the pieces are large, vividly colored and shiny. Being the oldest and having numerous introductions each year, it is also the largest village.

It represents Main Street Americana. From Drive-in Diners to Drive-in Movie Theaters, Football Stadiums to Filling Stations to Fire Stations: it's all here. Mom and Pop retail establishments are plentiful, but so are several familiar names. Special licensing agreements have brought several franchise opportunities to Snow Village entrepreneurs. Coca-Cola®, McDonald's®, Starbuck's®, Hershey's® and Krispy Kreme® are favorite places for the residents to patronize. Bikes from Harley-Davidson® and cars from Ford®, plus other Classic Cars, fill the roads and parking lots.

Residential homes are both simple and ornate. The American Architectural Series showcases several distinct architectural styles. Snow Village pieces can be displayed throughout the year to keep your display fresh and timely. Celebrate Valentine's Day, St. Patrick's Day, and Easter the D56 way. Patriotic pavilions and military recruitment centers make wonderful vignettes over the Fourth of July. Halloween has its own village.

Although there is plenty to do and see in town, the rural areas are not forgotten. The Fisherman's Nook Resort and Cabins, as well as the Buck's County Series and other unique pieces, provide plenty of outdoor activities and interest. This village may be huge, but that also provides the opportunity to pick and choose the pieces that have a personal meaning.

Mountain Lodge

50013

Dates	OSRP	VDTsv	Paid
1976 - 1979	**$20**	**$345**	$_____

- Colors on roof often vary.
- Must have a sunburst face on the end of the building to be authentic.
- Skis are sometimes broken or detached.

Gabled Cottage

50021

Dates	OSRP	VDTsv	Paid
1976 - 1979	**$20**	**$278**	$_____

- Color varies to the point where no two are alike.

The Inn

50039

Dates	OSRP	VDTsv	Paid
1976 - 1979	**$20**	**$420**	$_____

- Colors on roof often vary to the point where no two are alike.
- Watch for cracks in the porch supports.

Country Church

50047

Dates	OSRP	VDTsv	Paid
1976 - 1979	**$18**	**$217 - $345**	$_____

- Also known as Wayside Chapel.
- This is one of the most frequently imitated pieces in Snow Village. The lettering on the walls must be hand painted (as opposed to stamped on) to be authentic.

Steepled Church

50054

Dates	OSRP	VDTsv	Paid
1976 - 1979	**$25**	**$390**	$_____

- Colors on roof often vary.

Small Chalet

50062

Dates	OSRP	VDTsv	Paid
1976 - 1979	**$15**	**$395**	$_____

- Also known as Gingerbread Chalet.
- An often imitated design, it is difficult to authenticate.
- The color varies from tan to brown, and the number of flowers in window box varies.

Victorian House 50070

Dates	OSRP	VDTsv	Paid
1977 - 1979	**$30**	**$318 - $450**	$_____

- Color of building varies among rust/white, salmon/white, pink/white, and orange/yellow (no tree attached).
- Birds are often broken off, leaving lack of paint and glazing where the birds should be.

Mansion 50088

Dates	OSRP	VDTsv	Paid
1977 - 1979	**$30**	**$400 - $520**	$_____

- Color of roof often varies from forest green (first shipments) to turquoise.
- The amount of glaze on the forest green version varies while the turquoise version sometimes has flaking paint.

Stone Church (Version 1) 50096

Dates	OSRP	VDTsv	Paid
1977 - 1979	**$35**	**$595**	$_____

- Pale mint green building with very glossy finish.
- Right sides of front steps are flush.
- Steeple is approximately 10½" high as opposed to the 1979 version which is approximately 8½" high.

(Version 2)

	VDTsv	Paid
	$580	$_____

- Greenish-yellow building with less glossy finish.
- Right side of top front step is indented from bottom one.
- Both versions have felt glued to the bottom.
- The bell is sometimes missing from the bell tower.

Homestead 50112

Dates	OSRP	VDTsv	Paid
1978 - 1984	**$30**	**$178**	$_____

- Sometimes not painted or glazed well.
- Porch pillars, garland, and chimney are easily damaged.

General Store

50120

Dates	OSRP	VDTsv	Paid
1978 - 1980	$25	**See below**	

- Variations: white with gray roof (first shipments), tan with red roof, and gold with brown roof.
- Signs: on white "General Store Y & L Brothers," on tan "General Store S & L Brothers," on gold "General Store."

	VDTsv	Paid
White	$375-$420	$_____
Tan	$420-$440	$_____
Gold	$420-$475	$_____

Cape Cod

50138

Dates	OSRP	VDTsv	Paid
1978 - 1980	$20	$318	$_____

- The snow around the bottom of the piece detaches easily.

Nantucket

50146

Dates	OSRP	VDTsv	Paid
1978 - 1986	$25	$98	$_____

- Some pieces were manufactured with garland above front windows; others were not. Still others had the garland broken off. This is usually easy to determine.

Skating Rink / Duck Pond Set

50153

Dates	OSRP	VDTsv	Paid
1978 - 1979	$16	$700 - $995	$_____

- The trees are attached directly to the bases where their size and weight caused frequent breakage.
- The pieces in this set are often sold separately on the secondary market.
- Do not confuse this set with the 1982 Skating Pond set.
- Set of 2 includes the Skating Rink (features a snowman and a lighted tree) and the Duck Pond (features a bench, blue birds, and a lighted tree).

Small Double Trees (Blue Birds)   50161

Dates	OSRP	VDTsv	Paid
1978 - 1989	$13.50	$138	$_____

- Pieces with blue birds were shipped first.

(Red Birds Version)

	VDTsv	Paid
	$20	$_____

- Pieces with red birds began to appear in late 1979.
- Throughout the years there were mold changes with the design becoming more and more detailed.
- Amount of snow on the trees varies greatly.

Victorian   50542

Dates	OSRP	VDTsv	Paid
1979 - 1982	$30	$298	

- Peach (1st year) often has peeling paint.
- Gold with smooth walls (2nd year) ⎫ Defects are often
- Gold with clapboard walls (3rd year) ⎭ located along the bottom edges.

Knob Hill (Gray)   50559

Dates	OSRP	VDTsv	Paid
1979 - 1981	$30	$265 - $280	$_____

- This color is considered to be the first shipped.
- The paint on this version is commonly thin and bubbly.
- Cracks on the bottom are also common.
- Beware of chips along the steps.

(Yellow Version)

	VDTsv	Paid
	$200 - $245	$_____

- Beware of chips along the steps.
- The chimneys on both colors are very fragile.

Brownstone

50567

Dates	OSRP	VDTsv	Paid
1979 - 1981	**$36**	**$430 - $495**	

- Gray roof (first year) $_____
- Red roof (second year) $_____
- Beware of cracks near windows and chipped steps.

Log Cabin

50575

Dates	OSRP	VDTsv	Paid
1979 - 1981	**$22**	**$435 - $480**	$_____

- The skis by the door are very fragile and are often broken off.

Countryside Church

50583

Dates	OSRP	VDTsv	Paid
1979 - 1984	**$27.50**	**$182**	$_____

Stone Church

50591

Dates	OSRP	VDTsv	Paid
1979 - 1980	**$32**	**$500 - $875**	$_____

- Similar to 1977 Stone Church, this steeple is approximately 8½" high.
- Felt was glued to the bottom at the factory to conceal cracks and chips.

School House

50609

Dates	OSRP	VDTsv	Paid
1979 - 1982	**$30**	**$368**	$_____

- Varies from reddish-brown to dark brown.
- American flag is separate in box.

Tudor House

50617

Dates	OSRP	VDTsv	Paid
1979 - 1981	**$25**	**$180 - $295**	$_____

- Another design with the same name was issued in this village in 2001.

Mission Church

50625

Dates	OSRP	VDTsv	Paid
1979 - 1980	$30	$1295	$_____

• The bell is sometimes missing.

Mobile Home

50633

Dates	OSRP	VDTsv	Paid
1979 - 1980	$18	$1000 - $1595	$_____

• The paint is usually thin and bubbly.
• The trailer hitch is easily broken off and, therefore, is sometimes missing.

Giant Trees

50658

Dates	OSRP	VDTsv	Paid
1979 - 1982	$20	$138	$_____

Adobe House

50666

Dates	OSRP	VDTsv	Paid
1979 - 1980	$18	$1800 - $2350	$_____

• Factory imperfections such as dents and fingerprints are common.
• The extended roof beams are fragile.

Cathedral Church

50674

Dates	OSRP	VDTsv	Paid
1980 - 1981	$36	$2400 - $2900	$_____

• Inspired by St. Paul Cathedral in St. Paul, MN.
• Prone to crazing.
• Felt is sometimes glued on at the factory to conceal chips and cracks.

Stone Mill House

50682

Dates	OSRP	VDTsv	Paid
1980 - 1982	$30	$356	$_____

• Separate bag of oats (intended to be hung from block and tackle) is often missing and decreases value.
• Window areas are often thin and fragile.

Colonial Farm House   50709

Dates	OSRP	VDTsv	Paid
1980 - 1982	**$30**	**$220**	**$____**

• All Saints Church (1986) was also issued with this item number.

Town Church   50717

Dates	OSRP	VDTsv	Paid
1980 - 1982	**$33**	**$360**	**$____**

• Carriage House (1986) was also issued with this item number.

Train Station With 3 Train Cars   50856

Dates	OSRP	VDTsv	Paid
1980 - 1985	**$100**	**$375**	**$____**

• In the first year, the set included a Station with 6 windows in front (top, left). A year later, the Station was larger with 8 windows in front (bottom, left), and the OSRP increased to $110. Set of 4. All pieces light.

Train Station   50873

Dates	OSRP	VDTsv	Paid
1980 - 1981	**$42**	**$215**	**$____**

• Station has 6 windows in front and 1 in the door.
• It was sold individually as well as part of the above set.

3 Train Cars   50865

Dates	OSRP	VDTsv	Paid
1980 - 1982	**$65**	**$185**	**$____**

• It was sold individually as well as part of the above set.
• Set of 3. All pieces light.

Wooden Clapboard · 50725

Dates	OSRP	VDTsv	Paid
1981 - 1984	$32	$145	$_____

English Cottage · 50733

Dates	OSRP	VDTsv	Paid
1981 - 1982	$25	$220	$_____

• Toy Shop (1986) was also issued with this item number.

Barn · 50741

Dates	OSRP	VDTsv	Paid
1981 - 1984	$32	$255	$_____

• The cow at the side of the barn often has its ears and/or horns broken off.

Corner Store · 50768

Dates	OSRP	VDTsv	Paid
1981 - 1983	$30	$98	$_____

• Apothecary (1986) was also issued with this item number.

Bakery · 50776

Dates	OSRP	VDTsv	Paid
1981 - 1983	$30	$215	$_____

• Bakery (1986) was also issued with this item number.

English Church · 50784

Dates	OSRP	VDTsv	Paid
1981 - 1982	$30	$360	$_____

• Diner (1986) was also issued with this item number.
• Cross is separate in box.

Large Single Tree

50806

Dates	OSRP	VDTsv	Paid
1981 - 1989	**$17**	**$33**	$_____

• Throughout the years there were mold changes with the design becoming more and more detailed.
• Amount of snow on the trees varies greatly.

Skating Pond

50172

Dates	OSRP	VDTsv	Paid
1982 - 1984	**$25**	**$285**	$_____

• Snowman easily breaks off.
• Set of 2 includes pond and separate lighted trees.
• Do not confuse this piece with the 1978 Skating Pond/ Duck Set.

Street Car

50199

Dates	OSRP	VDTsv	Paid
1982 - 1984	**$16**	**$285**	$_____

• The "electrical hook-up" on roof often causes collectors to believe a pole should be included, but this is not so.
• Cathedral Church (1987) was also issued with this item number.

Centennial House

50202

Dates	OSRP	VDTsv	Paid
1982 - 1984	**$32**	**$245**	$_____

• The front steps and extension are fragile.

Carriage House

50210

Dates	OSRP	VDTsv	Paid
1982 - 1984	**$28**	**$200**	$_____

• Another design with the same name was issued in this village in 1986.

Pioneer Church

50229

Dates	OSRP	VDTsv	Paid
1982 - 1984	**$30**	**$305 - $395**	$_____

• The front steps are fragile.

Swiss Chalet

50237

Dates	OSRP	VDTsv	Paid
1982 - 1984	**$28**	**$250**	$_____

• Sometimes came from the factory with uneven and bubbly paint on the roof.

Bank

50245

Dates	OSRP	VDTsv	Paid
1982 - 1983	**$32**	**$295**	$_____

• Check areas around the staircase and revolving door.
• Dentist sign at stairway is often broken off.
• Cumberland House (1987) was also issued with this item number.

Gabled House

50814

Dates	OSRP	VDTsv	Paid
1982 - 1983	**$30**	**$395**	$_____

• Early samples are rust color; production pieces are white.
• Early release to GCC dealers.
• Red Barn (1987) was also issued with this item number.

Flower Shop

50822

Dates	OSRP	VDTsv	Paid
1982 - 1983	**$25**	**$418**	$_____

• Window frames vary from brown to green.
• Flowers are fragile.
• Jefferson School (1987) was also issued with this item number.

New Stone Church

50830

Dates	OSRP	VDTsv	Paid
1982 - 1984	**$32**	**$335**	$_____

• This is often not as glossy as most Snow Village pieces.
• Early release to GCC dealers.

Town Hall

50008

Dates	OSRP	VDTsv	Paid
1983 - 1984	**$32**	**$260 - $345**	$_____

• Metal weathervane is separate in box. It is rare to find a Town Hall with its weathervane.

Grocery

50016

Dates	OSRP	VDTsv	Paid
1983 - 1985	**$35**	**$345**	$_____

• The staircase is very fragile.

Victorian Cottage

50024

Dates	OSRP	VDTsv	Paid
1983 - 1984	**$35**	**$350**	$_____

Governor's Mansion

50032

Dates	OSRP	VDTsv	Paid
1983 - 1985	**$32**	**$198**	$_____

• The ironwork for the cupola is separate in box and is often missing.

Turn Of The Century

50040

Dates	OSRP	VDTsv	Paid
1983 - 1986	**$36**	**$175**	$_____

• Bottom inscription reads "Turn The Time Of Century."
• The three chimneys are very fragile, especially the one on the center peak.

Gingerbread House

50253

Dates	OSRP	VDTsv	Paid
1983 - 1984	**$24**	**$380**	$_____

• Besides lighted version, there is also a very rare non-lighted bank with a coin slot that was sold as a giftware item as opposed to part of Snow Village.

Village Church

50261

Dates	OSRP	VDTsv	Paid
1983 - 1984	**$30**	**$415**	$_____

• Very similar to Parish Church (1984).
• Early release to GCC dealers.

Gothic Church

50288

Dates	OSRP	VDTsv	Paid
1983 - 1986	**$36**	**$220**	$_____

• The cross at the top is easily broken off.

Parsonage

50296

Dates	OSRP	VDTsv	Paid
1983 - 1985	**$35**	**$325**	$_____

• The cross atop the gable is easily broken off.

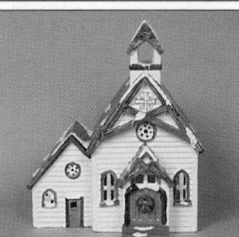

Wooden Church

50318

Dates	OSRP	VDTsv	Paid
1983 - 1985	**$30**	**$269**	$_____

Fire Station

50326

Dates	OSRP	VDTsv	Paid
1983 - 1984	**$32**	**$350 - $385**	$_____

• Varies with and without Dalmatian. Close examination should reveal whether a piece without a Dalmatian was made that way or if the dog was broken off.

English Tudor

50334

Dates	OSRP	VDTsv	Paid
1983 - 1985	**$30**	**$185**	$_____

• Chimneys are fragile.

Chateau

50849

Dates	OSRP	VDTsv	Paid
1983 - 1984	**$35**	**$375**	$_____

• This is often not as glossy as most Snow Village pieces.
• Early release to GCC dealers.

Main Street House
50059

Dates	OSRP	VDTsv	Paid
1984 - 1986	$27	$195	$_____

• Early release to GCC dealers.

Stratford House
50075

Dates	OSRP	VDTsv	Paid
1984 - 1986	$28	$155	$_____

Haversham House
50083

Dates	OSRP	VDTsv	Paid
1984 - 1987	$37	$110	$_____

• Early release to GCC dealers. These are larger, heavier, more impressive, and subject to more defects than those shipped later. **VDTsv: $240**   Paid:$_____

Galena House
50091

Dates	OSRP	VDTsv	Paid
1984 - 1985	$32	$370	$_____

• The front steps are fragile.

River Road House
50105

Dates	OSRP	VDTsv	Paid
1984 - 1987	$36	$136 - $146	$_____

• Early release to GCC dealers. These have window above door and transoms above lower front windows cut out. Later ones do not.

Delta House
50121

Dates	OSRP	VDTsv	Paid
1984 - 1986	$32	$245	$_____

• Ironwork for the top of the tower is separate in box and is often missing.

Bayport

50156

Dates	OSRP	VDTsv	Paid
1984 - 1986	**$30**	**$173 - $195**	**$_____**

Congregational Church

50342

Dates	OSRP	VDTsv	Paid
1984 - 1985	**$28**	**$490 - $535**	**$_____**

• It is rare to find one with a straight steeple.
• The steeple is easily broken.

Trinity Church

50350

Dates	OSRP	VDTsv	Paid
1984 - 1986	**$32**	**$295**	**$_____**

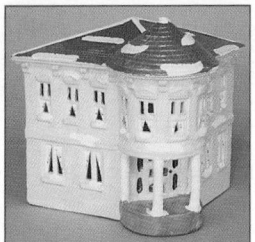

Summit House

50369

Dates	OSRP	VDTsv	Paid
1984 - 1985	**$28**	**$320 - $350**	**$_____**

• The porch columns are crooked on almost all examples of this design.
• Do not handle by porch columns.

New School House

50377

Dates	OSRP	VDTsv	Paid
1984 - 1986	**$35**	**$235**	**$_____**

• American flag is separate in box.

Parish Church

50393

Dates	OSRP	VDTsv	Paid
1984 - 1986	**$32**	**$248**	**$_____**

• Very similar to Village Church (1993).

Stucco Bungalow

50458

Dates	OSRP	VDTsv	Paid
1985 - 1986	$30	$300 - $365	$_____

Williamsburg House

50466

Dates	OSRP	VDTsv	Paid
1985 - 1988	$37	$133	$_____

- Entryway attachment is fragile.
- The paint on the building is known to suddenly develop cracks under the glaze after a period of time.

Plantation House

50474

Dates	OSRP	VDTsv	Paid
1985 - 1987	$37	$63 - $148	$_____

- Do not handle by porch columns.

Church Of The Open Door

50482

Dates	OSRP	VDTsv	Paid
1985 - 1988	$34	$105	$_____

- Despite its name, the door on this design is closed.

Spruce Place

50490

Dates	OSRP	VDTsv	Paid
1985 - 1987	$33	$198	$_____

- The area around the porch and steps is easily damaged.

Duplex

50504

Dates	OSRP	VDTsv	Paid
1985 - 1987	$35	$118	$_____

Depot And Train With 2 Train Cars

50512

Dates	OSRP	VDTsv	Paid
1985 - 1988	$65	$91 - $120	$_____

• There are 3 variations:
1. Brown Depot with gray cornerstones (top) and Train Car with yellow windows.
2. Brick Depot without cornerstones and Train Car with yellow windows (bottom).
3. Brick Depot without cornerstones and Train Car with white windows.
• Though referred to as a set of 2, it includes the Depot, 2-piece train, and a ceramic track.

Ridgewood

50520

Dates	OSRP	VDTsv	Paid
1985 - 1987	$35	$165	$_____

• Do not handle by porch columns.

Waverly Place

50415

Dates	OSRP	VDTsv	Paid
1986 - 1986	$35	$325	$_____

• Inspired by Gingerbread Mansion in Ferndale, CA.
• Early release to GCC dealers.
• Squirrel is often missing.

Twin Peaks

50423

Dates	OSRP	VDTsv	Paid
1986 - 1986	$32	$276	$_____

• The peaks are easily damaged.
• Early release to GCC dealers.

2101 Maple

50431

Dates	OSRP	VDTsv	Paid
1986 - 1986	$32	$280	$_____

• The turret peak is easily damaged.
• Early release to GCC dealers.

Lincoln Park Duplex 50601

Dates	OSRP	VDTsv	Paid
1986 - 1988	**$33**	**$98**	$_____

Sonoma House 50628

Dates	OSRP	VDTsv	Paid
1986 - 1988	**$33**	**$148**	$_____

• Early release to GCC dealers.

Highland Park House 50636

Dates	OSRP	VDTsv	Paid
1986 - 1988	**$35**	**$165**	$_____

• The chimney is fragile.
• Early release to GCC dealers.

Beacon Hill House 50652

Dates	OSRP	VDTsv	Paid
1986 - 1988	**$31**	**$175**	$_____

• This design is often confused with the Pacific Heights House because they were mislabeled in the Department 56 Snow Village Collectors Album.

Pacific Heights House 50660

Dates	OSRP	VDTsv	Paid
1986 - 1988	**$33**	**$88**	$_____

• This design is often confused with the Beacon Hill House because they were mislabeled in the Department 56 Snow Village Collectors Album.

Ramsey Hill House 50679

Dates	OSRP	VDTsv	Paid
1986 - 1989	**$36**	**$65 - $85**	$_____

• Early release to GCC dealers. Pieces in early release are brighter than those shipped later.

Saint James Church

50687

Dates	OSRP	VDTsv	Paid
1986 - 1988	$37	$85 - $96	$_____

• The cross on the center peak is easily broken off.

All Saints Church

50709

Dates	OSRP	VDTsv	Paid
1986 - 1997	$38	$25 - $58	$_____

• Colonial Farm House (1980) was also issued with this item number.

Carriage House

50717

Dates	OSRP	VDTsv	Paid
1986 - 1988	$29	$95	$_____

• Town Church (1980) was also issued with this item number.
• Another design with the same name was issued in this village in 1982.

Toy Shop

50733

Dates	OSRP	VDTsv	Paid
1986 - 1990	$36	$50 - $60	$_____

• Inspired by the Finch Building in Hastings, MN.
• Decorative attachments on the roof are fragile.
• English Cottage (1981) was also issued with this item number.

Apothecary

50768

Dates	OSRP	VDTsv	Paid
1986 - 1990	$34	$78	$_____

• Sleeves often read "Antique Shop."
• Inspired by the former City Hall in Hastings, MN.
• Corner Store (1981) was also issued with this item number.

Bakery

50776

Dates	OSRP	VDTsv	Paid
1986 - 1991	$35	$48 - $57	$_____

• Inspired by the Scofield Building in Northfield, MN.
• The awnings are fragile.
• Bakery (1981) was also issued with this item number.

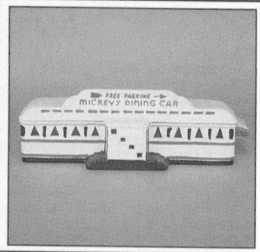

Diner 50784

Dates	OSRP	VDTsv	Paid
1986 - 1987	$22	$495	$_____

- Also known as Mickey's and Mickey's Diner.
- Inspired by Mickey's Diner in St. Paul, MN.
- English Church (1981) was also issued with this item number.

St. Anthony Hotel & Post Office 50067

Dates	OSRP	VDTsv	Paid
1987 - 1989	$40	$50 - $88	$_____

- American flag is separate in box.

Snow Village Factory 50130

Dates	OSRP	VDTsv	Paid
1987 - 1989	$45	$60 - $74	$_____

- Smokestack is a separate piece from building.
- The dark burgundy paint on the building is known to suddenly develop cracks under the glaze after a period of time.

Cathedral Church 50199

Dates	OSRP	VDTsv	Paid
1987 - 1990	$50	$71	$_____

- Street Car (1982) was also issued with this item number.

Cumberland House 50245

Dates	OSRP	VDTsv	Paid
1987 - 1995	$42	$40 - $65	$_____

- Do not handle by the columns.
- Bank (1982) was also issued with this item number.

Springfield House 50270

Dates	OSRP	VDTsv	Paid
1987 - 1990	$40	$53 - $125	$_____

Lighthouse

50300

Dates	OSRP	VDTsv	Paid
1987 - 1988	**$36**	**$375**	$_____

- There are 2 variations:
  Tower painted white and unglazed.
  Tower painted off-white and glazed.
- Do not handle by the tower.

Red Barn

50814

Dates	OSRP	VDTsv	Paid
1987 - 1992	**$38**	**$68 - $98**	$_____

- Early release to GCC dealers.
- Gabled House (1982) was also issued with this item number.

Jefferson School

50822

Dates	OSRP	VDTsv	Paid
1987 - 1991	**$36**	**$178**	$_____

- Early release to GCC dealers.
- Bell is sometimes missing from tower.
- Flower Shop (1982) was also issued with this item number.

Farm House

50890

Dates	OSRP	VDTsv	Paid
1987 - 1992	**$40**	**$45 - $78**	$_____

- Do not handle by porch columns or railings.

Fire Station No. 2

50911

Dates	OSRP	VDTsv	Paid
1987 - 1989	**$40**	**$145**	$_____

- Staircase is easily damaged.
- Early release to GCC dealers.

Snow Village Resort Lodge

50920

Dates	OSRP	VDTsv	Paid
1987 - 1989	**$55**	**$115**	$_____

Village Market   50440

Dates	OSRP	VDTsv	Paid
1988 - 1991	**$39**	**$45 - $78**	

- Color varies from mint green to cream.
- Sisal tree on top of roof is packaged separately in the box and is often missing.
- Early release to GCC dealers.

Kenwood House   50547

Dates	OSRP	VDTsv	Paid
1988 - 1990	**$50**	**$54 - $95**	$_____

- Do not handle by porch columns.
- Early release to GCC dealers.

Maple Ridge Inn   51217

Dates	OSRP	VDTsv	Paid
1988 - 1990	**$55**	**$30 - $60**	$_____

- Inspired by the actual Maple Ridge Inn in Cambridge, NY. The home once belonged to relatives of painter Grandma Moses who visited there often.
- Early release to GCC dealers.

Village Station And Train   51225

Dates	OSRP	VDTsv	Paid
1988 - 1992	**$65**	**$86**	$_____

- Train cars do not light.
- Set of 4.

Cobblestone Antique Shop   51233

Dates	OSRP	VDTsv	Paid
1988 - 1992	**$36**	**$35 - $53**	$_____

- On rare occasion, the silk-screened windows detach.

Corner Cafe
51241

Dates	OSRP	VDTsv	Paid
1988 - 1991	$37	$50 - $64	$_____

• On rare occasion, the silk-screened windows detach.

Single Car Garage
51250

Dates	OSRP	VDTsv	Paid
1988 - 1990	$22	$42 - $78	$_____

• In many cases, the box must be broken in order to safely remove the piece.
• The tree attached to the back is indeed supposed to have holes drilled in it.

Home Sweet Home
51268

Dates	OSRP	VDTsv	Paid
1988 - 1991	$60	$90	$_____

• Inspired by the East Hampton, NY historic home of John Howard Payne, composer of *Home Sweet Home*.
• The windmill blades are packaged separately in the box and are made of metal.
• Set of 2.

Redeemer Church
51276

Dates	OSRP	VDTsv	Paid
1988 - 1992	$42	$42 - $125	$_____

Service Station
51284

Dates	OSRP	VDTsv	Paid
1988 - 1991	$37.50	$79 - $125	$_____

• Also known as Big Bill's Service Station which is the inscription on the bottom.
• Set of 2 includes Station and pumps.

Stonehurst House   51403

Dates	OSRP	VDTsv	Paid
1988 - 1994	**$37.50**	**$20 - $48**	$_____

Palos Verdes   51411

Dates	OSRP	VDTsv	Paid
1988 - 1990	**$37.50**	**$49 - $58**	$_____

• A small potted tree is packaged separately in the box.

Jingle Belle Houseboat   51144

Dates	OSRP	VDTsv	Paid
1989 - 1991	**$42**	**$168**	$_____

• Bell is packaged separately in box and is often missing.

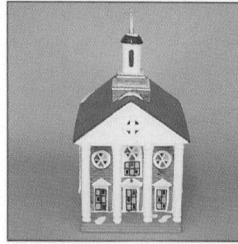

Colonial Church   51195

Dates	OSRP	VDTsv	Paid
1989 - 1992	**$60**	**$48 - $68**	$_____

• The gray paint at steps and porch sometimes curls up and peels off.
• Do not handle by the columns.
• Early release to GCC dealers.

North Creek Cottage   51209

Dates	OSRP	VDTsv	Paid
1989 - 1992	**$45**	**$49 - $75**	$_____

• Do not handle by the columns.
• Early release to GCC dealers.

Paramount Theater   51420

Dates	OSRP	VDTsv	Paid
1989 - 1993	**$42**	**$138**	$_____

• Decals make cleaning this piece a delicate job.

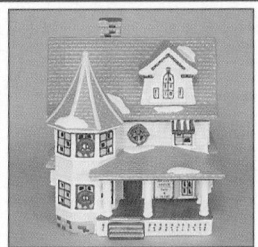

Doctor's House

51438

Dates	OSRP	VDTsv	Paid
1989 - 1992	**$56**	**$48 - $90**	$_____

• Do not handle by columns.

Courthouse

51446

Dates	OSRP	VDTsv	Paid
1989 - 1993	**$65**	**$118**	$_____

• Inspired by the Gibson County Courthouse in Princetown, IN.
• Do not handle by tower.

Village Warming House

51454

Dates	OSRP	VDTsv	Paid
1989 - 1992	**$42**	**$25 - $48**	$_____

• Includes 4 removable sisal trees.

J. Young's Granary

51497

Dates	OSRP	VDTsv	Paid
1989 - 1992	**$45**	**$38 - $53**	$_____

Pinewood Log Cabin

51500

Dates	OSRP	VDTsv	Paid
1989 - 1995	**$37.50**	**$30 - $58**	$_____

• Do not handle by porch columns.
• Early release to GCC dealers.

56 Flavors Ice Cream Parlor

51519

Dates	OSRP	VDTsv	Paid
1990 - 1992	**$42**	**$98**	$_____

• Stem on cherry is often broken off and is often missing.
• "Parlor" decal comes off easily.
• Early release to GCC dealers.

Morningside House
51527

Dates	OSRP	VDTsv	Paid
1990 - 1992	**$45**	**$38 - $95**	$_____

• Includes 5 removable sisal trees.

Mainstreet Hardware Store
51535

Dates	OSRP	VDTsv	Paid
1990 - 1993	**$42**	**$88**	$_____

• Sample pieces have blue awnings and window trim. They were changed to green for the actual production.

Village Realty
51543

Dates	OSRP	VDTsv	Paid
1990 - 1993	**$42**	**$42 - $58**	$_____

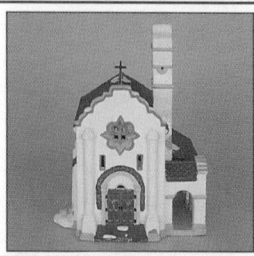

Spanish Mission Church
51551

Dates	OSRP	VDTsv	Paid
1990 - 1992	**$42**	**$55 - $98**	$_____

• Inspired by the then-named Enga Memorial Chapel in Minneapolis, MN.
• Bell in tower is easily lost.
• Crosses on roof and in graveyard are fragile.

Prairie House
51560

Dates	OSRP	VDTsv	Paid
1990 - 1993	**$42**	**$98**	$_____

• American Architecture Series.
• Includes 2 removable sisal trees.

Queen Anne Victorian
51578

Dates	OSRP	VDTsv	Paid
1990 - 1996	**$48**	**$59 - $115**	$_____

• American Architecture Series.
• Do not handle by columns.

The Christmas Shop
50970

Dates	OSRP	VDTsv	Paid
1991 - 1996	$37.50	$40 - $54	$_____

• Early release to GCC and Showcase dealers.

Oak Grove Tudor
54003

Dates	OSRP	VDTsv	Paid
1991 - 1994	$42	$35 - $65	$_____

• Early release to Showcase dealers.

The Honeymooner Motel
54011

Dates	OSRP	VDTsv	Paid
1991 - 1993	$42	$68 - $75	$_____

• The moon and stars symbol on the peak are easily damaged.
• Early release to Showcase dealers.

Village Greenhouse
54020

Dates	OSRP	VDTsv	Paid
1991 - 1995	$35	$37 - $78	$_____

• The greenhouse "glass" often discolors with age.

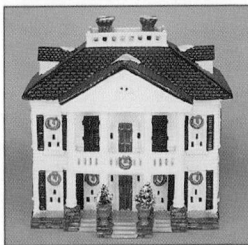

Southern Colonial
54038

Dates	OSRP	VDTsv	Paid
1991 - 1994	$48	$48	$_____

• American Architecture Series.
• 2 small sisal trees are separate in the box.
• Do not handle by columns or railings.

Gothic Farmhouse
54046

Dates	OSRP	VDTsv	Paid
1991 - 1997	$48	$58 - $70	$_____

• American Architecture Series.
• Do not handle by columns.

Finklea's Finery: Costume Shop   54054

Dates	OSRP	VDTsv	Paid
1991 - 1993	$45	$49 - $58	$_____

• Some decals detach easily.

Jack's Corner Barber Shop   54062

Dates	OSRP	VDTsv	Paid
1991 - 1994	$42	$60 - $95	$_____

• The turret is easily damaged.

Double Bungalow   54070

Dates	OSRP	VDTsv	Paid
1991 - 1994	$45	$45 - $58	$_____

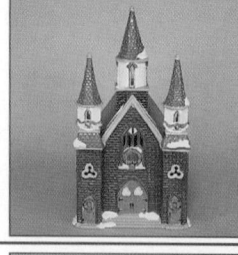

Grandma's Cottage   54208

Dates	OSRP	VDTsv	Paid
1992 - 1996	$42	$47 - $75	$_____

• Do not handle by columns or railings.
• Early release to GCC dealers.

St. Luke's Church   54216

Dates	OSRP	VDTsv	Paid
1992 - 1994	$45	$41 - $78	$_____

• Early release to GCC dealers.

Village Post Office   54224

Dates	OSRP	VDTsv	Paid
1992 - 1995	$35	$47 - $99	$_____

• Early release to Showcase dealers.

Al's TV Shop 54232

Dates	OSRP	VDTsv	Paid
1992 - 1995	$40	$38 - $48	$_____

• Television antenna is packaged separately in the box.

Good Shepherd Chapel & Church School 54240

Dates	OSRP	VDTsv	Paid
1992 - 1996	$72	$53 - $74	$_____

• Though designed to do so, the two pieces do not always fit together well.
• Decals fall off easily.
• Set of 2.

Print Shop & Village News 54259

Dates	OSRP	VDTsv	Paid
1992 - 1994	$37.50	$39 - $88	$_____

• Do not handle by columns.

Hartford House 54267

Dates	OSRP	VDTsv	Paid
1992 - 1995	$55	$48 - $100	$_____

• Do not handle by columns or railings.

Village Vet And Pet Shop 54275

Dates	OSRP	VDTsv	Paid
1992 - 1995	$32	$70 - $75	$_____

• Early pieces read "Vetrinary."
• Decals fall off easily.

Craftsman Cottage 54372

Dates	OSRP	VDTsv	Paid
1992 - 1995	$55	$44 - $54	$_____

• American Architecture Series.

Village Station

54380

Dates	OSRP	VDTsv	Paid
1992 - 1997	**$65**	**$76 - $92**	**$_____**

• Decals fall off easily.

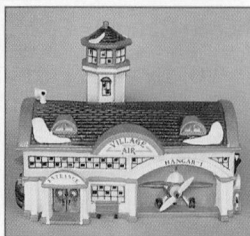

Airport

54399

Dates	OSRP	VDTsv	Paid
1992 - 1996	**$60**	**$158 - $188**	**$_____**

• Loudspeaker and propeller are easily damaged.
• Do not handle by tower.

Nantucket Renovation

54410

Dates	OSRP	VDTsv	Paid
1993 - 1993	**$55**	**$30 - $55**	**$_____**

• First limited (year of production) Snow Village design.
• Concept is how a "remodeled" Nantucket might appear 15 years after the original one was issued.
• Packaged in special "blueprint" sleeve.

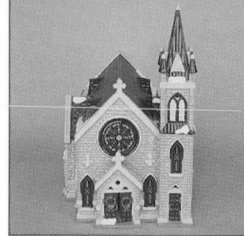

Mount Olivet Church

54429

Dates	OSRP	VDTsv	Paid
1993 - 1996	**$65**	**$57 - $78**	**$_____**

• Crosses on peaks are easily damaged.

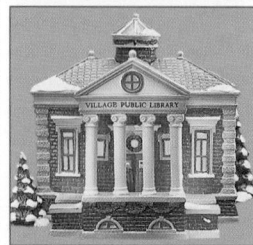

Village Public Library

54437

Dates	OSRP	VDTsv	Paid
1993 - 1997	**$55**	**$195**	**$_____**

• Do not handle by columns.

Woodbury House

54445

Dates	OSRP	VDTsv	Paid
1993 - 1996	**$45**	**$50 - $58**	**$_____**

• Do not handle by columns or railing.

Hunting Lodge — 54453

Dates	OSRP	VDTsv	Paid
1993 - 1996	**$50**	**$110 - $189**	$_____

• Antlers are easily damaged.

Dairy Barn — 54461

Dates	OSRP	VDTsv	Paid
1993 - 1997	**$55**	**$76 - $128**	$_____

• Weathervane is packaged separately in the box.

Dinah's Drive-In — 54470

Dates	OSRP	VDTsv	Paid
1993 - 1996	**$45**	**$110 - $134**	$_____

• The name "Dinah" was inspired by the line "Someone's in the kitchen with Dinah" in the song *I've Been Working on the Railroad.*
• The straw in the rooftop milk shake is easily damaged.

Snowy Hills Hospital — 54488

Dates	OSRP	VDTsv	Paid
1993 - 1996	**$48**	**$210**	$_____

• A portion of the proceeds benefited AmFAR—the American Foundation for AIDS Research.
• Do not handle by columns.

Fisherman's Nook Cabins — 54615

Dates	OSRP	VDTsv	Paid
1994 - 1999	**$50**	**$58 - $72**	$_____

• Cabins differ only by names "Bass" and "Trout."
• Railings are very fragile.
• Set of 2.

Fisherman's Nook Resort

54607

Dates	OSRP	VDTsv	Paid
1994 - 1999	**$75**	**$45 - $110**	$_____

- Sign on side is very fragile.

Snow Village Starter Set

54623

Dates	OSRP	VDTsv	Paid
1994 - 1996	**$50**	**$30 - $90**	$_____

- First available at GCC Open House event in November 1994.
- Set of 6 includes **Shady Oak Church** (named for street adjacent to Department 56's office complex), "Sunday School Serenade," trees, and snow.

Wedding Chapel

54640

Dates	OSRP	VDTsv	Paid
1994 - 2001	**$55**	**$85 - $168**	$_____

- Bell is attached in tower.

Federal House

54658

Dates	OSRP	VDTsv	Paid
1994 - 1997	**$50**	**$49 - $65**	$_____

- American Architecture Series.
- Do not handle by columns.

Carmel Cottage

54666

Dates	OSRP	VDTsv	Paid
1994 - 1997	**$48**	**$28 - $60**	$_____

Skate & Ski Shop — 54674

Dates	OSRP	VDTsv	Paid
1994 - 1998	$50	$38 - $56	$_____

• Sign and snow extending from front are easily damaged.

Glenhaven House — 54682

Dates	OSRP	VDTsv	Paid
1994 - 1997	$45	$45 - $98	$_____

• Do not handle by columns.

Coca-Cola® Brand Bottling Plant — 54690

Dates	OSRP	VDTsv	Paid
1994 - 1997	$65	$55 - $76	$_____

• First pieces do not have soda cases on loading platform, though some later pieces have lost theirs. Close examination should reveal this.
• Licensed by Coca-Cola®.

Marvel's Beauty Salon — 54704

Dates	OSRP	VDTsv	Paid
1994 - 1997	$37.50	$37 - $75	$_____

Christmas Cove Lighthouse — 54836

Dates	OSRP	VDTsv	Paid
1995M - 2001	$60	$74	$_____

• First lighthouse with separate bulb at top of tower.
• The top comes off easily and is susceptible to damage because it is a separate piece and does not fit tightly.

Coca-Cola® Brand Corner Drugstore — 54844

Dates	OSRP	VDTsv	Paid
1995M - 1998	$55	$74 - $89	$_____

• Early samples have red "label" around the bottle at the top of the sign.
• Licensed by Coca-Cola®.

Peppermint Porch Day Care

54852

Dates	OSRP	VDTsv	Paid
1995^M - 1997	$45	$57 - $78	$_____

• Early samples read "Peppermint Place."
• Do not handle by columns.

Snow Carnival Ice Palace

54850

Dates	OSRP	VDTsv	Paid
1995 - 1998	$95	$345	$_____

• Inspired by the snow castles constructed during carnivals in Minnesota.
• Acrylic turrets can become unglued or yellow with age.
• Set of 2 includes building and gate.

Pisa Pizza

54851

Dates	OSRP	VDTsv	Paid
1995 - 1998	$35	$53 - $78	$_____

Village Police Station

54853

Dates	OSRP	VDTsv	Paid
1995 - 1998	$48	$72 - $140	$_____

• Acrylic light globes are easily dislodged.
• Do not handle by attached doughnut shop.

Holly Brothers Garage

54854

Dates	OSRP	VDTsv	Paid
1995 - 1998	$48	$48 - $68	$_____

• Do not handle by columns or gas pumps.

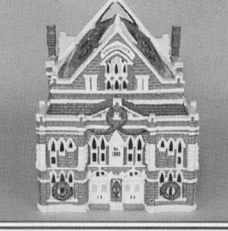

Ryman Auditorium

54855

Dates	OSRP	VDTsv	Paid
1995 - 1997	$75	$118	$_____

• Inspired by country music's Ryman Auditorium in Nashville, TN, once home to the Grand Ole Opry.
• Licensed by Opryland USA, Inc.

Dutch Colonial

54856

Dates	OSRP	VDTsv	Paid
1995 - 1996	**$45**	**$41 - $48**	$_____

• American Architecture Series.

Beacon Hill Victorian

54857

Dates	OSRP	VDTsv	Paid
1995 - 1998	**$60**	**$49 - $66**	$_____

• Do not handle by columns or railing.

Bowling Alley

54858

Dates	OSRP	VDTsv	Paid
1995 - 1998	**$42**	**$54**	$_____

Starbucks Coffee®

54859

Dates	OSRP	VDTsv	Paid
1995 - 2000	**$48**	**$148 - $295**	$_____

• Do not handle by roof pediment.
• Licensed by Starbucks Coffee®.

Nick's Tree Farm

54871

Dates	OSRP	VDTsv	Paid
1996ᴹ - 1999	**$40**	**$58**	$_____

• Set of 10 includes Nick, hut, and 8 sisal trees.
• The coat, hat, and lantern hanging on the hut often come unglued.

Smokey Mountain Retreat

54872

Dates	OSRP	VDTsv	Paid
1996ᴹ - 2000	**$65**	**$98**	$_____

• Chimney "smokes" when used with Village Magic Smoke®. Smoking element sometimes leaks, requiring something being placed under it for protection.
• Do not handle by railings or columns.

Boulder Springs House

54873

Dates	OSRP	VDTsv	Paid
1996^M - 1997	$60	$42 - $67	$_____

• Do not handle by columns or railing.

Reindeer Bus Depot

54874

Dates	OSRP	VDTsv	Paid
1996^M - 1997	$42	$45 - $64	$_____

• Do not handle by columns, sign, or bench.

Rockabilly Records

54880

Dates	OSRP	VDTsv	Paid
1996 - 1998	$45	$45	$_____

Christmas Lake High School

54881

Dates	OSRP	VDTsv	Paid
1996 - 1999	$52	$128	$_____

• Attached basketball hoop is easily damaged.

Birch Run Ski Chalet

54882

Dates	OSRP	VDTsv	Paid
1996 - 1999	$60	$145	$_____

• Do not handle by columns or railings.

Rosita's Cantina

54883

Dates	OSRP	VDTsv	Paid
1996 - 1999	$50	$225	$_____

• Lighting fixtures are easily damaged when removing piece from box.

Shingle Victorian   54884

Dates	OSRP	VDTsv	Paid
1996 - 1999	$55	$51 - $98	$_____

• American Architecture Series.
• Do not handle by columns or railings.

The Secret Garden Florist   54885

Dates	OSRP	VDTsv	Paid
1996 - 2001	$50	$58	$_____

• The awning is cloth.
• Sign is separate in box.
• A similar design was produced for Bachman's in 1997. See the Special Design section.

Harley-Davidson® Motorcycle Shop   54886

Dates	OSRP	VDTsv	Paid
1996 - 2002	$65	$132 - $138	$_____

• The gray paint on the front overhang's supports often peels. They are also very fragile.
• Licensed by Harley-Davidson®.

Mainstreet Gift Shop   54887

Dates	OSRP	VDTsv	Paid
1997ᴹ - 1997	$50	$30 - $59	$_____

• To commemorate the 20th Anniversary of GCC, this design was available only through GCC member stores.
• Two signs are included—one with the GCC logo, and a blank one so dealers could personalize the design.

Snow Village Start A Tradition Set   54902

Dates	OSRP	VDTsv	Paid
1997ᴹ - 1998	$100	$75 - $130	$_____

• It was first available for $75 during the 1997 Homes for the Holidays event.
• Set of 8 includes **Kringles Toy Shop**, **Nikki's Cocoa Shop**, "Saturday Morning Downtown" accessory, trees, snow, and road.
• Nikki's Cocoa Shop's hang-tag reads "Kringle's Cocoa Shop."
• The handle on the mug is fragile.

Old Chelsea Mansion
54903

Dates	OSRP	VDTsv	Paid
1997^M - 1998	$85	$64 - $98	$_____

• Inspired by the New York, NY home of Clement C. Moore, author of *A Visit from St. Nicholas*. Includes a book containing the classic poem and information about Moore and the mansion.

New Hope Church
54904

Dates	OSRP	VDTsv	Paid
1997^M - 1998	$60	$48 - $165	$_____

Ronald McDonald® House, The House That ♥ Built
08960

Dates	OSRP	VDTsv	Paid
1997^M - 1997	Promo	$190	$_____

• A limited edition design, this was made available as a fund raiser during the November 1997 Homes for the Holidays event. Proceeds benefited Ronald McDonald® House Charities.

Christmas Barn Dance
54910

Dates	OSRP	VDTsv	Paid
1997 - 1999	$65	$43 - $78	$_____

Italianate Villa
54911

Dates	OSRP	VDTsv	Paid
1997 - 2001	$55	$60	$_____

• American Architecture Series.
• Spire is separate in box.
• Do not handle by columns.

Farm House
54912

Dates	OSRP	VDTsv	Paid
1997 - 2000	$50	$58 - $65	$_____

• Do not handle by columns.

Hershey's® Chocolate Shop 54913

Dates	OSRP	VDTsv	Paid
1997 - 2000	$55	$145	$_____

• The billboard on the roof is very fragile.
• Licensed by Hershey Foods.

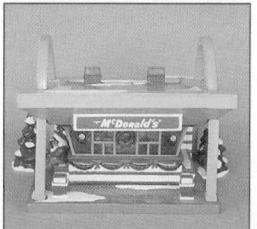

McDonald's® 54914

Dates	OSRP	VDTsv	Paid
1997 - 1999	$65	$168	$_____

• First time people were included as an attachment.
• Because of the attachments and the arches, extra care should be taken when handling this piece.
• Licensed by McDonald's®.

Gracie's Dry Goods & General Store 54915

Dates	OSRP	VDTsv	Paid
1997 - 2000	$70	$50 - $78	$_____

• Do not handle by columns.
• Set of 2 includes Store and gas pumps.
• Licensed by Rapala.

Rollerama Roller Rink 54916

Dates	OSRP	VDTsv	Paid
1997 - 1999	$56	$47 - $78	$_____

• The lights on the building are functional.
• Do not handle by the front entryway.

Linden Hills Country Club 54917

Dates	OSRP	VDTsv	Paid
1997 - 2001	$60	$57 - $75	$_____

• Metal lanterns light from within.
• Linden Hills is an area near downtown Minneapolis, close to Lake Harriet.
• Set of 2 includes building and sign.

The Brandon Bungalow 54918

Dates	OSRP	VDTsv	Paid
1997 - 1999	$55	$98	$_____

• Brandon is a small resort town in northern Minnesota.

Rock Creek Mill House

54932

Dates	OSRP	VDTsv	Paid
1998^M - 1998	$64	$57 - $88	$_____

• Early samples have a glossy finish. Production pieces have a matte finish.
• The water wheel comes loose on occasion.

Glossy Edition VDTsv = $95 $_____

Carnival Carousel

54933

Dates	OSRP	VDTsv	Paid
1998^M - 2001	$150	$145 - $295	$_____

• Images on screen created by carousel inside building.
• Plays 30 songs.
• Includes AC adapter. Optional lights enhance appearance.

Snowy Pines Inn Exclusive Gift Set

54934

Dates	OSRP	VDTsv	Paid
1998^M - 1998	$65	$55 - $138	$_____

• Available during the 1998 Homes for the Holiday event.
• Set of 9 includes building, a 2 piece accessory "Decorate The Tree," trees, road, and snow.

Ronald McDonald® House, The House That ♥ Built

02210

Dates	OSRP	VDTsv	Paid
1998^M - 1998	Promo	$175	$_____

• Limited to only 5,600 pieces, this was made available as a fund raiser during the November 1998 Homes for the Holidays event. Proceeds benefited Ronald McDonald® House Charities.

Center For The Arts

54940

Dates	OSRP	VDTsv	Paid
1998 - 2000	$64	$46 - $65	$_____

• Sign for Art Center is separate in box.

Uptown Motors Ford®   54941

Dates	OSRP	VDTsv	Paid
1998 - 2002	$95	$295	$_____

- Working turntable inside building displays red Mustang.
- Set of 3 incudes building, car, and sign.
- Pennants and hanging sign packaged separately in box.
- Licensed by Ford Motor Co.

Fire Station #3   54942

Dates	OSRP	VDTsv	Paid
1998 - 2003	$70	$98	$_____

- Turret peak is susceptible to damage when removing the piece from its box.

Stick Style House   54943

Dates	OSRP	VDTsv	Paid
1998 - 2000	$60	$43 - $68	$_____

- American Architecture Series.
- Do not handle by columns.

Hidden Ponds House   54944

Dates	OSRP	VDTsv	Paid
1998 - 2001	$50	$125	$_____

...Another Man's Treasure Garage   54945

Dates	OSRP	VDTsv	Paid
1998 - 2001	$60	$47 - $58	$_____

- Set of 22 includes building, items to be sold, and a string of pennants.

The Farmer's Co-Op Granary   54946

Dates	OSRP	VDTsv	Paid
1998 - 2000	**$64**	**$43 - $64**	$_____

• Lamp is separate in box.

Lionel® Electric Train Shop   54947

Dates	OSRP	VDTsv	Paid
1998 - 2000	**$55**	**$71 - $225**	$_____

• A similar design was produced for Allied Model Trains. See the Special Design section.
• Licensed by Lionel®.

Harley-Davidson® Manufacturing   54948

Dates	OSRP	VDTsv	Paid
1998 - 2000	**$80**	**$295**	$_____

• The address reflects that of Harley-Davidson's Milwaukee, WI headquarters.
• Set of three includes building and two motorcycles.
• Licensed by Harley-Davidson®.

The Secret Garden Greenhouse   54949

Dates	OSRP	VDTsv	Paid
1998 - 2001	**$60**	**$195**	$_____

• In addition to bulb and cord arrangement, interior lights along ceiling also light.
• A similar design was produced for Bachman's. See the Special Design section.

2000 Holly Lane   54977

Dates	OSRP	VDTsv	Paid
1999ᴹ - 1999	**$65**	**$195**	$_____

• Limited to year of production.
• This is the first Snow Village design to include a three-dimensional scene in the house.
• First available during the November 1999 Discover Department 56 event.
• Set of 11 includes house, gate, hedges, and snowman.

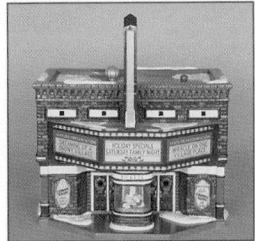

Cinema 56   54978

Dates	OSRP	VDTsv	Paid
1999^M - 2001	$85	$158	$_____

• Marquee is interchangeable with optional accessory marquees.
• The lights around the marquee are functional.
• Do not handle by marquee.

A Home In The Making   54979

Dates	OSRP	VDTsv	Paid
1999^M - 2001	$95	$110	$_____

• A portion of the proceeds benefited Habitat for Humanity.
• Midyear introduction to select stores.
• Set of 5 includes the house, man climbing ladder, two men cutting board, two women carrying lumber, and sign.

Champsfield Stadium   55001

Dates	OSRP	VDTsv	Paid
1999 - 2001	$195	$248	$_____

• Set of 24 includes two seating sections; two teams; two referees; fans; field; two goal posts; two billboards; U.S., Canadian, NFC, and AFC flags; and stickers and lettering for collector customization.

• Players' arms and waists move.
• Licensed by NFLP.

Village Bank & Trust   55002

Dates	OSRP	VDTsv	Paid
1999 - 2001	$75	$98	$_____

• Lanterns on either side of the main entrance are functional.

Holy Spirit Church 55003

Dates	OSRP	VDTsv	Paid
1999 - 2002	**$70**	**$145**	$_____

- Cross and plaque that can be personalized are separate in box.
- Do not handle by columns.
- Set of 2 includes church and sign.

Super Suds Laundromat 55006

Dates	OSRP	VDTsv	Paid
1999 - 2001	**$60**	**$49 - $58**	$_____

Shelly's Diner 55008

Dates	OSRP	VDTsv	Paid
1999 -	**$110**	**$88**	$_____

- Set of 2 includes Diner and lighted sign.

Cedar Point Cabin 55009

Dates	OSRP	VDTsv	Paid
1999 - 2002	**$66**	**$68 - $75**	$_____

- A bird house is separate in box.

WSNO Radio 55010

Dates	OSRP	VDTsv	Paid
1999 - 2002	**$75**	**$88**	$_____

- The light at the top of the antenna is functional.
- Lamp is separate in box.
- Customized version WCCO used as a promotional item at Twin Cities radio station.

Lucky Dragon Restaurant 55011

Dates	OSRP	VDTsv	Paid
1999 - 2000	**$75**	**$60 - $90**	$_____

- Early sample reads "The Golden Dragon Restaurant."
- 8 lanterns are separate in box.
- The hanging lanterns are fragile.

Last Stop Gas Station

55012

Dates	OSRP	VDTsv	Paid
1999 - 2001	**$72**	**$70**	$_____

• Set of 2 includes building and pumps.

Carpenter Gothic Bed & Breakfast

55043

Dates	OSRP	VDTsv	Paid
2000ᴹ - 2003	**$75**	**$210**	$_____

• American Architecture Series.
• Do not handle by columns or railings.
• Set of 2 includes building and sign.

Silver Bells Christmas Shop Gift Set

55040

Dates	OSRP	VDTsv	Paid
2000ᴹ - 2000	**$75**	**$38 - $95**	$_____

• Sold during the 2000 Discover Department 56 event.
• Limited to year of production.
• Silver bells commemorate Dept. 56's 25th anniversary.
• The lamppost at the tree lot is functional.
• Set of 4 includes Shop, "Oh, Christmas Tree" accessory, tree, and snow.

Elvis Presley's Graceland Gift Set

55041

Dates	OSRP	VDTsv	Paid
2000ᴹ - 2001	**$165**	**$228**	$_____

• Sold during the 2000 Discover Department 56 event.
• Retired on January 8, 2001, Elvis' 66th birthday.
• Set of 6 includes "Graceland", "1955 Pink Cadillac Fleetwood", wrought iron gate, original lawn decorations, and 2 sets of mylar twinkling trees.
• Licensed by EPE and GM.

Village Town Hall 55044

Dates	OSRP	VDTsv	Paid
2000 - 2003	**$96**	**$120**	**$_____**

- 6 "add-on" garland pieces and sign allow holiday decor to be added to this non-snow building.
- U. S. and Canadian flags are separate in box.
- Spires and lampposts are fragile.

Candlerock Lighthouse Restaurant 55045

Dates	OSRP	VDTsv	Paid
2000 - 2001	**$110**	**$82 - $125**	**$_____**

- 25th Anniversary Limited Edition of 30,000.
- The top of the light tower is separate and can easily fall and be damaged.
- Flag and 3 lanterns are separate in box.

Palm Lounge Supper Club 55046

Dates	OSRP	VDTsv	Paid
2000 - 2001	**$95**	**$56 - $78**	**$_____**

- Set of 2 includes building and walkway.
- Posts on the walkway are fragile.

Frost And Sons 5 & Dime 55047

Dates	OSRP	VDTsv	Paid
2000 - 2002	**$68**	**$88**	**$_____**

- Do not handle by sign.
- Licensed by SWIMC, Inc. and Eveready Battery Co., Inc.

The Holiday House 55048

Dates	OSRP	VDTsv	Paid
2000 - 2005	**$90**	**$158**	**$_____**

- Santa and 4 reindeer are separate in box.

Buck's County™ Horse Barn 55049

Dates	OSRP	VDTsv	Paid
2000 - 2002	**$72**	**$118**	**$_____**

- Weathervane and lantern are separate in box.

Buck's County™ Farmhouse

55051

Dates	OSRP	VDTsv	Paid
2000 - 2002	$75	$88	$_____

- Weathervane is separate in box.
- Tree limbs are very fragile and are easily broken when removing or putting the piece in its box.

Abner's Implement Co.

55052

Dates	OSRP	VDTsv	Paid
2000 - 2003	$85	$148	$_____

- Buck's County Series.
- Set of 2 includes building and gas pump.
- Flag and lantern are separate in box.
- Licensed by Deere & Co.

Totem Town Souvenir Shop

55053

Dates	OSRP	VDTsv	Paid
2000 - 2002	$68	$52	$_____

- Sign and lantern are separate in box.

Timberlake Outfitters

55054

Dates	OSRP	VDTsv	Paid
2000 - 2002	$75	$65	$_____

- Block and tackle is separate in box.
- Oars are extremely fragile.
- Licensed by Bob Timberlake, Inc.

Crosby House

55056

Dates	OSRP	VDTsv	Paid
2000 - 2002	$50	$98	$_____

Lowell Inn

55059

Dates	OSRP	VDTsv	Paid
2001^M - 2001	$85	$395	$_____

- Depicts the Stillwater, MN inn where the concept of the villages was conceived.
- Only available at Dept. 56's silver anniversary event.
- 16 flags (13 colonies, MN, US, D56) are separate in box.

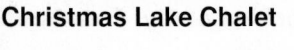

Christmas Lake Chalet 55061

Dates	OSRP	VDTsv	Paid
2001^M - 2001	$75	$140	$_____

- First available during the 2001 Holiday Discover Department 56 event.
- Fireplace flickers, and lanterns on porch light.
- Set of 5 includes Chalet, "The Final Touch" accessory, 2 sisal trees, and a bag of snow.

Tudor House 55062

Dates	OSRP	VDTsv	Paid
2001^M - 2002	$60	$138	$_____

- American Architecture Series.
- Another design with the same name was issued in this village in 1979.

Stardust Drive-In Theater 55064

Dates	OSRP	VDTsv	Paid
2001^M - 2003	$68	$295	$_____

- Animated screen with 12 different images.

Stardust Refreshment Stand 55065

Dates	OSRP	VDTsv	Paid
2001^M - 2003	$50	$178	$_____

- Set of 7 includes Refreshment Stand and 6 speakers.

Juliette's School Of French Cuisine 55063

Dates	OSRP	VDTsv	Paid
2001 - 2002	$65	$52 - $65	$_____

- Mother's Day Spring promotion.
- Set of 4 includes School, sign, 2 potted shrubs, and extra sign which can be personalized.
- 5% of proceeds donated to breast cancer research.

McGuire's Irish Pub

55066

Dates	OSRP	VDTsv	Paid
2001 - 2004	$50	$80 - $165	$_____

- Designed to celebrate St. Patrick's Day.
- Front banner is removable.
- Two lanterns are separate in the box.

Gus's Drive-In

55067

Dates	OSRP	VDTsv	Paid
2001 - 2003	$95	$95 - $98	$_____

- Set of 7 includes Drive-In, "Car Hop" accessory, 2 trays, 2 menus, and a sandwich board.

Woodlake Chapel Starter Set

55068

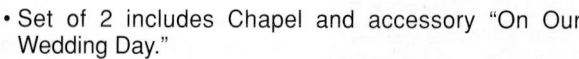

Dates	OSRP	VDTsv	Paid
2001 - 2003	$65	$49 - $65	$_____

- Set of 2 includes Chapel and accessory "On Our Wedding Day."
- Cross and brass plaque which can be engraved are separate in the box.
- Cross attached to roof is very fragile.

Cedar Ridge School

55070

Dates	OSRP	VDTsv	Paid
2001 - 2004	$60	$131	$_____

- Flag, lantern, and brass plaque which can be engraved are separate in the box.

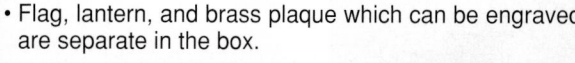

Krispy Kreme Doughnut Shop   55071

Dates	OSRP	VDTsv	Paid
2001 - 2004	**$85**	**$85 - $158**	$_____

• Set of 2 includes Shop and sign.
• Licensed by HDN Development Corporation.

Country Quilts And Pies   55072

Dates	OSRP	VDTsv	Paid
2001 - 2004	**$65**	**$185**	$_____

• Buck's County Series.
• Set of 2 includes building and "Handmade Quilts For Sale" accessory.

Polaris Snowmobile Dealership   55078

Dates	OSRP	VDTsv	Paid
2001 - 2003	**$85**	**$64 - $78**	$_____

• Sign is separate in the box.
• Licensed by Polaris Industries, Inc.

Village Legion Hall   55080

Dates	OSRP	VDTsv	Paid
2001 - 2003	**$55**	**$55 - $105**	$_____

• Set of 2 includes Hall and 2-piece accessory "Cannon And Flag."
• Second flag (with short staff) and lamppost are separate in the box.

Armed Forces Recruiting Station
55081

Dates	OSRP	VDTsv	Paid
2001 - 2002	**$55**	**$125**	$_____

• Two signs and 2 flags are separate in the box.

Happy Easter House
55090

Dates	OSRP	VDTsv	Paid
2001 - 2005	**$50**	**$235**	$_____

• Easter Series.
• "Happy Easter" sign is removable.
• Set of 3 includes house, 2-piece accessory "Egg Hunt."

Moonlight Bay Bunk And Breakfast
55074

Dates	OSRP	VDTsv	Paid
2002ᴹ - 2004	**$75**	**$98 - $118**	$_____

• Set of 2 includes building and sign.

1224 Kissing Claus Lane
55091

Dates	OSRP	VDTsv	Paid
2002ᴹ - 2002	**$75**	**$138**	$_____

• Holiday 2002 Special Edition.
• Animated and musical. Plays *I Saw Mommy Kissing Santa Claus*.
• Set of 4 includes house, "Christmas Eve Delivery" accessory, a frosted topiary, and a bag of snow.
• Spires on roof are fragile.

Lily's Nursery & Gifts

55095

Dates	OSRP	VDTsv	Paid
2002ᴹ - 2004	$65	$228	$_____

- Easter Series.
- Set of 3 includes building and 2 piece accessory, "Gifts For Easter."

Hearts & Blooms Cottage

55097

Dates	OSRP	VDTsv	Paid
2002ᴹ - 2005	$50	$78 - $98	$_____

- Intended to be used as a Valentine's Day design.
- Set of 2 includes Cottage and "Young Love" accessory.

The Cocoa Stop

55096

Dates	OSRP	VDTsv	Paid
2002ᴹ - 2002	$65	$245	$_____

- Club 56 dealer exclusive. Limited to 5,600 pieces.
- Many boxes and sleeves have a rippled effect.
- Certificate of authenticity and hot cocoa recipe are included in the box.

Red Owl Grocery Store

55303

Dates	OSRP	VDTsv	Paid
2002 - 2003	$70	$75 - $125	$_____

- Named after a Midwest grocery store.
- Licensed by Supervalu, Inc.

The Sweet Shop (Regular Issue) 55300

Dates	OSRP	VDTsv	Paid
2002 - 2004	**$65**	**$68**	$_____

• The Shop's hanging sign is extremely fragile.

(Early Release) 05923

Dates	OSRP	VDTsv	Paid
2002ᴹ - 2002	**$75**	**$100**	$_____

• This was an early release to department stores.
• Set of 5 includes the Shop, 2-piece lit accessory "Sampling The Treats" (pictured at left), frosted topiary with candy canes, and snow.

Harmony House 55302

Dates	OSRP	VDTsv	Paid
2002 - 2004	**$50**	**$44 - $88**	$_____

• Set of 3 includes the House, and 2 piece accessory, "Snowman Sonata And Fence."
• Can be personalized.

Rocky's 56 Filling Station 55305

Dates	OSRP	VDTsv	Paid
2002 - 2004	**$80**	**$88**	$_____

• Set of 3 includes the Station and 2 piece accessory, "56 Gasoline Pump And Sign."

Bungalow

55304

Dates	OSRP	VDTsv	Paid
2002 - 2004	**$55**	**$55 - $72**	**$_____**

• American Architecture Series.

Main Street Medical

55306

Dates	OSRP	VDTsv	Paid
2002 - 2004	**$68**	**$82**	**$_____**

• Can be personalized.

Jonathan The Bear Man's Carving Studio

55307

Dates	OSRP	VDTsv	Paid
2002 - 2003	**$75**	**$82**	**$_____**

• Limited to year of production.
• Named for an artist in Wyoming.

Dairy Land Creamery

55308

Dates	OSRP	VDTsv	Paid
2002 - 2004	**$75**	**$78**	**$_____**

Campbell's® Soup Counter

55309

Dates	OSRP	VDTsv	Paid
2002 - 2004	**$60**	**$50 - 68**	**$_____**

• Licensed by The Campbell Soup Co®.

The Frozen Swirl

55318

Dates	OSRP	VDTsv	Paid
2002 - 2004	**$65**	**$88**	**$_____**

Wright Bike Shop 55314

Dates	OSRP	VDTsv	Paid
2002 - 2003	**$65**	**$82 - $88**	**$____**

- Spring Gift Set.
- Set of 5 includes the Shop, "Let's Get A New Bike" accessory, 2 shrubs, and a summer tree.
- Can be personalized.
- Named for the Wright brothers.

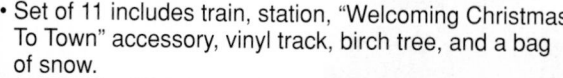

Home For The Holidays Express 55320

Dates	OSRP	VDTsv	Paid
2003ᴹ - 2003	**$110**	**$110 - $225**	**$____**

- Holiday 2003 Special Edition.
- Musical. Plays *Home For The Holidays* and train sounds.
- Set of 11 includes train, station, "Welcoming Christmas To Town" accessory, vinyl track, birch tree, and a bag of snow.
- A special edition Home For The Holidays Caboose was issued in 2004 as a complementary piece.

Year Round Holiday House 55321

Dates	OSRP	VDTsv	Paid
2003ᴹ - 2004	**$75**	**$168**	**$____**

- Christmas Lane Series.
- Includes attachable decorations for five holidays.

American Hero Comics 55322

Dates	OSRP	VDTsv	Paid
2003ᴹ - 2003	**$65**	**$38 - $65**	**$____**

- Club 56 dealer exclusive. Limited to 5,600 pieces.

Sweetheart Candy Shop 55323

Dates	OSRP	VDTsv	Paid
2003ᴹ - 2005	$50	$198	$_____

• Valentine's Series.
• Candy decorations light up and flash.

Hard Rock Café Snow Village 55324

Dates	OSRP	VDTsv	Paid
2003ᴹ - 2005	$85	$58 - $85	$_____

• Includes pin.
• Licensed by Hard Rock Cafe International (USA), Inc.

Happy Easter Church 55325

Dates	OSRP	VDTsv	Paid
2003ᴹ - 2005	$65	$195	$_____

• Easter Series.
• Set of 3 includes Church, "Joyful Greetings" accessory, and 2 removable banners.

High Roller Riverboat Casino 55330

Dates	OSRP	VDTsv	Paid
2003ᴹ - 2005	$110	$120	$_____

• Special lighting effect on paddle wheel.

Village Train Station 55331

Dates	OSRP	VDTsv	Paid
2003 - 2005	$85	$99	$_____

Mission Style House
55332

Dates	OSRP	VDTsv	Paid
2003 - 2005	$75	$65 - $75	$_____

• American Architecture Series.

Woody's Woodland Crafts
55333

Dates	OSRP	VDTsv	Paid
2003 - 2005	$45	$38	$_____

• Set of 2 includes building and "Wood Carvings For Sale" accessory.

Midtown Shops
55334

Dates	OSRP	VDTsv	Paid
2003 - 2005	$70	$70 - $88	$_____

Lot 56, Christmas Court
55335

Dates	OSRP	VDTsv	Paid
2003 - 2008	$65	$88	$_____

KBRR TV
55337

Dates	OSRP	VDTsv	Paid
2003 - 2005	$80	$78 - $80	$_____

• Can be personalized.
• Includes adapter.

Roosevelt Park Band Shell

55338

Dates	OSRP	VDTsv	Paid
2003 - 2005	$65	$78	$_____

- Set of 2 includes Band Shell and "Village Musicians" accessory.
- Adapter included.
- Christmas and Fourth Of July decorations are separate in box.

Vineland Estates Winery

55339

Dates	OSRP	VDTsv	Paid
2003 - 2004	$70	$265	$_____

- Numbered limited edition of 20,000.
- Can be personalized.

Friendly Used Car Sales

55340

Dates	OSRP	VDTsv	Paid
2003 - 2005	$60	$60	$_____

Pillsbury Doughboy™ Bake Shop

55342

Dates	OSRP	VDTsv	Paid
2003 - 2005	$75	$78 - $85	$_____

- Set of 2 includes Bake Shop and "Pillsbury Doughboy™" accessory.
- Licensed by The Pillsbury Company.

The Noel House 55341

Dates	OSRP	VDTsv	Paid
2003 - 2006	**$85**	**$195**	$_____

• Christmas Lane Series.
• Includes an adapter.

Home For The Holidays Caboose 02991

Dates	OSRP	VDTsv	Paid
2004 - 2004	**n/a**	**$975**	$_____

• Limited to 1,000 pieces, it was distributed to collectors whose 2003 Homes For The Holidays Gift Set boxes contained special Department 56 holograms.

City Lights Christmas Trimmings 55348

Dates	OSRP	VDTsv	Paid
2004^M - 2005	**$75**	**$75 - $110**	$_____

• Early release for City Lights in San Diego, CA.

Meadowbrook Church 55349

Dates	OSRP	VDTsv	Paid
2004^M - 2005	**$65**	**$65**	$_____

• Can be personalized.
• Removeable Christmas decorations.

The Peppermint House 55350

Dates	OSRP	VDTsv	Paid
2004^M - 2004	**$75**	**$150**	$_____

• Christmas Lane Series.
• Set of 5 includes building, "Buster Helps Out" accessory, lit tree, tree, and snow.
• Limited to year of production.

Winter Park Warming House

55351

Dates	OSRP	VDTsv	Paid
2004ᴹ - 2004	$65	$60 - $65	$_____

• Club 56 dealer exclusive. Limited edition of 5,000.

American Bandstand

55353

Dates	OSRP	VDTsv	Paid
2004ᴹ - 2006	$95	$78 - $95	$_____

• Animated.
• Plays *Bandstand Boogie*.
• Licensed by Dick Clark Productions.

Chapel Of Love

55354

Dates	OSRP	VDTsv	Paid
2004ᴹ - 2006	$50	$88	$_____

• Valentine's Series.
• Set of 2 includes the Chapel and "The Happy Couple" accessory.

Chocolate Bunny Factory

55355

Dates	OSRP	VDTsv	Paid
2004ᴹ - 2006	$65	-	$_____

• Easter Series.
• Set of 2 includes building and "The Best Part Of Easter" accessory.

Thanksgiving At Grandmother's House   55358

Dates	OSRP	VDTsv	Paid
2004 - 2006	**$75**	**$275**	$_____

- Decorating set.
- Long Life Cordless Lighting.
- Set of 12 includes building, "Dinner Guests" accessory, tree, hay bale, pumpkins, gourds, and leaves.

Santa's Wonderland House   55359

Dates	OSRP	VDTsv	Paid
2004 -	**$120**	**$96**	$_____

- Christmas Lane Series.
- Adapter included.
- Train moves around house.

Budweiser Brewery   55361

Dates	OSRP	VDTsv	Paid
2004 - 2006	**$75**	**$128**	$_____

- Inspired by real brewery in St. Louis, Missouri.
- Licensed by Anheuser-Busch, Inc.

Richardsonian Romanesque House   55362

Dates	OSRP	VDTsv	Paid
2004 - 2005	**$70**	**$118**	$_____

- American Architecture Series.
- Limited to year of production.

Main Street Office Building   55363

Dates	OSRP	VDTsv	Paid
2004 - 2006	**$55**	**$98**	$_____

- Can be personalized.

Christmas Time Post Office

55364

Dates	OSRP	VDTsv	Paid
2004 - 2006	$60	$118	$_____

• Can be personalized.

Village Pets - Sales & Service

55365

Dates	OSRP	VDTsv	Paid
2004 - 2008	$60	$60 - $88	$_____

St. Nick's Toy Land

55366

Dates	OSRP	VDTsv	Paid
2004 - 2006	$75	$75	$_____

• Decorating set.
• Long Life Cordless Lighting.

Hope Chest Consignment Shop

55367

Dates	OSRP	VDTsv	Paid
2004 - 2006	$65	$65 - $78	$_____

Long Haul Truck Stop

55368

Dates	OSRP	VDTsv	Paid
2004 - 2006	$80	$80	$_____

• Adapter included.
• Coffee cup sign blinks.

Grandpap's Cabin

55369

Dates	OSRP	VDTsv	Paid
2004 - 2006	$50	$115	$_____

• Weekend At The Lake Series.
• Includes a boat.

Cascades Marina

55370

Dates	OSRP	VDTsv	Paid
2004 - 2006	**$65**	**$65 - $78**	$_____

• Weekend At The Lake Series.
• Includes a boat.

Silent Night Church

55378

Dates	OSRP	VDTsv	Paid
2005ᴹ - 2005	**$75**	**$118**	$_____

• Set of 6 includes church, 2 votive holders w/candles, pine boughs, and snow.

The Jingle Bells House

55380

Dates	OSRP	VDTsv	Paid
2005ᴹ - 2007	**$85**	**$148**	$_____

• Set of 2 includes house and "Ring, Jingle, Ring" accessory.

NASCAR® Café

55381

Dates	OSRP	VDTsv	Paid
2005ᴹ - 2007	**$85**	**$85 - $95**	$_____

• Long Life Cordless Lighting.
• Licensed by The National Association for Stock Car Auto Racing, Inc.

Fire House No. 4

55382

Dates	OSRP	VDTsv	Paid
2005ᴹ - 2006	**$85**	**$138**	$_____

• Weekend At The Lake Series.
• Includes a boat.

Stillwater Collectibles & Antiques

55383

Dates	OSRP	VDTsv	Paid
2005ᴹ - 2005	$65	$95 - $144	$_____

• 30th Anniversary Special Edition.
• The idea of Snow Village was conceived in Stillwater, MN.

Cupid's Cardshop

55384

Dates	OSRP	VDTsv	Paid
2005ᴹ - 2006	$55	$55	$_____

• Valentine's Series.
• Long Life Cordless Lighting.

Easter Egg Painting Studio

55385

Dates	OSRP	VDTsv	Paid
2005ᴹ - 2006	$55	-	$_____

• Easter Series.
• Long Life Cordless Lighting.

Pearlson's Jewelry

55386

Dates	OSRP	VDTsv	Paid
2005 - 2006	$80	$80 - $88	$_____

• 30th Anniversary Special Edition.
• Limited to year of production.

Harvest Apple Orchard

55388

Dates	OSRP	VDTsv	Paid
2005 - 2006	$80	$120	$_____

• Limited to year of production.
• Set of 2 includes building and "A Fall Family Tradition" accessory.
• Long Life Cordless Lighting.

McKenzie's Chevrolet

55389

Dates	OSRP	VDTsv	Paid
2005 - 2007	**$85**	**$135**	$_____

• Long Life Cordless Lighting.

The Snowman House

55390

Dates	OSRP	VDTsv	Paid
2005 -	**$90**	**$72**	$_____

• Sign, lantern, and snowmen light.
• Christmas Lane Series.

Little Tots Baby Goods

55391

Dates	OSRP	VDTsv	Paid
2005 - 2007	**$75**	**$98**	$_____

• Long Life Cordless Lighting.

Happy Holidays Barn

55394

Dates	OSRP	VDTsv	Paid
2005 - 2007	**$90**	**$135**	$_____

Village Phone Company

55396

Dates	OSRP	VDTsv	Paid
2005 - 2007	**$60**	**$60**	$_____

• Limited to year of production.
• Set of 2 includes telephone pole.

Rock Point Lighthouse

55397

Dates	OSRP	VDTsv	Paid
2005 - 2006	**$100**	**$100 - $125**	$_____

• Numbered Limited Edition of 15,000.
• Beacon lights and spins.

Elmwood House

55398

Dates	OSRP	VDTsv	Paid
2005 - 2007	$85	$110	$_____

• Long Life Cordless Lighting.

Snow Village 30th Anniversary Ball

55399

Dates	OSRP	VDTsv	Paid
2006ᴹ - 2006	$85	$169	$_____

• Limited Edition 10,000.
• 30th Anniversary Series.

Mrs. Claus' Northwoods Nursery

55601

Dates	OSRP	VDTsv	Paid
2006ᴹ - 2006	$80	$98	$_____

• Set of 2 includes building and "How Do I Look" accessory.

The Santa Claus House

55602

Dates	OSRP	VDTsv	Paid
2006ᴹ - 2006	$110	$155	$_____

• Limited Edition of 12,000.
• Christmas Lane Series.
• Display Anywhere Lighting.

Big League Sports

55604

Dates	OSRP	VDTsv	Paid
2006ᴹ - 2009	$70	$49 - $74	$_____

Snow Village Gazette   55605

Dates	OSRP	VDTsv	Paid
2006^M - 2008	$75	$75 - $89	$_____

• Village Single Light Cord.

Harvest Farm Roadside Sales   55606

Dates	OSRP	VDTsv	Paid
2006 -	$85	-	$_____

Snow Village Mayor's Mansion   55607

Dates	OSRP	VDTsv	Paid
2006 - 2007	$100	$80 - $138	$_____

• Collectors' Edition.
• Limited Edition of 12,000.

Franky's Hot Dogs   55608

Dates	OSRP	VDTsv	Paid
2006 - 2009	$75	$75	$_____

• Lighted Interior Scene.

The Tinsel & Garland House   55609

Dates	OSRP	VDTsv	Paid
2006 - 2008	$85	$85 - $110	$_____

• Christmas Lane Series.
• Set of 2. Includes "Snowman" Accessory.

Stone Steeple Church

55610

Dates	OSRP	VDTsv	Paid
2006 - 2009	$85	$85 - $135	$_____

Bud's T.V. & Hi-Fi

55612

Dates	OSRP	VDTsv	Paid
2006 - 2009	$85	$60 - $85	$_____

• Lighted Interior Scene.

Mighty Fine BBQ

55613

Dates	OSRP	VDTsv	Paid
2006 - 2009	$85	$60 - $85	$_____

Sharky's Pool Hall

55614

Dates	OSRP	VDTsv	Paid
2006 -	$80	$64	$_____

• Lighted Interior Scene.

Main Street Pharmacy

55615

Dates	OSRP	VDTsv	Paid
2006 -	$80	$64	$_____

• Lighted Interior Scene.

Christmas Crafts Cottage

55616

Dates	OSRP	VDTsv	Paid
2006 - 2009	$80	$80	$_____

NASCAR® Garage   55617

Dates	OSRP	VDTsv	Paid
2006 - 2007	$85	$68 - $96	$_____

Snow Village Museum Of Art   55618

Dates	OSRP	VDTsv	Paid
2007ᴹ - 2007	$90	$90 - $125	$_____

- Numbered Limited Edition of 10,000.
- Features Carved Statue.

The Dutchman's Pancake House   55619

Dates	OSRP	VDTsv	Paid
2007ᴹ - 2007	$95	$95 -$135	$_____

- Collectors' Edition.
- Limited Edition of 10,000.
- Windmill Blades Rotate.

Kringle's Korner   55621

Dates	OSRP	VDTsv	Paid
2007ᴹ - 2007	$99	-	$_____

- Limited to year of production.
- Holiday Value Set of 2.
* Includes "Reindeer Rides" Accessory.

Miss Mae's Rooming House   55622

Dates	OSRP	VDTsv	Paid
2007ᴹ - 2008	$80	$64 - $80	$_____

Yuengling Tavern

55626

Dates	OSRP	VDTsv	Paid
2007 - 2009	$85	-	$_____

• Limited 2007 Early Release for Retailer Boscovs.

Chateau Valley Winery

799926

Dates	OSRP	VDTsv	Paid
2007 - 2009	$125	$125 - $162	$_____

Frost University

799927

Dates	OSRP	VDTsv	Paid
2007 - 2008	$90	$72 - $98	$_____

• Collectors' Edition.
• Limited Edition of 12,000.

Little Sunshine Daycare

799928

Dates	OSRP	VDTsv	Paid
2007 - 2008	$75	$75 - $89	$_____

Lot 57, Christmas Court

799929

Dates	OSRP	VDTsv	Paid
2007 -	$90	$72	$_____

•Garland & Shrubs have lit LED lights.

The Flamingo Motel

799930

Dates	OSRP	VDTsv	Paid
2007 - 2009	$125	$125	$_____

• Set of 2, includes "Roadside Sign" lit with holiday lights.

Sam's Butcher Shop

799931

Dates	OSRP	VDTsv	Paid
2007 -	**$80**	**$64**	$_____

• Detailed Window Displays.

Scarecrow Harvest Festival

799932

Dates	OSRP	VDTsv	Paid
2007 - 2008	**$100**	**$80 - $125**	$_____

• Requires 4 AA Batteries.

The Gingerbread House

799933

Dates	OSRP	VDTsv	Paid
2007 - 2009	**$100**	**$100**	$_____

• Christmas Lane Series.
• Over decorated with gingerbread theme and lit holiday lights.

The Angel House

799937

Dates	OSRP	VDTsv	Paid
2008ᴹ - 2008	**$100**	**$100 - $118**	$_____

• Collectors' Edition.
• Numbered Limited Edition of 8,000.
• House is designed with Angels, lit yard décor.

Lyndale Tree Lot

799938

Dates	OSRP	VDTsv	Paid
2008ᴹ - 2008	**$79**	**$79**	$_____

• Set of 2, with accessory "Just The Right Tree."
• Celebrate Holiday Value Set ($100 value).

Noah's Stuffed Animals 799990

Dates	OSRP	VDTsv	Paid
2008M - 2008	$85	$85 - $90	$_____

Nokomis House 804442

Dates	OSRP	VDTsv	Paid
2008M -	$85	-	$_____

Majorie's Blue Ribbon Baked Goods 805500

Dates	OSRP	VDTsv		Paid
2008 -	$95		-	$_____

• Honoring Marjorie Johnson & Her Blue Ribbon Baking

Colonial Revival 805501

Dates	OSRP	VDTsv	Paid
2008 - 2009	$90	$72 - $90	$_____

• American Archiecture Series.
•Numbered Limited Edition 8,000.

Dancing Lights House 805502

Dates	OSRP	VDTsv	Paid
2008 -	$145	-	$_____

• Christmas Lane Series.
• Flashing Lights are synchronized with the music.

Our Lady Of Grace Church 805503

Dates	OSRP	VDTsv	Paid
2008 -	$100	-	$_____

Northgate School   805504

Dates	OSRP	VDTsv	Paid
2008 -	$95	-	$_____

Rolling Acres Corn Maze   805506

Dates	OSRP	VDTsv	Paid
2008 -	$95	-	$_____

• Set of 2, Pictured.
• Includes "Popping The Kettle Corn" Accessory.

Rose's Flower Shop   805507

Dates	OSRP	VDTsv	Paid
2008 -	$90	-	$_____

White Castle   805508

Dates	OSRP	VDTsv	Paid
2008 -	$90	-	$_____

Richmond Holiday House   805509

Dates	OSRP	VDTsv	Paid
2009^M - 2009	$79	$79 - $95	$_____

• Limited to Year 2009 production.
• Includes "Dad's Little Helper".

The Elf House   805510

Dates	OSRP	VDTsv	Paid
2010 -	$115	-	$_____

* Christmas Lane Series.

Christmas At Grandma's   808943

Dates	OSRP	VDTsv	Paid
2010 -	$95	-	$_____

Nutcraker Playhouse   808944

Dates	OSRP	VDTsv	Paid
2010 -	$95	-	$_____

Red Cup Cafe   808946

Dates	OSRP	VDTsv	Paid
2010 -	$55	-	$_____

Tom's Foods   808947

Dates	OSRP	VDTsv	Paid
2010 -	$85	-	$_____

SVPD Precinct 76   808948

Dates	OSRP	VDTsv	Paid
2010 -	$90	-	$_____

Loon Lake Cabin

808949

Dates	OSRP	VDTsv	Paid
2010 -	$85	-	$____

Notes:

Carolers

50641 - Set of 4

1979 - 1986

OSRP: $12

VDTsv: $72-
$125

Paid: $_____

Ceramic Car

50690

1980 - 1986

OSRP: $5

VDTsv: $35-$45

Paid: $_____

Ceramic Sleigh

50792

1981 - 1986

OSRP: $5

VDTsv: $35-$45

Paid: $_____

Snowman With Broom

50180

1982 - 1990

OSRP: $3

VDTsv: $12-$15

Paid: $_____

• This is the first mixed
media accessory. It's
made of ceramic and
straw.

Monks-A-Caroling

64599

1983 - 1984

OSRP: $6

VDTsv: $32-$45

Paid: $_____

• Blush on cheeks is
lighter and diffused.
• 1982 giftware line had
unglazed set (64602) w/
paper books and cord
sashes. VDTsv: $145

Monks-A-Caroling

50407

1984 - 1988

OSRP: $6

VDTsv: $26-$45

Paid: $_____

• 1st: Bright red speck-
led rash on cheeks. 2nd:
Blush on cheeks is a
defined dot. Taller.

Scottie With Tree

50385

1984 - 1985

OSRP: $3

VDTsv: $170-
$225

Paid: $_____

• Is also available with a
white star on top of the
tree.

Singing Nuns

50539

1985 - 1987

OSRP: $6

VDTsv: $110-
$115

Paid: $_____

Auto With Tree

(Squashed Version)

50555

1985 - 2001

OSRP: $5

VDTsv: $6 - $12

Paid: $_____

• The first pieces are less round and less detailed. See picture to the right.

VDTsv: $110

Paid: $_____

Snow Kids Sled, Skis

50563 - Set of 2

1985 - 1987

OSRP: $11

VDTsv: $30-$40

Paid: $_____

• In 1987, this set was reduced in size and combined with Girl/ Snowman, Boy to form Snow Kids.

Family Mom / Kids, Goose / Girl

50571 - Set of 2

1985 - 1988

OSRP: $11

VDTsv: $17-$40

Paid: $_____

• The first year's pieces were larger and less detailed than those produced in the later years.

Santa / Mailbox

50598 - Set of 2

1985 - 1988

OSRP: $11

VDTsv: $36-$70

Paid: $_____

• The first year's pieces were larger and less detailed than those produced in the later years.

Kids Around The Tree

50946

1986 - 1990

OSRP: $15

VDTsv: $25-$50

Paid: $_____

• The first year's pieces were larger and less detailed than those produced in the later years.

Girl / Snowman, Boy

50954 - Set of 2

1986 - 1987

OSRP: $11

VDTsv: $20-$70

Paid: $_____

• In 1987, this set was reduced in size and combined with Snow Kids Sled, Skis to form Snow Kids.

Shopping Girls With Packages

50962 - Set of 2

1986 - 1988

OSRP: $11

VDTsv: $25-$50

Paid: $_____

• The first year's pieces were larger and less detailed than those produced in the later years.

3 Nuns With Songbooks

51020

1987 - 1988

OSRP: $6

VDTsv: $120-

$148

Paid: $_____

Praying Monks

51039

1987 - 1988

OSRP: $6

VDTsv: $35-60

Paid: $_____

Children In Band

51047

1987 - 1989

OSRP: $15

VDTsv: $16-$25

Paid: $_____

Caroling Family

51055 - Set of 3

1987 - 1990

OSRP: $20

VDTsv: $15-$30

Paid: $_____

Taxi Cab

51063

1987 - 2000

OSRP: $6

VDTsv: $6-$15

Paid: $_____

Christmas Children

51071 - Set of 4

1987 - 1990

OSRP: $20

VDTsv: $20-$45

Paid: $_____

House For Sale Sign

51080

1987 - 1989

OSRP: $3.50

VDTsv: $5-$9

Paid: $_____

• A similar design with no writing was produced for GCC and given to collectors who made $100 purchases.

Snow Kids

51136 - Set of 4

1987 - 1990

OSRP: $20

VDTsv: $28-$50

Paid: $_____

• This set combines smaller versions of Snow Kids Sled, Skis (1985) and Girl/ Snowman, Boy (1986).

Snow Village House For Sale Sign

Promo

1987 - 1987

OSRP: Promo

VDTsv: $25

Paid: $_____

• This was free to dealers who placed their orders at Department 56 showrooms. It is a very rare accessory.

Man On Ladder Hanging Garland

51160

1988 - 1992

OSRP: $7.50

VDTsv: $11-$25

Paid: $_____

• Includes mixed media —ceramic man, wooden ladder, and sisal garland.

Hayride

51179

1988 - 1990

OSRP: $30

VDTsv: $30-$45

Paid: $_____

School Children

51187 - Set of 3

1988 - 1990

OSRP: $15

VDTsv: $18-$24

Paid: $_____

Apple Girl / Newspaper Boy

51292 - Set of 2

1988 - 1990

OSRP: $11

VDTsv: $22

Paid: $_____

Woodsman And Boy

51306 - Set of 2

1988 - 1991

OSRP: $13

VDTsv: $14-$24

Paid: $_____

Doghouse / Cat In Garbage Can

51314 - Set of 2

1988 - 1992

OSRP: $15

VDTsv: $17

Paid: $_____

• Box reads "Cat And Dog."

Fire Hydrant & Mailbox

51322 - Set of 2

1988 - 1998

OSRP: $6

VDTsv: $12

Paid: $_____

Water Tower

51330

1988 - 1991

OSRP: $20

VDTsv: $55-$75

Paid: $_____

• Similar designs were produced for retailers. See the Special Design section.

Nativity

51357

1988 - 2000

OSRP: $7.50

VDTsv: $8-$16

Paid: $_____

Woody Station Wagon

51365

1988 - 1990

OSRP: $6.50

VDTsv: $16-$28

Paid: $_____

School Bus, Snow Plow

51373 - Set of 2

1988 - 1991

OSRP: $16

VDTsv: $48-$52

Paid: $_____

Tree Lot

51381

1988 - 1999

OSRP: $33.50

VDTsv: $30-$38

Paid: $_____

• Includes mixed media —small ceramic shed, wooden fence, and 7 sisal trees.

Sisal Tree Lot

81833

1988 - 1991

OSRP: $45

VDTsv: $45-$65

Paid: $_____

Village Gazebo

51462

1989 - 1995

OSRP: $27

VDTsv: $30-$68

Paid: $_____

Choir Kids

51470

1989 - 1992

OSRP: $15

VDTsv: $21-$28

Paid: $_____

Special Delivery

51489 - Set of 2

1989 - 1990

OSRP: $16

VDTsv: $35-$78

Paid: $_____

• Retired after one year due to unauthorized use of red, white, and blue colors of U.S. Postal Service.

For Sale Sign

51667

1989 - 1998

OSRP: $4.50

VDTsv: $5

Paid: $_____

• Similar designs were produced for retailers. See the Special Design section.

Street Sign

51675 - Set of 6

1989 - 1992

OSRP: $7.50

VDTsv: $8-$15

Paid: $_____

• Includes stickers (with street names and blank ones) for signs.
• Metal.

Kids Tree House

51683

1989 - 1991

OSRP: $25

VDTsv: $34-$39

Paid: $_____

• This was the first all resin accessory.

Bringing Home The Tree

51691

1989 - 1992

OSRP: $15

VDTsv: $15-$58

Paid: $_____

• Includes mixed media —ceramic sleigh and people with sisal tree.

Skate Faster Mom

51705

1989 - 1991

OSRP: $13

VDTsv: $15-$22

Paid: $_____

Crack The Whip

51713 - Set of 3

1989 - 1996

OSRP: $25

VDTsv: $17-$28

Paid: $_____

Through The Woods

51721 - Set of 2

1989 - 1991

OSRP: $18

VDTsv: $22-$28

Paid: $_____

Statue Of Mark Twain

51730

1989 - 1991

OSRP: $15

VDTsv: $19-$28

Paid: $_____

Calling All Cars

51748 - Set of 2

1989 - 1991

OSRP: $15

VDTsv: $30-$55

Paid: $_____

Village Stop Sign

51764 - Set of 2

1989 - 1998

OSRP: $5

VDTsv: $8

Paid: $_____

• Metal.

Flag Pole

51772

1989 - 1999

OSRP: $8.50

VDTsv: $25

Paid: $_____

• Metal, ceramic, and cloth.

Village Parking Meter

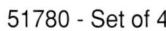

51780 - Set of 4

1989 - 1999

OSRP: $6

VDTsv: $6

Paid: $_____

• Metal.

Mailbox

51799

1989 - 1990

OSRP: $3.50

VDTsv: $15-$20

Paid: $_____

• Retired after one year due to unauthorized use of red and blue colors of U.S.P.S.

Snow Village Promotional Sign

99481

1989 - 1990

OSRP: Promo

VDTsv: $20

Paid: $_____

• Used as a promotional piece by Dept. 56 retailers.

Kids Decorating The Village Sign

51349

1990 - 1993

OSRP: $12.50

VDTsv: $15-$22

Paid: $_____

Down The Chimney He Goes

51586

1990 - 1993

OSRP: $6.50

VDTsv: $7-$14

Paid: $_____

• Adhesive strip allows this piece to be mounted on a building's roof.

Sno-Jet Snowmobile

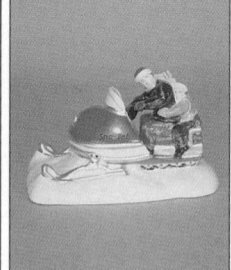

51594

1990 - 1993

OSRP: $15

VDTsv: $19-$28

Paid: $_____

Sleighride

51608

1990 - 1992

OSRP: $30

VDTsv: $35-$45

Paid: $_____

Here We Come A Caroling

51616 - Set of 3

1990 - 1992

OSRP: $18

VDTsv: $18-$24

Paid: $_____

Home Delivery

51624 - Set of 2

1990 - 1992

OSRP: $16

VDTsv: $28-$32

Paid: $_____

Fresh Frozen Fish

51632 - Set of 2

1990 - 1993

OSRP: $20

VDTsv: $24-$32

Paid: $_____

A Tree For Me

51640 - Set of 2

1990 - 1995

OSRP: $7.50

VDTsv: $10-$28

Paid: $_____

• Ceramic with sisal trees.

A Home For The Holidays

51659

1990 - 1996

OSRP: $6.50

VDTsv: $6-$10

Paid: $_____

Special Delivery

51977 - Set of 2

1990 - 1992

OSRP: $16

VDTsv: $25-$28

Paid: $_____

• Re-issue of first Special Delivery (1989) after changing the color of the truck to red, white, and green.

Village Mail Box

51985

1990 - 1998

OSRP: $3.50

VDTsv: $6

Paid: $_____

• Re-issue of Mailbox (1989) after changing the colors to red and green and putting "S.V. Mail" on front.

Christmas Trash Cans

52094 - Set of 2

1990 - 1998

OSRP: $7

VDTsv: $10

Paid: $_____

• Metal, paper, and plastic.

Wreaths For Sale

54089 - Set of 4

1991 - 1994

OSRP: $27.50

VDTsv: $30-$38

Paid: $_____

• Ceramic with sisal wreaths.

Winter Fountain

54097

1991 - 1993

OSRP: $25

VDTsv: $25-$42

Paid: $_____

• Includes mixed media —ceramic and acrylic.

Cold Weather Sports

54100 - Set of 4

1991 - 1994

OSRP: $27.50

VDTsv: $27-$35

Paid: $_____

Come Join The Parade

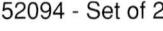

54119

1991 - 1992

OSRP: $12.50

VDTsv: $11-$18

Paid: $_____

Village Marching Band

54127 - Set of 3

1991 - 1992

OSRP: $30

VDTsv: $30-$55

Paid: $_____

Christmas Cadillac

54135

1991 - 1994

OSRP: $9

VDTsv: $12-$15

Paid: $_____

Snowball Fort

54143 - Set of 3

1991 - 1993

OSRP: $27.50

VDTsv: $31-$36

Paid: $_____

Country Harvest

54151

1991 - 1993

OSRP: $13

VDTsv: $16-$22

Paid: $_____

Village Used Car Lot

54283 - Set of 5

1992 - 1997

OSRP: $45

VDTsv: $40-$68

Paid: $_____

Village Phone Booth

54291

1992 -

OSRP: $7.50

VDTsv: -

Paid: $_____

Nanny And The Preschoolers

54305 - Set of 2

1992 - 1994

OSRP: $27.50

VDTsv: $20-$36

Paid: $_____

Early Morning Delivery

54313 - Set of 3

1992 - 1995

OSRP: $27.50

VDTsv: $21-$30

Paid: $_____

Christmas Puppies

54321 - Set of 2

1992 - 1996

OSRP: $27.50

VDTsv: $25-$33

Paid: $_____

Round & Round We Go!

54330 - Set of 2

1992 - 1995

OSRP: $18

VDTsv: $22-$25

Paid: $_____

A Heavy Snowfall

54348 - Set of 2

1992 - 2001

OSRP: $16

VDTsv: $16-$28

Paid: $_____

We're Going To A Christmas Pageant

54356

1992 - 1994

OSRP: $15

VDTsv: $13-$24

Paid: $_____

Winter Playground

54364

1992 - 1995

OSRP: $20

VDTsv: $25-$58

Paid: $_____

Spirit Of Snow Village Airplane

54402

1992 - 1996

OSRP: $32.50

VDTsv: $30-$40

Paid: $_____

• This is very difficult to put back in box. See 1993 for item by the same name.

Safety Patrol

54496 - Set of 4

1993 - 1997

OSRP: $27.50

VDTsv: $21-$32

Paid: $_____

Christmas At The Farm

54500 - Set of 2

1993 - 1996

OSRP: $16

VDTsv: $15-$25

Paid: $_____

Check It Out Bookmobile

54518 - Set of 3

1993 - 1995

OSRP: $25

VDTsv: $25-$32

Paid: $_____

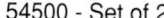

Tour The Village

54526

1993 - 1997

OSRP: $12.50

VDTsv: $13-$18

Paid: $_____

• Bayport on sign is spelled "Bay**q**ort."

Pint-Size Pony Rides

54534 - Set of 3

1993 - 1996

OSRP: $37.50

VDTsv: $35-$45

Paid: $_____

Pick-up And Delivery

54542

1993 - 2001

OSRP: $10

VDTsv: $10-$28

Paid: $_____

• See Special Design section.

A Herd Of Holiday Heifers

54550 - Set of 3

1993 - 1997

OSRP: $18

VDTsv: $28-$38

Paid: $_____

Windmill

54569

1993 - 1993

OSRP: $20

VDTsv: $25

Paid: $_____

Classic Cars

54577 - Set of 3

1993 - 1998

OSRP: $22.50

VDTsv: $8-$28

Paid: $_____

Spirit Of Snow Village Airplane

54585

1993 - 1996

OSRP: $12.50

VDTsv: $19-$68

Paid: $_____

• Available in blue or yellow. See 1992 for another item by the same name.

Village News Delivery

54593 - Set of 2

1993 - 1996

OSRP: $15

VDTsv: $15-$24

Paid: $_____

Caroling At The Farm

54631
1994ᴹ - 2000
OSRP: $35
VDTsv: $30-$42
Paid: $_____

Stuck In The Snow

54712 - Set of 3
1994 - 1998
OSRP: $30
VDTsv: $25-$32
Paid: $_____

Pets On Parade

54720 - Set of 2
1994 - 1998
OSRP: $16.50
VDTsv: $16-$38
Paid: $_____

Feeding The Birds

54739 - Set of 3
1994 - 1997
OSRP: $25
VDTsv: $23-$30
Paid: $_____

Mush!

54747 - Set of 2
1994 - 1997
OSRP: $20
VDTsv: $17-$25
Paid: $_____

Skaters & Skiers

54755 - Set of 3
1994 - 2001
OSRP: $27.50
VDTsv: $25-$35
Paid: $_____

Going To The Chapel

54763 - Set of 2
1994 - 2001ᴹ
OSRP: $20
VDTsv: $20-$25
Paid: $_____

Santa Comes To Town, 1995

54771
1994 - 1995
OSRP: $30
VDTsv: $26-$30
Paid: $_____

- Limited to year of production.
- First in a series.

Marshmallow Roast

54780 - Set of 3

1994 - 2002

OSRP: $32.50

VDTsv: $33-$58

Paid: $_____

• The fire is battery or adapter operated.

Coca-Cola® Brand Delivery Truck

54798

1994 - 1998

OSRP: $15

VDTsv: $18-$30

Paid: $_____

• Licensed by Coca-Cola.

Coca-Cola® Brand Delivery Men

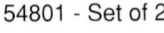

54801 - Set of 2

1994 - 1998

OSRP: $25

VDTsv: $20-$32

Paid: $_____

• Licensed by Coca-Cola.

Coca-Cola® Brand Billboard

54810

1994 - 1997

OSRP: $18

VDTsv: $11-$24

Paid: $_____

• Licensed by Coca-Cola.

Sunday School Serenade

54623

1994 - 1996

OSRP: *

VDTsv: *

• Accessory contained in The Original Snow Village Starter Set.

Frosty Playtime

54860 - Set of 3

1995 - 1997

OSRP: $30

VDTsv: $25-$37

Paid: $_____

Poinsettias For Sale

54861 - Set of 3

1995 - 1998

OSRP: $30

VDTsv: $26-$58

Paid: $_____

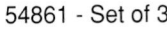

Santa Comes To Town, 1996

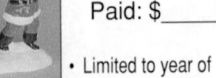

54862

1995 - 1996

OSRP: $32.50

VDTsv: $23-$65

Paid: $_____

• Limited to year of production.
• Second in a series.

Chopping Firewood

54863 - Set of 2

1995 - 2002

OSRP: $16.50

VDTsv: $17-$30

Paid: $_____

• This includes mixed media —ceramic and wood.

Firewood Delivery Truck

54864

1995 - 1999

OSRP: $15

VDTsv: $17-$30

Paid: $_____

• This includes mixed media —ceramic and wood.

Service With A Smile

54865 - Set of 2

1995 - 1998

OSRP: $25

VDTsv: $20-$30

Paid: $_____

Pizza Delivery

54866 - Set of 2

1995 - 1998

OSRP: $20

VDTsv: $18-$26

Paid: $_____

Grand Ole Opry Carolers

54867

1995 - 1997

OSRP: $25

VDTsv: $21-$36

Paid: $_____

• Licensed by Opry-land USA, Inc.

Snow Carnival Ice Sculptures

54868 - Set of 2

1995 - 1998

OSRP: $27.50

VDTsv: $20-$30

Paid: $_____

• Includes mixed media—ceramic and acrylic.

Snow Carnival King & Queen

54869

1995 - 1998

OSRP: $35

VDTsv: $25-$45

Paid: $_____

Starbucks Coffee® Cart

54870 - Set of 2

1995 - 2000

OSRP: $27.50

VDTsv: $35-$45

Paid: $_____

• Licensed by Starbucks Coffee.

Just Married

54879 - Set of 2
1995 - 2005
OSRP: $25
VDTsv: $25
Paid: $_____

A Ride On The Reindeer Lines

54875 - Set of 3
1996^M - 1997
OSRP: $35
VDTsv: $30-$85
Paid: $_____

Treetop Tree House

54890
1996 - 2004
OSRP: $35
VDTsv: $36
Paid: $_____

• Resin.

On The Road Again

54891 - Set of 2
1996 - 2002
OSRP: $20
VDTsv: $20-$34
Paid: $_____

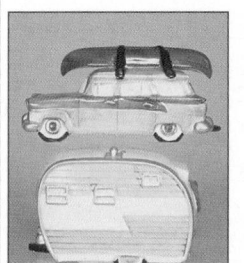

Moving Day

54892 - Set of 3
1996 - 1998
OSRP: $32.50
VDTsv: $24-$36
Paid: $_____

Holiday Hoops

54893 - Set of 3
1996 - 1999
OSRP: $20
VDTsv: $24-$38
Paid: $_____

Men At Work

54894 - Set of 5
1996 - 1998
OSRP: $27.50
VDTsv: $22-$30
Paid: $_____

Terry's Towing

54895 - Set of 2
1996 - 1999
OSRP: $20
VDTsv: $20-$28
Paid: $_____

Caroling Through The Snow

54896

1996 - 1999

OSRP: $15

VDTsv: $15-$32

Paid: $_____

Heading For The Hills

54897

1996 - 2002

OSRP: $8.50

VDTsv: $9-$19

Paid: $_____

• Available in blue or yellow.

A Harley-Davidson® Holiday

54898 - Set of 2

1996 - 1999

OSRP: $25

VDTsv: $19-$25

Paid: $_____

• Licensed by Harley-Davidson.

Santa Comes To Town, 1997

54899

1996 - 1997

OSRP: $35

VDTsv: $26-$40

Paid: $_____

• Limited to year of production.
• Third in a series.

Harley-Davidson® Fat Boy & Softail

54900

1996 - 2001^M

OSRP: $16.50

VDTsv: $18-$25

Paid: $_____

• Licensed by Harley-Davidson.

Harley-Davidson® Sign

54901

1996 - 2002

OSRP: $18

VDTsv: $22-$30

Paid: $_____

• Licensed by Harley-Davidson.

Saturday Morning Downtown

54902 - Set of 2

1997^M - 1998

OSRP: *

VDTsv: *

* Accessory contained in The Original Snow Village Start A Tradition Set.

The Whole Family Goes Shopping

54905 - Set of 3

1997^M - 1999

OSRP: $25

VDTsv: $25

Paid: $_____

A Holiday Sleigh Ride Together

54921

1997 - 2001ᴹ

OSRP: $32.50

VDTsv: $32-$48

Paid: $_____

Christmas Kids

54922 - Set of 5

1997 - 1999

OSRP: $27.50

VDTsv: $20-$32

Paid: $_____

Let It Snow, Let It Snow

54923

1997 - 2000

OSRP: $20

VDTsv: $18-$24

Paid: $_____

Kids Love Hershey's®!

54924 - Set of 2

1997 - 2000

OSRP: $30

VDTsv: $28-$42

Paid: $_____

• Licensed by Hershey Foods.

McDonald's®...Lights Up The Night

54925

1997 - 1999

OSRP: $30

VDTsv: $35-$48

Paid: $_____

• Sign is battery/adapter operated.
• Licensed by McDonald's.

Kids, Candy Canes...& Ronald McDonald®

54926 - Set of 3

1997 - 1999

OSRP: $30

VDTsv: $27-$35

Paid: $_____

• Licensed by McDonald's.

He Led Them Down The Streets Of Town

54927 - Set of 3

1997 - 1999

OSRP: $30

VDTsv: $27-$32

Paid: $_____

Everybody Goes Skating At Rollerama

54928 - Set of 2

1997 - 1999

OSRP: $25

VDTsv: $22-$28

Paid: $_____

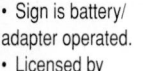

At The Barn Dance, It's Allemande Left

54929 - Set of 2

1997 - 1999

OSRP: $30

VDTsv: $35

Paid: $_____

Hitch-Up The Buckboard

54930

1997 - 1999

OSRP: $40

VDTsv: $28-$40

Paid: $_____

Farm Accessory Set

54931 - Set of 35

1997 - 2002

OSRP: $75

VDTsv: $75-$85

Paid: $_____

• Includes 8 trees, 12 hay bales, 4 fence, and 11 ceramic pieces.

Santa Comes To Town, 1998

54920

1997 - 1998

OSRP: $30

VDTsv: $24-$36

Paid: $_____

• Limited to year of production.
• Fourth in a series.

Snow Village Utility Accessories

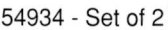

52775

1998 - 2001

OSRP: $15

VDTsv: $15

Paid: $_____

Decorate The Tree

54934 - Set of 2

1998^M - 1998

OSRP: *

VDTsv: *

* Accessory contained in the Snowy Pines Inn Gift Set.

First Round Of The Year

54936 - Set of 3

1998^M - 2001^M

OSRP: $30

VDTsv: $30

Paid: $_____

Carnival Tickets & Cotton Candy

54938 - Set of 3

1998^M - 2000

OSRP: $30

VDTsv: $20-$33

Paid: $_____

• Ceramic and cloth.

Two For The Road

54939

1998^M - 2002

OSRP: $20

VDTsv: $25-$28

Paid: $_____

• Available in three color schemes—red, yellow, and blue.
• Licensed by Harley-Davidson.

Uptown Motors Ford® Billboard

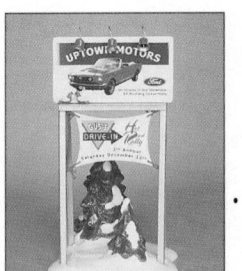

52780

1998 - 2001^M

OSRP: $20

VDTsv: $15-$29

Paid: $_____

• Licensed by Ford.

1955 Ford® Automobiles

54950

1998 - 2001

OSRP: $10 ea.

VDTsv: $14-$30

Paid: $_____

• 6 assorted, each with a sign.
• Licensed by Ford.

1964½ Ford® Mustang

54951

1998 - 2001

OSRP: $10 ea.

VDTsv: $12-$20

Paid: $_____

• 3 assorted, each with a sign.
• Licensed by Ford.

Village Fire Truck

54952

1998 - 2003

OSRP: $22.50

VDTsv: $25

Paid: $_____

• Lighted headlights and emergency beacon are battery operated.

Fireman To The Rescue

54953 - Set of 3

1998 - 2001^M

OSRP: $30

VDTsv: $28-$34

Paid: $_____

Fun At The Firehouse

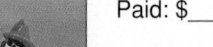

54954 - Set of 2

1998 - 2004

OSRP: $27.50

VDTsv: $26

Paid: $_____

Farmer's Flatbed

54955

1998 - 2000

OSRP: $17.50

VDTsv: $16-$20

Paid: $_____

The Catch Of The Day

54956

1998 - 2001^M

OSRP: $30

VDTsv: $27-$34

Paid: $_____

• Fishing line is easily broken.

Christmas Visit To The Florist

54957 - Set of 3

1998 - 2001

OSRP: $30

VDTsv: $24-$35

Paid: $_____

• A similar design was also produced for Bachman's. See the Special Design section.

Santa Comes To Town, 1999

54958

1998 - 1999

OSRP: $30

VDTsv: $26-$35

Paid: $_____

• Limited to year of production.
• Fifth in a series.

Village Service Vehicles

54959

1998 - 2001

OSRP: $15 ea.

VDTsv: $15-$16

Paid: $_____

• 3 assorted—garbage truck, tow truck, and snow plow were often sold separately.

Quality Service At Ford®

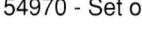

54970 - Set of 2

1998 - 2001^M

OSRP: $27.50

VDTsv: $24-$28

Paid: $_____

• Licensed by Ford.

Patrolling The Road

54971

1998 - 2001^M

OSRP: $20

VDTsv: $20-$30

Paid: $_____

• Licensed by Harley-Davidson.

Couldn't Wait Until Christmas

54972

1998 - 2000

OSRP: $17

VDTsv: $15-$22

Paid: $_____

• Licensed by Lionel.

Uncle Sam's Fireworks Stand

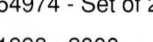
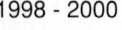

54974 - Set of 2

1998 - 2000

OSRP: $45

VDTsv: $45-$78

Paid: $_____

• July 1999 event piece.

Harley-Davidson® Water Tower

54975

1998 - 2002

OSRP: $32.50

VDTsv: $42-$95

Paid: $_____

• Licensed by Harley-Davidson.

Another Man's Treasure Accessories

54976 - Set of 3

1998 - 2001ᴹ

OSRP: $27.50

VDTsv: $23-$34

Paid: $_____

A Home In The Making Accessories

54979 - Set of 4

1999ᴹ - 2001

OSRP: *

VDTsv: *

* This accessory is contained in A Home In The Making.
• Licensed by Habitat For Humanity

Looney Tunes® Film Festival

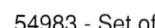

54983 - Set of 4

1999ᴹ - 2001ᴹ

OSRP: $40

VDTsv: $22-$44

Paid: $_____

• Marquee can be placed on Cinema 56.
• Licensed by Warner Bros.

The Backyard Patio

52836 - Set of 2

1999 - 2002

OSRP: $40

VDTsv: $28-$42

Paid: $_____

It's Time For An Icy Treat

55013 - Set of 2

1999 - 2001

OSRP: $30

VDTsv: $30-$36

Paid: $_____

• Licensed by Good Humor-Breyers Ice Cream.

Welcome To The Congregation

55014

1999 - 2001ᴹ

OSRP: $15

VDTsv: $15-$24

Paid: $_____

Santa Comes To Town, 2000

55015

1999 - 2000

OSRP: $37.50

VDTsv: $31-$40

Paid: $_____

• Limited to year of production.
• Sixth in a series.

Laundry Day

55017

1999 - 2001[M]

OSRP: $13

VDTsv: $13-$18

Paid: $_____

Before The Big Game

55019 - Set of 4

1999 - 2001

OSRP: $37.50

VDTsv: $32-$40

Paid: $_____

Finding The Bird's Song

55020 - Set of 2

1999 - 2001[M]

OSRP: $25

VDTsv: $20-$26

Paid: $_____

Send In The Clown!

55021

1999 - 2001[M]

OSRP: $13.50

VDTsv: $12-$18

Paid: $_____

• Stickers are included
so plaque can be
personalized.

Holy Spirit Baptistery

55022

1999 - 2001

OSRP: $37.50

VDTsv: $38

Paid: $_____

• Music box plays
"Jesus Loves The Little
Children."

First Deposit

55023

1999 - 2001

OSRP: $14

VDTsv: $14-$17

Paid: $_____

Angels In The Snow

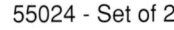

55024 - Set of 2

1999 - 2008

OSRP: $30

VDTsv: -

Paid: $_____

Santa's Little Helpers

55025

1999 - 2001

OSRP: $27.50

VDTsv: $26-$32

Paid: $_____

Is That Frosty?

55030
1999 - 2007
OSRP: $22.50
VDTsv: -
Paid: $_____

On The Way To Ballet Class

55031 - Set of 3
1999 - 2001ᴹ
OSRP: $27.50
VDTsv: $24-$30
Paid: $_____

The Dragon Parade

55032
1999 - 2001
OSRP: $35
VDTsv: $35-$65
Paid: $_____

Gifts On The Go

55035 - Set of 2
1999 -2001ᴹ
OSRP: $30
VDTsv: $24-$30
Paid: $_____

Backwoods Outhouse

55036
1999 - 2007
OSRP: $20
VDTsv: -
Paid: $_____

• Battery operated.

Oh, Christmas Tree

55040
2000ᴹ - 2000
OSRP: *
VDTsv: *

* Accessory contained
in the Silver Bells
Christmas Shop Gift Set.

1955 Pink Cadillac® Fleetwood™

55041
2000ᴹ - 2000
OSRP: *
VDTsv: *

* Accessory contained
in the Elvis Presley's
Graceland Gift Set.
• Licensed by GM.

Sitting In The Park

55100 - Set of 4
2000ᴹ - 2002
OSRP: $28
VDTsv: $26-$30
Paid: $_____

How The Grinch Stole Christmas — Movie Premiere

55103-Setof2

2000^M - 2001
OSRP: $17.50
VDTsv: $20-$58
Paid: $_____

• Marquee can be placed on Cinema 56.
• Licensed by Dr. Seuss Enterprises.

Windmill By The Chicken Coop

52867

2000 - 2003
OSRP: $55
VDTsv: $50
Paid: $_____

• Buck's County Series.

The Old Pickup Truck

52868

2000 - 2002
OSRP: $30
VDTsv: $30-$40
Paid: $_____

• Buck's County Series.

Yesterday's Tractor

52869

2000 - 2002
OSRP: $30
VDTsv: $30-$38
Paid: $_____

• Buck's County Series.

The Tree Lighting Ceremony

55104 - Set of 3

2000 - 2002
OSRP: $65
VDTsv: $65-$65
Paid: $_____

• Lights are battery/adapter operated.

Now Showing — Elvis Presley Sign

55105

2000 - 2001
OSRP: $30
VDTsv: $32-$58
Paid: $_____

• Licensed by Elvis Presley Enterprises.
• Adapter operated.

Elvis Presley's Autograph

55106 - Set of 3

2000 - 2001
OSRP: $25
VDTsv: $28-$70
Paid: $_____

• Licensed by Elvis Presley Enterprises.

Pedal Cars For Christmas

55108 - Set of 2

2000 - 2003
OSRP: $27.50
VDTsv: $28
Paid: $_____

Roadside Billboards

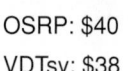

55109 - Set of 3

2000 - 2003

OSRP: $40

VDTsv: $38

Paid: $_____

• Licensed by the Campbell Soup Co., SWIMC, Inc., and Eveready Batt. Co, Inc.
• Battery/adapter.

Christmastime Trimming

55110

2000 -

OSRP: $15

VDTsv: -

Paid: $_____

Buck's County™ Water Tower

55111

2000 - 2003

OSRP: $32.50

VDTsv: $37

Paid: $_____

• Buck's County Series.

Buck's County™ Stables

55112 - Set of 9

2000 - 2002

OSRP: $65

VDTsv: $62-$70

Paid: $_____

• Buck's County Series.

Family Canoe Trip

55116 - Set of 3

2000 - 2002

OSRP: $48

VDTsv: $34-$48

Paid: $_____

2001 Space Oddity

55118 - Set of 11

2000 - 2001

OSRP: $125

VDTsv: $125-
$195

Paid: $_____

• Includes adapter.

On The Beat

55119 - Set of 2

2000 - 2006

OSRP: $35

VDTsv: -

Paid: $_____

• Battery/adapter operated.

Santa Comes To Town, 2001

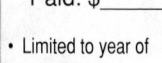

55120

2000 - 2001

OSRP: $40

VDTsv: $40-$40

Paid: $_____

• Limited to year of production.
• Seventh in a series.
• Batt./adapt. operated.

The Abandoned Gas Pump

55121

2000 - 2002

OSRP: $37.50

VDTsv: $36-$44

Paid: $_____

• Buck's County Series.

1958 Corvette® Roadster

55281

2000 - 2007

OSRP: $20

VDTsv: -

Paid: $_____

• Classic Cars Series.
• Licensed by General Motors.

50's Hot Rod

55282

2000 - 2006

OSRP: $20

VDTsv: -

Paid: $_____

• Classic Cars Series.

1957 Chevrolet® Bel Air

55283

2000 - 2006

OSRP: $20

VDTsv: -

Paid: $_____

• Classic Cars Series.
• Licensed by General Motors.

1958 John Deere® 730 Diesel Tractor

55284

2000 - 2003

OSRP: $20

VDTsv: $25

Paid: $_____

• Classic Cars Series.
• Licensed by Deere & Co.

1950 Ford® F-1 Pickup

55285

2000 - 2003

OSRP: $20

VDTsv: $22

Paid: $_____

• Classic Cars Series.
• Licensed by Ford Motor Co and Deere & Co.

Buck's County™ Horse Trailer

55286

2000 - 2002

OSRP: $17.50

VDTsv: $18-$40

Paid: $_____

• Buck's County Series.
• Coordinates with 1950 Ford F-1 Pickup.

1954 Willy's CJ3 Jeep®

55287

2000 - 2002

OSRP: $20

VDTsv: $20-$55

Paid: $_____

• Classic Cars Series.
• Licensed by Daimler-Chrysler Corp.

1949 Ford® Woody Wagon

55288

2000 - 2006

OSRP: $20

VDTsv: -

Paid: $_____

• Classic Cars Series.
• Licensed by Ford Motor Co.

1959 Chevrolet® Impala Convertible

55289

2000 - 2007

OSRP: $20

VDTsv: -

Paid: $_____

• Classic Cars Series.
• Licensed by General Motors.

The Final Touch

55061

2001^M - 2001

OSRP: *

VDTsv: *

* The accessory contained in the Christmas Lake Chalet Gift Set.

Happy New Year

55124 - Set of 4

2001^M - 2002

OSRP: $25

VDTsv: $17-$26

Paid: $_____

• Includes sign that can be placed on Town Hall (#55044).

Fun In The Snow

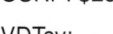

55125 - Set of 2

2001^M - 2006

OSRP: $25

VDTsv: -

Paid: $_____

Holiday Reindeer Run

55126

2001^M - 2002

OSRP: $25

VDTsv: $25-$28

Paid: $_____

• Originally was titled Holiday Fun Run.

Car Hop

55067

2001 - 2003

OSRP: *

VDTsv: *

* The accessory contained in Gus's Drive-In.

On Our Wedding Day

55068

2001 -

OSRP: *

VDTsv: *

* The accessory contained in the Woodlake Chapel Starter Set.

Handmade Quilts For Sale

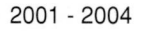

55072

2001 - 2004

OSRP: *

VDTsv: *

* The accessory contained in Country Quilts And Pies.

Cannon And Flag

55080

2001 - 2003

OSRP: *

VDTsv: *

* The accessory contained in Village Legion Hall.

Egg Hunt

55090

2001 - 2005

OSRP: *

VDTsv: *

* The accessory contained in Happy Easter House.

Feeding The Ducks

55122

2001 - 2003

OSRP: $40

VDTsv: $44

Paid: $_____

• Buck's County Series.

Santa Comes To Town, 2002

55127

2001 - 2002

OSRP: $85

VDTsv: $70-$90

Paid: $_____

• Limited to year of production, 2002.
• Eighth in a series.
• Battery operated.

Bringing The Irish Cheer

55128

2001 - 2005

OSRP: $12.50

VDTsv: $13

Paid: $_____

School's Out!

55129

2001 - 2003

OSRP: $20

VDTsv: $20

Paid: $_____

Start Your Engines

55132 - Set of 2

2001 - 2003

OSRP: $25

VDTsv: $28

Paid: $_____

Hiking In The North Woods

55133
2001 - 2003
OSRP: $20
VDTsv: $22
Paid: $_____

Main Street Villagers

55134 - Set of 3
2001 - 2006
OSRP: $25
VDTsv: -
Paid: $_____

College Kids At Krispy Kreme®

55135
2001 - 2004
OSRP: $17.50
VDTsv: $18
Paid: $_____

• Licensed by
HDN Development Corp.

Snowmobile Racers

55136 - Set of 2
2001 - 2006
OSRP: $15
VDTsv: -
Paid: $_____

Oh, Brother!

55137 - Set of 2
2001 - 2003
OSRP: $18
VDTsv: $18
Paid: $_____

Door-To-Door Sales

55139 - Set of 2
2001 - 2003
OSRP: $20
VDTsv: $22
Paid: $_____

4th of July Celebration

55141 - Set of 3
2001 -
OSRP: $25
VDTsv: -
Paid: $_____

Rest Stop?

55142
2001 - 2003
OSRP: $15
VDTsv: $17
Paid: $_____

Sunday Football With Dad

55143

2001 - 2003

OSRP: $15

VDTsv: $17

Paid: $_____

Ben & Buddy's Lemonade Stand

55144

2001 - 2003

OSRP: $20

VDTsv: $28

Paid: $_____

Brand New Recruit

55152

2001 - 2003

OSRP: $20

VDTsv: $22

Paid: $_____

Congratulations...Recruit!

55153 - Set of 2

2001 - 2002

OSRP: $17.50

VDTsv: $19

Paid: $_____

Snow Village Raising The Flag

55154

2001 - 2005

OSRP: $15

VDTsv: $15

Paid: $_____

Welcome To Snow Village
Population Sign

55155

2001 - 2005

OSRP: $10

VDTsv: $10

Paid: $_____

School Bus

55292

2001 - 2004

OSRP: $20

VDTsv: $20

Paid: $_____

• Classic Cars Series.

1950 Studebaker

55293

2001 - 2004

OSRP: $20

VDTsv: $20

Paid: $_____

• Classic Cars Series.

1951 Custom Mercury

55294

2001 - 2004

OSRP: $20

VDTsv: $22

Paid: $_____

- Classic Cars Series.
- Licensed by Ford Motor Co.

1959 Cadillac Eldorado

55295

2001 - 2003

OSRP: $20

VDTsv: $20

Paid: $_____

- Classic Cars Series.
- Licensed by General Motors.

Sampling The Treats

05923 - Set of 2

2002^M - 2002

OSRP: *

VDTsv: *

* The accessory contained in The Sweet Shop.

Christmas Eve Delivery

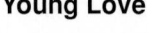

55091

2002^M - 2002

OSRP: *

VDTsv: *

* The accessory contained in 1224 Kissing Claus Lane.

Gifts For Easter

55095 - Set of 2

2002^M - 2004

OSRP: *

VDTsv: *

- Easter Series.
- * The accessory contained in Lily's Nursery & Gifts.

Young Love

55097

2002^M - 2005

OSRP: *

VDTsv: *

* The accessory contained in Hearts & Blooms Cottage.

Nature Walk

55156 - Set of 2

2002^M - 2004

OSRP: $27.50

VDTsv: $28

Paid: $_____

Lucky's Irish Souvenirs

55157 - Set of 2

2002^M - 2004

OSRP: $45

VDTsv: $40

Paid: $_____

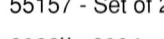

- Battery/adapter operated.

Mainstreet Snowman

55159

2002^M - 2002

OSRP: $32.50

VDTsv: $98

Paid: $_____

• Limited to year of production.
• Available only at Gold Key dealers.

One Hop Walk

55160

2002^M - 2004

OSRP: $40

VDTsv: $38

Paid: $_____

• Easter Series.

It's The Easter Bunny!

55164 - Set of 2

2002^M - 2004

OSRP: $17.50

VDTsv: $85

Paid: $_____

• Easter Series.

Krispy Kreme® Doughnut Deliveries

55165

2002^M - 2004

OSRP: $20

VDTsv: $62

Paid: $_____

• Licensed by HDN Development Corp. and General Motors.

1956 Hook & Ladder

55296

2002^M - 2005

OSRP: $30

VDTsv: $58

Paid: $_____

• Classic Cars Series.

1956 Mainline Police Sedan

55297

2002^M - 2005

OSRP: $20

VDTsv: $40

Paid: $_____

• Classic Cars Series.
• Box reads "1956 Ford Mainline Police Sedan."
• Licensed by Ford.

Village Snow Clown

55161

2002 - 2003

OSRP: $17.50

VDTsv: $18

Paid: $_____

At Your Service

55168

2002 - 2004

OSRP: $12.50

VDTsv: $12-$18

Paid: $_____

Violin Serenade

55169

2002 - 2004

OSRP: $17.50

VDTsv: $17-$18

Paid: $_____

Making A House Call

55170

2002 - 2004

OSRP: $12.50

VDTsv: $18

Paid: $_____

Home Away From Home

55171

2002 - 2006

OSRP: $27.50

VDTsv: $75

Paid: $_____

• Battery/adapter operated.

Weekend Getaway

55172 - Set of 2

2002 - 2004

OSRP: $25

VDTsv: $25-$36

Paid: $_____

Let's Play House

55173

2002 - 2006

OSRP: $22.50

VDTsv: $48

Paid: $_____

• Lighted.

Village Utilities

55175 - Set of 10

2002 - 2005

OSRP: $15

VDTsv: $25

Paid: $_____

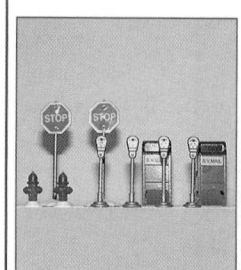

Best Friends

55176

2002 - 2006

OSRP: $20

VDTsv: -

Paid: $_____

Car Wash Fundraiser

55177 - Set of 2

2002 - 2004

OSRP: $20

VDTsv: $20-$35

Paid: $_____

• Can be personalized.

Carry Out Boy

55178

2002 - 2003

OSRP: $17.50

VDTsv: $12

Paid: $_____

Mm! Mm! Good!

55179

2002 - 2004

OSRP: $25

VDTsv: $23-$25

Paid: $_____

• Licensed by the
Campbell Soup Co.

Summertime Family Picnic

55180 - Set of 3

2002 - 2004

OSRP: $37.50

VDTsv: $37-$38

Paid: $_____

Kiddie Parade

55181 - Set of 3

2002 - 2004

OSRP: $30

VDTsv: $30-$89

Paid: $_____

Merrily Round We Go

55183

2002 - 2004

OSRP: $45

VDTsv: $34-$65

Paid: $_____

• Animated.
• Battery/adapter oper-
ated.

Santa Comes To Town, 2003

55194

2002 - 2003

OSRP: $45

VDTsv: $30-$45

Paid: $_____

• Limited to year of
production, 2003.
• Ninth in a series.

Fresh Dairy Delivery

55195 - Set of 2

2002 - 2004

OSRP: $25

VDTsv: $24-$50

Paid: $_____

Ice Cream For Everyone

55196 - Set of 2

2002 - 2004

OSRP: $22.50

VDTsv: $30

Paid: $_____

Sitting In The Village

55197 - Set of 3

2002 -

OSRP: $25

VDTsv: -

Paid: $_____

• Benches are not included.

Animals On The Farm

55199 - Set of 9

2002 - 2004

OSRP: $25

VDTsv: $38

Paid: $_____

Jonathan The Bear Man

55202

2002 - 2003

OSRP: $12.50

VDTsv: $18

Paid: $_____

• Named for a Wyoming artist.

1957 Ambulance

55299

2002 - 2005

OSRP: $20

VDTsv: $115

Paid: $_____

• Classic Cars Series.

Snowman Sonata And Fence

55302

2002 - 2004

OSRP: *

VDTsv: *

* The accessory contained in Harmony House.

56 Gasoline Pump And Sign

55305

2002 - 2004

OSRP: *

VDTsv: *

* The accessory contained in Rocky's 56 Filling Station.

Let's Get A New Bike

55314

2002 - 2003

OSRP: *

VDTsv: $65

* The accessory contained in Wright Bike Shop.

1961 Ford Ranchero

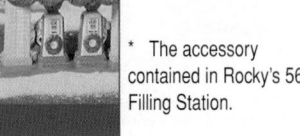

55532

2002 - 2004

OSRP: $20

VDTsv: $40

Paid: $_____

• Classic Cars Series.
• Licensed by Ford Motor Co.

Main Street Christmas Tree

55205

2003^M - 2003

OSRP: $35

VDTsv: $98

Paid: $_____

• Adapter included.
• Limited to year of production.
• Available only at Gold Key dealers.

St. Patrick's Day Parade

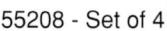

55207

2003^M - 2004

OSRP: $20

VDTsv: $20-$36

Paid: $_____

• Can be personalized.

Work A Little, Play A Little

55208 - Set of 4

2003^M - 2004

OSRP: $25

VDTsv: $23-$25

Paid: $_____

• Includes two sets of figures dressed for four seasons.

I'm Home!

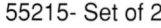

55209

2003^M - 2005

OSRP: $13

VDTsv: $ 32

Paid: $_____

Kisses - 25 Cents

55215- Set of 2

2003^M - 2005

OSRP: $25

VDTsv: $35-$68

Paid: $_____

• Valentine's Day design.
• Special lighting effects.

Welcoming Christmas To Town

55320

2003^M - 2003

OSRP: *

VDTsv: *

* The accessory contained in Home For The Holidays Express.

Joyful Greetings

55325

2003^M - 2005

OSRP: *

VDTsv: *

• Easter Series.
* The accessory contained in Happy Easter Church.

Easter Egg Hunt

55326 - Set of 3

2003^M - 2005

OSRP: $50

VDTsv: $80

Paid: $_____

• Easter Series.
• Includes adapter.

Dressed In Our Easter Best

55327 - Set of 2

2003M - 2006

OSRP: $25

VDTsv: $25-$48

Paid: $_____

• Easter Series.

1956 Pumper

55533

2003M - 2005

OSRP: $25

VDTsv: $55

Paid: $_____

• Classic Cars.

Personalized School Bus

55534

2003M - 2006

OSRP: $20

VDTsv: $41

Paid: $_____

• Classic Cars.

No Girls Allowed

55217

2003 - 2005

OSRP: $20

VDTsv: $20-$38

Paid: $_____

We're Going By Train!

55218 - Set of 2

2003 - 2005

OSRP: $25

VDTsv: $48

Paid: $_____

Santa Comes To Town, 2004

55222

2003 - 2004

OSRP: $50

VDTsv: $50

Paid: $_____

• Limited to year of production, 2004.
• Tenth in a series.

Brand New Shoes!

55224 - Set of 2

2003 - 2005

OSRP: $17.50

VDTsv: $12

Paid: $_____

News Flash!

55225

2003 - 2005

OSRP: $17.50

VDTsv: $14-$18

Paid: $_____

Listening To A Summer Concert

55227 - Set of 2

2003 - 2005

OSRP: $20

VDTsv: $16-$20

Paid: $_____

A Day At The Beach

55228

2003 - 2005

OSRP: $25

VDTsv: $28

Paid: $_____

Billboard Surprise

55229

2003 - 2005

OSRP: $22.50

VDTsv: $22.50-$38

Paid: $_____

Here Comes The Birdie!

55230

2003 - 2005

OSRP: $17.50

VDTsv: $16-18

Paid: $_____

More

Decorations?

55231 - Set of 2

2003 - 2008

OSRP: $17.50

VDTsv: -

Paid: $_____

• Chrsitmas Lane Series.

Pleasing The Palate!

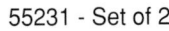

55232

2003 - 2005

OSRP: $20

VDTsv: $30-$55

Paid: $_____

Christmas Is Coming

55233

2003 - 2006

OSRP: $25

VDTsv: -

Paid: $_____

Neighborhood Poinsettia Salesman

55235 - Set of 2

2003 - 2008

OSRP: $22.50

VDTsv: -

Paid: $_____

Wood Carvings For Sale

55333

2003 - 2005

OSRP: *

VDTsv: *

Paid: $_____

* The accessory contained in Woody's Woodland Crafts.

Village Musicians

55338

2003 - 2005

OSRP: *

VDTsv: *

Paid: $_____

* The accessory contained in Roosevelt Park Band Shell.

The Pillsbury Doughboy™

55342

2003 - 2005

OSRP: *

VDTsv: *

Paid: $_____

* The accessory contained in Pillsbury Doughboy Bake Shop.
• Licensed by The Pillsbury Company.

1955 Ford® Thunderbird

55535

2003 - 2006

OSRP: $20

VDTsv: $112

Paid: $_____

• Classic Cars Series.
• Licensed by Ford Motor Co.

1957 Cadillac® Eldorado Brougham

55536

2003 - 2005

OSRP: $20

VDTsv: $75

Paid: $_____

• Classic Cars Series.
• Licensed by General Motors.

We'll Win For Sure!

55251

2004M - 2005

OSRP: $15

VDTsv: $15

Paid: $_____

Townspeople

55252 - Set of 5

2004M - 2005

OSRP: $32.50

VDTsv: $38

Paid: $_____

Neighborhood Christmas Scene

55253

2004M - 2004

OSRP: $50

VDTsv: $50-$65

Paid: $_____

• Limited to year of production.

Main Street Town Santa

55254

2004^M - 2004

OSRP: $32.50

VDTsv: $28-$33

Paid: $_____

• Limited to year of production.

Buster Helps Out

55350

2004^M - 2004

OSRP: *

VDTsv: *

Paid: $_____

* The accessory contained in The Peppermint House.

The Happy Couple

55354

2004^M - 2006

OSRP: *

VDTsv: *

Paid: $_____

* The accessory contained in Chapel Of Love.

The Best Part Of Easter

55355

2004^M - 2006

OSRP: *

VDTsv: *

Paid: $_____

* The accessory contained in Chocolate Bunny Factory.

1965 Ford® Mustang 2+2 Fastback

55537

2004^M - 2006

OSRP: $20

VDTsv: $46

Paid: $_____

• Classic Cars Series.
• Licensed by Ford® Motor Co.

Budweiser Clydesdales

55256

2004 - 2006

OSRP: $65

VDTsv: $137

Paid: $_____

• Licensed by Anheuser-Busch®, Inc.

Harvest Yard Fun

55258 - Set of 2

2004 - 2006

OSRP: $25

VDTsv: $25-$40

Paid: $_____

Who's Walking Who?

55260

2004 - 2008

OSRP: $20

VDTsv: $30

Paid: $_____

We Have A Deal!

55261

2004 - 2006

OSRP: $17.50

VDTsv: $18-$30

Paid: $_____

Something For Me?

55262

2004 - 2006

OSRP: $17.50

VDTsv: $44

Paid: $_____

Can I Open One Now?

55264

2004 - 2006

OSRP: $18.50

VDTsv: $19-$28

Paid: $_____

What A Great Find!

55265 - Set of 2

2004 - 2006

OSRP: $17.50

VDTsv: $18-$28

Paid: $_____

Santa Comes to Town, 2005

55266

2004 - 2005

OSRP: $35

VDTsv: $35-$58

Paid: $_____

- Limited to year of production.
- Licensed by Coca-Cola.

Christmas Lights Tour

55267

2004 -

OSRP: $25

VDTsv: $20

Paid: $_____

- Christmas Lane Series.

Future Hockey Stars

55268

2004 - 2007

OSRP: $17.50

VDTsv: -

Paid: $_____

Gone Fishing

55269

2004 - 2006

OSRP: $20

VDTsv: $20-$46

Paid: $_____

- Weekend At The Lake Series.

Dinner Guests

55358 - Set of 2

2004 - 2006

OSRP: *

VDTsv: *

* The accessory contained in Thanksgiving at Grandmother's House.

Freight Truck

55538

2004 - 2006

OSRP: $20

VDTsv: -

Paid: $_____

• Classic Cars Series.

Hurry Up, It's Picture Time

55278

2005^M - 2006

OSRP: $15

VDTsv: $68

Paid: $_____

A Day At The Races

55279

2005^M - 2006

OSRP: $17.50

VDTsv: $17.50-30

Paid: $_____

Ring, Jingle, Ring

55380

2005^M - 2007

OSRP: *

VDTsv: *

* The accessory contained in The Jingle Bells House.
• Chistmas Lane Series

Sparky's New Doghouse

55401

2005^M - 2007

OSRP: $15

VDTsv: -

Paid: $_____

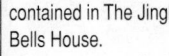

A Fall Family Tradition

55388

2005 - 2006

OSRP: *

VDTsv: *

* The accessory contained in Harvest Apple Orchard.

Santa Comes To Town, 2006

55402

2005 - 2006

OSRP: $27.50

VDTsv: -

Paid: $_____

• Limited to year of production.

Flash Photo Hut

55403

2005 - 2008

OSRP: $27.50

VDTsv: $28-$30

Paid: $_____

Will You Marry Me?

55404

2005 - 2006

OSRP: $15

VDTsv: $60

Paid: $_____

- Limited to year of production.

Budweiser Delivery Truck

55406

2005 - 2006

OSRP: $25

VDTsv: $20-$38

Paid: $_____

Like Father, Like Son

55407

2005 -

OSRP: $20

VDTsv: $16

Paid: $_____

What An Adorable Baby!

55408

2005 - 2007

OSRP: $18.50

VDTsv: $19

Paid: $_____

Decorating Elsie For Christmas

55412

2005 - 2008

OSRP: $20

VDTsv: $38

Paid: $_____

Telephone Line Repairman

55413

2005 - 2007

OSRP: $15

VDTsv: -

Paid: $_____

Toy Boat Whittling Lesson

55414

2005 - 2007

OSRP: $17.50

VDTsv: $18

Paid: $_____

Dad's Christmas Tradition

55415
2006^M - 2007
OSRP: $17.50
VDTsv: $18-$30
Paid: $_____

Soccer Moms Rule!

55416
2006^M - 2007
OSRP: $18.50
VDTsv: -
Paid: $_____

Roadside Produce Stand

55411
2006 - 2009
OSRP: $32.50
VDTsv: $33
Paid: $_____

Candy Canes From The Mayor

55418
2006 -
OSRP: $18.50
VDTsv: -
Paid: $_____

Weiner Dogs To Go

55419
2006 - 2009
OSRP: $12.50
VDTsv: $13
Paid: $_____

Everyone Decorates The Tinsel Tree

55420
2006 -
OSRP: $18.50
VDTsv: $15
Paid: $_____

Children's Nativity

55421
2006 - 2009
OSRP: $12.50
VDTsv: $13
Paid: $_____

Our First Television

55422
2006 - 2009
OSRP: $15.00
VDTsv: $11-$15
Paid: $_____

Grill Master & Friend

55423

2006 - 2009

OSRP: $18.50

VDTsv: $13-$19

Paid: $_____

A Pool Tournament At Sharky's

55424

2006 -

OSRP: $17.50

VDTsv: $14

Paid: $_____

One Malt - Two Straws

55426

2006 - 2008

OSRP: $15

VDTsv: $28

Paid: $_____

Kitten Wants New Mittens

55427

2006 - 2009

OSRP: $15

VDTsv: $15

Paid: $_____

Santa Comes To Town - 2007

55428

2006 - 2007

OSRP: $27.50

VDTsv: $28-$65

Paid: $_____

• Limited to year of production.

They Have A Room For Us

55430

2007^M - 2008

OSRP: $15

VDTsv: $15

Paid: $_____

The Windmill Wishing Well

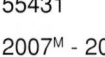

55431

2007^M - 2007

OSRP: $20

VDTsv: $16-$36

Paid: $_____

Reindeer Rides

55621

2007^M - 2007

OSRP: $99

VDTsv: -

Paid: $_____

• Accessory to set "Kringle's Korner"

His Name Will Be Pumpkinhead

799967
2007 - 2009
OSRP: $27.50
VDTsv: $28
Paid: $_____

Homework Can't Wait

799968
2007 - 2008
OSRP: $22.50
VDTsv: $23-$31
Paid: $_____

Nursery School Outing

799969
2007 - 2009
OSRP: $32.50
VDTsv: $33
Paid: $_____

Over The Threshold

799970
2007 - 2009
OSRP: $22.50
VDTsv: $23
Paid: $_____

Ready For Picking

799971
2007 - 2009
OSRP: $30
VDTsv: $24-$30
Paid: $_____

Santa Comes To Town - 2008

799972
2007 - 2008
OSRP: $32.50
VDTsv: $33
Paid: $_____

• Limited to 2008 production.

The Yuengling Champs

799973
2007 - 2009
OSRP: $30
VDTsv: $24-$30
Paid: $_____

Welcome To Christmas Court

799974
2007 - 2009
OSRP: $20
VDTsv: $20
Paid: $_____

Welcome To Snow Village

799975

2007 - 2009

OSRP: $20

VDTsv: $20

Paid: $_____

An Angelic Scene

804453

2008^M -

OSRP: $20

VDTsv: -

Paid: $_____

A Letter To Santa

804454

2008^M -

OSRP: $15

VDTsv: -

Paid: $_____

It's A Tough Choice

804455

2008^M -

OSRP: $22.50

VDTsv: -

Paid: $_____

Ginger's House

799966

2007 -

OSRP: $20

VDTsv: -

Paid: $_____

Christmas Lane Lit Gate

800005

2007 -

OSRP: $27.50

VDTsv: -

Paid: $_____

•Includes battery pack

Just The Right Tree

799938

2008^M - 2008

OSRP: $27.50

VDTsv: -

Paid: $_____

• Accessory Contained
in Lyndale Tree Lot

Yuengling Delivery

805025 - Set of 2

2008 - 2009

OSRP: $30

VDTsv: $30

Paid: $_____

Popping The Kettle Corn

805506

2008^M -

OSRP: $75

VDTsv: -

Paid: $_____

• "Rolling Acres Corn Maze" Accessory

Santa Comes to Town, 2009

807285

2008 - 2009

OSRP: $35

VDTsv: $28-$35

Paid: $_____

• Limited to 2009 Year of Production

Blue Ribbon Treats

807286

2008 -

OSRP: $30

VDTsv: -

Paid: $_____

Unfair Advantage

807287 - Set of 2

2008 -

OSRP: $27.50

VDTsv: -

Paid: $_____

Tour Tickets Here

807288

2008 -

OSRP: $37.50

VDTsv: -

Paid: $_____

• Christmas Lane Series

Making Luminaries

807289

2008 -

OSRP: $17.50

VDTsv: -

Paid: $_____

Gifts For The Teacher

807290

2008 -

OSRP: $22.50

VDTsv: -

Paid: $_____

Help With The Decorations

807291

2008 -

OSRP: $18.50

VDTsv: -

Paid: $_____

I Hope She Likes Them

807292

2008 -

OSRP: $22.50

VDTsv: -

Paid: $_____

What You Crave

807293

2008 -

OSRP: $25

VDTsv: -

Paid: $_____

Dad's Little Helper

805509

2009^M - 2009

OSRP: $79

VDTsv: -

Paid: $_____

Out For A Drive

808736

2009^M -

OSRP: $18.50

VDTsv: -

Paid: $_____

The Finishing Touch

807294

2010 -

OSRP: $18.50

VDTsv: -

Paid: $_____

Santa Comes To Town, 2010

808877

2010 -

OSRP: $37.50

VDTsv: -

Paid: $_____

Grandma's Favorite Present

808952

2010 -

OSRP: $22.50

VDTsv: -

Paid: $_____

Nutcracker Ballerinas

808953

2010 -

OSRP: $25

VDTsv: -

Paid: $_____

Four Cups Of 'Joe' To Go

808954

2010 -

OSRP: $18.50

VDTsv: -

Paid: $_____

Shopping With Mom

808957

2010 -

OSRP: $22.50

VDTsv: -

Paid: $_____

Lost And Found

808958

2010 -

OSRP: $22.50

VDTsv: -

Paid: $_____

Thanks For The Help, Boy

808959

2010 -

OSRP: $18.50

VDTsv: -

Paid: $_____

Waiting For The Bus

809010

2010 -

OSRP: $30

VDTsv: -

Paid: $_____

Notes:

Haunted Mansion (Green Roof)   54935

Dates	OSRP	VDTsv	Paid
1998ᴹ - 2000ᴹ	$110	$469 - $695	$_____

- This is the SV version.
- Images on screen created by carousel inside building.
- Includes AC adapter.

(Black Roof)   34050

Dates	OSRP	VDTsv	Paid
1998ᴹ - 1999	$110	$1350 - $1975	$_____

- This is the giftware version and came in a black box.
- Images on screen created by carousel inside building.
- Includes AC adapter.

Grimsly Manor   55004

Dates	OSRP	VDTsv	Paid
1999 - 2009	$120	$120	$_____

- Features special effects including horror sounds and lightning supplied by separate unit in box.
- The earliest pieces have a jack-o'-lantern on the porch. Later ones do not. Care must be taken in selecting one with a jack-o'-lantern since some collectors have added it to a piece that originally did not have one.
- Four bats hang from eaves, rocker is on porch, and a tree is attached in back. Matte finish.
- The box can separate even while in the sleeve so the box must be carried by the bottom.

Creepy Creek Carriage House   55055

Dates	OSRP	VDTsv	Paid
2000 - 2003	$75	$185	$_____

- Bat mobile is separate in box.

Hauntsburg House   55058

Dates	OSRP	VDTsv	Paid
2000 - 2002	$95	$95 - $98	$_____

- Grass platform is separate in box.
- Be careful removing from box; the tree is easily broken.

Haunted Barn

55060

Dates	OSRP	VDTsv	Paid
2001^M - 2001	$75	$135 -$195	$_____

- Halloween Discover Department 56 design. Limited to year of production.
- Set of 4 includes Barn, "Scarecrow Jack" accessory, fence, and tree.

The Spooky Schooner

55087

Dates	OSRP	VDTsv	Paid
2001 - 2002	$95	$98	$_____

- Limited to year of production, 2002.
- Has sound effects and green light.

Shipwreck Lighthouse

55088

Dates	OSRP	VDTsv	Paid
2001 - 2003	$110	$209 - $265	$_____

- Features animated ghost that glows in the dark.

Haunted Fun House Gift Set

55094

Dates	OSRP	VDTsv	Paid
2002^M - 2002	$75	$112 - $138	$_____

- Limited to year of production.
- Several features are animated.
- Set of 4 includes the Fun House, "Dressed Up For Fun" accessory, tree, and leaves.

Spooky Farmhouse

55315

Dates	OSRP	VDTsv	Paid
2002 - 2004	$55	$165	$_____

Helga's House Of Fortunes

55316

Dates	OSRP	VDTsv	Paid
2002 - 2004	$95	$120 - $160	$_____

• Tells fortunes.

Ghostly Carousel

55317

Dates	OSRP	VDTsv	Paid
2002 - 2005	$130	$395	$_____

• Animated with sounds.

Black Cat Diner

55319

Dates	OSRP	VDTsv	Paid
2002 - 2003	$75	$245	$_____

• Holiday Program.
• Limited to year of production.
• Set of 4 includes the Diner, "You Go First!" accessory, 10" tree, and leaves.

Haunted Windmill

55345

Dates	OSRP	VDTsv	Paid
2003 - 2006	$95	$295	$_____

• Working windmill.
• Makes horror sounds

1031 Trick-Or-Treat Drive 55343

Dates	OSRP	VDTsv	Paid
2003 - 2004	$75	$350	$_____

- Limited to year of production.
- Set of 8 includes the house, "Just Treats, No Tricks, Please" accessory, and Halloween decorations.

Castle Blackstone 55346

Dates	OSRP	VDTsv	Paid
2003 - 2005	$125	$250	$_____

- Makes horror sounds.

Witch Way? Flight School 55347

Dates	OSRP	VDTsv	Paid
2003 - 2004	$60	$225	$_____

- Limited to year of production.
- Set of 7 includes the School, "Practice Makes Perfect" accessory, and Halloween decorations.

Mickey's Haunted House 55375

Dates	OSRP	VDTsv	Paid
2004 - 2006	$85	$125	$_____

- Licensed by Disney.

LaGhosti Movie Theater

55374

Dates	OSRP	VDTsv	Paid
2004 - 2005	$75	$220	$_____

- Limited to year of production.
- Set of 7 includes the Theater and "Hurry — The Movie's About To Start!" accessory, tree, bench, fence, and leaves.
- Plays scary movie sounds, and threater marquee lights.

Witchs' Brew Pub

55376

Dates	OSRP	VDTsv	Paid
2004 - 2006	$80	$275	$_____

- Adapter included.
- Multi-color effect in caldron.

Dead End Motel

55377

Dates	OSRP	VDTsv	Paid
2004 - 2007	$60	$89	$_____

- Adapter included.
- Motel Sign lights and blinks.

Jack's Pumpkin Carving Studio

54600

Dates	OSRP	VDTsv	Paid
2005 - 2006	$80	-	$_____

- Limited to year of production.
- Set of 2 includes the Studio and "Jack And His Apprentice" accessory.
- Long Life Cordless Lighting.

Halloween Victorian House

54601

Dates	OSRP	VDTsv	Paid
2005 - 2007	$85	-	$_____

• Long Life Cordless Lighting.

Dr. Lunatic's Laboratory

54602

Dates	OSRP	VDTsv	Paid
2005 - 2008	$110	$110 - $188	$_____

• Long Life Cordless Lighting.

Hair Today, Gone Tomorrow

54603

Dates	OSRP	VDTsv	Paid
2005 - 2007	$70	$70 - $128	$_____

Be Witching Costume Shop

54604

Dates	OSRP	VDTsv	Paid
2006^M - 2006	$85	$279 - $345	$_____

• Limited Edition of 8,000.
• 30th Anniversary Series.

Zelda's Wax Museum

54605

Dates	OSRP	VDTsv	Paid
2006 - 2008	$90	$90 - $128	$_____

Dead Creek Mill

54606

Dates	OSRP	VDTsv	Paid
2006 - 2007	$100	$185	$_____

• Collectors' Edition.
• Limited Edition of 13,000.

Rest In Peace Tombstones 54608

Dates	OSRP	VDTsv	Paid
2006 -	$125	-	$_____

The Candy Cauldron 54609

Dates	OSRP	VDTsv	Paid
2006 -	$85	-	$_____

HOWL Radio 54610

Dates	OSRP	VDTsv	Paid
2007 - 2007	$90	$90 - $112	$_____

Rickety Railroad Station 800000

Dates	OSRP	VDTsv	Paid
2007 -	$120	-	$_____

Haunted Rails Engine & Coal Car 800001

Dates	OSRP	VDTsv	Paid
2007 -	$70	-	$_____

Ghoul School 799934

Dates	OSRP	VDTsv	Paid
2007 - 2009	$90	$72 - $90	$_____

Grimsly's House Of Oddities

799935

Dates	OSRP	VDTsv	Paid
2007 - 2009	$110	$88 - $110	$_____

Monsters Of The Deep

799936

Dates	OSRP	VDTsv	Paid
2007 - 2008	$125	$125 - $188	$_____

• Collectors' Edition.
• Limited Edition of 13,000.

Screech Owl Farm

804443

Dates	OSRP	VDTsv	Paid
2008^M -	$110	-	$_____

• With Sound

Croak-N-Haggard Mortuary

805673

Dates	OSRP	VDTsv	Paid
2008 - 2009	$125	$125	$_____

• Collectors' Edition.

Gravely Estate

805674

Dates	OSRP	VDTsv	Paid
2008 -	$130	-	$_____

Deep Woods Haunt

805675

Dates	OSRP	VDTsv	Paid
2008 -	$90	-	$_____

Black Widow Dating Service — 805676

Dates	OSRP	VDTsv	Paid
2008 -	$115	-	$_____

Haunted Rails Dining Car — 805677

Dates	OSRP	VDTsv	Paid
2008 -	$55	-	$_____

• Halloween 10th Anniversary.

Voodoo Lounge — 805678

Dates	OSRP	VDTsv	Paid
2010 -	$125	-	$_____

Rusty's Used Cars — 808965

Dates	OSRP	VDTsv	Paid
2010 -	$125	-	$_____

Critter's Pets & Pelts — 808986

Dates	OSRP	VDTsv	Paid
2010 -	$95	-	$_____

Screech Owl Farmhouse — 808988

Dates	OSRP	VDTsv	Paid
2010 -	$87.50	-	$_____

Haunted Rails Passenger Car

808992

Dates	OSRP	VDTsv	Paid
2010 -	$55	-	$_____

Notes:

Trick Or Treat Kids

54937 - Set of 3

1998^M - 2005

OSRP: $33

VDTsv: $25-$46

Paid: $_____

Costumes For Sale

54973 - Set of 2

1998 - 2002

OSRP: $60

VDTsv: $65

Paid: $_____

• Pumpkin lights are battery/adapter operated.

Preparing For Halloween

54982 - Set of 2

1999^M - 2002

OSRP: $40

VDTsv: $28-$29

Paid: $_____

Treats for The Kids

55016 - Set of 3

1999 - 2002

OSRP: $33

VDTsv: $66-$69

Paid: $_____

Lighting The Jack-O'-Lanterns

55117 - Set of 3

2000 - 2003

OSRP: $32.50

VDTsv: $20-$32

Paid: $_____

• Battery/adapter operated.

Scarecrow Jack

55060

2001^M - 2001

OSRP: *

VDTsv: *

* This accessory is contained in the Haunted Barn Gift Set.

Halloween Hayride

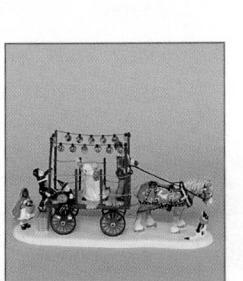

55148

2001 - 2006

OSRP: $45

VDTsv: $96

Paid: $_____

Captain Black Bart's Ghost

55149

2001 - 2002

OSRP: $18

VDTsv: $65-$69

Paid: $_____

Haunted Tree House

55150

2001 - 2006

OSRP: $45

VDTsv: $88

Paid: $_____

Dressed Up For Fun

55094

2002^M - 2002

OSRP: *

VDTsv: *

* The accessory contained in Haunted Fun House Gift Set.

Bobbing For Apples

55185

2002 - 2004

OSRP: $22.50

VDTsv: $16-$22

Paid: $_____

Halloween Kids

55186 - Set of 3

2002 - 2004

OSRP: $27.50

VDTsv: $65

Paid: $_____

Halloween Dance

55189

2002 - 2004

OSRP: $85

VDTsv: $158

Paid: $_____

• Musical and animated.

Strangers Beware

55192

2002 - 2006

OSRP: $17.50

VDTsv: $40

Paid: $_____

Campbell's® Trick-Or-Treat

55198

2002 - 2003

OSRP: $17.50

VDTsv: $27-$30

Paid: $_____

• Licensed by The Campbell Soup Co.

Gathering Pumpkins

55200

2002 - 2004

OSRP: $30

VDTsv: $26

Paid: $_____

Costume Parade

55201

2002 - 2003

OSRP: $50

VDTsv: $50-160

Paid: $_____

• Limited to year of production.
• Musical and animated.

Building The Scarecrow

55203

2002 - 2003

OSRP: $32.50

VDTsv: $98

Paid: $_____

• Limited to year of production.

You Go First!

55319

2002 - 2003

OSRP: *

VDTsv: *

* The accessory contained in Black Cat Diner.

Lighting Up Halloween

55238

2003 - 2006

OSRP: $27.50

VDTsv: $38

Paid: $_____

• Lights up; battery operated.

A Gravely Haunting - 2004

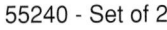

55240 - Set of 2

2003 - 2004

OSRP: $22.50

VDTsv: $23-45

Paid: $_____

• Limited to year of production, 2004.

Canine Trick-Or-Treaters

55241 - Set of 2

2003 - 2005

OSRP: $20

VDTsv: $34

Paid: $_____

Pick Your Own Pumpkin

55244

2003 - 2006

OSRP: $30

VDTsv: -

Paid: $_____

Haunted Harvest

55245

2003 - 2005

OSRP: $17.50

VDTsv: $78

Paid: $_____

Creative Carvings

55246

2003 - 2005

OSRP: $32.50

VDTsv: $65

Paid: $_____

• Battery/adapter operated.

Forever On Guard

55248

2003 - 2005

OSRP: $17.50

VDTsv: $40

Paid: $_____

• Battery/adapter operated.

Just Treats, No Tricks, Please

55343

2003 - 2004

OSRP: *

VDTsv: *

* The accessory contained in 1031 Trick-Or-Treat Drive.

Practice Makes Perfect

55347

2003 - 2004

OSRP: *

VDTsv: *

* The accessory contained in Witch Way? Flight School.

Haunted Coal Car

53156 - Set of 3

2004^M - 2009

OSRP: $85

VDTsv: -

Paid: $_____

• Animated

Haunted Tower Tours

55257

2004 - 2006

OSRP: $35

VDTsv: $98

Paid: $_____

• Adapter included.

A Gravely Haunting - 2005

55270

2004 - 2005

OSRP: $20

VDTsv: $20-42

Paid: $_____

• Limited to year of production.

Can't Wait For Halloween!

55272 - Set of 2

2004 - 2006

OSRP: $20

VDTsv: $20-48

Paid: $_____

Happy Haunting

55273

2004 - 2006

OSRP: $22.50

VDTsv: $42

Paid: $_____

• Licensed by Disney.

Brew Ha-Ha

55274

2004 - 2007

OSRP: $15

VDTsv: $15-28

Paid: $_____

Caramel Apple Stand

55275

2004 - 2007

OSRP: $27.50

VDTsv: $36

Paid: $_____

• Battery/adapter compatible.

Black Kittens For Sale

55276

2004 - 2008

OSRP: $10

VDTsv: $13-22

Paid: $_____

Halloween Hot Rod

55277

2004 - 2009

OSRP: $18.50

VDTsv: -

Paid: $_____

Hurry The Movie's About To Start!

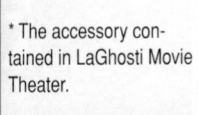

55374 - Set of 7

2004 - 2005

OSRP: *

VDTsv: *

* The accessory contained in LaGhosti Movie Theater.

Haunted Taxi

53213

2005 - 2008

OSRP: $17.50

VDTsv: -

Paid: $_____

Jack And His Apprentice

54600

2005 - 2006

OSRP: *

VDTsv: *

* The accessory contained in Jack's Pumpkin Carving Studio.

Topping Off The Scarecrow

54701

2005 - 2007

OSRP: $17.50

VDTsv: $14-$32

Paid: $_____

Dr. Lunatic, The Mad Scientist

54702

2005 - 2008

OSRP: $17.50

VDTsv: $17-$38

Paid: $_____

Bats In My Belfry!

54703

2005 - 2007

OSRP: $17.50

VDTsv: $17-$30

Paid: $_____

A Gravely Haunting - 2006

54705

2005 - 2006

OSRP: $25

VDTsv: $36

Paid: $_____

• Limited to year of production.

Grimsley's Garage

54706

2005 -

OSRP: $45

VDTsv: -

Paid: $_____

• Complements Grimsley's Manor.

Building Fort Frightful

54707

2005 - 2007

OSRP: $20

VDTsv: $20-$28

Paid: $_____

Little Space Explorers

54708

2005 - 2007

OSRP: $18.50

VDTsv: $18-$38

Paid: $_____

A Vampire's Best Friend

54709

2005 - 2007

OSRP: $15

VDTsv: $30

Paid: $_____

Madame Zelda At Work

54710

2006 - 2008

OSRP: $18.50

VDTsv: $18-$32

Paid: $_____

How About Our Lay-Away Plan?

54711

2006 - 2008

OSRP: $22.50

VDTsv: $22-$27

Paid: $_____

Candy Kids

54713

2006 - 2008

OSRP: $22.50

VDTsv: $22-$27

Paid: $_____

A Gravely Haunting - 2007

54714

2006 - 2007

OSRP: $25

VDTsv: $25-$35

Paid: $_____

• Limited to year of production.

Dead Creek Mill Delivery

54715

2006 - 2009

OSRP: $35

VDTsv: $35

Paid: $_____

Getting Candy For Halloween

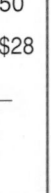

54716

2006 - 2008

OSRP: $17.50

VDTsv: $17-$28

Paid: $_____

Grimsly's Tool Shed

54717

2006 - 2009

OSRP: $35

VDTsv: $28-$35

Paid: $_____

Time's-A-Wastin'

800216

2007 -

OSRP: $22.50

VDTsv: -

Paid: $_____

A Gravely Haunting, 2008

799976

2007 - 2008

OSRP: $25

VDTsv: $20-$46

Paid: $_____

Autographs With Dracula

799977

2007 - 2009

OSRP: $32.50

VDTsv: $23-$33

Paid: $_____

A Grimsly Family

799978

2007 -

OSRP: $29.50

VDTsv: -

Paid: $_____

Come In If You Dare

799979

2007 -

OSRP: $45

VDTsv: $36

Paid: $_____

Photos With Frankenstein

799980

2007 - 2009

OSRP: $32.50

VDTsv: $33

Paid: $_____

Little Ghouls' Field Trip

799981

2007 - 2009

OSRP: $29.50

VDTsv: $30

Paid: $_____

Time To Feed The Monsters

799982

2007 - 2009

OSRP: $17.50

VDTsv: $18

Paid: $_____

An Ax To Grind

804456

2008^M -

OSRP: $22.50

VDTsv: -

Paid: $_____

Halloween 10th Anniversary Sign

805026

2008^M - 2008

OSRP: $20

VDTsv: $20-$28

Paid: $_____

A Grave Undertaker

807301

2008 - 2009

OSRP: $22.50

VDTsv: $23

Paid: $_____

Grimsly's Family Crypt

807302

2008 -

OSRP: $37.50

VDTsv: -

Paid: $_____

Made For Each Other

807303

2008 -

OSRP: $30

VDTsv: -

Paid: $_____

The Old Hermit In The Woods

807304

2008 -

OSRP: $18.50

VDTsv: -

Paid: $_____

Dinner Is Served

807305

2008 -

OSRP: $15

VDTsv: -

Paid: $_____

•Halloween 10th
Anniversary

Gravely Haunting, 2009

807306

2008 - 2009

OSRP: $32.50

VDTsv: $33

Paid: $_____

Let's Go To The Moon

807307

2008 -

OSRP: $30

VDTsv: -

Paid: $_____

•Halloween 10th Anniversary

Go Team! Trick-Or-Treaters

807308

2008 - 2009

OSRP: $30

VDTsv: $30

Paid: $_____

Rusty Scares Up A Deal

808998

2010 -

OSRP: $18.50

VDTsv: -

Paid: $_____

Midnight's Last Ride

808999

2010 -

OSRP: $25

VDTsv: -

Paid: $_____

Deranged Chickens

809002

2010 -

OSRP: $23.50

VDTsv: -

Paid: $_____

Service With A Smile

809003

2010 -

OSRP: $20

VDTsv: -

Paid: $_____

Halloween Kittens

809004

2010 -

OSRP: $25

VDTsv: -

Paid: $_____

Don't Forget To Tip Your Server

809361

2010 -

OSRP: $22.50

VDTsv: -

Paid: $_____

The Zombies

811779
2010 -
OSRP: $32.50
VDTsv: -
Paid: $_____

Notes:

Several Halloween buildings and accessories have been produced within the Original Snow Village Collection.

These General Village pieces can be used by themselves or in combination with those items.

String Of 12 Pumpkin Lights
$13   52700
1998 - 2001

Jack-O' Lanterns
$10   52701
1998 - 2002

Up, Up & Away Witch - Animated
$50   52711
1998 - 2003

Halloween Luminaries
$44   52738
1998 - 2002

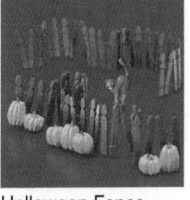

Halloween Fence
$12.50   52702
1998 - 2004

Halloween Accessories
$50   52704
1998 - 2001

Halloween Spooky Tree
$48   52770
1998 - 2002

Witch By The Light Of The Moon
$30   52879
2000 - 2004

Lit Spooky Tree
$30   52896
2000 - 2007

Haunted Front Yard
$65   52924
2001ᴹ - 2006

Halloween Scene
$45   52933
2001ᴹ - 2004

Haunted Graveyard
$36   52513
2001 - 2004

Village Swinging Skeleton - Animated
$36   52514
2001 - 2003

Hocus Pocus Witch - Animated
$30   52516
2001 - 2007

Halloween Pumpkin Stand
$35   52956
2001 - 2004

Halloween Village
Set, s/24
$35   52957
2001 - 2003

Halloween Full Moon
$30   52960
2001 - 2003

Gothic Street Lamp,
s/2
$17.50   52961
2001 - 2004

Spooky Black Bare
Branch Trees, s/3
$12.50   52964
2001 - 2002

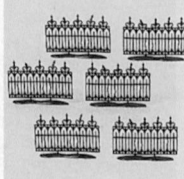

Spooky Wrought Iron
Fence, s/6
$15   52982
2001 -

Autumn/Halloween
Landscape Set, s/6
$35   52992
2001 - 2002

Jack-O'-Lantern
String of 12 Lights
$7.50   53000
2001 - 2004

Candy Corn String of
20 Lights
$10   53013
2001 - 2003

Halloween Village
Sign
$7.50   53044
2002 - 2003

Witch Crash
$36   53056
2002 - 2004

Haunted Hearse
$42.50   53057
2002 - 2006

Skeleton Fence
$12.50   53059
2002 - 2005

Gravely Landscape
Set, s/8
$45   53060
2002 - 2006

Lighted Halloween
Scarecrows, s/2
$25   53061
2002 - 2004

Halloween Topiaries,
s/3
$17.50   53062
2002 - 2003

Spooky Totem
$12.50   53063
2002 - 2003

Tombstones, s/6
$10   53065
2002 -

Spooky Black Glitter
Tree, s/3
$17.50   53067
2002 - 2005

Haunted Outhouse
$25   53068
2002 - 2007

Creepy Creek Bridge
$35   53071
2002 - 2006

Over The Hill
Tombstone
$12   53072
2002 - 2004

Haunted Fiber Optic
Backdrop
$65   53075
2002 - 2004

Jack-O-Lantern
Pumpkins, s/12
$7.50   53077
2002 - 2004

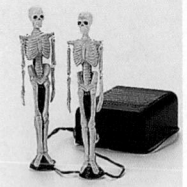

Skull Street Lamps,
s/4
$17.50   53079
2002 - 2007

Glowing String of
Scary Lights, 2 Astd
$12.50   53080
2002 - 2004

Spooky Willows, s/2
$17.50   53087
2002 - 2004

Ghostly Landscape
Set, s/12 (Exclusive)
$35   04771
2003 - 2003

Eerie Rocks & Road,
s/8
$35   53119
2003 - 2005

Phantom Of The
Organ
$65   53126
2003 - 2006

Rock-A-Bye Vampire
$36   53128
2003 - 2006

Lit Graveyard Tree
$17.50   53129
2003 - 2005

Halloween Yard
Decorations, s/22
$12.50   53130
2003 -

Scary Twisted Trees,
s/2
$20   53131
2003 - 2005

Scaredy Bat
$45   53132
2003 - 2005

Swinging Ghoulies
$55   53133
2003 -

Ghostly Landscape
Set, s/12
$35   53143
2003 - 2005

Spooky Village Sign
$7.50   53144
2003 - 2004

Harvest Gourds, s/10
$7.50   53145
2003 - 2005

Resting My Bones
$25   53146
2003 -

Mummy Mischief
$30   53148
2003 - 2005

Bubble Light Ghosts
s/2
$25   53149
2003 - 2004

Pumpkin Street
Lamps, s/2
$12.50   53150
2003 - 2005

Halloween Parade
$32.50   53157
2004 - 2006

Honest, This Tree
Came Out Of Nowhere!
$17.50   53158
2004 - 2007

Taking Bones For A
Walk
$55   53159
2004 - 2006

Escape From The
Crypt
$55   53160
2004 - 2006

Shaking Graveyard
$45   53162
2004 - 2006

Killing Time
$25   53164
2004 - 2007

Halloween Scenery,
s/9
$12.50   53165
2004 - 2009

Monster Park Statues
$20   53166
2004 - 2006

Bat Lights, s/2
$17.50   53167
2004 - 2009

Halloween Twinkle
Brite Tree
$20   53168
2004 - 2008

Harvest Mailbox
$12.50   53169
2004 - 2008

Creepy Village Sign
$7.50   53170
2004 - 2006

Spinning Pumpkins
$75   53173
2004 - 2009

Bats & Spooks Tree,
s/2
$17.50   53176
2004 - 2007

Spooky Yard Scene
$27.50   53177
2004 - 2007

Candy Corn Trees,
s/2
$15   53205
2004 - 2006

Scaredy Cat Ferris
Wheel
$85^M - 2009   53208
2005

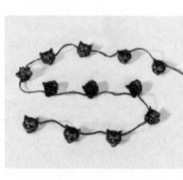

String Of 12 Black
Cat Lights
$10   53209
2005^M - 2006

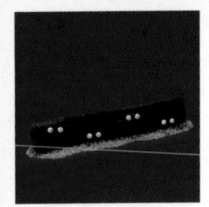

Lighted Spooky
Eyeball Hedge
$20   53211
2005 - 2008

Scarecrow & His
Feathered Friends
$50   53212
2005 - 2007

Hanging Around
$32   53214
2005 - 2008

Halloween Sounds
Scene
$50   53215
2005 - 2008

Bewitched Street
Lights
$17.50   53216
2005 - 2008

Spooky Lemonade
Stand
$20   53217
2005 - 2008

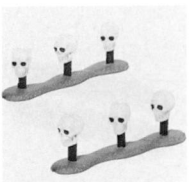

Skull Lawn Lights
$17.50   53218
2005 - 2008

Runaway Monster &
Bride
$65   53219
2005 - 2007

Witch Rides
$50   53220
2005 - 2007

Bone To Be Wild
$20   53221
2005 -

Ghastly Organ
Grinder
$18.50   53222
2005 - 2008

Halloween Water
Tower
$32.50   53223
2005 -

Halloween Creepy
Street
$20   53224
2005 - 2009

String Of 12 Orange
& Purple Lights
$15   53225
2005 -

Halloween Rat Race
$65   53226
2006 - 2008

Ship Of Sea
Phantoms
$75   53227
2006 - 2008

Halloween Festival
$75   53229
2006 - 2008

Campfire Scary
Stories
$18.50   53240
2006 - 2008

Halloween Festival
Billboard
$25   53241
2006 - 2008

Creepy Lighted Front
Yard
$70   53242
2006 - 2008

Skeleton Crew
$25   53243
2006 - 2009

Halloween Monsters
Rock Band
$32.50   53245
2006 - 2008

Halloween Accessory
Set, S/5
$20   53246
2006 - 2008

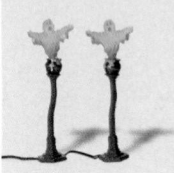

Ghostly Glow Street
Lights, S/2
$17.50   53260
2006 - 2008

Lighted Jack-O-
Lantern Tree
$17.50   53270
2006 - 2009

Halloween Twinkle
Brite Hedge, S/2
$22.50   53271
2006 -

Halloween Purple
Twinkle Brite Tree
$25   53272
2006 -

Halloween Orange
Twinkle Brite Tree
$20   53273
2006 -

Airborne Witch
$16 - $25   800022
2007 - 2009

Bone Appetite
$33   800023
2007 - 2009

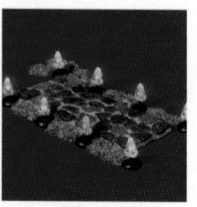

Candy Corn Lawn
Lights
$19   800024
2007 - 2009

Corn Stalk Lanterns
Set of 2
$20   800025
2007 -

Halloween Decorating
Set 5
$16 - $25   800026
2007 - 2008

Gothic Gate
$35   800027
2007 -

Halloween Oak Tree
$14 - $18   800028
2007 - 2009

Pumpkin Heads
Set of 5
$12.50   800029
2007 -

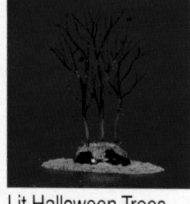

Lit Halloween Trees
$33   800030
2007 - 2009

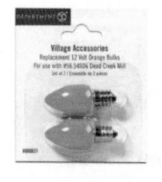

Replacement 12 Volt
Orange Bulbs
$5   800031
2007 -

Scary Street Lights
Set of 2
$18 - $23   800032
2007 - 2009

Scary Walk
Includes Adapter Cord
$85   800033
2007 -

Spooky Spider Trees
Set of 2
$17.50   800034
2007 -

String Of 8 Spooky
Eyeball Lights
$15   800035
2007 - 2009

Swampy Boat Ride
$90   810632
2008 -

Up, Up, & Away Witch
With Ghosts
$50   810633
2008 -

Lazy Bones
$32.50   810634
2008 -

The Grim Reaper
$18.50   810636
2008 -

Graveyard Shift
$27.50   810637
2008 -

Creatures of the
Night, Set of 6
$12.50   810638
2008 -

Haunted Rails Water
Tower
$40   810639
2008 -

Haunted Rails
Crossing Sign
$22.50   810640
2008 -

Halloween Park
Bench
$5   810641
2008 -

Gothic Gate Fence
Sections
$22.50   810642
2008 -

Hanging Ghosts
Set of 6
$5   810643
2008 -

Halloween Street
Lamps
$20   810795
2008 -

Spooky Sidewalk
Luminaries
$15   810797
2008 -

Lit Jack-O-Lanterns
$22.50   810798
2008 -

String Of 12 Oozing
Slime Lights
$15   810799
2008 -

String Of 12 Jack-O-
Lantern Lights
$15   810800
2008 -

String of 12 Purple
Lights
$18.50   810801
2008 -

Replacement Light
Bulbs, Or. & Pur.
$5   810803
2008 -

Spooky Shadows Oak
Tree
$20   810806
2008 -

Animated Haunted
Wall
$55   809362
2010 -

Foggy Point Platform
$125   809379
2010 -

Chilled To The Bone
$25   809380
2010 -

Made To Be Wild
$28.50   809381
2010 -

Scary Warning Signs
$15   809386
2010 -

Spooky Mailboxes
$20   809387
2010 -

Lady & The Vamp
$28.50   809390
2010 -

Eyeball Street Lights
$20   809399
2010 -

Lit Cauldrons
$20   809400
2010 -

Purple Glitter Sisal
Trees
$15   809455
2010 -

Purple Glitter Bare
Branch Tree
$8.50   809456
2010 -

Copper Glitter Bare
Branch Tree
$8.50   809457
2010 -

Dickens' Village Series®

"It was the best of times, it was the worst of times."
— *Charles Dickens (1812 – 1870) A Tale of Two Cities*

The original buildings from Dickens' Village — the first Heritage Village collection — were issued in 1984. Contrast those to the current introductions in the same village and it is definitely *A Tale of Two Cities*. The tiny butcher, baker, and candlestick maker, as well as the other four within the original set of seven, are simple, but oh so charming, and coveted by Dickens' collectors. Charles John Huffman Dickens, after whom this village was named, was the premiere English novelist of the Victorian Era. He achieved worldwide acclaim in his own lifetime. His 1843 novel *A Christmas Carol* rekindled the joy and traditions of Christmas celebrations throughout the western world.

Several of Dickens' short stories and novels are portrayed in Dickens' Village. Besides pieces illustrating *A Christmas Carol*, several other stories are represented including *David Copperfield*, *Nicholas Nickleby*, *Oliver Twist*, and the *Old Curiosity Shop*. Dickens' himself is featured in accessory pieces.

The village depicts England in the late 1800s: the rich and the poor. Numerous merchant shops and pubs; thatched roofed cottages and stately rural manors; and country inns and lodges are prevalent. Several sub-series have been issued including the Abington Canal, A Victorian Christmas, Queens Port, and All Hallow's Eve™. Each is designed to be all inclusive as a display vignette. Beautiful cathedrals and delightful country churches abound. Formal rail stations and modest rural depots help travelers traverse the diverse landscape, while royalty board their fancy carriages and coaches.

Some of England's most famous buildings add reality to the setting or stand alone as a tribute to historic London. "Big Ben," "Tower Bridge of London," "Old Globe Theater," "Windsor Castle," and "Buckingham Palace" are replicas of the actual buildings. They are also designated as Historical Landmark Series™ buildings. Dickens' Village has always been one of the most diverse, charming, and popular villages.

THE ORIGINAL SHOPS OF DICKENS' VILLAGE - Set of 7

65153

Dates	OSRP	VDTsv	Paid
1984 - 1988	$175	$668	$_____

• None of the seven buildings have names on the bottom.

Crowntree Inn

65153

Dates	OSRP	VDTsv	Paid
1984 - 1988	$25	$150	$_____

Candle Shop

65153

Dates	OSRP	VDTsv	Paid
1984 - 1988	$25	$210	$_____

• Early pieces have gray roofs. Later ones have blue.

Green Grocer

65153

Dates	OSRP	VDTsv	Paid
1984 - 1988	$25	$98	$_____

• Though there is snow at the base and above the front window, there is no snow on the roof.

Golden Swan Baker

65153

Dates	OSRP	VDTsv	Paid
1984 - 1988	$25	$115	$_____

Bean And Son Smithy Shop

65153

Dates	OSRP	VDTsv	Paid
1984 - 1988	$25	$72 - $88	$_____

Abel Beesley Butcher

65153

Dates	OSRP	VDTsv	Paid
1984 - 1988	$25	$88	$_____

Jones & Co. Brush & Basket Shop

65153

Dates	OSRP	VDTsv	Paid
1984 - 1988	$25	$214	$_____

Dickens' Village Church

65161

Dates	OSRP	VDTsv	Paid
1985 - 1989	$35	**See below**	

- There are 5 recognized versions of the Village Church.
- White: Very pale walls and brown cornerstones and roof.
  VDTsv: **$395**   Paid: $_____
- Yellow: Yellowish walls with butterscotch stones and roof.
  VDTsv: **$100**   Paid: $_____
- Green: Pale green walls with butterscotch stones and roof.
  VDTsv: **$195**   Paid: $_____
- Tan: Tan walls with butterscotch stones and roof.
  VDTsv: **$110-$135** Paid: $_____
- Butterscotch: Walls and roof are nearly the same butterscotch color. Only sleeve to read "Village Church." All others read "Shops of Dickens' Village."
  VDTsv: **$80**   Paid: $_____

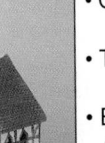

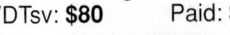

Dickens' Village Mill

65196

Dates	OSRP	VDTsv	Paid
1985 - 1986	$35	$3600 - $4725	$_____

- Limited Edition of 2,500.
- Early pieces have sleeves that read "Dickens' Village Cottage."
- Early release to GCC dealers.

DICKENS' COTTAGES — Set of 3   65188

Dates	OSRP	VDTsv	Paid
1985 - 1988	**$75**	**$528**	$_____

- None of the three buildings have names on the bottom.
- Early release to GCC dealers.

Thatched Cottage   65188

Dates	OSRP	VDTsv	Paid
1985 - 1988	**$25**	**$88**	$_____

- Early release to GCC dealers.

Stone Cottage   65188

Dates	OSRP	VDTsv	Paid
1985 - 1988	**$25**	**$128**	

- The Tan version is considered to be the first shipped.
- The Green version's walls vary from light green to a pea green.
- The chimneys are very fragile.
- Early release to GCC dealers.

	VDTsv	Paid
Tan	-	$_____
Green	-	$_____

Tudor Cottage   65188

Dates	OSRP	VDTsv	Paid
1985 - 1988	**$25**	**$128**	$_____

- The chimneys are very fragile and are often crooked.
- Early release to GCC dealers.

Norman Church   65021

Dates	OSRP	VDTsv	Paid
1986 - 1987	**$40**	**$2900**	$_____

- Limited Edition of 3,500.
- Early Churches are light gray, and they got increasingly darker as production continued.
- Early release to GCC dealers.

CHRISTMAS CAROL COTTAGES — Set of 3   65005

Dates	OSRP	VDTsv	Paid
1986 - 1995	$75	-	$_____

• Originally marketed as its own sub-series of Dickens' Village with sleeves and hangtags that read "*A Christmas Carol.*" The early pieces were made in Taiwan, and later ones were made in the Philippines.

Fezziwig's Warehouse   65005

Dates	OSRP	VDTsv	Paid
1986 - 1995	$25	$64 - $68	$_____

• Early pieces have panes cut out of the front door. Later ones have a solid front door.

Scrooge & Marley Counting House   65005

Dates	OSRP	VDTsv	Paid
1986 - 1995	$25	$18 - $39	$_____

• First of two pieces with this name. Re-issued in 2000.

The Cottage of Bob Cratchit & Tiny Tim   65005

Dates	OSRP	VDTsv	Paid
1986 - 1995	$25	$47 - $58	$_____

• Many scholars believe that Dickens modeled his version of this home after his own childhood home on Bayham St. in Camden Town.

Blythe Pond Mill House   65080

Dates	OSRP	VDTsv	Paid
1986 - 1990	$37	See below	

• Early shipments are commonly referred to as the "Correct" version. "Blythe Pond" is correctly inscribed in the bottom of the building.
• This is the rarer of the two versions.
• Later shipments are commonly referred to as the "By The Pond" version. "BY THE POND" is incorrectly inscribed in the bottom of the building.
• The sign above the door is correct on both versions.

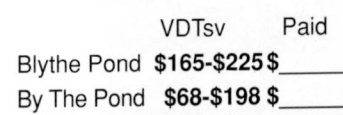

	VDTsv	Paid
Blythe Pond	$165-$225	$_____
By The Pond	$68-$198	$_____

DICKENS' LANE SHOPS - Set of 3   65072

Dates	OSRP	VDTsv	Paid
1986 - 1989	$80	$185	$_____

Thomas Kersey Coffee House   65072

Dates	OSRP	VDTsv	Paid
1986 - 1989	$27	$75 - $135	$_____

• Bottomstamp reads "Coffee House."

Cottage Toy Shop   65072

Dates	OSRP	VDTsv	Paid
1986 - 1989	$27	$90 - $98	$_____

• Bottomstamp reads "Toy Shop."

Tuttle's Pub   65072

Dates	OSRP	VDTsv	Paid
1986 - 1989	$27	$145	$_____

• Bottomstamp reads "Pub."

Chadbury Station And Train — Set of 4   65285

Dates	OSRP	VDTsv	Paid
1986 - 1989	$65	$345	$_____

• The front of the platform on the first version of the station is 9" wide.
• The front of the platform on the second version is 9½" wide.
• Early sleeve reads "Train And Lighted Station." The later sleeve reads "Chadbury Station And Train."

BARLEY BREE — Set of 2   59005

Dates	OSRP	VDTsv	Paid
1987 - 1989	$60	$128	$_____

- Though the pieces of this set were originally priced at $30 each, they are boxed together. It is extremely rare for them to be sold separately on the secondary market.
- Early pieces have dark roofs. Later ones have lighter roofs.

The Old Curiosity Shop   59056

Dates	OSRP	VDTsv	Paid
1987 - 1999	$32	$28 - $44	$_____

- Designed after the Old Curiosity Shop on Portsmouth Street in London.
- First of two pieces with this name. Re-issued in 2000.

Kenilworth Castle   59161

Dates	OSRP	VDTsv	Paid
1987 - 1988	$70	$455 - $475	$_____

- Bottom reads "Castle."
- Early pieces are approx. 9" tall, later ones approx. 8½".
- It's not unusual for this piece to have concave walls. One with straight walls is considered more valuable.

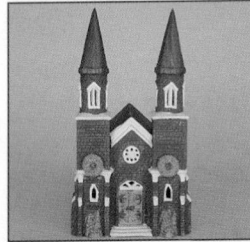

Brick Abbey   65498

Dates	OSRP	VDTsv	Paid
1987 - 1989	$33	$168	$_____

- Many pieces have spires that lean inward. One with straight spires is considered more valuable.

Chesterton Manor House   65684

Dates	OSRP	VDTsv	Paid
1987 - 1988	$45	$540	$_____

- Limited Edition of 7,500.
- Both the bottomstamp and box read "Manor."
- Early release to GCC dealers.

Counting House & Silas Thimbleton Barrister

59021

Dates	OSRP	VDTsv	Paid
1988 - 1990	$32	$38-$72	$___

- Early pieces have lamps with natural porcelain panes. Later ones have lamps with panes painted yellow.
- Box reads "Silas Thimbleton Barrister." Bottomstamp reads "Counting House."

C. Fletcher Public House

59048

Dates	OSRP	VDTsv	Paid
1988 - 1989	$35	$250 - $285	$___

- Limited Edition of 12,500.
- Box and bottomstamp read "Public House."
- There are some proofs available, though they are rare.
- Early release to GCC dealers.

COBBLESTONE SHOPS — Set of 3

59242

Dates	OSRP	VDTsv	Paid
1988 - 1990	$95	$220	$___

The Wool Shop

59242

Dates	OSRP	VDTsv	Paid
1988 - 1990	$32	$128 - $135	$___

Booter And Cobbler

59242

Dates	OSRP	VDTsv	Paid
1988 - 1990	$32	$48 - $68	$___

- Some sleeves picture T. Wells Fruit & Spice Shop though they read "Booter & Cobbler" as they should.
- Some others picture Booter & Cobbler as they should and read "T. Wells Fruit & Spice Shop."

T. Wells Fruit & Spice Shop

59242

Dates	OSRP	VDTsv	Paid
1988 - 1990	$32	$45 - $78	$___

- Some sleeves picture Booter & Cobbler though they read "T. Wells Fruit & Spice Shop" as they should.
- Some others picture T. Wells Fruit & Spice Shop as they should and read "Booter & Cobbler."

MERCHANT SHOPS — Set of 5   59269

Dates	OSRP	VDTsv	Paid
1988 - 1993	$150	$45 - $135	$_____

Poulterer   59269

Dates	OSRP	VDTsv	Paid
1988 - 1993	$32.50	$35 - $65	$_____

Geo. Weeton Watchmaker   59269

Dates	OSRP	VDTsv	Paid
1988 - 1993	$32.50	$24 - $45	$_____

The Mermaid Fish Shoppe   59269

Dates	OSRP	VDTsv	Paid
1988 - 1993	$32.50	$48 - $54	$_____

White Horse Bakery   59269

Dates	OSRP	VDTsv	Paid
1988 - 1993	$32.50	$40 - $68	$_____

Walpole Tailors   59269

Dates	OSRP	VDTsv	Paid
1988 - 1993	$32.50	$24 - $34	$_____

NICHOLAS NICKLEBY — Set of 2   59250

Dates	OSRP	VDTsv	Paid
1988 - 1991	$72	$100	$_____

**Set with the "K" version of
Nicholas Nickleby Cottage:** $110 $_____

Nicholas Nickleby Cottage   59250

Dates	OSRP	VDTsv	Paid
1988 - 1991	$36	$44 - $62	$_____

• Early pieces have a bottomstamp that reads "Nickolas
Nickleby."   **VDTsv: $72** $_____

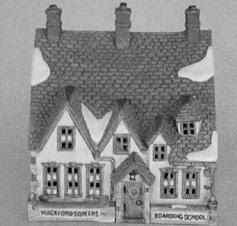

Wackford Squeers Boarding School   59250

Dates	OSRP	VDTsv	Paid
1988 - 1991	$36	$30 - $45	$_____

• Dickens based his version of the school on the Bowes
Academy that once stood in Yorkshire.
• The majority of these have a sagging roof.

Ivy Glen Church   59277

Dates	OSRP	VDTsv	Paid
1988 - 1991	$35	$38 - $58	$_____

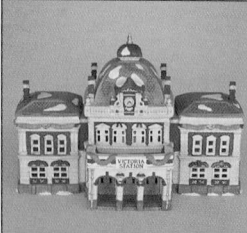

Victoria Station   55743

Dates	OSRP	VDTsv	Paid
1989 - 1998	$100	$112 - $119	$_____

• Inspired by the famous station in London.
• Early release to Showcase and NALED dealers.

Knottinghill Church   55824

Dates	OSRP	VDTsv	Paid
1989 - 1995	$50	$40 - $70	$_____

DAVID COPPERFIELD — Set of 3 — 55506

Dates	OSRP	VDTsv	Paid
1989 - 1992	$125	-	$_____

**Set with the Tan version of
Peggotty's Seaside Cottage:** $160 $_____

• Early release to Showcase dealers.

Mr. Wickfield Solicitor — 55506

Dates	OSRP	VDTsv	Paid
1989 - 1992	$42.50	$54 - $68	$_____

• Dickens based his version of this house on one that stands at 71 St. Dunstan's St. in Canterbury, England.
• Early release to Showcase dealers.

Betsy Trotwood's Cottage — 55506

Dates	OSRP	VDTsv	Paid
1989 - 1992	$42.50	$20 - $46	$_____

• Dickens based his version of this cottage on one owned by Mary Strong in Broadstairs, England. It is now a Dickens museum.
• Early release to Showcase dealers.

Peggotty's Seaside Cottage — 55506

Dates	OSRP	VDTsv	Paid
1989 - 1992	$42.50	See below	

• The Tan version was the earlier of the two. Its hull is not painted. Department 56 stated that the green paint it intended to use would not adhere to the porcelain.
• The problem was resolved by using a different green paint.
• This was an early release to Showcase dealers.
• Dickens based his version of the cottage on an actual boat-turned dwelling at the canal at Gravesend.

	VDTsv	Paid
Tan	$65-$79	$_____
Green	$28-$59	$_____

Cobles Police Station — 55832

Dates	OSRP	VDTsv	Paid
1989 - 1991	$37.50	$115 - $124	$_____

Theatre Royal 55840

Dates	OSRP	VDTsv	Paid
1989 - 1992	$45	$46 - $56	$_____

• Inspired by the Theatre Royal in Rochester, England where Dickens saw his first Shakespearean play.

Ruth Marion Scotch Woolens 55859

Dates	OSRP	VDTsv	Paid
1989 - 1990	$65	$224-$295	$_____

• Limited Edition of 17,500.
• Proofs have "Proof" stamped on the bottom and on the sleeve instead of a number. **$125** $_____
• Early release to GCC dealers.

Green Gate Cottage 55867

Dates	OSRP	VDTsv	Paid
1989 - 1990	$65	$105 - $158	$_____

• Limited Edition of 22,500.
• Proofs have "Proof" stamped on the bottom and on the sleeve instead of a number. **$125** $_____
• Early release to Showcase Dealers.

The Flat Of Ebenezer Scrooge 55875

Dates	OSRP	VDTsv	Paid
1989 - 2001	$37.50	$45 - $79	$_____

• Version 1:
• Window panes on the second and third floor are painted yellow. The fourth floor's far left shutter is slightly open.
• Gray trim is darker than on subsequent editions.
• Early release to NALED dealers.

• Version 2:
• All panes have been cut out of the windows on the second and third floors.
• Like Version 1, this was made in Taiwan.

• Version 3:
• Window panes are yellow. The far left shutter on the 4th floor is closed. Made in Philippines and China.
• *A Christmas Carol* Series.
• Ebenezer Scrooge's House introduced in 2001.

	VDTsv	Paid
Version 1	-	$_____
Version 2	-	$_____
Version 3	-	$_____

Bishops Oast House

55670

Dates	OSRP	VDTsv	Paid
1990 - 1992	$45	$38 - $52	$_____

• "Bishops" refers to a surname, not a religious figure.
• Oast houses dot the Kent countryside. Many have been converted into private homes.

King's Road — Set of 2

55689

Dates	OSRP	VDTsv	Paid
1990 - 1996	$72	$74	$_____

Tutbury Printer

55690

Dates	OSRP	VDTsv	Paid
1990 - 1996	$36	$28 - $42	$_____

C. H. Watt Physician

55691

Dates	OSRP	VDTsv	Paid
1990 - 1996	$36	$56 - $106	$_____

Fagin's Hide-A-Way

55522

Dates	OSRP	VDTsv	Paid
1991 - 1995	$68	$39 - $84	$_____

• Dickens based his Fagin's Hide-A-Way and its characters in Oliver Twist on the people who frequented the series of underground passages in London.

Ashbury Inn

55557

Dates	OSRP	VDTsv	Paid
1991 - 1995	$55	$38 - $58	$_____

OLIVER TWIST — Set of 2   55530

Dates	OSRP	VDTsv	Paid
1991 - 1993	$75	$56	$_____

Brownlow House   55530

Dates	OSRP	VDTsv	Paid
1991 - 1993	$37.50	$30 - $85	$_____

• Early samples have charcoal gray roof and trim.
• Dickens based his version of this house on the one at 39 Craven Street in London.

Maylie Cottage   55530

Dates	OSRP	VDTsv	Paid
1991 - 1993	$37.50	$30 - $48	$_____

Nephew Fred's Flat   55573

Dates	OSRP	VDTsv	Paid
1991 - 1994	$35	$64 - $68	$_____

• *A Christmas Carol* Series.
• Early pieces were manufactured in Taiwan and are darker than the later ones from China.
• Later version, Fred Holiwell's House, introduced in 2001.

Crown & Cricket Inn   57509

Dates	OSRP	VDTsv	Paid
1991 - 1992	$100	$78 - $88	$_____

• Limited to year of production.
• The first of the Charles Dickens' Signature Series™.
• Early pieces have light trim, later ones darker gray trim.

Old Michaelchurch   55620

Dates	OSRP	VDTsv	Paid
1992 - 1996	$42	$41 - $88	$_____

• Early release to Showcase and GCC dealers.

The Pied Bull Inn

57517

Dates	OSRP	VDTsv	Paid
1992 - 1993	$100	$70 - $72	$_____

- Limited to year of production.
- Charles Dickens' Signature Series™.
- Sign is separate in box.

Hembleton Pewterer

58009

Dates	OSRP	VDTsv	Paid
1992 - 1995	$72	$38 - $72	$_____

- The right side of the early pieces is composed of two small additions. On the later ones it is one large addition.

King's Road Post Office

58017

Dates	OSRP	VDTsv	Paid
1992 - 1998	$45	$31 - $48	$_____

- Flag is separate in box.

Boarding & Lodging School — #18

58092

Dates	OSRP	VDTsv	Paid
1992 - 1993	$48	$82 - $88	$_____

- Limited to year of production. See also 1994 release.
- This Signature Series piece commemorates the 150th anniversary of the publishing of *A Christmas Carol*.
- Early release to Showcase dealers and buying groups.

Dedlock Arms

57525

Dates	OSRP	VDTsv	Paid
1993 - 1994	$100	$45 - $98	$_____

- Limited to year of production.
- Charles Dickens' Signature Series™.
- Dickens based his version of this tavern from *Bleak House* on the Sondes Arms in Rockingham, England.

Kingsford's Brew House

58114

Dates	OSRP	VDTsv	Paid
1993 - 1996	$45	$29 - $54	$_____

- Sign is separate in box.

PUMP LANE SHOPPES — Set of 3   58084

Dates	OSRP	VDTsv	Paid
1993 - 1996	$112	$100	$_____

Bumpstead Nye Cloaks & Canes   58085

Dates	OSRP	VDTsv	Paid
1993 - 1996	$37.50	$30 - $44	$_____

Lomas Ltd. Molasses   58086

Dates	OSRP	VDTsv	Paid
1993 - 1996	$37.50	$28 - $44	$_____

W. M. Wheat Cakes & Puddings   58087

Dates	OSRP	VDTsv	Paid
1993 - 1996	$37.50	$31 - $52	$_____

• The name on the front of the building reads "WM," the abbreviation of William.

Great Denton Mill   58122

Dates	OSRP	VDTsv	Paid
1993 - 1997	$50	$38 - $54	$_____

Whittlesbourne Church   58211

Dates	OSRP	VDTsv	Paid
1994M - 1998	$85	$78 - $106	$_____

Giggelswick Mutton & Ham

58220

Dates	OSRP	VDTsv	Paid
1994^M - 1997	$48	$28 - $52	$_____

Boarding & Lodging School — #43

58106

Dates	OSRP	VDTsv	Paid
1994 - 1998	$48	$33 - $38	$_____

• This School with 43 as its address is similar to the 1992 limited edition that has 18 as its address. Putting the addresses together forms 1843, the year *A Christmas Carol* was published.

PORTOBELLO ROAD THATCHED COTTAGES — Set of 3

58246

Dates	OSRP	VDTsv	Paid
1994 - 1997	$120	-	$_____

Mr. & Mrs. Pickle

58247

Dates	OSRP	VDTsv	Paid
1994 - 1997	$40	$28 - $48	$_____

Cobb Cottage

58248

Dates	OSRP	VDTsv	Paid
1994 - 1997	$40	$30 - $110	$_____

Browning Cottage

58249

Dates	OSRP	VDTsv	Paid
1994 - 1997	$40	$45 - $46	$_____

Sir John Falstaff Inn

57533

Dates	OSRP	VDTsv	Paid
1994 - 1995	$100	$43 - $84	$_____

- Limited to year of production.
- Charles Dickens' Signature Series™.
- Inspired by the inn across from Dickens' last home, Gad's Hill Place.

Hather Harness

58238

Dates	OSRP	VDTsv	Paid
1994 - 1997	$48	$34 - $58	$_____

Dickens' Village Start A Tradition Set

58327

Dates	OSRP	VDTsv	Paid
1995ᴹ - 1996	$85	$40 - $109	$_____

- First available at the 1995 Homes for the Holidays event.
- During that event and the 1996 Homes for the Holidays event, it was specially priced at $65.

- Set of 13 includes the "Town Square Shops"— **Faversham Lamps & Oil** (top) and **Morston Steak And Kidney Pie** (bottom)—the 3 piece accessory "Town Square Carolers," 6 trees, Cobblestone Road, and a bag of snow.

The Maltings

58335

Dates	OSRP	VDTsv	Paid
1995ᴹ - 1998	$50	$24 - $52	$_____

Dudden Cross Church

58343

Dates	OSRP	VDTsv	Paid
1995ᴹ - 1997	$45	$32 - $58	$_____

- Early pieces have a bell that hangs in actual cutout in bell tower. Later ones have bell as part of porcelain.

The Grapes Inn

57534

Dates	OSRP	VDTsv	Paid
1995 - 1996	$120	$42 - $112	$_____

- Limited to year of production.
- Charles Dickens' Signature Series™.
- Dickens based the Porters in *Our Mutual Friend* on this inn located in the Limehouse section of London.

J. D. Nichols Toy Shop

58328

Dates	OSRP	VDTsv	Paid
1995 - 1998	$48	$39 - $148	$_____

- Sign is separate in box.

Dursley Manor

58329

Dates	OSRP	VDTsv	Paid
1995 - 1999	$50	$38 - $68	$_____

Blenham Street Bank

58330

Dates	OSRP	VDTsv	Paid
1995 - 1998	$60	$49 - $98	$_____

WRENBURY SHOPS — Set of 3

58331

Dates	OSRP	VDTsv	Paid
1995 - 1997/98	$100	$110	$_____

Wrenbury Baker

58332

Dates	OSRP	VDTsv	Paid
1995 - 1997	$35	$48	$_____

- Sign is separate in box.

The Chop Shop

58333

Dates	OSRP	VDTsv	Paid
1995 - 1997	$35	$30 - $38	$_____

• Sign is separate in box.

T. Puddlewick Spectacle Shop

58334

Dates	OSRP	VDTsv	Paid
1995 - 1998	$35	$125	$_____

• Sign is separate in box.

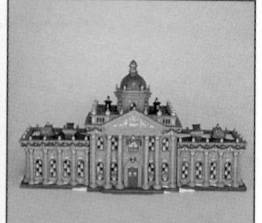

Ramsford Palace

58336

Dates	OSRP	VDTsv	Paid
1996^M - 1996	$175	$239 - $250	$_____

• Limited Edition of 27,500.
• Inspired by the Castle Howard in York, England.
• Set of 17 includes the Palace, the 2 piece accessory "Palace Guards," gate, fountain, 8 wall hedges, and 4 corner topiaries.

Butter Tub Farmhouse

58337

Dates	OSRP	VDTsv	Paid
1996^M - 1999	$40	$44 - $98	$_____

• Butter Tub refers to the Buttertub Pass in Yorkshire, England where pools known as buttertubs form in pot-holes.

Butter Tub Barn

58338

Dates	OSRP	VDTsv	Paid
1996^M - 1999	$48	$38 - $79	$_____

• Butter Tub refers to the Buttertub Pass in Yorkshire, England where pools known as buttertubs form in pot-holes.

The Christmas Carol Cottage — 58339

Dates	OSRP	VDTsv	Paid
1996^M - 2000	$60	$118	$_____

- Christmas Carol Revisited Series.
- Uses Magic Smoke to create smoking effect rising from the chimney.
- Sign is separate in box.

Gad's Hill Place — 57535

Dates	OSRP	VDTsv	Paid
1996 - 1997	$98	$40 - $82	$_____

- Limited to year of production.
- Inspired by Dickens' last home, Gad's Hill Place.
- Sign is separate in box.
- Charles Dickens' Signature Series™.

Nettie Quinn Puppets & Marionettes — 58344

Dates	OSRP	VDTsv	Paid
1996 - 2001	$50	$39 - $88	$_____

- This is the first Heritage Village Collection design to feature multiple weathervanes, and they are very fragile.
- Sign and 2 marionettes are separate in box.

Mulberrie Court Brownstones — 58345

Dates	OSRP	VDTsv	Paid
1996 - 1999	$90	$69 - $128	$_____

- This piece is frequently adopted into Christmas In The City by collectors.
- Includes 7 sisal bushes to be placed around building.

The Olde Camden Town Church — 58346

Dates	OSRP	VDTsv	Paid
1996 - 1999	$55	$50 - $88	$_____

- Dickens may have based his version of the Church on St. Stephen's Church in Camden, England.
- Christmas Carol Revisited Series.

The Melancholy Tavern — 58347

Dates	OSRP	VDTsv	Paid
1996 - 1999	$45	$37 - $84	$_____

- Dickens may have based his version of the Tavern on the Baker's Chop Shop that once stood in London.
- First of two pieces with this name. Re-issued in 2003.
- Christmas Carol Revisited Series. Sign is separate in box.

Quilly's Antiques   58348

Dates	OSRP	VDTsv	Paid
1996 - 1999	$46	$43 - $47	$_____

Dickens' Village Start A Tradition Set   58322

Dates	OSRP	VDTsv	Paid
1997ᴹ - 1998	$100	$65 - $88	$_____

• First available during the November 1997 Homes for the Holidays event. The price was reduced to $65 during the event.

• Set of 13 includes **Sudbury Church** (top), **Old East Rectory** (bottom), a 3 piece accessory "The Spirit Of Giving," 6 sisal trees, Cobblestone Road, and a bag of snow.

J. Lytes Coal Merchant   58323

Dates	OSRP	VDTsv	Paid
1997ᴹ - 1999	$50	$39 - $45	$_____

• Early pieces have bottomstamps that read "Dickens' **Vallage** Series."

Tower Of London   58500

Dates	OSRP	VDTsv	Paid
1997ᴹ - 1997	$165	$259	$_____

• Limited to year of production.
• The first Historical Landmark Series™ design. See this series in the Small Collection section.
• This, the White Tower, is one of the many towers that comprise the Tower of London, famous for housing a prison as well as the Crown Jewels. Legend says six ravens must be at the tower to preserve the monarchy.
• The actual Tower of London is located along the Thames River in London.
• Set of 5 includes the Tower, a gate with tower, the raven master, a sign, and a wall with ravens.

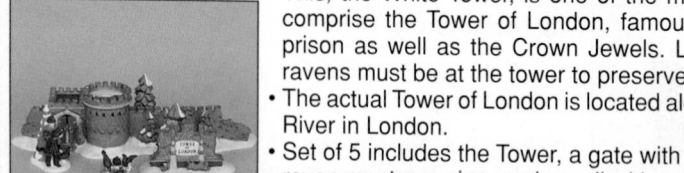

Barmby Moor Cottage   58324

Dates	OSRP	VDTsv	Paid
1997ᴹ - 2000	$48	$34 - $38	$_____

• Barmby Moor is a village located east of York, England.

Manchester Square   58301

Dates	OSRP	VDTsv	Paid
1997 - 2000	$250	$195 - $250	$_____

• Early pieces have bottomstamps that read "Dickens' Village **Seires**."
• Set of 25 includes **Custom House** (top), **Frogmore Chemist** (center), **G. Choir's Weights & Scales** (bottom), **Lydby Trunk & Satchel Shop** (below), the 7 piece accessory "Manchester Square Accessory Set," 12 trees, Cobblestone Road, and a bag of snow.
• Frogmore's sign and G. Choir's scales are separate in box.
• Man's walking stick is fragile.

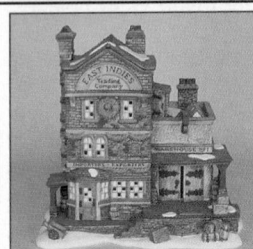

East Indies Trading Co.   58302

Dates	OSRP	VDTsv	Paid
1997 - 1999	$65	$41 - $118	$_____

• Similar to the Canadian Trading Co., but with a change of colors.

Canadian Trading Co.   58306

Dates	OSRP	VDTsv	Paid
1997 - 1998	$65	$109	$_____

• Similar to the East Indies Trading Co., but with a slight change of colors.
• Available only in Canada.
• Sign is separate in box.

Leacock Poulterer

58303

Dates	OSRP	VDTsv	Paid
1997 - 1999	**$48**	**$48 - $58**	$_____

• Christmas Carol Revisited Series.

Crooked Fence Cottage

58304

Dates	OSRP	VDTsv	Paid
1997 - 2000	**$60**	**$58**	$_____

• Early pieces have bottomstamps that read "Dickens' Village Series."
• Bird cage is separate in box.
• The tree branches in front are very fragile.

Ashwick Lane Hose & Ladder

58305

Dates	OSRP	VDTsv	Paid
1997 - 2005	**$54**	**$135**	$_____

• 2 ladders are separate in box.
• This design was also the primary piece in a special GCC gift set in 2000.

The Old Globe Theatre

58501

Dates	OSRP	VDTsv	Paid
1997 - 1998	**$175**	**$52-$125**	$_____

• Limited to year of production.
• The second Historical Landmark Series™ design. See this series in the Small Collection section.
• First samples of the building were made as two pieces. For production it is one piece.
• Some early pieces have "The City Globe" stamped on the bottom.
• The Globe Theatre, located along the Thames River in London, was demolished in 1644 and was rebuilt in 1996 near the original site.
• Set of 4 includes the Theatre, two trumpeters, and a sign.

Thomas Mudge Timepieces

58307

Dates	OSRP	VDTsv	Paid
1998ᴹ - 2000	**$60**	**$43 - $68**	$_____

• Clock is separate in box.
• Lamppost is fragile.

Seton Morris Spice Merchant Gift Set   58308

Dates	OSRP	VDTsv	Paid
1998ᴹ - 1998	$65	$49 - $89	$_____

- Limited to year of production.
- First available during the November 1998 Homes for the Holidays event.
- Set of 10 includes the shop, a 3 piece accessory "Christmas Apples," 4 sisal trees, Cobblestone Road, and a bag of snow.

Kensington Palace   58309

Dates	OSRP	VDTsv	Paid
1998ᴹ - 1998	$195	$125 - $198	$_____

- Limited to year of production.
- Introduced during the 1998 International Collectible Expo, this special edition of the famous London royal residence was first available during the November 1998 Homes for the Holidays event.
- A portion of the proceeds benefited the Ronald McDonald Houses across the U.S. and Canada.
- Early pieces had boxes that read "Princess of Whales." When discovered, stickers that read "Princess of Wales" were placed over the mistake.
- Set includes the Palace, palace gates, a statue of William III, a flag of Great Britain, 4 sisal trees, 4 sisal hedges, adhesive adornments, and Cobblestone Road.

Tattyeave Knoll   58311

Dates	OSRP	VDTsv	Paid
1998ᴹ - 1999	$55	$42 - $65	$_____

Heathmoor Castle   58313

Dates	OSRP	VDTsv	Paid
1998 - 1999	$90	$53 - $90	$_____

- Limited to year of production.
- 2 pennants are separate in box.
- 1 lion on each of the two center turrets is supposed to appear as if it is broken.

Teaman & Crupp China Shop

58314

Dates	OSRP	VDTsv	Paid
1998 - 2003	$64	$88	$_____

• Sign is separate in box.

Lynton Point Tower

58315

Dates	OSRP	VDTsv	Paid
1998 - 2001	$80	$105 - $148	$_____

• 2 small attachments are separate in box.
• Oars at boat are fragile.

North Eastern Sea Fisheries Ltd.

58316

Dates	OSRP	VDTsv	Paid
1998 - 1999	$70	$41 - $65	$_____

The Horse And Hounds Pub

58340

Dates	OSRP	VDTsv	Paid
1998 - 2004	$70	$138	$_____

• Two signs are separate in box.

Great Expectations Satis Manor

58310

Dates	OSRP	VDTsv	Paid
1998 - 2001	$110	$58 - $65	$_____

• The first Literary Classics design. See this series in the Small Collection section.
• Charles Dickens used Restoration House in Rochester, England as the model for his Satis Manor.
• Set of 4 plus book includes the Manor and the accessory "Miss Havisham, Estella, and Pip."

Big Ben

58341

Dates	OSRP	VDTsv	Paid
1998 - 2003	$95	$98	$_____

- The fourth Historical Landmark Series™ design. See this series in the Small Collection section.
- It is a replica of London's Big Ben along the Thames River.
- Set of 2 includes Big Ben with working clock and sign.

Chancery Corner

58352

Dates	OSRP	VDTsv	Paid
1999ᴹ - 1999	$65	$68	$_____

- Limited to year of production.
- This was the first Dickens' Village design to include a three-dimensional scene in the house.
- First available during the 1999 Discover Department 56 event.
- Set of 8 includes the house, 2 sisal trees, 2 fence sections with gate, walkway, birdbath, and snow.

Dudley Docker

58353

Dates	OSRP	VDTsv	Paid
1999ᴹ - 2000	$70	$36 - $74	$_____

Old Queensbridge Station

58443

Dates	OSRP	VDTsv	Paid
1999 - 2002	$100	$120 - $223	$_____

- 6 hanging plants and a clock are separate in box.
- Do not handle by the metal canopies.
- Set of 2 includes the Station and a platform.

Margrove Orangery 58440

Dates	OSRP	VDTsv	Paid
1999 - 2001	$98	$64 - $98	$_____

Aldeburgh Music Box Shop 58441

Dates	OSRP	VDTsv	Paid
1999 - 2000	$60	$65 - $70	$_____

- Dream House Sweepstakes Grand Prize winner assisted in the design.
- Music box plays Chopin's *Fantaisie-Impromptu*.
- Named after a seaside town in England.

Aldeburgh Music Box Shop Gift Set 58442

Dates	OSRP	VDTsv	Paid
1999 - 2000	$85	$70 - $85	$_____

- Limited Edition of 35,000.
- First available during the Spring 2000 Discover Department 56 event.
- Music box plays *Heindenroselin*.
- Set of 3 includes Shop, "The Mother's Gift" accessory, walkway with pediments, floral hedges and topiaries, and 2 hanging baskets.
- Sign is separate in box for this and the design above.

McShane Cottage 58444

Dates	OSRP	VDTsv	Paid
1999 - 2001	$55	$21 - $55	$_____

- Set of 2 includes the Cottage and a duck house.

Staghorn Lodge 58445

Dates	OSRP	VDTsv	Paid
1999 - 2002	$72	$188	$_____

- Early pieces have brown antlers above the front door or antlers that were simply painted on. Later ones have gold antlers.

Leed's Oyster House

58446

Dates	OSRP	VDTsv	Paid
1999 - 2001	$68	$51 - $66	$_____

• The positions of the holes for the signs are reversed from the ones shown on the sleeve. This requires that the location of the signs be switched.

The China Trader

58447

Dates	OSRP	VDTsv	Paid
1999 - 2000	$72	$42 - $89	$_____

The Spider Box Locks

58448

Dates	OSRP	VDTsv	Paid
1999 - 2001	$60	$42 - $78	$_____

• Sign and key are separate in box.

Wingham Lane Parrot Seller

58449

Dates	OSRP	VDTsv	Paid
1999 - 2001	$68	$56 - $88	$_____

• Sign and 5 bird cages are separate in box.
• This shop derives its name from the Wingham Bird Park located near Canterbury, England.

The Old Royal Observatory
Gold Dome Edition

58451

Dates	OSRP	VDTsv	Paid
1999 - 2000	Promo	$336	$_____

• Limited to 5,500, Department 56 sent one to its valued retailers as a thank you for their support.
• The fifth Historical Landmark Series™ design. See this series in the Small Collection section.

The Old Royal Observatory

58453

Dates	OSRP	VDTsv	Paid
1999 - 2000	$95	$48	$_____

• Limited Edition of 35,000.
• The fifth Historical Landmark Series™ design. See this series in the Small Collection section.
• Set of 2 includes Observatory and sign.

Fezziwig's Ballroom Animated Gift Set   58470

Dates	OSRP	VDTsv	Paid
2000^M - 2000	$75	$375 - $385	$_____

- First available during the 2000 Discover Dept. 56 event.
- The silver bell honors Department 56's 25th anniversary.
- The dancers inside the building spin on a revolving turntable.
- Set of 6 includes the warehouse, the accessory "Scrooge At Fezziwig's Ball," 3 sisal trees, and a bag of snow.
- Christmas Carol Revisited Series.

St. Martin-In-The-Fields Church   58471

Dates	OSRP	VDTsv	Paid
2000^M - 2002	$96	$188	$_____

- Inspired by the famous church in London's Trafalgar Sq.
- The Roman numerals on the portico of Department 56's version read 1716 instead of 1726.
- Ornamental top for spire is separate in box.

Ashwick Lane Gift Set   05700

Dates	OSRP	VDTsv	Paid
2000^M - 2000	$65	$65	$_____

- Gold accents have been added to the hinges and rail posts of the 1997 version of this building.
- This set is an exclusive for GCC dealers.
- Set of 10 includes the fire house, a 3 piece accessory "At The Firehouse" that has a brass plaque that can be personalized, 4 trees, Cobblestone Road, and a bag of snow.

Crowntree Freckleton Windmill   58472

Dates	OSRP	VDTsv	Paid
2000 - 2001	$80	$69 - $105	$_____

- 25th Anniversary Limited Edition of 30,000.
- Abington Canal Series.
- Windmill is animated.
- The open door and fence are very fragile.

Abington Lockside Inn 58473

Dates	OSRP	VDTsv	Paid
2000 - 2003	$68	$40 - $145	$_____

• Abington Canal Series.

Abington Lockkeeper's Residence 58474

Dates	OSRP	VDTsv	Paid
2000 - 2002	$58	$62 - $70	$_____

• Abington Canal Series.
• Bell is separate in box.

Lilycott Garden Conservatory 58475

Dates	OSRP	VDTsv	Paid
2000 - 2001	$65	$70 - $118	$_____

• Discover Department 56 Spring Event Piece.
• Set of 5 includes building, "Sweet Roses" accessory, and 3 topiary trees.
• Fountain is separate in box.

Hedgerow Garden Cottage 58476

Dates	OSRP	VDTsv	Paid
2000 - 2002	$57	$33 - $38	$_____

Burwickglen Golf Clubhouse 58477

Dates	OSRP	VDTsv	Paid
2000 - 2002	$96	$76 - $88	$_____

• Sign, 9 pennants, and "pin" are separate in box.

Glendun Cocoa Works

58478

Dates	OSRP	VDTsv	Paid
2000 - 2003	$80	$71 - $160	$_____

- Lantern is separate in box.
- Smokestack and ironwork brace are fragile.

Rockingham School

58479

Dates	OSRP	VDTsv	Paid
2000 - 2002	$85	$79 - $135	$_____

- Sign is separate in box.
- Spires and small stacks are fragile.

Royal Stock Exchange

58480

Dates	OSRP	VDTsv	Paid
2000 - 2001	$110	$67 - $110	$_____

- Urns are fragile.

Royal Staffordshire Porcelains

58481

Dates	OSRP	VDTsv	Paid
2000 - 2002	$65	$42 - $70	$_____

- Sign is separate in box.

The Old Curiosity Shop

58482

Dates	OSRP	VDTsv	Paid
2000 - 2005	$50	$40	$_____

- This is the updated version of the same piece originally issued in 1987.
- Do not handle by hitching posts.

Scrooge & Marley Counting House

58483

Dates	OSRP	VDTsv	Paid
2000 - Current	$80	$80	$_____

- This is the updated version of the same piece originally issued in 1986.
- Sign is separate in box.
- *A Christmas Carol* Series.

Sherlock Holmes — 221B Baker Street   58601

Dates	OSRP	VDTsv	Paid
2000 - 2003	$90	$295	$_____

- This is the fifth Literary Classics piece. See this series in the Small Collection section.
- Inspired by Arthur Conan Doyle's famous works, this is Department 56's interpretation of the home of England's greatest fictional detective.
- Set of 3 plus book includes the house and 2 piece accessory "Elementary My Dear Watson."

Brightsmith & Sons, Queens Jewellers   58484

Dates	OSRP	VDTsv	Paid
2001^M - 2001	$75	$495-$498	$_____

- Special Swarovski crystals are featured on the building.
- Only available at Dept. 56 25th Anniversary celebration.
- Sign separate in box.

Somerset Valley Church   58485

Dates	OSRP	VDTsv	Paid
2001^M - 2001	$75	$80 - $98	$_____

- First available during the 2001 Holiday Discover Department 56 event.
- Church bell can be set to chime hourly.
- Set of 9 includes the Church, the accessory "Christmas Eve Celebration," 3 sisal trees, 2 fieldstone wall sections, and a bag of snow.

Cratchit's Corner   58486

Dates	OSRP	VDTsv	Paid
2001^M -	$80	$80	$_____

- *A Christmas Carol* Series.

Mrs. Brimm's Tea Room Gift Set — 58487

Dates	OSRP	VDTsv	Paid
2001 - 2002	$65	$88	$_____

- First available during the Mother's Day Spring Program.
- Set of 4 includes building, sign that can be personalized, tree, and accessory "High Tea."
- Hanging sign and 2 hanging plants are separate in box.
- 5% of proceeds goes to fight against breast cancer.

Dickens' Gad's Hill Chalet — 58488

Dates	OSRP	VDTsv	Paid
2001 - 2003	$65	$41-$44	$_____

- Set of 2 includes Chalet and "Dickens Writing" accessory.

Bidwell Windmill #2 — 58489

Dates	OSRP	VDTsv	Paid
2001 - 2003	$80	$88	$_____

- Abington Canal Series.
- Windmill is animated.

Ebenezer Scrooge's House — 58490

Dates	OSRP	VDTsv	Paid
2001 -	$85	$85	$_____

- *A Christmas Carol* Series.
- Hanging sack is separate in the box.
- This is an updated version of The Flat of Ebenezer Scrooge (1989).

Fred Holiwell's House

58492

Dates	OSRP	VDTsv	Paid
2001 - 2004	$62	$245	$_____

- *A Christmas Carol* Series.
- This is an updated version of Nephew Fred's Flat (1991).

Sheffield Manor

58493

Dates	OSRP	VDTsv	Paid
2001 - 2002	$130	$98 - $111	$_____

- Limited to year of production, 2002.

The Slone Hotel

58494

Dates	OSRP	VDTsv	Paid
2001 - 2003	$90	$72 - $90	$_____

- Set of 2 includes includes Hotel and "Doorman" accessory.
- Spire is separate in the box.
- Awning supports are very fragile.

Bayly's Blacksmith

58495

Dates	OSRP	VDTsv	Paid
2001 - 2004	$70	$96	$_____

- Sign is separate in the box.

St. Ives Lock House

58496

Dates	OSRP	VDTsv	Paid
2001 - 2003	$75	$48 - $88	$_____

- Abington Canal series.
- The ladder is extremely fragile.

Piccadilly Gallery

58498

Dates	OSRP	VDTsv	Paid
2001 - 2002	**$75**	**$46 - $75**	**$_____**

• Lamps are fragile.

Thornbury Chapel

58502

Dates	OSRP	VDTsv	Paid
2001 - 2003	**$60**	**$52 - $58**	**$_____**

Christmas At Codington Cottage

05925

Dates	OSRP	VDTsv	Paid
2002ᴹ - 2002	**$75**	**$75**	**$_____**

• Department store exclusive.
• Limited to year of production.
• The "Winter Frolic" accessory is animated.
• The railing and water pump are very fragile.
• Set of 7 includes the Cottage, "Winter Frolic" accessory, 3 Natural Evergreens, a Bare Branch Tree, and snow.
• A similar design, Codington Cottage with a different accessory and no trees or snow, was released as a regular issue in 2002.

1 Royal Tree Court

58506

Dates	OSRP	VDTsv	Paid
2002ᴹ - 2002	**$75**	**$235**	**$_____**

• Holiday 2002 Special Edition.
• Limited to year of production.
• Animated.
• Set of 8 includes the house, "Bearing Gifts" accessory, 2 riverstone walls, 2 frosted topiaries, a Bare Branch Tree, and snow.
• Spires are fragile.

Norfolk Biffins Bakery

58491

Dates	OSRP	VDTsv	Paid
2002ᴹ - 2004	$65	$64 - $65	$_____

• *A Christmas Carol* Series.

Hop Castle Folly

58633

Dates	OSRP	VDTsv	Paid
2002ᴹ - 2002	$65	$88 - $129	$_____

• Club 56 dealer exclusive.
• Limited to 5,600 numbered pieces.
• Inspired by an actual building in northern England.
• Set of 2 includes the building and "Lord Of The Follies" accessory.
• Weathervane is separate in the box.
• Certificate of authenticity is included in the box.

Regent Street Coffeehouse

58507

Dates	OSRP	VDTsv	Paid
2002 - 2004	$70	$70	$_____

Antiquarian Bookseller

58508

Dates	OSRP	VDTsv	Paid
2002 - 2004	$57	$195	$_____

Mordecai Mould Undertaker

58509

Dates	OSRP	VDTsv	Paid
2002 - 2004	$70	$69 - $108	$_____

• All Hallows' Eve™ design.
• Named for the undertaker in Dickens' "Life And Adventures Of Martin Chuzzlewit."

Collyweston Post Office 58510

Dates	OSRP	VDTsv	Paid
2002 - 2003	$50	$43 - $98	$_____

The Leather Bottle 58511

Dates	OSRP	VDTsv	Paid
2002 - 2003	$65	$42 - $65	$_____

- Abington Canal Series.
- Charles Dickens frequented a pub named The Leather Bottle.

Belle's House 58512

Dates	OSRP	VDTsv	Paid
2002 - 2004	$55	$175	$_____

- *A Christmas Carol* Series.
- A special 20th Anniversary edition of this design was issued in 2004.

The Daily News 58513

Dates	OSRP	VDTsv	Paid
2002 - 2004	$75	$75 - $110	$_____

- Set of 2 includes the building and "The First Edition" accessory.
- Named after the newspaper where Charles Dickens was the editior.

Westminster Abbey 58517

Dates	OSRP	VDTsv	Paid
2002 - 2005	$95	$195	$_____

- This is a replica of one of England's most famous landmarks.
- Historical information is printed on the back of facade.

Codington Cottage

58514

Dates	OSRP	VDTsv	Paid
2002 - 2003	$65	$44	$_____

- Set of 2 includes the Cottage and "Bringing Home The Holly" accessory.
- A similar design, Christmas At Codington Cottage with a different accessory, trees, and snow, was released as a department store exclusive in 2002.
- Fragile railing and water pump.

Shakespeare's Birthplace

58515

Dates	OSRP	VDTsv	Paid
2002 - 2003	$85	$85	$_____

- Limited to 25,000 numbered pieces.
- Inspired by the author's birthplace in Stratford-Upon-Avon.
- Set of 4 includes the building and "All The World's A Stage" accessory.

Sweetbriar Cottage

58518

Dates	OSRP	VDTsv	Paid
2002 - 2003	$65	$48	$_____

- Spring Gift Set.
- Set of 3 includes the Cottage, "Rose Garden Beauty" accessory, and a spring tree.

London Skating Club 58700

Dates	OSRP	VDTsv	Paid
2003^M - 2003	$75	$75	$_____

- Holiday Gift Set.
- Set of 5 includes "Victorian Skaters" accessory, birch tree, and snow.
- Skaters move around rink.

Gunnersbury Park Folly 58702

Dates	OSRP	VDTsv	Paid
2003^M - 2003	$65	$48 - $65	$_____

- Club 56 dealer exclusive. Limited to 5,600 pieces.

Melancholy Tavern 58703

Dates	OSRP	VDTsv	Paid
2003^M - 2005	$65	$56 - $65	$_____

- This is the updated version of the piece originally issued in 1996.
- *A Christmas Carol* Series.

Green's Park Nosegays 58704

Dates	OSRP	VDTsv	Paid
2003 - 2005	$65	$63 - $65	$_____

- Spring Gift Set.
- Set of 2 includes the building and "For You, My Lady" accessory.

Tower Bridge Of London 58705

Dates	OSRP	VDTsv	Paid
2003 - 2004	$165	$165 - $179	$_____

- Historical Landmark Series™. Numbered L.E. of 20,000.
- Dickens' Village 20th Anniversary Series. Includes pin.
- It is a replica of London's Tower Bridge.
- Set of 4.

Theatre Of The Macabre 58706

Dates	OSRP	VDTsv	Paid
2003 - 2005	$65	$56 - $75	$_____

- All Hallows' Eve™ Series.

All Saints Church 58707

Dates	OSRP	VDTsv	Paid
2003 - 2005	$70	$125	$_____

- All Hallows' Eve™ Series.

Notting Hill Water Tower 58708

Dates	OSRP	VDTsv	Paid
2003 - 2005	$55	$68	$_____

- Spire and lamp are separate in box.

Williams Gas Works 58709

Dates	OSRP	VDTsv	Paid
2003 - 2005	$70	$70 - $78	$_____

Dickens' Birthplace 58710

Dates	OSRP	VDTsv	Paid
2003 - 2004	$50	$78	$_____

- Limited to year of production. Includes lantern and plaque.
- Dickens' Village 20th Anniversary Series. Includes pin.
- It is a replica of the house in which Dickens was born in Portsmouth, England.

Stump Hill Gatehouse 58711

Dates	OSRP	VDTsv	Paid
2003 - 2005	**$50**	**$50 - $78**	$_____

Hospital For Sick Children At Ormond Street 58712

Dates	OSRP	VDTsv	Paid
2003 - 2004	**$65**	**$245**	$_____

- Limited to year of production.
- Dickens' Village 20th Anniversary Series. Includes pin.
- This was inspired by the hospital in London.

Naval Academy, Queens Port 58713

Dates	OSRP	VDTsv	Paid
2003 - 2005	**$75**	**$78 - 84**	$_____

- Queens Port Series.

Lighthouse, Queens Port 58714

Dates	OSRP	VDTsv	Paid
2003 - 2005	**$70**	**$78**	$_____

- Queens Port Series.

Belle's House — Special Edition 02973

Dates	OSRP	VDTsv	Paid
2004^M - 2004	**n/a**	**$800**	$_____

- Numbered limited of 500 pieces.
- This edition differs from the original (2002) in that it has a Dickens' Village 20th Anniversary stamp on the bottom, has an intricate bay window, and features Belle looking out an upper window at Scrooge.
- A number limited of 500 pieces, the first 250 were distributed when Department 56 randomly drew names from its *celebrations* magazine subscription list. Another 200 were sold on eBay in late 2004.

The Red Lion Pub

58715

Dates	OSRP	VDTsv	Paid
2004ᴹ - 2004	$65	$85 - $98	$_____

- Limited to year of production.
- Dickens' Village 20th Anniversary Series.
- Includes pin.

Canadian Pub

58716

Dates	OSRP	VDTsv	Paid
2004ᴹ - 2004	$91 CA	$65	$_____

- Limited to year of production.
- Available only in Canada.
- Includes pin.

Victorian Family Christmas House

58717

Dates	OSRP	VDTsv	Paid
2004ᴹ - 2004	$75	$95 - $128	$_____

- Limited to year of production.
- A Victorian Christmas™ Series.
- Set of 6 includes the House, "Kissing Under The Mistletoe" accessory, sign, two trees, and snow.

T. Smith Christmas Crackers

58719

Dates	OSRP	VDTsv	Paid
2004ᴹ - 2006	$65	$65 - $85	$_____

- Limited to year of production.
- A Victorian Christmas™ Series.
- Set of 2 includes the building and "Popping The Cracker" accessory.

Windsor Castle

58720

Dates	OSRP	VDTsv	Paid
2004 - 2007	$95	$235	$_____

• Historical Landmark Series™.
• This lighted facade is a replica of the world's largest occupied castle.

Tower Bridge Of London

58721

Dates	OSRP	VDTsv	Paid
2004 - 2006	$135	-	$_____

• Re-issue of the Historical Landmark Series™ limited edition that was issued in 2003.

St. Stephen's Church

58722

Dates	OSRP	VDTsv	Paid
2004 - 2006	$75	-	$_____

• A Victorian Christmas™ Series.
• Decorating Set.
• Long Life Cordless Lighting.
• Set of two includes building and tree.

J. Horsley Christmas Cards

58723

Dates	OSRP	VDTsv	Paid
2004 - 2007	$65	$88	$_____

• A Victorian Christmas™ Series.

Turner's Spice & Mustard Shop

58724

Dates	OSRP	VDTsv	Paid
2004 - 2007	$60	$60	$_____

E. Tipler, Agent For Wines & Spirits

58725

Dates	OSRP	VDTsv	Paid
2004 -	$60	$60	$_____

• Sign separate in box.

T. C. Chester Clocks & Watches

58726

Dates	OSRP	VDTsv	Paid
2004 - 2007	$55	$65	$_____

• Sign separate in box.

Customs House, Queens Port

58727

Dates	OSRP	VDTsv	Paid
2004 - 2006	$65	$65 - $118	$_____

• Queens Port Series.

Howard Street Row Houses

58728

Dates	OSRP	VDTsv	Paid
2004 - 2007	$70	$82	$_____

• Removable Christmas decorations.

Hollyberry Cottage

58729

Dates	OSRP	VDTsv	Paid
2004 -	$45	$45	$_____

Scotland Yard Station

58730

Dates	OSRP	VDTsv	Paid
2004 - 2005	$70	$66	$_____

• Limited to year of production.
• Named for the famous home to the Metropolitan Police Department.

Barleycorn Manor

58731

Dates	OSRP	VDTsv	Paid
2004 - 2006	$70	$70 - $138	$_____

• All Hallows' Eve™ Series.

Christmas At Ashby Manor 58732

Dates	OSRP	VDTsv	Paid
2005^M - 2005	$75	$75	$_____

- Limited to year of production.
- Set of 6 includes Manor, "Shall We Dance Tonight?" accessory, trees, hedge, and snow.

Admiral's House, Queens Port 58733

Dates	OSRP	VDTsv	Paid
2005^M - 2006	$55	$55 - $65	$_____

- Long Life Cordless Lighting.
- Queens Port Series.

Chalk Cottage 58734

Dates	OSRP	VDTsv	Paid
2005^M - 2006	$55	$55 - $68	$_____

- Long Life Cordless Lighting.

Victoria Park Theatre 58735

Dates	OSRP	VDTsv	Paid
2005 - 2006	$90	$90 - $118	$_____

- 30th Anniversary Series.
- Limited to year of production.
- Long Life Cordless Lighting.

Plumstead Market House 58737

Dates	OSRP	VDTsv	Paid
2005 - 2007	$75	$75 - $85	$_____

Buckingham Palace

58736

Dates	OSRP	VDTsv	Paid
2005 - 2006	**$125**	**$125 - $195**	**$_____**

- Numbered Limited Edition of 12,000.
- Set of 4 includes the Palace, "Household Guards" set of 2 accessory, and front gate.
- Replica of Buckingham Palace in London.

H. Smythe, Publisher

58739

Dates	OSRP	VDTsv	Paid
2005 - 2007	**$70**	**$70 - $78**	**$_____**

A.G. Scott Hats & Walking Sticks

58741

Dates	OSRP	VDTsv	Paid
2005 - 2008	**$60**	**$60 - $74**	**$_____**

The Timbers Hotel

58742

Dates	OSRP	VDTsv	Paid
2005 - 2006	**$100**	**$100**	**$_____**

- Numbered Limited Edition of 15,000.

Hickman Wells Gentlemen's Club

58743

Dates	OSRP	VDTsv	Paid
2005 - 2007	**$80**	**$80 - $115**	**$_____**

- Long Life Cordless Lighting.

London Gin Distillery — 58746

Dates	OSRP	VDTsv	Paid
2005 -	$85	$85	$_____

• Long Life Cordless Lighting.

Thomas Gainsworth, Portrait Artist To The Queen — 58747

Dates	OSRP	VDTsv	Paid
2006ᴹ - 2006	$85	$115 - $139	$_____

• Limited Edition of 10,000.
• 30th Anniversary Series.

Beckingham's Christmas Candles — 58748

Dates	OSRP	VDTsv	Paid
2006ᴹ - 2006	$80	$198	$_____

• Set of 6.
• Includes "May Your Christmas Season Be Bright". and 2 trees

Mead & Mutton Public House — 58749

Dates	OSRP	VDTsv	Paid
2006ᴹ - 2008	$70	$70 - $88	$_____

Victorian University — 58750

Dates	OSRP	VDTsv	Paid
2006 - 2007	$110	$110	$_____

• Collectors' Edition.
• Limited Edition of 12,000.
• Includes "University Gate."

William & Robert Glaser, Stained Glass — 58751

Dates	OSRP	VDTsv	Paid
2006 - 2008	$70	$70 - $90	$_____

T. Watling Ships & Sails

58752

Dates	OSRP	VDTsv	Paid
2006 - 2008	$85	$85 - $118	$_____

Swift's Stringed Instruments

58753

Dates	OSRP	VDTsv	Paid
2006 -	$65	$65	$_____

Fraiser Family Farmhouse

58754

Dates	OSRP	VDTsv	Paid
2006 - 2008	$65	$ 65 - $96	$_____

Fraiser Family Barn

58755

Dates	OSRP	VDTsv	Paid
2006 - 2008	$75	$75 - $120	$_____

Charles Darby Perfumery

58756

Dates	OSRP	VDTsv	Paid
2006 - 2009	$70	$49 - $70	$_____

Prettywell Sisters Lace Makers

58757

Dates	OSRP	VDTsv	Paid
2006 - 2009	$70	$49 - $70	$_____

Pearce & Crump Silversmiths 58758

Dates	OSRP	VDTsv	Paid
2007^M - 2007	$85	$85	$____

• Limited Edition of 10,000.

Cartwright Coach Builders 58759

Dates	OSRP	VDTsv	Paid
2007^M - 2007	$105	$105 - $178	$____

• Collectors' Edition.
• Limited Edition of 8,000.
• Limited To Year Of Production.
• Set of 2, Includes "Royal Coach" Accessory.

Abbey Lane Chocolates 58760

Dates	OSRP	VDTsv	Paid
2007^M - 2007	$79	$79	$____

• Limited To Year Of Production.
• Holiday Value Set of 2.
• Includes "Delivering Holiday Chocolates."
• Lanterns are lit and has interior scene.

Canton Tea Trading 799910

Dates	OSRP	VDTsv	Paid
2007 - 2009	$90	$85 - $90	$____

Barrow Manor

799909

Dates	OSRP	VDTsv	Paid
2007 - 2008	$110	$110 - $185	$_____

- Collectors' Edition.
- Limited Edition of 10,000.
- Set of 2.
- Includes Fountain accessory.

Peale's Bell Casting

799911

Dates	OSRP	VDTsv	Paid
2007 - 2009	$85	$85	$_____

Wellbourn Bros. Lanterns

799912

Dates	OSRP	VDTsv	Paid
2007 - 2009	$95	$66 - $95	$_____

Walter Key, Scrivener

799913

Dates	OSRP	VDTsv	Paid
2007 - 2009	$80	$56 - $80	$_____

Wilkenson & Kidd Saddlery

799914

Dates	OSRP	VDTsv	Paid
2007 -	$115	$115	$_____

Barton's Holiday Greens 799991

Dates	OSRP	VDTsv	Paid
2008^M - 2008	$79	$79 - $115	$_____

2008^M - 2008 $79 $79 - $115 $_____

- Set of 2, accessory "Delivering The Holiday Greenery."
- Celebrate Holiday Value Set. ($100 value)
- Limited To Year Of Production.

Victoria & Albert Museum 799992

Dates	OSRP	VDTsv	Paid
2008^M - 2009	$125	$125 - $198	$_____

- Collectors' Edition.
- Limited Edition of 9,000.
- Historical Landmark Series™.

West Lott Chapel 799993

Dates	OSRP	VDTsv	Paid
2008^M -	$85	$85	$_____

Buckleberry Cottage 804439

Dates	OSRP	VDTsv	Paid
2008^M - 2009	$85	$60 - $85	$_____

The Neilan Lund Gallery 805512

Dates	OSRP	VDTsv	Paid
2008 -	$90	$90	$_____

- Dickens' 25th Anniversary.
- Front windows feature artist's paintings.

Boz's Books

805513

Dates	OSRP	VDTsv	Paid
2008 -	$90	$90	$_____

Glensford School

805514

Dates	OSRP	VDTsv	Paid
2008 -	$95	$95	$_____

• *A Christmas Carol* Series.

Crowntree Inn — Anniversary Edition

805515

Dates	OSRP	VDTsv	Paid
2008 -	$90	$90	$_____

• Dickens' 25th Anniversary.

Abel Beesley Butcher — Anniversary Edition

805516

Dates	OSRP	VDTsv	Paid
2008 -	$85	$85	$_____

• Dickens' 25th Anniversary.

Golden Swan Baker — Anniversary Edition

805517

Dates	OSRP	VDTsv	Paid
2008 -	$85	$85	$_____

• Dickens' 25th Anniversary

The Flying Horse Tavern

805518

Dates	OSRP	VDTsv	Paid
2008 -	$90	$90	$_____

M. Pickering Finest Persian Rugs 805519

Dates	OSRP	VDTsv	Paid
2008 -	$80	$80	$_____

Christmas at Regent's Park House 805520

Dates	OSRP	VDTsv	Paid
2009ᴹ - 2009	$79	$79	$_____

• Limited To Year of Production.
• Set of 2 with accessory "Park House Carriage."

48 Doughty St. 805521
Home to Charles Dickens

Dates	OSRP	VDTsv	Paid
2009ᴹ - 2009	$85	$85	$_____

• Dickens' Village Series 25th Anniversary.

Jones & Co. Brush & Basket Shop 805522
— Anniversary Edition

Dates	OSRP	VDTsv	Paid
2009ᴹ - 2009	$90	$90	$_____

• Dickens' Village Series 25th Anniversary.

Bean And Son Smithy Shop —
Anniversary Edition 808841

Dates	OSRP	VDTsv	Paid
2010 -	$80	$80	$_____

• Dickens' 25th Anniversary

Candle Shop —
Anniversary Edition

808848

Dates	OSRP	VDTsv	Paid
2010 -	$75	$75	$_____

• Dickens' 25th Anniversary

Green Grocer —
Anniversary Edition

808856

Dates	OSRP	VDTsv	Paid
2010 -	$85	$85	$_____

• Dickens' 25th Anniversary

St. Luke's Church

808858

Dates	OSRP	VDTsv	Paid
2010 -	$125	-	$_____

Splendid Cod Fish n' Chips

808868

Dates	OSRP	VDTsv	Paid
2010 -	$70	-	$_____

Lea Hurst House

808869

Dates	OSRP	VDTsv	Paid
2010 -	$95	-	$_____

Regent's Park Punt Rental

808876

Dates	OSRP	VDTsv	Paid
2010 -	$75	-	$_____

Want to connect with friends who share your passion for Villaging?

Check our Village Resources section to get more information about the National Council of 56 Clubs (NCC). Learn how you can attend and enjoy collector events, buy exclusive club pieces and pins, get plugged into a local club, and expand your knowledge base through online forums and club seminars. See how NCC can enhance your enjoyment of your hobby!

Village Resources
Starts on page 583

Carolers (White Post Version)

(Black Post Version)

65269 - Set of 3

1984 - 1990

OSRP: $10

VDTsv: $55

Paid: $_____

• Made for a short time, the white post set includes a viola that is very light with dark brown trim.

65269 - Set of 3

VDTsv: $27

Paid: $_____

• Early pieces of the black post set have a viola that is one color and made in Taiwan. The second viola has dark trim and was made in the Philippines.

Village Train

65277 - Set of 3

1985 - 1985

OSRP: $12

VDTsv: $125

Paid: $_____

• Also called the "Brighton Train" due to the name on the side of the middle car.

Christmas Carol Figures

65013 - Set of 3

1986 - 1990

OSRP: $12.50

VDTsv: $2-$78

Paid: $_____

• *A Christmas Carol* Series. Sleeve shows Tiny Tim with crutch, but there isn't one in the figurine.

Farm People & Animals

59013 - Set of 5

1987 - 1989

OSRP: $24

VDTsv: $58-$62

Paid: $_____

• Early pieces had box that read "Heritage Village Farm Set."

Blacksmith

59340 - Set of 3

1987 - 1990

OSRP: $20

VDTsv: $32-$48

Paid: $_____

Silo & Hay Shed

59501 - Set of 2

1987 - 1989

OSRP: $18

VDTsv: $98-116

Paid: $_____

• Early versions have roofs with rust, gold, and brown stripes. Later ones are brown.

Dickens' Village Sign

65692

1987 - 1993

OSRP: $6

VDTsv: $10-$18

Paid: $_____

• Bottomstamp reads "Handcrafted by Jiean Fung Porcelains, Taiwan."

• The early signs have a dark background.

Ox Sled (Tan Pants)

59510

1987 - 1989

OSRP: $20

VDTsv: $159

Paid: $_____

• The driver has tan pants and is seated on a green cushion.

(Blue Pants Version)

VDTsv: $40-$85

Paid: $_____

• The driver has blue pants and is seated on a black cushion.

(Blue Pants/Mold Change Version)

VDTsv: $56

Paid: $_____

• Blue pants, black cushion, and the snow under the oxen is not attached to hind legs.

Dover Coach (Version 1)

65900

1987 - 1990

OSRP: $18

VDTsv: $78

Paid: $_____

• The coachman is clean shaven, and the wheels are very crude. Made in Taiwan.
• Box reads "Horse With Coach."

(Version 2)

VDTsv: $56-$58

Paid: $_____

• The coachman has a mustache; the wheels are more round. Made in Taiwan.

(Version 3)

VDTsv: $56-$58

Paid: $_____

• The coachman has a mustache, and the wheels are round. Made in Sri Lanka.

Shopkeepers

59668 - Set of 4

1987 - 1988

OSRP: $15

VDTsv: $10-$22

Paid: $_____

• One of only two accessories to have "snow" sprinkled on them.

City Workers

59676 - Set of 4

1987 - 1988

OSRP: $15

VDTsv: $18-$48

Paid: $_____

• One of only two acc. to have "snow" sprinkled on them.
• Some boxes read "City People"; some have no name.

Village Well & Holy Cross

65471 - Set of 2

1987 - 1989

OSRP: $13

VDTsv: $60-129

Paid: $_____

• Early versions have blue water, dark birds. Later ones have colorless water, light birds.

Childe Pond And Skaters

59030 - Set of 4

1988 - 1991

OSRP: $30

VDTsv: $30-$68

Paid: $_____

• Color of the warming hut varies, but does not affect the value.

Fezziwig And Friends

59285 - Set of 3

1988 - 1990

OSRP: $12.50

VDTsv: $35-$51

Paid: $_____

• *A Christmas Carol* Series.

Nicholas Nickleby Characters

59293 - Set of 4

1988 - 1991

OSRP: $20

VDTsv: $10-$36

Paid: $_____

• Sleeves have misspelling—"Nicholas Nick**el**by."

David Copperfield Characters

55514 - Set of 5

1989 - 1992

OSRP: $32.50

VDTsv: $23-$52

Paid: $_____

Lamplighter With Lamp

55778 - Set of 2

1989 - 2004

OSRP: $9

VDTsv: $8-$32

Paid: $_____

Royal Coach

55786

1989 - 1992

OSRP: $55

VDTsv: $47-$75

Paid: $_____

• Early release to NALED dealers.

Constables

55794 - Set of 3

1989 - 1991

OSRP: $17.50

VDTsv: $54-$65

Paid: $_____

Violet Vendor / Carolers / Chestnut Vendor

55808 - Set of 3
1989 - 1992
OSRP: $23
VDTsv: $16-$38
Paid: $_____

King's Road Cab

55816
1989 - 1998
OSRP: $30
VDTsv: $20-$60
Paid: $_____

Christmas Carol Christmas Morning Figures

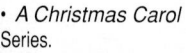

55883 - Set of 3
1989 - 2002
OSRP: $18
VDTsv: $20-$36
Paid: $_____

• *A Christmas Carol* Series.
• Early release to NALED dealers.

Christmas Carol Christmas Spirits Figures

55891 - Set of 4
1989 - 2001
OSRP: $27.50
VDTsv: $25-$39
Paid: $_____

• *A Christmas Carol* Series.

Town Crier & Chimney Sweep

55697 - Set of 2
1990 - 2001^M
OSRP: $15
VDTsv: $9-$19
Paid: $_____

Carolers On The Doorstep

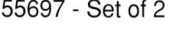

55700 - Set of 4
1990 - 1993
OSRP: $25
VDTsv: $14-$25
Paid: $_____

Holiday Travelers

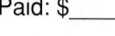

55719 - Set of 3
1990 - 1999
OSRP: $22.50
VDTsv: $15-$28
Paid: $_____

The Flying Scot Train

55735 - Set of 4
1990 - 1998
OSRP: $48
VDTsv: $56-$58
Paid: $_____

Victoria Station Train Platform

55751

1990 - 1999

OSRP: $20

VDTsv: $13-$38

Paid: $_____

- Porcelain and metal.
- Reads "Platform 1" on one side; "Platform 2" on the other.

Oliver Twist Characters

55549 - Set of 3

1991 - 1993

OSRP: $35

VDTsv: $23-$32

Paid: $_____

Bringing Home The Yule Log

55581 - Set of 3

1991 - 1998

OSRP: $27.50

VDTsv: $17-$30

Paid: $_____

Poultry Market

55590 - Set of 3

1991 - 1995

OSRP: $30

VDTsv: $18-$40

Paid: $_____

- Early samples have patches on the left hand side of the drape.
- 3 geese are separate in box.

Come Into The Inn

55603 - Set of 3

1991 - 1994

OSRP: $22

VDTsv: $13-$27

Paid: $_____

Holiday Coach

55611

1991 - 1998

OSRP: $68

VDTsv: $52-$74

Paid: $_____

- Early pieces have gold chains, and later ones have silver chains.

Gate House

55301

1992 - 1992

OSRP: $22.50

VDTsv: $12 - $39

Paid: $_____

- Brick varies from gray to blue.
- Event piece for 1992 dealer Open Houses.

The Old Puppeteer

58025 - Set of 3

1992 - 1995

OSRP: $32

VDTsv: $21-$35

Paid: $_____

- 2 marionettes are separate in box and can easily be lost.

The Bird Seller

58033 - Set of 3

1992 - 1995

OSRP: $25

VDTsv: $17-$32

Paid: $_____

Village Street Peddlers

58041 - Set of 2

1992 - 1994

OSRP: $16

VDTsv: $12-$18

Paid: $_____

English Post Box

58050

1992 - 2000

OSRP: $4.50

VDTsv: $12-$18

Paid: $_____

• Metal.

Lionhead Bridge

58645

1992 - 1997

OSRP: $22

VDTsv: $15-$22

Paid: $_____

Chelsea Market Fruit Monger & Cart

58130 - Set of 2

1993 - 1997

OSRP: $25

VDTsv: $18-$28

Paid: $_____

• Lantern and staff are separate in box.

Chelsea Market Fish Monger & Cart

58149 - Set of 2

1993 - 1997

OSRP: $25

VDTsv: $15-$44

Paid: $_____

• Lantern and staff are separate in box.

Chelsea Market Flower Monger & Cart

58157 - Set of 2

1993 - 2000

OSRP: $27.50

VDTsv: $27-$34

Paid: $_____

• A similar design was produced for Lord & Taylor. See the Special Design section.

Chelsea Lane Shoppers

58165 - Set of 4

1993 - 1999

OSRP: $30

VDTsv: $22-$38

Paid: $_____

Vision Of A Christmas Past

58173 - Set of 3

1993 - 1996

OSRP: $27.50

VDTsv: $19-$26

Paid: $_____

• *A Christmas Carol* Series.

C. Bradford, Wheelwright & Son

58181 - Set of 2

1993 - 1996

OSRP: $24

VDTsv: $12-$24

Paid: $_____

Bringing Fleeces To The Mill

58190 - Set of 2

1993 - 1998

OSRP: $35

VDTsv: $22-$29

Paid: $_____

Dashing Through The Snow

58203

1993 - 2002

OSRP: $32.50

VDTsv: $22-$25

Paid: $_____

Winter Sleighride

58254

1994 - 2001

OSRP: $18

VDTsv: $15-$32

Paid: $_____

• In early samples, the handle is attached to the sleigh with wires that curl before entering the sleigh.

Chelsea Market Mistletoe Monger & Cart

58262 - Set of 2

1994 - 1998

OSRP: $25

VDTsv: $35-$36

Paid: $_____

• Lantern and staff are separate in box.

Chelsea Market Curiosities Monger & Cart

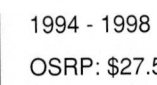

58270 - Set of 2

1994 - 1998

OSRP: $27.50

VDTsv: $19-$36

Paid: $_____

• Violin is separate in box.

Portobello Road Peddlers

58289 - Set of 3

1994 - 1998

OSRP: $27.50

VDTsv: $15-$21

Paid: $_____

Thatchers

58297 - Set of 3

1994 - 1997

OSRP: $35

VDTsv: $10-$30

Paid: $_____

• Frequently displayed with Cobb Cottage which has its roof undergoing repair.

A Peaceful Glow On Christmas Eve

58300 - Set of 3

1994 - 2003

OSRP: $30

VDTsv: $21-$38

Paid: $_____

Christmas Carol Holiday Trimming Set

58319 - Set of 21

1994 - 1997

OSRP: $65

VDTsv: $60

Paid: $_____

• *A Christmas Carol* Series.

Postern

98710

1994 - 1994

OSRP: $17.50

VDTsv: $15-$17

Paid: $_____

• Special imprint on bottom commemorates the village's 10th anniversary.

A Partridge In A Pear Tree – #I

58351

1995 - 1999

OSRP: $35

VDTsv: $21-$28

Paid: $_____

• 12 Days of Dickens' Village Series.
• 3 sets of bells are separate in box.

Two Turtle Doves – #II

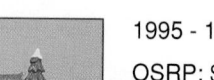

58360 - Set of 4

1995 - 1999

OSRP: $32.50

VDTsv: $20-$30

Paid: $_____

• 12 Days of Dickens' Village Series.

Three French Hens – #III

58378 - Set of 3

1995 - 1999

OSRP: $32.50

VDTsv: $28-$39

Paid: $_____

• 12 Days of Dickens' Village Series.

Four Calling Birds – #IV

58379 - Set of 2

1995 - 1999

OSRP: $32.50

VDTsv: $24

Paid: $_____

• 12 Days of Dickens' Village Series.

Five Golden Rings – #V

58381 - Set of 2

1995 - 1999

OSRP: $27.50

VDTsv: $15-$30

Paid: $_____

• 12 Days of Dickens' Village Series.

Six Geese A-Laying – #VI

58382 - Set of 2

1995 - 1999

OSRP: $30

VDTsv: $27-$42

Paid: $_____

• 12 Days of Dickens' Village Series.

Brixton Road Watchman

58390 - Set of 2

1995 - 1999

OSRP: $25

VDTsv: $12-$20

Paid: $_____

• Man's walking stick is fragile.

Tallyho!

58391 - Set of 5

1995 - 1998

OSRP: $50

VDTsv: $35-$50

Paid: $_____

Chelsea Market Hat Monger & Cart

58392 - Set of 2

1995 - 2000

OSRP: $27.50

VDTsv: $30

Paid: $_____

• Lantern and staff are separate in box.

Ye Olde Lamplighter Dickens' Village Sign

58393

1995 - 2001^M

OSRP: $20

VDTsv: $20-$48

Paid: $_____

Cobbler & Clock Peddler

58394 - Set of 2

1995 - 1997

OSRP: $25

VDTsv: $12-$27

Paid: $_____

• Though designed for Dickens', many collectors believe it more appropriate for Alpine.

Town Square Carolers

58327 - Set of 3

1995 - 1996

OSRP: *

VDTsv: *

* Accessory contained in the Dickens' Village Start A Tradition Set.

Palace Guards

58336 - Set of 2

1996ᴹ - 1996

OSRP: *

VDTsv: *

* Accessory contained in the Ramsford Palace Set.

Tending The New Calves

58395 - Set of 3

1996ᴹ - 1999

OSRP: $33

VDTsv: $18-$30

Paid: $_____

Caroling With The Cratchit Family

58396 - Set of 3

1996ᴹ -

OSRP: $37.50

VDTsv: -

Paid: $_____

• Christmas Carol Revisited Series.

Yeomen Of The Guard

58397 - Set of 5

1996ᴹ - 1997

OSRP: $30

VDTsv: $45-$65

Paid: $_____

• Lances and swords are fragile.

Seven Swans A-Swimming – #VII

58383 - Set of 4

1996 - 2000

OSRP: $27.50

VDTsv: $19-$43

Paid: $_____

• 12 Days of Dickens' Village Series.

Eight Maids A-Milking – #VIII

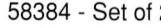

58384 - Set of 2

1996 - 2000

OSRP: $25

VDTsv: $28-$65

Paid: $_____

• 12 Days of Dickens' Village Series.

The Fezziwig Delivery Wagon

58400

1996 - 2006

OSRP: $32.50

VDTsv: $42-$98

Paid: $_____

• Christmas Carol Revisited Series.
• Similar design made for Lord & Taylor. See Special Design section.

Red Christmas Sulky

58401

1996 - 2001

OSRP: $30

VDTsv: $70

Paid: $_____

Gingerbread Vendor

58402 - Set of 2

1996 - 2001

OSRP: $22.50

VDTsv: $22-$40

Paid: $_____

A Christmas Carol Reading By Charles Dickens

58403 - Set of 4

1996 - 2001

OSRP: $45

VDTsv: $45-$49

Paid: $_____

• Christmas Carol Revisited Series.
• Sign is separate in box.

A Christmas Carol Reading By Charles Dickens

58404 - Set of 7

1996 - 1997

OSRP: $75

VDTsv: $55-$75

Paid: $_____

• Limited to 42,500.
• Charles Dickens' Signature Series™
• 4 lanterns and 2 signs separate in box.

Delivering Coal For The Hearth

58326 - Set of 2

1997ᴹ - 1999

OSRP: $32.50

VDTsv: $25-$68

Paid: $_____

• Early pieces have maroon wheels and buckets attached. Later ones have red wheels and buckets on hooks.

Nine Ladies Dancing – #IX

58385 - Set of 3

1997 - 2000

OSRP: $30

VDTsv: $33-$52

Paid: $_____

• 12 Days of Dickens' Village Series.

Ten Pipers Piping – #X

58386 - Set of 3

1997 - 2000

OSRP: $30

VDTsv: $40-$95

Paid: $_____

• 12 Days of Dickens' Village Series.

Ashley Pond Skating Party

58405 - Set of 6

1997 - 1999

OSRP: $70

VDTsv: $47-110

Paid: $_____

• One side of hanging sign reads "Ashley Pond," the other "Ashley Road Pond."

The Fire Brigade Of London Town

58406 - Set of 5

1997 - 2005

OSRP: $70

VDTsv: $68

Paid: $_____

Father Christmas's Journey

58407 - Set of 2

1997 - 2001

OSRP: $30

VDTsv: $30

Paid: $_____

• A similar design was produced for North Pole City. See the Special Design section.

Christmas Pudding Costermonger

58408 - Set of 3

1997 - 2001ᴹ

OSRP: $32.50

VDTsv: $24-$45

Paid: $_____

• Lantern is separate in box.

The Spirit Of Giving

58322 - Set of 3

1997 - 1998

OSRP: *

VDTsv: *

* Accessory contained in the Dickens' Village Start A Tradition Set.

Manchester Square Accessory Set

58301 - Set of 7

1997 - 2000

OSRP: *

VDTsv: $185

* Accessory contained in the Manchester Square Set.
• Man's walking stick is fragile.

Christmas Apples

58308 - Set of 3

1998ᴹ - 1998

OSRP: *

VDTsv: *

* Accessory contained in the Seton Morris Spice Merchant Set.

Miss Havisham, Estella, And Pip

58310 - Set of 3

1998 - 2001

OSRP: *

VDTsv: *

* Accessory contained in the Great Expectations Set.
• Literary Classic Series.

Here We Come A-Wassailing

58410 - Set of 5

1998 - 2001ᴹ

OSRP: $45

VDTsv: $33

Paid: $_____

Sitting In Camden Park

58411 - Set of 4

1998 - 2005

OSRP: $35

VDTsv: $90

Paid: $_____

Eleven Lords A-Leaping – #XI

58413

1998 - 2000

OSRP: $27.50

VDTsv: $31-$100

Paid: $_____

• 12 Days of Dickens' Village Series.

Until We Meet Again

58414 - Set of 2

1998 - 2001

OSRP: $27.50

VDTsv: $18-$19

Paid: $_____

Child's Play

58415 - Set of 2

1998 - 2001^M

OSRP: $25

VDTsv: $18

Paid: $_____

Tending The Cold Frame

58416 - Set of 3

1998 - 1999

OSRP: $32.50

VDTsv: $12-$25

Paid: $_____

• A similar design was also produced for Bachman's. See the Special Design section.

Ale Mates

58417 - Set of 2

1998 - 2004

OSRP: $25

VDTsv: $25

Paid: $_____

Twelve Drummers Drumming – #XII

58387

1999^M - 2000

OSRP: $65

VDTsv: $170-$400

Paid: $_____

• 12 Days of Dickens' Village Series.

A Good Day's Catch

58420 - Set of 2

1999^M - 2000

OSRP: $27.50

VDTsv: $16

Paid: $_____

The Mother's Gift

58442

1999 - 2000

OSRP: *

VDTsv: *

* Accessory contained in the Aldeburgh Music Box Shop Gift Set.

The Queen's Parliamentary Coach

58454

1999 - 2000

OSRP: $60

VDTsv: $38

Paid: $_____

• Limited to year of production.

Members Of Parliament

58455 - Set of 2

1999 - 2000

OSRP: $19

VDTsv: $15-$19

Paid: $_____

• Paper in man's hand is real.

King's Road Market Cross

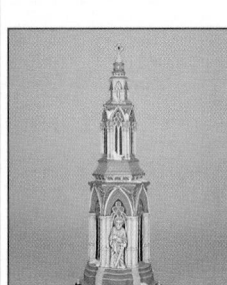

58456

1999 - 2000

OSRP: $25

VDTsv: $19-$28

Paid: $_____

• Dream House Sweepstakes Deluxe Prize winner assisted in the design.

Meeting Family At The Railroad Station

58457 - Set of 4

1999 - 2001ᴹ

OSRP: $32.50

VDTsv: $32

Paid: $_____

Master Gardeners

58458 - Set of 2

1999 - 2001ᴹ

OSRP: $30

VDTsv: $18-$30

Paid: $_____

Under The Bumbershoot

58460

1999 - 2002

OSRP: $20

VDTsv: $28

Paid: $_____

• Similar designs were produced for the NCC. See the Special Design section.

A Treasure From The Sea

58461 - Set of 2

1999 - 2001ᴹ

OSRP: $22.50

VDTsv: $14-$16

Paid: $_____

Fine Asian Antiques

58462 - Set of 2

1999 - 2001^M

OSRP: $27.50

VDTsv: $18-$48

Paid: $_____

Busy Railway Station

58464 - Set of 3

1999 - 2001^M

OSRP: $27.50

VDTsv: $18-$25

Paid: $_____

Locomotive Shed & Water Tower

58465

1999 - 2001

OSRP: $32.50

VDTsv: $27-$50

Paid: $_____

Queensbridge Railroad Yard Acc.

58466 - Set of 3

1999 - 2001^M

OSRP: $37.50

VDTsv: $49

Paid: $_____

12 Days Of Dickens' Village Sign

58467

1999 - 2000

OSRP: $20

VDTsv: $35

Paid: $_____

• 12 Days of Dickens' Village Series.

Scrooge At Fezziwig's Ball

58470

2000^M - 2000

OSRP: *

VDTsv: *

* Accessory contained in the Fezziwig's Ballroom Gift Set.
• Christmas Carol Revisited Series.

Holiday Quintet

58520 - Set of 6

2000^M - 2009

OSRP: $37.50

VDTsv: $26-$48

Paid: $_____

• Lamppost is battery/ adapter operated.
• Bow and baton are fragile.

At The Fire House

05700 - Set of 3

2000^M - 2000

OSRP: *

VDTsv: *

* Accessory contained in the GCC Ashwick Lane Gift Set.

Sweet Roses

58475 - Set of 5

2000 - 2001

OSRP: *

VDTsv: *

* Accessory contained
in the Lilycott Garden
Conservatory Gift Set.

Abington Locks

58521 - Set of 2

2000 - 2003

OSRP: $48

VDTsv: $85

Paid: $_____

• Abington Canal Series.

Abington Canal Boat

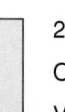

58522 - Set of 2

2000 - 2002

OSRP: $35

VDTsv: $14

Paid: $_____

• Abington Canal Series.

Gourmet Chocolates Delivery
Wagon

58523

2000 - 2003

OSRP: $45

VDTsv: $46

Paid: $_____

Hedgerow Dovecote

58524 - Set of 2

2000 - 2002

OSRP: $32.50

VDTsv: $30

Paid: $_____

Par For The Course

58525 - Set of 3

2000 - 2002

OSRP: $27.50

VDTsv: $58

Paid: $_____

Following The Leader

58526 - Set of 2

2000 - 2002

OSRP: $32.50

VDTsv: $34

Paid: $_____

Master Potter

58527

2000 - 2002

OSRP: $18

VDTsv: $48

Paid: $_____

Sliding Down Cornhill With Bob Cratchit

58528

2000 - 2005

OSRP: $25

VDTsv: $18-$28

Paid: $_____

• *A Christmas Carol* Series.

Polo Players

58529 - Set of 2

2000 - 2002

OSRP: $40

VDTsv: $28-$30

Paid: $_____

These Are For You

58530 - Set of 2

2000 - 2002

OSRP: $25

VDTsv: $75

Paid: $_____

Horses At The Lampguard

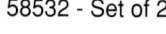

58531 - Set of 3

2000 - 2006

OSRP: $45

VDTsv: -

Paid: $_____

Keeping The Streets Clean

58532 - Set of 2

2000 - 2002

OSRP: $18

VDTsv: $18

Paid: $_____

Merry Go Roundabout

58533

2000 - 2004

OSRP: $32.50

VDTsv: $115

Paid: $_____

Sherlock Holmes – The Hansom Cab

58534

2000 - 2003

OSRP: $35

VDTsv: $40-118

Paid: $_____

Abington Canal

58535 - Set of 2

2000 - 2003

OSRP: $30

VDTsv: $65

Paid: $_____

• Abington Canal Series.

Abington Bridge

58536

2000 - 2003

OSRP: $37.50

VDTsv: $35

Paid: $_____

• Abington Canal Series.

Elementary My Dear Watson

58601

2000 - 2003

OSRP: *

VDTsv: *

* Accessory contained
in Sherlock Holmes -
221B Baker Street set.
• Literary Classic Series.

Christmas Eve Celebration

58485

2001ᴹ - 2001

OSRP: *

VDTsv: *

* Accessory contained
in the Somerset Valley
Church Gift Set.

Bob Cratchit And Tiny Tim

58537

2001ᴹ -

OSRP: $15

VDTsv: $47-$58

Paid: $_____

• *A Christmas Carol*
Series.

Ghost Of Christmas Present
Visits Scrooge

58538

2001ᴹ - 2001

OSRP: $15

VDTsv: $35

Paid: $_____

• *A Christmas Carol*
Series.

High Tea

58487

2001 - 2002

OSRP: *

VDTsv: *

* The accessory con-
tained in Mrs. Brimm's
Tea Room Gift Set.

Dickens Writing

58488

2001 - 2003

OSRP: *

VDTsv: *

* The accessory
contained in the Dickens'
Gad's Hill Chalet.

Doorman

58494

2001 - 2003

OSRP: *

VDTsv: *

* The accessory
contained in The Slone
Hotel.

The Big Prize Turkey

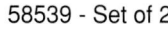

58539 - Set of 2

2001 - 2008

OSRP: $27.50

VDTsv: $27-$36

Paid: $_____

• *A Christmas Carol* Series.

Cobbler's Corner Stand

58540 - Set of 2

2001 - 2004

OSRP: $27.50

VDTsv: $60

Paid: $_____

Blacksmith To The Rescue

58541

2001 - 2004

OSRP: $22.50

VDTsv: $23

Paid: $_____

• Originally was named "Shoeing The Horse."

A Christmas Carol Visit

58542 - Set of 4

2001 -

OSRP: $27.50

VDTsv: $27.40

Paid: $_____

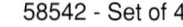

• *A Christmas Carol* Series.

Taking Grain To The Mill

58545

2001 - 2003

OSRP: $20

VDTsv: $20-$22

Paid: $_____

• Abington Canal Series.

A Family Tradition

58546 - Set of 2

2001 - 2002

OSRP: $20

VDTsv: $55

Paid: $_____

Lock Keeper

58547

2001 - 2003

OSRP: $12.50

VDTsv: $12-$15

Paid: $_____

• Abington Canal Series.

Chimney Sweep & Son

58548

2001 - 2004

OSRP: $18.50

VDTsv: $20

Paid: $_____

An Elegant Ride

58549

2001 - 2009

OSRP: $30

VDTsv: $29-$52

Paid: $_____

Street Merchants

58550 - Set of 3

2001 - 2004

OSRP: $17.50

VDTsv: $40

Paid: $_____

Formal Gardens

58551

2001 - 2003

OSRP: $65

VDTsv: $65-$118

Paid: $_____

Holiday Joy

58552

2001 - 2003

OSRP: $32.50

VDTsv: $45

Paid: $_____

• Battery/ adapter operated.

Dickens' Raising The Flag

58555

2001 - 2003

OSRP: $15

VDTsv: $8

Paid: $_____

• Includes British and Canadian flags.

Winter Frolic

05925

2002ᴹ - 2002

OSRP: *

VDTsv: *

* The accessory contained in Christmas At Codington Cottage.

Bearing Gifts

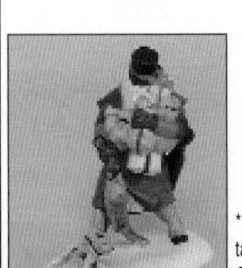

58506

2002ᴹ - 2002

OSRP: *

VDTsv: *

* The accessory contained in 1 Royal Tree Court.

Lord Of The Follies

58633

2002ᴹ - 2002

OSRP: *

VDTsv: *

* The accessory contained in Hop Castle Folly.

Chestnut Vendor

58557

2002^M -

OSRP: $32.50

VDTsv: $32-78

Paid: $_____

• *A Christmas Carol* Series.
• Battery/ adapter operated.

The First Edition

58513

2002 - 2004

OSRP: *

VDTsv: *

* The accessory contained in The Daily News.

Bringing Home The Holly

58514

2002 - 2003

OSRP: *

VDTsv: *

* The accessory contained in Codington Cottage.

All The World's A Stage

58515

2002 - 2003

OSRP: *

VDTsv: *

* The accessory contained in Shakespeare's Birthplace.

Rose Garden Beauty

58518

2002 - 2003

OSRP: *

VDTsv: *

* The accessory contained in Sweetbriar Cottage.

A Gentleman and Lady

58559

2002 - 2009

OSRP: $15

VDTsv: $10

Paid: $_____

London Newspaper Stand

58560 - Set of 2

2002 -

OSRP: $25

VDTsv: -

Paid: $_____

Jack-Of-The-Lantern

58561

2002 - 2005

OSRP: $25

VDTsv: $30

Paid: $_____

• All Hallows' Eve™ design.

Last Mail Call Of The Day

58562

2002 - 2004

OSRP: $10

VDTsv: $16-$17

Paid: $_____

Love or Money?

58563

2002 - 2004

OSRP: $15

VDTsv: $15-$78

Paid: $_____

• *A Christmas Carol* Series.

Temple Bar

58564

2002 - 2003

OSRP: $60

VDTsv: $23-$78

Paid: $_____

• Historical Landmark Series.

Covered Bridge At The Manor

58565

2002 - 2004

OSRP: $45

VDTsv: $25-$60

Paid: $_____

The Charitable Vicar

58566 - Set of 2

2002 - 2006

OSRP: $25

VDTsv: $58

Paid: $_____

A Rare Find

58567

2002 - 2004

OSRP: $15

VDTsv: $80

Paid: $_____

• Battery/ adapter operated.

A Christmas Beginning

58568

2002 -

OSRP: $17.50

VDTsv: $28

Paid: $_____

Omnibus

58569

2002 - 2005

OSRP: $55

VDTsv: $65

Paid: $_____

The Coffee-Stall

58571 - Set of 2

2003^M -

OSRP: $27.50

VDTsv: -

Paid: $_____

Victorian Skaters

58700 - Set of 3

2003^M - 2003

OSRP: *

VDTsv: *

* The accessory contained in London Skating Club.

The Halfpenny Showman

58572

2003 - 2005

OSRP: $17.50

VDTsv: $25

Paid: $_____

The Strange Case Of Dr. Jekyll & Mr. Hyde

58573

2003 - 2005

OSRP: $15

VDTsv: $17

Paid: $_____

• All Hallows' Eve™ Series.
• Inspired by Robert Louis Stevenson's novel.

Horse Drawn Hearse

58574

2003 - 2006

OSRP: $35

VDTsv: $88

Paid: $_____

• All Hallows' Eve™ Series.

Christmas Morning Parade

58575 - Set of 2

2003 - 2006

OSRP: $17.50

VDTsv: $40

Paid: $_____

London Gas Worker

58576

2003 - 2005

OSRP: $15

VDTsv: $24

Paid: $_____

Dickens Learns To Read

58577

2003 - 2009

OSRP: $12.50

VDTsv: $12-35

Paid: $_____

• Dickens' Village 20th Anniversary Series.

A Story For The Children

58578

2003 - 2005

OSRP: $12.50

VDTsv: $20

Paid: $_____

• Dickens' Village 20th Anniversary Series.

Ready For Duty, Queens Port

58579

2003 - 2005

OSRP: $15

VDTsv: $16-$20

Paid: $_____

• Queens Port Series.

Bringing Christmas Cheer, Queens Port

58580

2003 - 2005

OSRP: $20

VDTsv: $40

Paid: $_____

• Queens Port Series.

A Busy Day In Town

58581 - Set of 3

2003 - 2006

OSRP: $25

VDTsv: $25

Paid: $_____

• Dickens' Village 20th Anniversary Series.

A Basket Full Of Blooms

58583

2003 - 2005

OSRP: $16.50

VDTsv: $28

Paid: $_____

For You, My Lady

58704

2003 - 2005

OSRP: *

VDTsv: *

• The accessory contained in Green's Park Nosegays.

Scrooge

02973

2004 - 2004

OSRP: *

VDTsv: *

* The accessory contained in Belle's House - Special Edition.

Decorating With Holiday Greenery

58584 - Set of 2

2004^M - 2009

OSRP: $18.50

VDTsv: $18.50

Paid: $_____

• A Victorian Christmas™ Series.

Victorian Father Christmas

58585

2004^M - 2004

OSRP: $32.50

VDTsv: $62

Paid: $_____

• Limited to year of production.
• A Victorian Christmas™ Series.

A Toast To Our Anniversary

58587

2004^M - 2005

OSRP: $15

VDTsv: $50

Paid: $_____

• Dickens' Village 20th Anniversary Series.

Victorian Christmas Scene

58588

2004^M - 2004

OSRP: $50

VDTsv: $45

Paid: $_____

• Limited to year of production, 2004.
• A Victorian Christmas™ Series.

Kissing Under The Mistletoe

58717

2004^M - 2004

OSRP: *

VDTsv: *

* The accessory contained in Victorian Family Christmas House.

Popping The Cracker

58719

2004^M - 2006

OSRP: *

VDTsv: *

• A Victorian Christmas™ Series.
• The accessory contained in T. Smith Christmas Crackers.

Strolling Down Howard Street

58409

2004 - 2009

OSRP: $17.50

VDTsv: $12-$25

Paid: $_____

Begging For Soul Cakes

58412 - Set of 2

2004 - 2006

OSRP: $17.50

VDTsv: $32

Paid: $_____

• All Hallows' Eve™ Series.

A Caroling We Shall Go

58589

2004 - 2007

OSRP: $80

VDTsv: -

Paid: $_____

• Animated.
• Plays "Good King Wenceslas."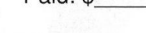

Town Square Market

58590

2004 - 2007

OSRP: $70

VDTsv: -

Paid: $_____

• Animated.

HMS Britannia, Queens Port

58591

2004 - 2006

OSRP: $55

VDTsv: $55-$75

Paid: $_____

• Queens Port Series.
• AC/DC adapter compatible.

Our Best Vintage, Sir

58593

2004 - 2008

OSRP: $15

VDTsv: $15-$25

Paid: $_____

Guarding The Castle

58594

2004 - 2006

OSRP: $15

VDTsv: -

Paid: $_____

• Historical Landmark Series.

A Boxing Day Tradition

58595

2004 - 2006

OSRP: $17.50

VDTsv: $17-$42

Paid: $_____

• A Victorian Christmas™ Series.

One More Christmas Card To Post, Please

58596

2004 - 2009

OSRP: $15

VDTsv: $10-$15

Paid: $_____

• A Victorian Christmas™ Series.

Get Your Spices 'Ere!

58597

2004 - 2007

OSRP: $10

VDTsv: -

Paid: $_____

On Time Delivery

58598

2004 - 2007

OSRP: $12.50

VDTsv: -

Paid: $_____

Checking The Ship's Manifest, Queens Port

58599
2004 - 2006
OSRP: $17.50
VDTsv: $17-$36
Paid: $_____

• Queens Port Series.

Future

Admiral, Queens Port

58418
2005ᴹ - 2006
OSRP: $12
VDTsv: $16
Paid: $_____

• Queens Port Series.

Charles And Catherine Dickens

58419
2005ᴹ -
OSRP: $12
VDTsv: $12
Paid: $_____

Red Lion Pub Beer Wagon

58421
2005ᴹ -
OSRP: $30
VDTsv: $30
Paid: $_____

• Available only in U.S.

Canadian Pub Beer Wagon

58422
2005ᴹ - 2006
OSRP: $30
VDTsv: -
Paid: $_____

• Available only in Canada.

Shall We Dance Tonight?

58732
2005ᴹ - 2005
OSRP: *
VDTsv: *

* The accessory contained in Christmas At Ashby Manor.

Lavender Costermonger

58424
2005 - 2008
OSRP: $18.50
VDTsv: $18
Paid: $_____

Advertising A Reading By Mr. Dickens

58425
2005 - 2006
OSRP: $17.50
VDTsv: $38
Paid: $_____

• Limited to year of production.
• 30th Anniversary Series.

Posy's Perfumes

58426
2005 - 2008
OSRP: $18.50
VDTsv: $12-$27
Paid: $_____

Dickens Submitting His First Manuscript

58428
2005 - 2008
OSRP: $15
VDTsv: $15-$32
Paid: $_____

The Best In Hats & Walking Sticks

58435
2005 - 2007
OSRP: $17.50
VDTsv: -
Paid: $_____

A Fine Shoe Shine

58436
2005 - 2007
OSRP: $20
VDTsv: -
Paid: $_____

Pausing For A Leisurely Pipe

58437
2005 - 2007
OSRP: $15
VDTsv: $30
Paid: $_____

Masquerading On All Hallows' Eve

58439 - Set of 2
2005 - 2007
OSRP: $20
VDTsv: $14-$20
Paid: $_____

• All Hallows' Eve™ Series.

A Fine Batch Of Gin

58450
2005 - 2009
OSRP: $17.50
VDTsv: $12-$28
Paid: $_____

Hadley's Currency Exchange

58452
2005 - 2007
OSRP: $25
VDTsv: -
Paid: $_____

Household Guards

58736 - Set of 2

2005 - 2006

OSRP: *

VDTsv: *

*The accessory contained in Buckingham Palace.

London's Finest Gin Delivery

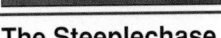

58459

2006 - 2008

OSRP: $17.50

VDTsv: $17-26

Paid: $_____

The Steeplechase

58468

2006 - 2007

OSRP: $30

VDTsv: $56

Paid: $_____

Congratulations, Graduate

58801

2006 - 2007

OSRP: $15

VDTsv: $30

Paid: $_____

Stained Glass Artisan

58802

2006 - 2008

OSRP: $17.50

VDTsv: $17.50

Paid: $_____

Ship Figurehead Carver

58803

2006 - 2008

OSRP: $17.50

VDTsv: -

Paid: $_____

Making Wonderful Music

58804

2006 - 2009

OSRP: $18.50

VDTsv: $13-$18

Paid: $_____

Fetching The Day's Water

58805

2006 - 2008

OSRP: $17.50

VDTsv: -

Paid: $_____

Victorian Perfumer

58806

2006 - 2009

OSRP: $18.50

VDTsv: $18.50

Paid: $_____

Making Bobbin Lace

58810

2006 - 2009

OSRP: $15

VDTsv: $10-$26

Paid: $_____

Playing With A Puppy

58811

2006 -

OSRP: $17.50

VDTsv: -

Paid: $_____

Snowball Fun

58812

2006 -

OSRP: $18.50

VDTsv: -

Paid: $_____

Royal Coach

58759 - Set of 2

2007ᴹ - 2007

OSRP: $105

VDTsv: -

Paid: $_____

• Limited Edition 8,000.
• Limited To Year of Production.

Delivering Holiday Chocolates

58760 - Set of 2

2007ᴹ - 2007

OSRP: $105

VDTsv: -

Paid: $_____

• Holiday Value Set of 2.
• Limited To Year of Production.

Tending The Royal Horses

58813

2007ᴹ - 2008

OSRP: $22.50

VDTsv: $22-$33

Paid: $_____

Fountain, Barrow Manor

799909 - Set of 2

2007 - 2008

OSRP: $110

VDTsv: -

Paid: $_____

• Limited Edition 10,000.

Skating Couple

799944
2007 - 2009
OSRP: $50
VDTsv: $50
Paid: $_____

To The Manor Born

799945
2007 -
OSRP: $20
VDTsv: -
Paid: $_____

Lanterns For Sale

799946
2007 - 2009
OSRP: $17.50
VDTsv: $17.50
Paid: $_____

Ye Royal Scrivener

799947
2007 - 2009
OSRP: $17.50
VDTsv: $17.50
Paid: $_____

Finishing The Christmas Bell

799948
2007 - 2009
OSRP: $17.50
VDTsv: $17.50
Paid: $_____

Master & Apprentice

799949
2007 - 2009
OSRP: $20
VDTsv: $20
Paid: $_____

Tea Time

799950
2007 - 2009
OSRP: $22.50
VDTsv: $15-$23
Paid: $_____

Welcome To Dickens' Village

799951
2007 - 2009
OSRP: $17.50
VDTsv: $17.50
Paid: $_____

Delivering The Holiday Greens

799991-Set of 2

2008^M - 2008

OSRP: $79

VDTsv: -

Paid: $_____

• Holiday Value Set of 2.
• Limited To Year of Production.

An Artist At Work

804447

2008^M - 2009

OSRP: $20

VDTsv: $20

Paid: $_____

Hallelujah

804448-Set of 2

2008^M -

OSRP: $15

VDTsv: $15

Paid: $_____

Heading Home From The Market

804449

2008^M - 2009

OSRP: $20

VDTsv: $12-$18

Paid: $_____

Welcome To Lund's Art Show

807225

2008 -

OSRP: $22.50

VDTsv: $22.50

Paid: $_____

• Dickens' 25th Anniversary.

A Dickens Book Signing

807226

2008 -

OSRP: $20

VDTsv: $20

Paid: $_____

Fan Visits Ebenezer

80722 -Set of 2

2008 -

OSRP: $27.50

VDTsv: $27.50

Paid: $_____

• A Christmas Carol.

Crowntree Coach

807228

2008 -

OSRP: $45

VDTsv: $45

Paid: $_____

• Dickens' 25th Anniversary.

Dickens' Shopkeepers

807229-Set of 3

2008 -

OSRP: $18.50

VDTsv: -

Paid: $_____

• Dickens' 25th Anniversary.

Dickens' Carolers

807230

2008 -

OSRP: $28.50

VDTsv: -

Paid: $_____

Tipping A Pint

807231

2008 -

OSRP: $20

VDTsv: $20

Paid: $_____

Persian Rugs For Sale

807232

2008 -

OSRP: $22.50

VDTsv: $22.50

Paid: $_____

Regent's Park Footbridge

807233

2008 -

OSRP: $42.50

VDTsv: $42.50

Paid: $_____

Park House Carriage

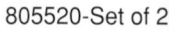

805520-Set of 2

2009^M - 2009

OSRP: $79

VDTsv: -

Paid: $_____

• Holiday Set of 2.
• Limited To Year of Production.

Dickens Family Stroll

811775

2009^M -

OSRP: $22.50

VDTsv: -

Paid: $_____

Sweeping Up

811776

2009^M -

OSRP: $15

VDTsv: -

Paid: $_____

Decorating The Lamp Post

808725

2010 -

OSRP: $20

VDTsv: -

Paid: $_____

Getting The Christmas Yule Log

808884

2010 -

OSRP: $20

VDTsv: -

Paid: $_____

Shoeing The Horse

808892

2010 -

OSRP: $28.50

VDTsv: -

Paid: $_____

Dickens' Merchants

808894-Set of 2

2010 -

OSRP: $16.50

VDTsv: -

Paid: $_____

Fish n' Chips To Go

808896

2010 -

OSRP: $27.50

VDTsv: -

Paid: $_____

Florence Nightingale

808897

2010 -

OSRP: $12.50

VDTsv: -

Paid: $_____

An Afternoon On Ice

808904-Set of 3

2010 -

OSRP: $35

VDTsv: -

Paid: $_____

Relaxing In Regent's Park

808905

2010 -

OSRP: $18.50

VDTsv: -

Paid: $_____

New England Village® Series

"Over the river and through the wood, to grandfather's house we go; the horse knows the way to carry the sleigh, Through the white and drifted snow." — Lydia Maria Child (1802-1880)

New England's original seven were issued in 1986. They were small in scale, but highly desired to complete this charming village dedicated to the northeastern states. The diversity of the area is showcased in the variety associated with this village. Small towns grow around white steepled churches. Barns, farm houses, grain elevators and sawmills create interesting rural settings. The coastline / waterfront themed pieces such as lighthouses, canneries, ship builders and quaint cottages — plus rustic cabins — make this a favorite village to display. The most coveted piece is the limited edition Smythe Woolen Mill, which most collectors have never seen, much less touched.

While most villages concentrate on winter and the holidays, New England's appeal begins as the leaves change to yellows, oranges, and reds. Town folk harvest apples, maple sugar, cranberries, and pumpkins. Pigs, cows, horses, ducks, and chickens populate the farm-lands. And, what would autumn be without local bazaars to sell hand-made quilts, knitted items, and toys; and yummy jams, jellies, pies, or flapjacks.

There have been expansions to the geographic area. The Amish Farm House and Barn reflect Pennsylvania. The Susquehanna Station is named after the river running through the state. One of the most popular sub-series is Sleepy Hollow, based on Washington Irving's legend which took place along the Hudson River in New York. This group adorns many tables during the fall months and many of the harvest related buildings are featured as Thanksgiving decorations. Several buildings have also been designed without patches of snow, Christmas wreaths and garland to enable them to be displayed throughout the year.

When the temperature drops and the snow falls, horse drawn sleighs take to the roads. Children grab their sleds to slide down the hills and skaters head to the frozen lakes. New England is a very special area. The New England Village® portrays it well.

NEW ENGLAND VILLAGE- Set of 7   65307

Dates	OSRP	VDTsv	Paid
1986 - 1989	$170	$880	$_____

• None of the seven buildings have names on the bottom.

Apothecary   65307

Dates	OSRP	VDTsv	Paid
1986 - 1989	$25	$70	$_____

General Store   65307

Dates	OSRP	VDTsv	Paid
1986 - 1989	$25	$155 - $245	$_____

• Do not handle by porch posts; they are very fragile.

Nathaniel Bingham Fabrics   65307

Dates	OSRP	VDTsv	Paid
1986 - 1989	$25	$118 - $148	$_____

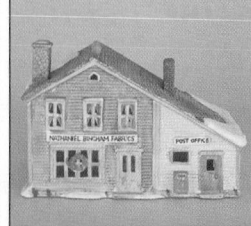

Livery Stable & Boot Shop   65307

Dates	OSRP	VDTsv	Paid
1986 - 1989	$25	$118	$_____

Brick Town Hall   65307

Dates	OSRP	VDTsv	Paid
1986 - 1989	$25	$85 - $160	$_____

Steeple Church (Version 1)   65307

Dates	OSRP	VDTsv	Paid
1986 - 1989	$25	$110	$_____

• Front tree is attached with porcelain slip.
• Sleeve is open on sides.

(Version 2)

	VDTsv	Paid
	$78 - $120	$_____

• Front tree is attached with glue.
• Sleeve is open at top and bottom.
• This design was re-issued in 1989 with item # 65390.

Red Schoolhouse   65307

Dates	OSRP	VDTsv	Paid
1986 - 1989	$25	$265 - $275	$_____

Jacob Adams Farmhouse & Barn   65382

Dates	OSRP	VDTsv	Paid
1986 - 1989	$65	$280 - $425	$_____

• Early pieces have sleeves that read "New England Village Farm." Later ones read "Jacob Adams Farmhouse and Barn."

• Because the animals were simply in tissue and placed in the box with no separate compartments, they are often damaged.
• Set of 5 includes Farmhouse, Barn, 2 cows, and a horse.
• Do not handle house by columns.

Craggy Cove Lighthouse   59307

Dates	OSRP	VDTsv	Paid
1987 - 1994	$35	$28 - $88	$_____

• Early pieces have a drain hole at the bottom of the tower. Later ones do not. Not only does the hole help collectors decide how early their piece was manufactured, but it also allows them to insert a "beacon."

Weston Train Station

59315

Dates	OSRP	VDTsv	Paid
1987 - 1989	$42	$174	$_____

• This station looks very much like the now-dilapidated station in the Boston, MA suburb of Weston.

Smythe Woolen Mill

65439

Dates	OSRP	VDTsv	Paid
1987 - 1988	$42	$995 - $1175	$_____

• Limited Edition of 7,500.

Timber Knoll Log Cabin

65447

Dates	OSRP	VDTsv	Paid
1987 - 1990	$28	$85 - $165	$_____

• Bottomstamp reads "Log Cabin."
• Do not handle by columns.

Old North Church

59323

Dates	OSRP	VDTsv	Paid
1988 - 1998	$40	$31 - $105	$_____

• Inspired by the historic landmark in Boston, Christ Church, where sexton Robert Newman hung lanterns in its steeple to warn colonists in Charlestown that the British were on their way to Lexington and Concord.

CHERRY LANE SHOPS - Set of 3

59390

Dates	OSRP	VDTsv	Paid
1988 - 1990	$80	$67 - $115	$_____

Ben's Barbershop

59390

Dates	OSRP	VDTsv	Paid
1988 - 1990	$27	$92 - $98	$_____

Otis Hayes Butcher Shop 59390

Dates	OSRP	VDTsv	Paid
1988 - 1990	$27	$55 - $82	$_____

• Do not handle by columns.

Anne Shaw Toys 59390

Dates	OSRP	VDTsv	Paid
1988 - 1990	$27	$102 - $120	$_____

Ada's Bed And Boarding House 59404
(Version 1)

Dates	OSRP	VDTsv	Paid
1988 - 1991	$36	$190 - $355	$_____

• Rear Steps: Part of the building's mold.
• 2nd Floor Windows: Alternating yellow panes.
• Color: Lemon yellow.
• Samples are pink/wine.   **VDTsv: $400**   Paid: $_____

(Version 2)

VDTsv	Paid
$120 - $145	$_____

• Rear Steps: Part of the building's mold.
• 2nd Floor Windows: Alternating yellow panes.
• Color: Pale yellow.

(Version 3)

VDTsv	Paid
$67	$_____

• Rear Steps: Separate attachment.
• 2nd Floor Windows: Top halves solid, bottom halves cut out.
• Color: Pale yellow.
• This version also has less snow on the roof and at base.

Steeple Church (Version 3) 65390

Dates	OSRP	VDTsv	Paid
1989 - 1990	$30	$98	$_____

• Front tree is attached with porcelain slip.
• Notice the different item number from original 1986 piece.

Berkshire House (Williamsburg Blue)   59420

Dates	OSRP	VDTsv	Paid
1989 - 1991	**$40**	**$85**	**$____**

- This version has pale shutters and porch rail spindles.
- Be careful when removing this piece from the box as it is very easy to break off the porch railing.
- Samples are forest green. **VDTsv: $90** Paid: $____

(Teal Version)

		VDTsv	Paid
		$75 - $88	**$____**

- This version has yellow shutters and porch rail spindles.
- Be careful when removing this piece from the box as it is very easy to break off the porch railing.

Jannes Mullet Amish Farm House   59439

Dates	OSRP	VDTsv	Paid
1989 - 1992	**$32**	**$49 - $98**	**$____**

Jannes Mullet Amish Barn   59447

Dates	OSRP	VDTsv	Paid
1989 - 1992	**$48**	**$59 - $89**	**$____**

Shingle Creek House   59463

Dates	OSRP	VDTsv	Paid
1990 - 1994	**$37.50**	**$21 - $78**	**$____**

- Early release to Showcase and NALED dealers.

Captain's Cottage   59471

Dates	OSRP	VDTsv	Paid
1990 - 1996	**$40**	**$31 - $48**	**$____**

- Do not handle by columns.

SLEEPY HOLLOW - Set of 3   59544

Dates	OSRP	VDTsv	Paid
1990 - 1993	$96	$150	$_____

• This set was inspired by Washington Irving's classic, *The Legend of Sleepy Hollow*. The story takes place along the Hudson River in North Tarrytown, NY.

Sleepy Hollow School   59544

Dates	OSRP	VDTsv	Paid
1990 - 1993	$32	$88 - $96	$_____

• A bell hangs in the tower.

Van Tassel Manor   59544

Dates	OSRP	VDTsv	Paid
1990 - 1993	$32	$30 - $43	$_____

Ichabod Crane's Cottage   59544

Dates	OSRP	VDTsv	Paid
1990 - 1993	$32	$30 - $48	$_____

Sleepy Hollow Church   59552

Dates	OSRP	VDTsv	Paid
1990 - 1993	$36	$40 - $68	$_____

McGrebe — Cutters & Sleighs   56405

Dates	OSRP	VDTsv	Paid
1991 - 1995	$45	$27 - $88	$_____

Bluebird Seed And Bulb

56421

Dates	OSRP	VDTsv	Paid
1992 - 1996	$48	$29 - $54	$_____

Yankee Jud Bell Casting

56430

Dates	OSRP	VDTsv	Paid
1992 - 1995	$44	$26 - $35	$_____

Stoney Brook Town Hall

56448

Dates	OSRP	VDTsv	Paid
1992 - 1995	$42	$30 - $66	$_____

A. BIELER FARM — Set of 2

56480

Dates	OSRP	VDTsv	Paid
1993 - 1996	$92	$64	$_____

Pennsylvania Dutch Farmhouse

56481

Dates	OSRP	VDTsv	Paid
1993 - 1996	$42	$31 - $88	$_____

Pennsylvania Dutch Barn

56482

Dates	OSRP	VDTsv	Paid
1993 - 1996	$50	$39 - $80	$_____

Blue Star Ice Co. 56472

Dates	OSRP	VDTsv	Paid
1993 - 1997	$45	$34 - $62	$_____

• Acrylic ice blocks easily come unglued.

Arlington Falls Church 56510

Dates	OSRP	VDTsv	Paid
1994ᴹ - 1997	$40	$25 - $52	$_____

• Do not handle by columns.

Cape Keag Fish Cannery 56529

Dates	OSRP	VDTsv	Paid
1994 - 1998	$48	$24 - $68	$_____

Pigeonhead Lighthouse 56537

Dates	OSRP	VDTsv	Paid
1994 - 1998	$50	$64	

• Posts near beacon and at front of building are extremely fragile.

BREWSTER BAY COTTAGES — Set of 2 56570

Dates	OSRP	VDTsv	Paid
1995ᴹ - 1997	$90	$72	$_____

Jeremiah Brewster House 56568

Dates	OSRP	VDTsv	Paid
1995ᴹ - 1997	$45	$48 - $70	$_____

• Early pieces have sleeves that read "Thomas T. Julian House." Later ones have stickers with the correct name placed over the mistake.

Thomas T. Julian House 56569

Dates	OSRP	VDTsv	Paid
1995^M - 1997	$45	$35 - $78	$_____

- Early pieces have sleeves that read "Jeremiah Brewster House." Later ones have stickers with the correct name placed over the mistake.
- Do not handle by columns.

Chowder House 56571

Dates	OSRP	VDTsv	Paid
1995 - 1998	$40	$24 - $55	$_____

- Sign is separate in box.

Woodbridge Post Office 56572

Dates	OSRP	VDTsv	Paid
1995 - 1998	$40	$37 - $78	$_____

Pierce Boat Works 56573

Dates	OSRP	VDTsv	Paid
1995 - 2000	$55	$29 - $84	$_____

Apple Valley School 56172

Dates	OSRP	VDTsv	Paid
1996^M - 2008	$35	$28 - $54	$_____

J. Hudson Stoveworks 56574

Dates	OSRP	VDTsv	Paid
1996 - 1998	$60	$41 - $67	$_____

- Black metal kettle is separate in box.

Navigational Charts & Maps

56575

Dates	OSRP	VDTsv	Paid
1996 - 1999	$48	$33 - $110	$_____

• Several attachments are very fragile.

Bobwhite Cottage

56576

Dates	OSRP	VDTsv	Paid
1996 - 2001	$50	$54 - $68	$_____

• A bobwhite is a small quail native to North America.
• Spires are fragile.

Van Guilder's Ornamental Ironworks

56577

Dates	OSRP	VDTsv	Paid
1997ᴹ - 1999	$50	$33 - $35	$_____

• This is the first New England Village design with multiple weathervanes.

East Willet Pottery

56578

Dates	OSRP	VDTsv	Paid
1997 - 1999	$45	$27 - $45	$_____

• Do not handle by columns.

Steen's Maple House

56579

Dates	OSRP	VDTsv	Paid
1997 - 2001	$60	$60 - $148	$_____

• Uses Magic Smoke to create smoking effect rising from the chimney.
• Buckets are separate in box.

Semple's Smokehouse

56580

Dates	OSRP	VDTsv	Paid
1997 - 1999	$45	$31 - $45	$_____

The Emily Louise

56581

Dates	OSRP	VDTsv	Paid
1998^M - 2000	$70	$78 - $88	$_____

- The wreath is "free-floating" and is easily damaged.
- 2 flags are separate in box.
- Set of 2 includes the ship and a dock.

Franklin Hook & Ladder Co.

56601

Dates	OSRP	VDTsv	Paid
1998 - 2000	$55	$41 - $69	$_____

Moggin Falls General Store

56602

Dates	OSRP	VDTsv	Paid
1998 - 2004	$60	$47 - $65	$_____

- Picture on sleeve is reversed.
- Flag and 2 signs are separate in box.

Deacon's Way Chapel

56604

Dates	OSRP	VDTsv	Paid
1998 - 2000	$68	$49 - $72	$_____

Harper's Farm

56605

Dates	OSRP	VDTsv	Paid
1998 - 2000	$65	$51 - $75	$_____

- Weathervane and 2 spires are separate in box.

Little Women – The March Residence — 56606

Dates	OSRP	VDTsv	Paid
1999^M - 2000	$90	$78	$_____

- Second in the Literary Classic Series. See this series in the Small Collection section.
- Louisa May Alcott based the March Residence on the Orchard House in Concord, MA where she grew up.
- Set of 4 plus book includes the Residence and the accessory "A Letter From Papa" which depicts Marmie, Jo, Amy, Beth, and Meg.
- The water pump's handle is very fragile.

Hale & Hardy House — 56610

Dates	OSRP	VDTsv	Paid
1999 - 2001	$60	$44 - $60	$_____

- 2 signs are separate in box.

Trinity Ledge — 56611

Dates	OSRP	VDTsv	Paid
1999 - 2002	$85	$59 - $85	$_____

- The three pinafore flags attached signal U - S - A.
- Includes U.S. and Canadian flags.

Harper's Farmhouse — 56612

Dates	OSRP	VDTsv	Paid
1999 - 2006	$57	$42 - $80	$_____

- Dream House Sweepstakes Grand Prize winner assisted in the design.
- 3 lightning rods are separate in box.

P. L. Wheeler's Bicycle Shop — 56613

Dates	OSRP	VDTsv	Paid
1999 - 2002	$57	$59 - $75	$_____

- This is one of the first New England pieces not to have snow.
- Sign and weathervane are packaged separately.

Platt's Candles & Wax

56614

Dates	OSRP	VDTsv	Paid
1999 - 2001	**$60**	**$38 - $60**	$_____

• Candelabra and weathervane are separate in box.

Susquehanna Station

56624

Dates	OSRP	VDTsv	Paid
2000ᴹ - 2002	**$60**	**$46 - $89**	$_____

• Set of 2 includes the Station and signal with coal car.

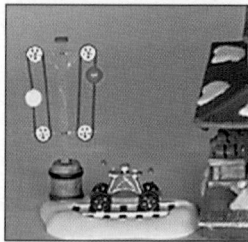

Mountain View Cabin

56625

Dates	OSRP	VDTsv	Paid
2000 - 2001	**$55**	**$295 - $296**	$_____

• 25th Anniversary Limited Edition of 10,000.

Verna Mae's Boutique Gift Set

56626

Dates	OSRP	VDTsv	Paid
2000 - 2001	**$65**	**$38 - $65**	$_____

• Discover Department 56 Spring Event Piece.
• Set of 3 includes building, "New Spring Finery" accessory, and flowering tree.
• Sign is separate in box.

The Cranberry House

56627

Dates	OSRP	VDTsv	Paid
2000 - 2002	$60	$72 - $98	$_____

• Weathervane and 3 utensils are separate in the box.

Wm. Walton Fine Clocks & Pocket Pieces

56628

Dates	OSRP	VDTsv	Paid
2000 - 2002	$60	$44 - $72	$_____

• Clock and 2 lanterns are separate in the box.
• Hitching post is fragile.

Laurel Hill Church

56629

Dates	OSRP	VDTsv	Paid
2000 - 2003	$68	$51 - $98	$_____

• This is the first church to include a cemetery.
• Do not handle by fence when removing from box.
• Gravestones are fragile.

Revere Silver Works

56632

Dates	OSRP	VDTsv	Paid
2001^M - 2002	$60	$60 - $60	$_____

• Set of 2 includes shop and "Creating Silver Keepsakes."
• Pitcher ornament is included separately in the box.

Breakers Point Lighthouse

56636

Dates	OSRP	VDTsv	Paid
2001 - 2005	$85	$195	$_____

• Seaside Series.
• Weathervane is separate in the box.

Springfield Studio Gift Set

56634

Dates	OSRP	VDTsv	Paid
2001 - 2002	**$65**	**$62 - $75**	**$_____**

• First available during the Mother's Day Spring program.
• Set of 5 includes Studio, 2 piece accessory "Spring Portrait," sign, and tree.
• Hanging plant is separate in the box.
• 5% of proceeds goes to fight against breast cancer.

Captain Kensey's House

56651

Dates	OSRP	VDTsv	Paid
2001 - 2003	**$55**	**$48 - $62**	**$_____**

• Seaside Series.

Whale Tale Pub & Inn

56652

Dates	OSRP	VDTsv	Paid
2001 - 2003	**$62**	**$60 - $70**	**$_____**

• Seaside Series.
• Sign is separate in the box.

Otter Creek Sawmill

56653

Dates	OSRP	VDTsv	Paid
2001 - 2003	**$70**	**$56 - $128**	**$_____**

• Mountain Lake Lodge Series.

Whitehill Round Barn

56654

Dates	OSRP	VDTsv	Paid
2001 - 2005	**$65**	**$54 - $68**	**$_____**

• Four weathervanes are separate in the box.

Chapman's Cider House

56655

Dates	OSRP	VDTsv	Paid
2002^M - 2005	$65	$78	$_____

• Named in honor of Johnny Appleseed.
• Sign is separate in the box.
• Do not handle by porch posts.

Salt Bay Lobster Co.

56658

Dates	OSRP	VDTsv	Paid
2002 - 2006	$57	$120	$_____

Warren Homestead And Walden Cottage

56659

Dates	OSRP	VDTsv	Paid
2002 - 2005	$85	$138	$_____

• Set of 2.
• Warren Homestead sign is separate in box. (But Walden Cottage sign is attached.)

Hutchison Grain Elevator

56660

Dates	OSRP	VDTsv	Paid
2002 - 2004	$55	$68	$_____

Castle Glassworks

56661

Dates	OSRP	VDTsv	Paid
2002 - 2003	$75	$67 - $87	$_____

• Limited to 15,000 numbered pieces.

Connacher's Nursery 56662

Dates	OSRP	VDTsv	Paid
2002 - 2004	$70	$66 - $70	$_____

Benjamin Bowman Violin Maker 56663

Dates	OSRP	VDTsv	Paid
2002 - 2004	$60	$76	$_____

Mt. Gibb Congregational Church 56664

Dates	OSRP	VDTsv	Paid
2003^M - 2006	$50	$155	$_____

- Set of 2 includes "Announcements Sign" accessory and removable wedding trim.
- Can be personalized.

The Red Fox 56665

Dates	OSRP	VDTsv	Paid
2003 - 2006	$55	$66	$_____

Waterbury Button Company 56666

Dates	OSRP	VDTsv	Paid
2003 - 2004	$65	$53 - $65	$_____

- Limited to year of production.

Drummond Bank 56667

Dates	OSRP	VDTsv	Paid
2003 - 2005	$55	$55	$_____

- Can be personalized.

Woodbridge Town Hall

56670

Dates	OSRP	VDTsv	Paid
2004^M - 2005	$55	$55 - $60	$_____

Sawyer Family Tree Farm

56671

Dates	OSRP	VDTsv	Paid
2004^M - 2004	$75	$68	$_____

- Limited to year of production.
- Set of 5 includes house, "Taking The Tree Home" accessory, trees, and snow.

J. Noyes Mill

56672

Dates	OSRP	VDTsv	Paid
2004 - 2006	$75	$115	$_____

- Windmill blades turn.
- Adapter included.

Woodbridge Gazette & Printing Office

56673

Dates	OSRP	VDTsv	Paid
2004 - 2007	$55	$55 - $68	$_____

- Sign is separate in box.

Chas. Hoyt Blacksmith

56674

Dates	OSRP	VDTsv	Paid
2004 - 2008	$60	$72	$_____

Christmas Homecoming At Havenport 56675

Dates	OSRP	VDTsv	Paid
2005^M - 2005	$75	$125	$____

• Set of 8 includes house "Coming Home For Christmas" accessory, walls, trees, and snow.

Mt. Gibb Parsonage 56676

Dates	OSRP	VDTsv	Paid
2005^M - 2007	$55	$55	$____

• Sign is separate in box.

Christmas Valley Toys & Dolls 56677

Dates	OSRP	VDTsv	Paid
2005 - 2006	$80	-	$____

• 30th Anniversary Series.
• Limited to year of production.
• Long Life Cordless Lighting.

Green Dragon Coffeehouse 56678

Dates	OSRP	VDTsv	Paid
2005 - 2006	$70	$70	$____

• NEV 20th Anniversary Series.
• Limited to year of production.

Salt Bay Life Saving Station 56679

Dates	OSRP	VDTsv	Paid
2005 - 2007	$60	$118	$____

Wheaton Christmas Bakery

57001

Dates	OSRP	VDTsv	Paid
2006 - 2006	$80	-	$_____

- Set of 5 includes house "Cookies For Everyone" accessory.
- Limited to year of production.

Knickerbocker Flag Company

57003

Dates	OSRP	VDTsv	Paid
2006 - 2007	$70	$65	$_____

Union Oyster House

57004

Dates	OSRP	VDTsv	Paid
2006 - 2008	$80	$80 - $118	$_____

Pine Creek Hunting Lodge

57005

Dates	OSRP	VDTsv	Paid
2006 - 2009	$80	$80 - $128	$_____

W. Bartell, Physician

57006

Dates	OSRP	VDTsv	Paid
2006 - 2008	$75	$75 - $120	$_____

Christmas At Salt Bay Lighthouse

57007

Dates	OSRP	VDTsv	Paid
2007^M - 2007	$79	$126	$_____

• Limited to year of production.

Bennington Manor

57008

Dates	OSRP	VDTsv	Paid
2007 - 2009	$75	$75	$_____

Pawtuck Furniture Maker

799923

Dates	OSRP	VDTsv	Paid
2007 - 2009	$75	$75	$_____

Roundel Cottage

799924

Dates	OSRP	VDTsv	Paid
2007 - 2009	$65	$65	$_____

C. Cope & Co. Tin Jobber

799925

Dates	OSRP	VDTsv	Paid
2007 -	$75	$75	$_____

Pembroke Textile Mill

805525

Dates	OSRP	VDTsv	Paid
2008 -	$115	$115	$_____

Providence Church   805526

Dates	OSRP	VDTsv	Paid
2008 -	$80	$80	$_____

Colonial Post & Telegraph   805527

Dates	OSRP	VDTsv	Paid
2008 -	$85	$85	$_____

Welcome to Windham Country Inn   805528

Dates	OSRP	VDTsv	Paid
2009^M - 2009	$79	-	$_____

- Limited to year of production.
- Set of 2.
- Celebrate Holiday Set.
- Includes "Arriving At Windham."

Tilton Station   808914

Dates	OSRP	VDTsv	Paid
2010 -	$95	-	$_____

South Deerfield Livery Stable   808915

Dates	OSRP	VDTsv	Paid
2010 -	$85	-	$_____

Covered Wooden Bridge

65315

1986 - 1990

OSRP: $10

VDTsv: $9-$15

Paid: $_____

• The sleeve reads "Covered Bridge."

New England Winter Set

65323 - Set of 5

1986 - 1990

OSRP: $18

VDTsv: $30-$69

Paid: $_____

• Sleeves on early pieces read "Winter Village Accessories."

New England Village Sign

65706

1987 - 1993

OSRP: $6

VDTsv: $6-$10

Paid: $_____

NEW ENGLAND VILLAGE

• Bottomstamp reads "Handcrafted by Jiean Fung Porcelains, Taiwan."
• Early signs have more detail and richer colors.

Maple Sugaring Shed

65897 - Set of 3

1987 - 1989

OSRP: $19

VDTsv: $125-$238

Paid: $_____

• Smokestack and pegs in trees are very fragile.

Village Harvest People

59412 - Set of 4

1988 - 1991

OSRP: $27.50

VDTsv: $25-$52

Paid: $_____

• The sleeves read "Harvest Time."

Woodcutter And Son

59862 - Set of 2

1988 - 1990

OSRP: $10

VDTsv: $38-$48

Paid: $_____

Red Covered Bridge

59870

1988 - 1994

OSRP: $15

VDTsv: $10-$20

Paid: $_____

Farm Animals

59455 - Set of 4

1989 - 1991

OSRP: $15

VDTsv: $16 - $35

Paid: $_____

• Another item with the same name was produced in 1995.

Amish Family (With Mustache)   (Without Mustache)

59480 - Set of 3

1990 - 1992

OSRP: $20

VDTsv: $64-$68

Paid: $_____

VDTsv: $24-$30

Paid: $_____

• Father has mustache which is against Amish customs.
• Early release: NALED and Showcase dealers.

• Re-issued with father without mustache.

Amish Buggy

59498

1990 - 1992

OSRP: $22

VDTsv: $27-$52

Paid: $_____

Sleepy Hollow Characters

59560 - Set of 3

1990 - 1992

OSRP: $27.50

VDTsv: $18-$54

Paid: $_____

• From characters in Washington Irving's "Legend of Sleepy Hollow."

Skating Party

55239 - Set of 3

1991 - 2001

OSRP: $27.50

VDTsv: $16-$68

Paid: $_____

Market Day

56413 - Set of 3

1991 - 1993

OSRP: $35

VDTsv: $16-$30

Paid: $_____

Harvest Seed Cart

56456 - Set of 3

1992 - 1995

OSRP: $27.50

VDTsv: $12-$25

Paid: $_____

Town Tinker

56464 - Set of 2

1992 - 1995

OSRP: $24

VDTsv: $12-$20

Paid: $_____

• Pots and pans are separate in box, and are easily lost.

Knife Grinder

56499 - Set of 2

1993 - 1996

OSRP: $22.50

VDTsv: $14-$22

Paid: $_____

• A pair of ice skates is separate in box.

Blue Star Ice Harvesters

56502 - Set of 2

1993 - 1997

OSRP: $27.50

VDTsv: $10-$29

Paid: $_____

• Porcelain and acrylic.
• Acrylic ice blocks easily come unglued.

Over The River And Through The Woods

56545

1994 - 1998

OSRP: $35

VDTsv: $53

Paid: $_____

The Old Man And The Sea

56553 - Set of 3

1994 - 1998

OSRP: $25

VDTsv: $10-$16

Paid: $_____

Two Rivers Bridge

56561

1994 - 1997

OSRP: $35

VDTsv: $25-$58

Paid: $_____

• Porcelain and resin.

Farm Animals

56588 - Set of 8

1995 - 2006

OSRP: $32.50

VDTsv: $25 -$38

Paid: $_____

• Another item with the same name was produced in 1989.
• Also has 8 hay bales.

Lobster Trappers

56589 - Set of 4

1995 - 2000

OSRP: $35

VDTsv: $31-$78

Paid: $_____

• 3 "cooked" lobsters are separate in box.
• Lobster in man's hand often breaks off.

Lumberjacks

56590 - Set of 2

1995 - 1998

OSRP: $30

VDTsv: $17-$25

Paid: $_____

• Porcelain and wood.

Harvest Pumpkin Wagon

56591

1995 - 1999

OSRP: $45

VDTsv: $38-$54

Paid: $_____

• Similar designs were produced for Heinz and Bachman's. See the Special Design section.

Fresh Paint New England Village Sign

56592

1995 - 2001^M

OSRP: $20

VDTsv: $14-$32

Paid: $_____

A New Potbellied Stove For Christmas

56593 - Set of 2

1996 - 1998

OSRP: $35

VDTsv: $24-$55

Paid: $_____

Christmas Bazaar Handmade Quilts

56594 - Set of 2

1996 - 1999

OSRP: $25

VDTsv: $19-$28

Paid: $_____

Christmas Bazaar Woolens & Preserves

56595 - Set of 2

1996 - 1999

OSRP: $25

VDTsv: $14-$20

Paid: $_____

• Early shipments read "Jame & Jellies" on the sign.

Christmas Bazaar Flapjacks & Hot Cider

56596 - Set of 2

1997 - 1999

OSRP: $27.50

VDTsv: $14-$21

Paid: $_____

Christmas Bazaar Toy Vendor & Cart

56597 - Set of 2

1997 - 1999

OSRP: $27.50

VDTsv: $10-$21

Paid: $_____

Christmas Bazaar Sign

56598 - Set of 2

1997 - 1999

OSRP: $16

VDTsv: $110-$15

Paid: $_____

Tapping The Maples

56599 - Set of 7

1997 - 2001^M

OSRP: $85

VDTsv: $51-$75

Paid: $_____

Sea Captain & His Mates

56587 - Set of 4

1998^M - 2000

OSRP: $32.50

VDTsv: $18 - $32

Paid: $_____

Load Up The Wagon

56630 - Set of 2

1998 - 2002

OSRP: $40

VDTsv: $29-$58

Paid: $_____

• Actual wood is used for the logs.

Under The Mistletoe

56631

1998 - 2001

OSRP: $16.50

VDTsv: $12-$26

Paid: $_____

Fly-casting In The Brook

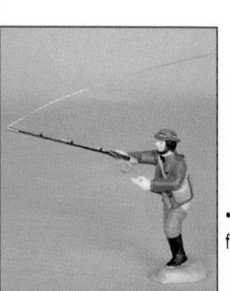

56633

1998 - 2002

OSRP: $15

VDTsv: $22

Paid: $_____

• Caution: Wire is very fragile.

Volunteer Firefighters

56635 - Set of 2

1998 - 2000

OSRP: $37.50

VDTsv: $18-$26

Paid: $_____

Farmer's Market

56637 - Set of 2

1998 - 2003

OSRP: $55

VDTsv: $41-$72

Paid: $_____

An Artist's Touch

56638

1998 - 2001^M

OSRP: $17

VDTsv: $11

Paid: $_____

• "Canvas" is porcelain with a decal, and easel is metal.

A Letter From Papa

56606 - Set of 3

1999^M - 2000

OSRP: *

VDTsv: *

* Accessory contained in Little Women - The March Residence.

It's Almost Thanksgiving

56639 - Set of 4

1999^M - 2005

OSRP: $60

VDTsv: $58-$60

Paid: $_____

• Porcelain and resin.

Pennyfarthing Pedaling

56615

1999 - 2003

OSRP: $13.50

VDTsv: $14

Paid: $_____

Doctor's House Call

56616 - Set of 2

1999 - 2001

OSRP: $27.50

VDTsv: $25-$68

Paid: $_____

The Sailors' Knot

56617

1999 - 2003

OSRP: $27.50

VDTsv: $17-$40

Paid: $_____

The Woodworker

56619

1999 - 2003

OSRP: $35

VDTsv: $24-$45

Paid: $_____

• The Dream House Sweepstakes Deluxe Prize winner assisted in the design.

Making The Christmas Candles

56620 - Set of 2

1999 - 2002

OSRP: $25

VDTsv: $18-$30

Paid: $_____

Let's Go One More Time

56621 - Set of 3

1999 - 2001

OSRP: $30

VDTsv: $58

Paid: $_____

Dairy Delivery Sleigh

56622

1999 - 2005

OSRP: $37.50

VDTsv: $22-$42

Paid: $_____

Mill Creek Crossing

56623

1999 - 2003

OSRP: $32.50

VDTsv: $27

Paid: $_____

Postal Pick-up

56641

2000^M - 2001^M

OSRP: $14

VDTsv: $12-$45

Paid: $_____

New Spring Finery

56626

2000 - 2001

OSRP: *

VDTsv: *

* Accessory contained in the Verna Mae's Boutique Gift Set.

A Day At The Cabin

56642 - Set of 2

2000 - 2003

OSRP: $25

VDTsv: $25-$38

Paid: $_____

Gathering Cranberries

56644

2000 - 2002

OSRP: $30

VDTsv: $17-$39

Paid: $_____

The Perfect Tree

56645

2000 - 2009

OSRP: $20

VDTsv: $20-$32

Paid: $_____

Here Comes Sinter Klaus

56646

2000 - 2002

OSRP: $17

VDTsv: $12

Paid: $_____

Best Of The Harvest

56647 - Set of 2

2000 - 2002

OSRP: $25

VDTsv: $16

Paid: $_____

Creating Silver Keepsakes

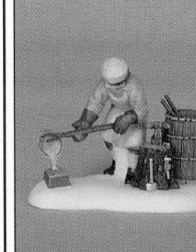

56632

2001ᴹ - 2002

OSRP: *

VDTsv: $44-$73

* Accessory contained in Revere Silver Works.

Silver For Sale

56650 - Set of 2

2001ᴹ - 2002

OSRP: $20

VDTsv: $15-$20

Paid: $_____

Spring Portrait

56634

2001 - 2002

OSRP: *

VDTsv: $47-$65

* The accessory contained in Springfield Studio Gift Set.

On The Boardwalk

56680 - Set of 3

2001 - 2005

OSRP: $27.50

VDTsv: $78

Paid: $_____

• Seaside Series.

Boardwalk Sunday Stroll

56681 - Set of 2

2001 - 2004

OSRP: $20

VDTsv: $40

Paid: $_____

• Seaside Series.

Lumberjack

56682

2001 - 2005

OSRP: $27.50

VDTsv: $42

Paid: $_____

Milking The Cow

56683

2001 - 2005

OSRP: $20

VDTsv: $20 - $48

Paid: $_____

Running The Apple Press

56684

2001 - 2005

OSRP: $24

VDTsv: $58

Paid: $_____

New England Raising The Flag

56687

2001 - 2004

OSRP: $15

VDTsv: $25

Paid: $_____

Loading The Grain

56688 - Set of 2

2002 - 2004

OSRP: $37.50

VDTsv: $59

Paid: $_____

Glassworks Craftsman

56689

2002 - 2003

OSRP: $15

VDTsv: $20

Paid: $_____

Admiring Nature's Beauty

56690

2002 - 2004

OSRP: $15

VDTsv: $12

Paid: $_____

Maestro And His Protégé

56691

2002 - 2004

OSRP: $18

VDTsv: $35

Paid: $_____

Salty's Live Bait Shack

56692 - Set of 2

2002 - 2006

OSRP: $35

VDTsv: $98

Paid: $_____

Today's Catch

56693

2002 - 2005

OSRP: $17.50

VDTsv: $34

Paid: $_____

Delivering The Christmas Spirit

56694

2002 - 2005

OSRP: $20

VDTsv: $42

Paid: $_____

New England Town Tree

56695

2002 - 2008

OSRP: $25

VDTsv: $58

Paid: $_____

Good Day, Reverend

56697 - Set of 2

2003^M - 2007

OSRP: $18.50

VDTsv: $26

Paid: $_____

Masonry Bake Oven

56698

2003 - 2005

OSRP: $16.50

VDTsv: $50

Paid: $_____

Dancing An Irish Jig

57102 - Set of 2

2003 - 2006

OSRP: $20

VDTsv: $50

Paid: $_____

A Penny Saved Is A Penny Earned

57103

2003 - 2005

OSRP: $12.50

VDTsv: $35

Paid: $_____

Family Sleigh Ride

57105

2003 - 2009

OSRP: $30

VDTsv: $30

Paid: $_____

The Hitching Post

57106

2003 - 2008

OSRP: $18

VDTsv: -

Paid: $_____

Pitching Horseshoes

57107

2003 - 2005

OSRP: $15

VDTsv: $15 - $28

Paid: $_____

Taking The Tree Home

56671 - Set of 2

2004^M - 2004

OSRP: *

VDTsv: *

* The accessory contained in Sawyer Family Tree Farm.

Hear Ye Citizens

57108

2004^M - 2005

OSRP: $15

VDTsv: $18

Paid: $_____

Ambrose Adder's Tonics & Curatives

57109

2004 - 2006

OSRP: $20

VDTsv: $20 - $30

Paid: $_____

Not Too Fast, Please

57110

2004 - 2008

OSRP: $12.50

VDTsv: $28

Paid: $_____

Town Blacksmith

57112

2004 - 2008

OSRP: $12.50

VDTsv: $12 - $24

Paid: $_____

Coming Home For Christmas

56675

2005^M - 2005

OSRP: *

VDTsv: *

* The accessory contained in Christmas Homecoming At Havenport.

• Lmt. to Year of Prod.

Hot Off The Press

57111

2005^M - 2007

OSRP: $12

VDTsv: $12

Paid: $_____

Teaching The Lesson

57113

2005^M - 2006

OSRP: $15

VDTsv: $15 - $30

Paid: $_____

Feeding The Birds

57114

2005^M - 2006

OSRP: $40

VDTsv: $40 - $82

Paid: $_____

The Winner By A Nose

57115

2005 - 2006

OSRP: $15

VDTsv: $15 - $25

Paid: $_____

• 30th Anniversary Series.
• Limited to year of production.

Conversation Over Coffee

57116

2005 - 2006

OSRP: $20

VDTsv: $20 - $30

Paid: $_____

• NEV 20th Anniversary Series.
• Limited to year of production.

Life Saving Volunteers

57117

2005 - 2007

OSRP: $25

VDTsv: $42

Paid: $_____

Minuteman Statue

57119

2005 - 2007

OSRP: $12.50

VDTsv: $12

Paid: $_____

Little Patriots At Play

57120

2005 - 2007

OSRP: $20

VDTsv: $20 - $32

Paid: $_____

Cookies For Everyone

57001 Set of 5

2006^M - 2006

OSRP: $80

VDTsv: -

Paid: $_____

• Limited To Year Of Production.
• Contained in "Wheaton Christmas Bakery."

Sewing The Stars & Stripes

57122
2006 - 2007
OSRP: $15
VDTsv: -
Paid: $_____

Fresh Oysters

57123
2006 - 2008
OSRP: $18.50
VDTsv: $18 - $38
Paid: $_____

Learning To Hunt

57124
2006 - 2009
OSRP: $17.50
VDTsv: -
Paid: $_____

Baby Doll's First Check-Up

57125
2006 - 2008
OSRP: $15.00
VDTsv: $13 - $18
Paid: $_____

New England Lamplighter

57127
2007 -
OSRP: $16.50
VDTsv: -
Paid: $_____

Hope For The Future

799961
2007 - 2009
OSRP: $18.50
VDTsv: $18
Paid: $_____

Making Friends

799962
2007 -
OSRP: $17.50
VDTsv: -
Paid: $_____

Tin Goods For Sale

799964
2007 - 2009
OSRP: $22.50
VDTsv: $22
Paid: $_____

Welcome To New England Village

799965
2007 - 2009
OSRP: $17.50
VDTsv: $17
Paid: $_____

The Latest Pembroke Fabrics

807246
2008 -
OSRP: $22.50
VDTsv: $22
Paid: $_____

Setting Up The Nativity

807247
2008 -
OSRP: $28.50
VDTsv: -
Paid: $_____

Collecting The Mail

807248
2008 -
OSRP: $16.50
VDTsv: $16
Paid: $_____

Loading The Cutter For Christmas

807249
2008 -
OSRP: $45
VDTsv: $45
Paid: $_____

Arriving At Windham

805528-Set of 2
2009ᴹ - 2009
OSRP: $79
VDTsv: -
Paid: $_____
• Limited To Year Of Production.
• Contained in Welcome to Windham Country Inn."

Waiting For The Train

808917
2010 -
OSRP: $25
VDTsv: -
Paid: $_____

A Christmas Pony

808918
2010 -
OSRP: $25
VDTsv: -
Paid: $_____

Caroling On Christmas Eve

808919

2010 -

OSRP: $25

VDTsv: -

Paid: $_____

Notes:

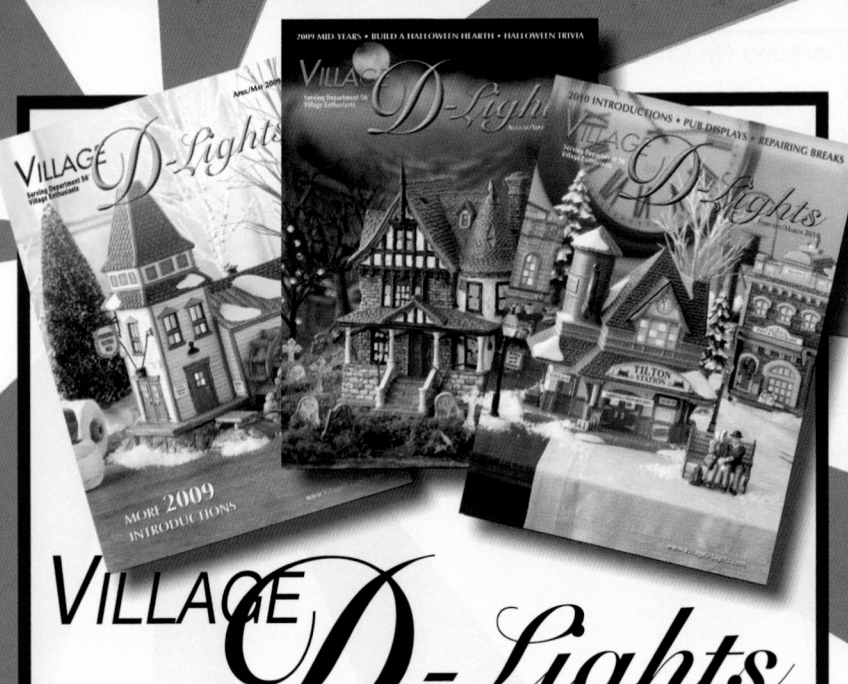

VILLAGE D-Lights

The "Village" Publication Serving Collectors and Display Builders

Read Village D-Lights for

- How-to articles
- New releases from Deparment 56®
- Updates from Melinda Seegers
- Events Calendar
- Collector Displays
- Information on unique building variations
- News from the National Council of 56 Clubs

Subscriptions Only $26.95 • 1 Year • 6 Issues

Call 800.352.8039
Visit www.VillageD-Lights.com

Mention that you saw this ad in Village D-tails and receive a free sample copy!

A Pioneer Communications, Inc. Publication

Alpine Village Series®

"Edelweiss... Edelweiss... Every morning you greet me. Small and white, clean and bright. You look happy to meet me." — *Oscar Hammerstein II, (1895 – 1960) lyrics from* The Sound of Music

Many collectors are attracted to this village because of their personal heritage. Others are drawn to it because of its charm. Many can appreciate both. It's inaugural year was 1986 when five diminutive buildings and one accessory were introduced. Only one or two buildings were added each year there after, with the exception of 1989 when there were no new pieces. It is the smallest of the Heritage Villages, which is another reason why many collectors desire to collect this village. Chalets are designed to be placed high on mountain slopes overlooking a small village in the valleys below which are centered around the striking onion domed steepled church(es). It reflects mountain living in the European Alps and Black Forest area of Germany as it has been for resident villagers for centuries. Mills grind corn and oats, or prepare the wool from sheep grazing along the hillsides. Gasthofs and bierkellers (quaint hotels and delightful drinking / eating establishments) and a ski resort for visitors arriving at the Bahnhof (railroad station) make this a great place for visitors, too! They come to enjoy the cool, fresh air and pristine snow, streams and mountain trails.

The rare and coveted Josef Engel Farmhouse is modeled in true Black Forest tradition — the home and barn are one. St. Nikolaus Kirche was designed after the church in Oberndorf, Austria where the Christmas favorite *Silent Night* was composed. Buildings names are written mainly in German.

In 1998, licensing rights to replicate buildings featured in the *Sound of Music* were obtained. Inspired by the Austrian setting in the movie, this series is larger, more formal and elegant then most of the village. Two accessories lend a musical touch — a gazebo playing *Something Good* from the movie; and the *Silent Night* memorial.

The newer pieces are colorful with emphasized half-timber designed architecture. A prime example of the land's feudal history was added in the 2008 introduction of the Castle Wolfstein. This village is charming, historical and fun to display. By the way, although a prominent part of the movie set in Austria, the edelweiss is actually the national flower of Switzerland.

ALPINE VILLAGE — Set of 5   65404

Dates	OSRP	VDTsv	Paid
1986 - 1996/97	$125	$120	$_____

• None of the buildings in this set have names on their bottoms or their sleeves.
• Early release to NALED dealers.

Besson Bierkeller   65405

Dates	OSRP	VDTsv	Paid
1986 - 1996	$25	$38 - $45	$_____

• English translation: Beer Cellar.
• Early release to NALED dealers.

Gasthof Eisl   65406

Dates	OSRP	VDTsv	Paid
1986 - 1996	$25	$34 - $48	$_____

• English translation: Guest House.
• Early release to NALED dealers.

Apotheke   65407

Dates	OSRP	VDTsv	Paid
1986 - 1997	$25	$27 - $110	$_____

• English translation: Apothecary.
• Early release to NALED dealers.

E. Staubr Backer   65408

Dates	OSRP	VDTsv	Paid
1986 - 1997	$25	$26 - $68	$_____

• English translation: Bakery.
• Early release to NALED dealers.

Milch-Kase   65409

Dates	OSRP	VDTsv	Paid
1986 - 1996	$25	$27 - $42	$_____

• English translation: Milk-Cheese.
• Early release to NALED dealers.

Josef Engel Farmhouse — 59528

Dates	OSRP	VDTsv	Paid
1987 - 1989	$33	$625 - $895	$_____

Alpine Church (White Trim) — 65412

Dates	OSRP	VDTsv	Paid
1987 - 1991	$32	$395	$_____

• This version was available in the early shipments and is the rarer of the two versions.

(Tan Trim)

VDTsv	Paid
$129 - $169	$_____

• This version was available in later shipments.

Grist Mill — 59536

Dates	OSRP	VDTsv	Paid
1988 - 1997	$42	$21 - $46	$_____

Bahnhof — 56154

Dates	OSRP	VDTsv	Paid
1990 - 1993	$42	$75 - $140	$_____

• English translation: Train Station.
• The early pieces had gilded trim. The later ones had a yellow-mustard trim.

St. Nikolaus Kirche — 56170

Dates	OSRP	VDTsv	Paid
1991 - 1999	$37.50	$49 - $76	$_____

• Designed after Church of St. Nikolaus in Oberndorf, Austria, the home of the Christmas hymn *Silent Night*.

ALPINE SHOPS — Set of 2   56189

Dates	OSRP	VDTsv	Paid
1992 - 1997/98	$75	$50	$_____

Metterniche Wurst   56190

Dates	OSRP	VDTsv	Paid
1992 - 1997	$37.50	$25 - $43	$_____

• English translation: Sausage Shop.

Kukuck Uhren   56191

Dates	OSRP	VDTsv	Paid
1992 - 1998	$37.50	$26 - $39	$_____

• English translation: Clock Shop.

Sport Laden   56120

Dates	OSRP	VDTsv	Paid
1993 - 1998	$50	$21 - $56	$_____

• English translation: Sports Shop.

Konditorei Schokolade   56146

Dates	OSRP	VDTsv	Paid
1994 - 1998	$37.50	$38 - $52	$_____

• English translation: Bakery & Chocolate Shop.
• The bottomstamp and the sleeve read "Bakery & Chocolate Shop."

Kamm Haus   56171

Dates	OSRP	VDTsv	Paid
1995 - 1999	$42	$37.50	$_____

• English translation: House On The Crest.

Danube Music Publisher 56173

Dates	OSRP	VDTsv	Paid
1996 - 2000	$55	$64 - $98	$_____

- The German translation of the building's name, Donau Musik Verlag, is found above its front door.
- A sign is separate in the box.

Bernhardiner Hundchen 56174

Dates	OSRP	VDTsv	Paid
1997^M - 2000	$50	$46 - $140	$_____

- English translation: St. Bernard Kennel.

Spielzeug Laden 56192

Dates	OSRP	VDTsv	Paid
1997 - 2000	$65	$42 - $64	$_____

- English translation: Toy Shop.
- Sign, doll, and 2 jack-in-the-boxes are separate in box.

Federbetten Und Steppdecken 56176

Dates	OSRP	VDTsv	Paid
1998^M - 2001	$48	$24 - $48	$_____

- English translation: Featherbeds And Quilts.
- A sign is separate in the box.

The Sound Of Music® von Trapp Villa 56178

Dates	OSRP	VDTsv	Paid
1998 - 2002	$130	$97 - $148	$_____

- Inspired by the stately mansion where Maria, the Captain, and their children lived in the *Sound Of Music*®.
- 2 lanterns are separate in the box.
- Set of 5 includes Villa, the von Trapps, and a gate.
- Licensed by R&H Org., Argyle & Fox.

Heidi's Grandfather's House 56177

Dates	OSRP	VDTsv	Paid
1998 - 2001	$64	$64 - $165	$_____

• Inspired by Johanna Spyri's classic novel.
• Antlers are separate in the box.

Glockenspiel 56210

Dates	OSRP	VDTsv	Paid
1999 - 2003	$80	$80 - $145	$_____

• Music box plays *Emperor Waltz*.

The Sound Of Music® Wedding Church 56211

Dates	OSRP	VDTsv	Paid
1999 - 2002	$60	$70 - $110	$_____

• Inspired by the church where Maria and the Captain got married in the *Sound Of Music*®.
• A star-shaped spire is separate in the box.
• Licensed by R&H Org., Argyle & Fox.

Hofburg Castle 56216

Dates	OSRP	VDTsv	Paid
2000ᴹ - 2002	$68	$78 - $120	$_____

• 3 flags are separate in the box.

Nussknacker Werkstatt 56217

Dates	OSRP	VDTsv	Paid
2000 - 2001	$60	$325 - $345	$_____

• English translation: Nutcracker Workshop.
• 25th Anniversary Limited Edition of 5,600.
• Sign and tin soldier are separate in the box.

Altstädter Bierstube 56218

Dates	OSRP	VDTsv	Paid
2000 - 2005	$65	$65	$_____

• English translation: Altstadter Beerhouse.
• 2 signs are separate in the box.

Schwarzwalder Kuckucksuhren 56220

Dates	OSRP	VDTsv	Paid
2001^M - 2003	$65	$128	$_____

• English translation: Cuckoo Clock Shop.

Getreidemühle Zwettl 56221

Dates	OSRP	VDTsv	Paid
2001 - 2004	$85	$68 - $126	$_____

• English translation: Grain Mill.
• Animated.

Käsehändler Schmitt 56222

Dates	OSRP	VDTsv	Paid
2001 - 2003	$55	$52 - $75	$_____

• English translation: Cheese Shop.
• Sign is separate in the box.

Nikolausfiguren 56223

Dates	OSRP	VDTsv	Paid
2002^M - 2005	$65	$159	$_____

• English translation: Nicholas Figurines.
• Sign and 3 hanging ornaments are separate in the box.

Bauernhof Drescher 56229

Dates	OSRP	VDTsv	Paid
2002 - 2005	$95	$95 - $158	$_____

• English translation: Barn and Farmhouse.
• Set of 2.

Rathaus Neudorf

56230

Dates	OSRP	VDTsv	Paid
2002 - 2005	**$65**	**$65 - $75**	**$_____**

• English translation: Town Hall.

Jägerutte — Hunting Cabin

56231

Dates	OSRP	VDTsv	Paid
2003ᴹ - 2005	**$65**	**$65 - $125**	**$_____**

Alpen Akademie der Musik

56232

Dates	OSRP	VDTsv	Paid
2003 - 2006	**$65**	**$98**	**$_____**

• English translation: Alpen Academy Of Music.

Burgermeister's House

56233

Dates	OSRP	VDTsv	Paid
2004 - 2008	**$65**	**$65 - $159**	**$_____**

• English translation: Mayor's House.

Weihnachten Glashutte

56234

Dates	OSRP	VDTsv	Paid
2005ᴹ - 2007	**$70**	**$179**	**$_____**

• English translation: Glass Ornament Factory

Alpine Elementary School

56236

Dates	OSRP	VDTsv	Paid
2005 - 2006	**$80**	**$80 - $135**	**$_____**

• 30th Anniversary Series.
• Limited to year of production 2006.

Merry Christmas Church 56237

Dates	OSRP	VDTsv	Paid
2005 - 2006	**$75**	**$75**	$_____

• Alpine Village 20th Anniversary Series.
• Limited to year of production.
• Set of two includes "Merry Christmas Creche" accessory.

Christmas House 56238

Dates	OSRP	VDTsv	Paid
2006 - 2007	**$75**	**$75 - $110**	$_____

Wolfsteiner Brewery 56239

Dates	OSRP	VDTsv	Paid
2006 - 2007	**$90**	**$90 - $118**	$_____

Castle Wolfstein 799903

Dates	OSRP	VDTsv	Paid
2007 -	**$125**	**$125**	$_____

Schultz's – Frankfurt's Wurst Restaurant 799904

Dates	OSRP	VDTsv	Paid
2007 - 2009	**$75**	**$75**	$_____

Christkindl Church

805530

Dates	OSRP	VDTsv	Paid
2008 -	$125	$125	$_____

Christkindl Post Office

805531

Dates	OSRP	VDTsv	Paid
2008 -	$80	$80	$_____

Wolfstein Beer Hall

808754

Dates	OSRP	VDTsv	Paid
2010 -	$95	$95	$_____

Snowdrop Cottage

808755

Dates	OSRP	VDTsv	Paid
2010 -	$70	$70	$_____

Notes:

Alpine Villagers

65420 - Set of 3

1986 - 1992

OSRP: $13

VDTsv: $20-$33

Paid: $_____

• Figures became thinner in later years of production.

Alpine Village Sign

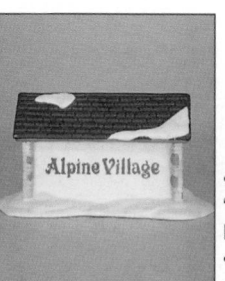

65714

1987 - 1993

OSRP: $6

VDTsv: $7-$18

Paid: $_____

• Bottomstamp reads "Handcrafted by Jiean Fung Porcelains, Taiwan."
• Early signs have more detail and richer colors.

The Toy Peddler

56162 - Set of 3

1990 - 1998

OSRP: $22

VDTsv: $12-$19

Paid: $_____

Buying Bakers Bread

56197 - Set of 2

1992 - 1995

OSRP: $20

VDTsv: $8-$26

Paid: $_____

Climb Every Mountain

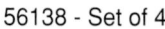

56138 - Set of 4

1993 - 2001^M

OSRP: $27.50

VDTsv: $18-$38

Paid: $_____

Polka Fest

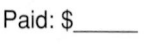

56073 - Set of 3

1994 - 1999

OSRP: $30

VDTsv: $21-$30

Paid: $_____

Silent Night Music Box

56180

1995 - 1999

OSRP: $32.50

VDTsv: $27-$78

Paid: $_____

• Based on the Silent Night Memorial Chapel in Oberndorf, Austria.
• First HV music box.

Alpenhorn Player Alpine Village Sign

56182

1995 - 2001^M

OSRP: $20

VDTsv: $17-$35

Paid: $_____

Nutcracker Vendor & Cart

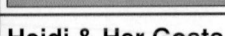

56183
1996 - 2002
OSRP: $20
VDTsv: $25-$78
Paid: $_____

A New Batch Of Christmas Friends

56175 - Set of 3
1997ᴹ - 2000
OSRP: $27.50
VDTsv: $24-$48
Paid: $_____

Heidi & Her Goats

56201 - Set of 4
1997 - 2001ᴹ
OSRP: $30
VDTsv: $15-$29
Paid: $_____

Trekking In The Snow

56202 - Set of 3
1998 - 2002
OSRP: $27.50
VDTsv: $21-$38
Paid: $_____

St. Nicholas

56203
1998 - 2005
OSRP: $12
VDTsv: $13-$18
Paid: $_____

The Sound Of Music® Gazebo

56212
1999 - 2002
OSRP: $40
VDTsv: $78
Paid: $_____

• Plays *Something Good*.
• R & H Org., Argyle & Fox.

Sisters Of The Abbey

56213 - Set of 2
1999 -
OSRP: $20
VDTsv: $20
Paid: $_____

Leading The Bavarian Cow

56214
1999 - 2002
OSRP: $20
VDTsv: $17-$25
Paid: $_____

Alpine Villagers

56215 - Set of 5

1999 - 2005

OSRP: $32.50

VDTsv: $33

Paid: $_____

Here Comes The Bride

56300

2000ᴹ - 2002

OSRP: $18

VDTsv: $18-$35

Paid: $_____

At The October Fest

56302 - Set of 3

2000 - 2005

OSRP: $27.50

VDTsv: $28

Paid: $_____

Cuckoo Clock Vendor & Cart

56303 - Set of 2

2001ᴹ - 2004

OSRP: $20

VDTsv: $20

Paid: $_____

Home From The Mill

56304

2001 - 2003

OSRP: $20

VDTsv: $20

Paid: $_____

A Head of Cheese

56305

2001 - 2003

OSRP: $12.50

VDTsv: $55

Paid: $_____

The Finishing Touch

56306

2002ᴹ - 2004

OSRP: $20

VDTsv: $50

Paid: $_____

Back From The Fields

56309

2002 - 2005

OSRP: $17.50

VDTsv: $24

Paid: $_____

Tap The First Barrel

56310
2002 - 2005
OSRP: $17.50
VDTsv: $18
Paid: $_____

The Bierfest Judge

56311 - Set of 2
2002 - 2005
OSRP: $25
VDTsv: $25
Paid: $_____

Going Hunting

56312
2003^M - 2005
OSRP: $15
VDTsv: $15
Paid: $_____

Mozart Monument

56313
2003 - 2005
OSRP: $15
VDTsv: $15
Paid: $_____

Hear Ye, Citizens

56314
2004 - 2005
OSRP: $15
VDTsv: $25
Paid: $_____

Making Beautiful Ornaments

56315
2005^M - 2006
OSRP: $24
VDTsv: $35
Paid: $_____

Happy Tree Hunting

56317
2005^M - 2006
OSRP: $22.50
VDTsv: $38
Paid: $_____

Merry Christmas Creche

56237
2005 - 2006
OSRP: *
VDTsv: *

* Accessory contained in Merry Christmas Church.
* Lmt. to Year of Prod.

Little Scholars

56318

2005 - 2006

OSRP: $17.50

VDTsv: -

Paid: $_____

• 30th Anniversary Series.
• Limited to year of production.

Alpine Traveling Band

56319

2005 - 2008

OSRP: $25

VDTsv: -

Paid: $_____

Decorating The Wayside Shrine

56320

2005 - 2006

OSRP: $17.50

VDTsv: $98

Paid: $_____

• Alpine Village 20th Anniversary Series.
• Limited to year of production.

Alpine Santa

56321

2006 - 2007

OSRP: $12.50

VDTsv: -

Paid: $_____

The Brew Master

56322 - Set of 2

2006 - 2007

OSRP: $22.50

VDTsv: -

Paid: $_____

Welcome To Alpine Village

799905

2007 - 2009

OSRP: $17.50

VDTsv: $17.50

Paid: $_____

The Night Watchman

801154

2007 - 2009

OSRP: $15.00

VDTsv: $15.00

Paid: $_____

Wursts For The Dachshund

801155

2007 - 2009

OSRP: $15.00

VDTsv: $15.00

Paid: $_____

Christmas Market, The Ornament Booth, Set of 2

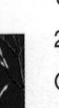

804441

2008^M -

OSRP: $40.00

VDTsv: $40.00

Paid: $_____

• First Issue in Christmas Market Series

The Christkindl Miracle

806283

2008 -

OSRP: $25

VDTsv: $25-125

Paid: $_____

Sharing An Alpine Christmas

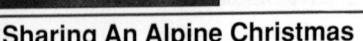

806284

2008 -

OSRP: $27.50

VDTsv: $27-80

Paid: $_____

Christmas Market, The Gingerbread Booth, Set of 2

807296

2009^M -

OSRP: $45

VDTsv: -

Paid: $_____

• Second Issue in Christmas Market Series

Wolfstein Beer Wagon

808756

2010 -

OSRP: $40

VDTsv: -

Paid: $_____

Pretzels And Beer, Set of 2

808777

2010 -

OSRP: $25

VDTsv: $25

Paid: $_____

Notes:

Christmas In The City® Series

"Oh! the snow, the beautiful snow, Filling the sky and earth below, Over the housetops, over the street, Over the heads of the people you meet." — J.W. (Joseph Warren) Watson (1849–1872)

A Department 56 building boom occurred in the mid 1980s as Christmas in the City became the fourth Heritage Village to be introduced in three years. The original set of three, plus CIC's big three — Sutton Place Brownstones, The Cathedral, and Palace Theater made their initial appearance in 1987. Representing New York City in the early years of the 20th century, it can be a childhood remembrance of any large city; bringing back memories of lit town trees, decorated department store windows, and the hustle and bustle of busy sidewalks. Numerous New York landmarks include Ellis Island, the Brooklyn Bridge, Rockefeller Center, Grand Central Station, The Empire State Building, and Flatiron Building. And, what would New Year's Eve be without Times Square?

There are numerous churches, cathedrals and a Synagogue to worship; museums, an art academy, dance studios and theaters for cultural activities; and a university for higher learning. A hospital is available for medical care. City Hall, banks and brokerages; car dealerships and motorcycle showrooms: the growing City is a hub of all sorts of activity.

Townhomes, row houses and apartments house residents, while visiting tourists seek out the Ritz. Add three together to form the Grand Hotel Ritz! All can patronize a variety of ethnic restaurants, shop at numerous merchants, ride the ferry and enjoy the waterfront. Baseball fans can attend a Yankee's game. Some collectors transform their City by rooting for the Dodgers, Red Sox, White Sox, or Cubs.

The holiday season is hectic and exciting. The streets are filled with vendors, musicians, carolers, shoppers, and workers. Horse-drawn carriages clip-clop through the park, while early model cars and taxis rush along the boulevards. The City is indeed a wonderful place to spend the holidays.

CHRISTMAS IN THE CITY — Set of 3   65129

Dates	OSRP	VDTsv	Paid
1987 - 1990	$112	$400 - $450	$_____

• All 3 pieces have "Christmas In The City" inscribed on the bottoms. Individual names do not appear.

Bakery   65129

Dates	OSRP	VDTsv	Paid
1987 - 1990	$37.50	$56	$_____

• Early pieces are light. Later ones are darker.
• Has 2 large and 2 small window grates.
• The chimneys are fragile.

Tower Restaurant   65129

Dates	OSRP	VDTsv	Paid
1987 - 1990	$37.50	$175 - $276	$_____

• Sleeve reads "Tower Cafe." Bottom has no name.
• Early pieces are very dark. Later ones are lighter.
• Has 11 window grates.

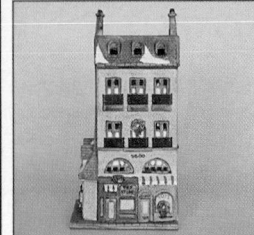

Toy Shop And Pet Store   65129

Dates	OSRP	VDTsv	Paid
1987 - 1990	$37.50	$148	$_____

• Early pieces are very dark. Later ones are lighter.
• Has 6 window grates.
• The chimneys are fragile.

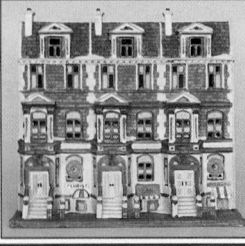

Sutton Place Brownstones   59617

Dates	OSRP	VDTsv	Paid
1987 - 1989	$80	$495	$_____

• Bottom is inscribed with "Sutton Place Rowhouse."
• Earliest pieces have grates at attic windows.
• It's not unusual for this piece to have concave walls. One with straight walls is considered more valuable.

The Cathedral   59625

Dates	OSRP	VDTsv	Paid
1987 - 1990	$60	$179 - $185	$_____

• Early pieces are smaller (10½" high), darker, and have snow on the steps. Later ones are larger (11½" high), lighter, and have no snow on the steps.

Palace Theatre

59633

Dates	OSRP	VDTsv	Paid
1987 - 1989	$45	$648 - $675	$_____

• Early pieces have gilded trim and more snow on roof. Later ones have yellow/mustard trim.
• It's not unusual for this piece to have concave walls. One with straight walls is considered more valuable.

Chocolate Shoppe

59684

Dates	OSRP	VDTsv	Paid
1988 - 1991	$40	$68- $98	$_____

• Early pieces are dark. Later ones are lighter.
• Has 2 window grates on second story.
• The roof of the attached bookstore is often not level.

City Hall

59692

Dates	OSRP	VDTsv	Paid
1988 - 1991	$65	$118 - $129	$_____

• Do not handle by the tower.
• The City Hall "Proof" is smaller than the regular City Hall edition. It came in a box with no sleeve or lightcord.
Proof VDTsv = $138 $_____

Hank's Market

59706

Dates	OSRP	VDTsv	Paid
1988 - 1992	$40	$35	$_____

• This is also referred to as the "Corner Grocer."
• Early samples have the vertical "Grocery" sign attached to the pillar to the right of the door and no 59¢ sign in the lettuce bin.

Variety Store And Barber Shop

59722

Dates	OSRP	VDTsv	Paid
1988 - 1990	$45	$78	$_____

• The design was inspired by a store in Stillwater, MN.
• The mold was also used for the Bachman's Hometown Series Drugstore. See the Special Design section.
• Sleeve reads "Variety Store & Barbershop."

Ritz Hotel

59730

Dates	OSRP	VDTsv	Paid
1989 - 1994	$55	$60 - $98	$_____

• Early pieces have yellow/mustard accents. Later ones have gilded accents and are smaller.
• Columns are easily broken.

Dorothy's Dress Shop

59749

Dates	OSRP	VDTsv	Paid
1989 - 1990	$70	$295	$_____

• Limited Edition of 12,500.

5607 Park Avenue Townhouse

59773

Dates	OSRP	VDTsv	Paid
1989 - 1992	$48	$89 - $120	$_____

• Early pieces have gilded trim at the top edge of the roof. Later ones have yellow/mustard trim.

5609 Park Avenue Townhouse

59781

Dates	OSRP	VDTsv	Paid
1989 - 1992	$48	$42 - $89	$_____

• Early pieces have gilded trim at the top edge of the roof. Later ones have yellow/mustard trim.

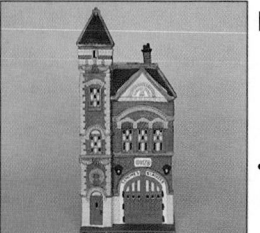

Red Brick Fire Station

55360

Dates	OSRP	VDTsv	Paid
1990 - 1995	$55	$98	$_____

• Cornerstones vary from gray to light blue.

Wong's In Chinatown

55379

Dates	OSRP	VDTsv	Paid
1990 - 1994	$55	$89 - $97	$_____

• Early pieces have red top windows. Later ones have gilded windows.
• Includes fire escape and ladder packaged separately in the box.

Hollydale's Department Store

55344

Dates	OSRP	VDTsv	Paid
1991 - 1997	$75	$148 - $168	$_____

• Early pieces are from Taiwan then China and have holly on first floor canopies only. Later ones are from China and then the Philippines and have holly on all canopies.
• Includes 4 porcelain topiaries and 6 metal flags in box.

"Little Italy" Ristorante 55387

Dates	OSRP	VDTsv	Paid
1991 - 1995	$50	$78 - $84	$_____

- Chimney on pizzeria oven can easily be broken when inserting in box.

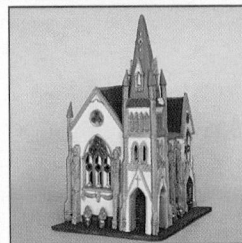

All Saints Corner Church 55425

Dates	OSRP	VDTsv	Paid
1991 - 1998	$96	$85 - $110	$_____

- The spires and the steeple are very fragile.

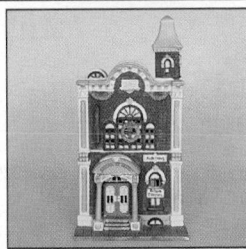

Arts Academy 55433

Dates	OSRP	VDTsv	Paid
1991 - 1993	$45	$36 - $58	$_____

The Doctor's Office 55441

Dates	OSRP	VDTsv	Paid
1991 - 1994	$60	$75 - $95	$_____

- Includes fire escape and ladder separately in the box.

Cathedral Church Of St. Mark 55492

Dates	OSRP	VDTsv	Paid
1991 - 1992	$120	$798 - $1675	$_____

- Limited Edition of 3,024 instead of the intended 17,500 due to production problems.
- Commonly referred to as St. Mark's Church.
- Early release to GCC, the only dealers to receive them.
- This design was originally intended for Dickens' Village.
- This building is very susceptible to firing cracks and other flaws. When purchasing one, you should examine it very closely, being certain to insert a light in it while in a darkened room.

UPTOWN SHOPPES - Set of 3   55310

Dates	OSRP	VDTsv	Paid
1992 - 1996	$150	$135 - $135	$_____

Haberdashery   55311

Dates	OSRP	VDTsv	Paid
1992 - 1996	$40	$38 - $40	$_____

• Has 1 window grate.

Music Emporium   55312

Dates	OSRP	VDTsv	Paid
1992 - 1996	$54	$50 - $62	$_____

• Music on the side of the building was inspired by a similar idea on the side of a music store in Minneapolis, MN.

City Clockworks   55313

Dates	OSRP	VDTsv	Paid
1992 - 1996	$56	$32 - $66	$_____

• Clock is easily broken, especially when removing or inserting building in box.

Town Tree   55654

Dates	OSRP	VDTsv	Paid
1993 - 2005	$45	$40 - $80	$_____

• Set of 5 includes Tree and 4 porcelain benches.

WEST VILLAGE SHOPS — Set of 2   58807

Dates	OSRP	VDTsv	Paid
1993 - 1996	$90	$75 - $96	$_____

Potter's Tea Seller

58808

Dates	OSRP	VDTsv	Paid
1993 - 1996	$45	$56 - $58	$_____

Spring St. Coffee House

58809

Dates	OSRP	VDTsv	Paid
1993 - 1996	$45	$39 - $56	$_____

• Sign is separate in the box.

Brokerage House

58815

Dates	OSRP	VDTsv	Paid
1994 - 1997	$48	$72	$_____

• "18" is the price of Dept. 56's initial stock offering at $18.
• "Price & Price" is in honor of Judith Price—Dept. 56's Ms. Lit Town—and her husband.
• "1960" is in honor of the year they were married.

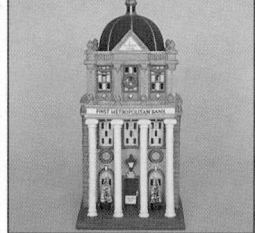

First Metropolitan Bank

58823

Dates	OSRP	VDTsv	Paid
1994 - 1997	$60	$130	$_____

• Do not handle by columns.

Heritage Museum Of Art

58831

Dates	OSRP	VDTsv	Paid
1994 - 1998	$96	$85 - $120	$_____

• Includes 2 red banners packaged separately in the box.
• Gold flags are easily broken when removing this piece from its box.
• Do not handle by columns.

Ivy Terrace Apartments

58874

Dates	OSRP	VDTsv	Paid
1995^M - 1997	$60	$88	$_____

• Includes a sisal garden on the penthouse terrace.

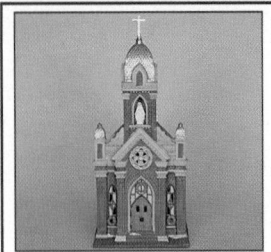

Holy Name Church — 58875

Dates	OSRP	VDTsv	Paid
1995 - 2003	$96	$118	$____

• Inspired by the Cathedral of the Immaculate Conception in Kansas City, MO.
• Gold cross packaged separately in the box.

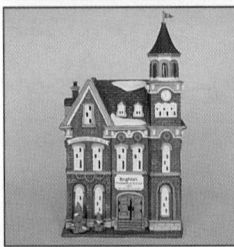

Brighton School — 58876

Dates	OSRP	VDTsv	Paid
1995 - 1998	$52	$145	$____

• The flag on top of roof is easily broken, especially when removing the piece from its box.

BROWNSTONES ON THE SQUARE — Set of 2 — 58877

Dates	OSRP	VDTsv	Paid
1995 - 1998/2000	$90	$80 - $90	$____

Beekman House — 58878

Dates	OSRP	VDTsv	Paid
1995 - 2000	$45	$45 - $75	$____

• Has 1 window grate.
• Includes fire escape and ladder, as well as a lantern packaged separately in the box.

Pickford Place — 58879

Dates	OSRP	VDTsv	Paid
1995 - 1998	$45	$58	$____

• Has 3 window grates.
• Includes lantern packaged separately in the box.

Washington Street Post Office — 58880

Dates	OSRP	VDTsv	Paid
1996^M - 1998	$52	$68 - $75	$____

• Includes two mail boxes packaged separately in the box — one for local mail and one for air mail.

Grand Central Railway Station 58881

Dates	OSRP	VDTsv	Paid
1996 - 1999	$90	$280 - $295	$_____

- Inspired by New York City's Grand Central Terminal.
- Includes 2 lanterns packaged separately in the box.
- The spires are easily broken, especially when removing the piece from its box.

Café Caprice French Restaurant 58882

Dates	OSRP	VDTsv	Paid
1996 - 2001	$45	$35 - $59	$_____

- The sample pieces have a different color scheme, including striped awnings.

The City Globe 58883

Dates	OSRP	VDTsv	Paid
1997^M - 2000	$65	$60 - $98	$_____

- The globe on the top of the building is very fragile and will easily break off.

Hi-De-Ho Nightclub 58884

Dates	OSRP	VDTsv	Paid
1997^M - 1999	$52	$68	$_____

- The club name highlights a Cab Calloway jazz riff.

Johnson's Grocery & Deli 58886

Dates	OSRP	VDTsv	Paid
1997 - 2002	$60	$75 - $168	$_____

- Includes sign packaged separately in the box.

The Capitol 58887

Dates	OSRP	VDTsv	Paid
1997 - 1998	$110	$78 - $95	$_____

Riverside Row Shops
58888

Dates	OSRP	VDTsv	Paid
1997 - 1999	**$52**	**$69 - $90**	$_____

• Includes bank, barber shop, stationery store.

The Grand Movie Theater
58870

Dates	OSRP	VDTsv	Paid
1998^M - 1999	**$50**	**$85**	$_____

Scottie's Toy Shop Exclusive Gift Set
58871

Dates	OSRP	VDTsv	Paid
1998^M - 1998	**$65**	**$98**	$_____

• First available during the 1999 Homes for the Holidays event.
• This was the first Village design to include a three-dimensional scene in a building.
• Set of 10 includes the Toy Shop, the 3-piece accessory "5¢ Pony Rides," 4 sisal trees, Cobblestone Road, and a bag of Fresh Fallen Snow.

Old Trinity Church
58940

Dates	OSRP	VDTsv	Paid
1998 - 2000	**$96**	**$88**	$_____

Precinct 25 Police Station
58941

Dates	OSRP	VDTsv	Paid
1998 - 2003	**$56**	**$138**	$_____

• The globes on the front of the Station are fragile.

The Wedding Gallery

58943

Dates	OSRP	VDTsv	Paid
1998 - 2002	$60	$192	$_____

• Includes a brass plaque that can be personalized and affixed to the building.

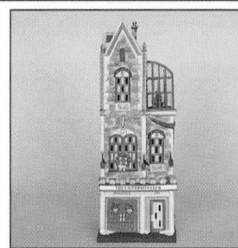

The University Club

58945

Dates	OSRP	VDTsv	Paid
1998 - 2000	$60	$40 - $65	$_____

• Includes 3 green flags packaged separately in the box.

The Times Tower

55510

Dates	OSRP	VDTsv	Paid
1999^M - 1999	$185	$312 -$325	$_____

• Inspired by the Times Tower in Times Square.
• Includes numerals that can be substituted for those atop the building up to the year 2009.

• Set of 3 includes the Tower, the accessory "The New Year's Kiss," and confetti.
• There is also limited edition "party set" of 2000 numbered pieces. **VDTsv for LE: $280**
• Licensed by Jamestown One Times Square, L.P.

Parkview Hospital

58947

Dates	OSRP	VDTsv	Paid
1999^M - 2000	$65	$96	$_____

Wintergarten Café

58948

Dates	OSRP	VDTsv	Paid
1999^M - 1999	$60	$35 - $84	$_____

• This piece is frequently adopted into Alpine Village by collectors.

5th Avenue Salon   58950

Dates	OSRP	VDTsv	Paid
1999 - 2001	**$68**	**$96 - $125**	$_____

- The two lanterns on the back wall are easily damaged.
- Interior Scene, 5th Avenue Series

The Consulate   58951

Dates	OSRP	VDTsv	Paid
1999 - 2000	**$95**	**$48 - $85**	$_____

- Limited to year of production.
- Main spire is packaged separately in the box.
- Spires are easily damaged when removing from box.
- Set of 2 includes Consulate, flag pole, and 25 flags.

Molly O'Brien's Irish Pub   58952

Dates	OSRP	VDTsv	Paid
1999 -	**$62**	**$50 - $62**	$_____

- Includes a lantern as well as a brass plaque that can be personalized. Both are packaged separately in the box.

Lafayette's Bakery   58953

Dates	OSRP	VDTsv	Paid
1999 - 2002	**$62**	**$98**	$_____

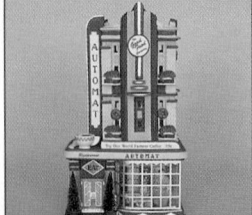

Clark Street Automat   58954

Dates	OSRP	VDTsv	Paid
1999 - 2000	**$68**	**$78**	$_____

- Includes special bulb that must be inserted on an angle.

Paramount Hotel   58911

Dates	OSRP	VDTsv	Paid
2000ᴹ - 2003	**$85**	**$125**	$_____

- Lighting includes traditional bulb at base plus flickering lights in ballroom and gold star on top of building.
- Includes separate cord for flickering lights.

Jenny's Corner Book Shop

58912

Dates	OSRP	VDTsv	Paid
2000^M - 2004	$65	$65 - $80	$_____

- Sign, bird cage, and weathervane are separate in the box.

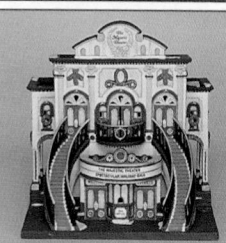

The Majestic Theater

58913

Dates	OSRP	VDTsv	Paid
2000 - 2001	$100	$279 - $295	$_____

- 25th Anniversary Limited Edition of 15,000.

42nd St. Fire Company

58914

Dates	OSRP	VDTsv	Paid
2000 - 2005	$80	$125	$_____

- Includes lantern packaged separately in the box.
- Includes separate cord for flashing red lights above the overhead doors.
- The dog on the base is fragile.

Gardengate House

58915

Dates	OSRP	VDTsv	Paid
2000 - 2002	$68	$68 - $88	$_____

Foster Pharmacy

58916

Dates	OSRP	VDTsv	Paid
2000 - 2002	$85	$160	$_____

- Includes 3 lanterns packaged separately in the box.
- The separate sign is very easily broken when inserting or removing.

Mrs. Stover's Bungalow Candies

58917

Dates	OSRP	VDTsv	Paid
2000 - 2003	$75	$68 - $75	$_____

- Includes sign packaged separately in the box.
- Licensed by Russell Stover Candies, Inc.

Department 56 Studio, 1200 Second Ave. 58918

Dates	OSRP	VDTsv	Paid
2001ᴹ - 2001	$100	$445	$_____

- Replica of Architect's and Engineer's Building where Dept. 56 was once located in Minneapolis, MN .
- Special issue for Department 56's silver anniversary.
- Only available at that event. Lantern separate in box.

Baker Bros. Bagel Bakery 58920

Dates	OSRP	VDTsv	Paid
2001ᴹ - 2002	$75	$65	$_____

- Includes table with umbrella packaged separately in the box.
- Several attachments can be easily broken when removing from box.

Paradise Travel Company 58921

Dates	OSRP	VDTsv	Paid
2001ᴹ - 2002	$75	$48 - $75	$_____

- Includes sign packaged separately in the box.

Yankee Stadium™ 58923

Dates	OSRP	VDTsv	Paid
2001ᴹ - 2005	$85	$158	$_____

- Legendary Ballparks Series.
- Replica of the facade of Yankee Stadium™ in New York.
- Includes two flags packaged separately in the box.
- Licensed by Major League Baseball Properties, Inc.

The Monte Carlo 58925

Dates	OSRP	VDTsv	Paid
2001 - 2002	$85	$85 - $95	$_____

- Numbered limited edition of 15,000.
- Garland and 2 wreaths are separate in the box.

Sterling Jewelers 58926

Dates	OSRP	VDTsv	Paid
2001 - 2003	$70	$264 - $278	$_____

Architectural Antiques 58927

Dates	OSRP	VDTsv	Paid
2001 - 2003	$75	$85	$_____

• Set of 17 includes house and various antiques.

Tavern In The Park Restaurant 58928

Dates	OSRP	VDTsv	Paid
2001 - 2004	$75	$198	$_____

• Christmas In The Park Series.
• Flag is separate in the box.

Nicholas & Co. Toys Starter Set 58929

Dates	OSRP	VDTsv	Paid
2001 - 2003	$65	$85	$_____

• Set of 2 includes building and "Look At All The Toys" accessory.
• Sign is separate in the box.

Cathedral Of St. Paul 58930

Dates	OSRP	VDTsv	Paid
2001 - 2005	$150	$150	$_____

• Re-issue of the Historical Landmark Series™ limited edition with copper colored roof. See that edition in the Small Collections section.

Fenway Park™ 58932

Dates	OSRP	VDTsv	Paid
2001 - 2005	$75	$125	$_____

• Legendary Ballparks Series.
• Replica of the façade of Fenway Park™ in Boston.
• Includes flag and banners packaged separately in box.
• Licensed by Major League Baseball Properties, Inc.

Wrigley Field™   58933

Dates	OSRP	VDTsv	Paid
2001 - 2005	$95	$275	$_____

• Legendary Ballparks Series.
• Replica of the façade of Wrigley Field™ in Chicago.
• Includes three flags packaged separately in the box.
• Licensed by Major League Baseball Properties, Inc.

Radio City Music Hall   58924

Dates	OSRP	VDTsv	Paid
2002ᴹ - 2006	$95	$150	$_____

• Replica of Radio City Music Hall in New York City.
• A separate cord lights the marquee.
• Licensed by Radio City Trademarks L.L.C.

Parkside Holiday Brownstone   58937

Dates	OSRP	VDTsv	Paid
2002ᴹ - 2002	$75	$75	$_____

• Holiday 2002 Special Edition.
• A separate cord lights decorative Christmas lights.
• Set of 4 includes building and "Last String Of Lights" accessory, City Lit Bare Branch Tree with adapter, and snow.
• Lamp and rooftop tree separate in the box.

Chez Monet   58938

Dates	OSRP	VDTsv	Paid
2002ᴹ - 2003	$65	$78	$_____

• Intended to be used as a Valentine's Day design.

Hudson Public Library   58942

Dates	OSRP	VDTsv	Paid
2002 - 2004	$80	$195 - $198	$_____

Midtown Barbershop 58944

Dates	OSRP	VDTsv	Paid
2002 - 2004	$65	$65 - $78	$____

• Sign is separate in the box.

East Harbor Fish Co. 58946

Dates	OSRP	VDTsv	Paid
2002 - 2005	$85	$110	$____

• Two signs and two "lamps" are separate in box.
• Special adapter is included to activate building's bulb and decorative Christmas lights.
• Do not handle by posts.

DeFazio's Pizzeria 58949

Dates	OSRP	VDTsv	Paid
2002 - 2004	$65	$76 - $78	$____

• Set of 2 includes the Pizzeria and "Pizza Pick-Up" accessory.

Seasons Department Store 59201

Dates	OSRP	VDTsv	Paid
2002 - 2004	$70	$70 - $80	$____

Harley-Davidson® City Dealership 59202

Dates	OSRP	VDTsv	Paid
2002 - 2006	$85	$115 - $138	$____

• Sign is separate in box.
• Licensed by Harley-Davidson®.

Ebbets Field™   59203

Dates	OSRP	VDTsv	Paid
2002 - 2004	$75	$75 - $105	$_____

- Legendary Ballparks Series.
- Replica of façade of Ebbets Field™ that stood in Brooklyn.
- Flag separate in box.
- Licensed by Major League Baseball Properties, Inc.

Central Synagogue   59204

Dates	OSRP	VDTsv	Paid
2002 - 2003	$110	$124 - $168	$_____

- Limited to year of production.
- Historical Landmark Series™.
- This is a replica of Central Synagogue in New York City.

1234 Four Seasons Parkway   59205

Dates	OSRP	VDTsv	Paid
2003^M - 2004	$75	$75 - $78	$_____

- Seasonal decorations and flowering trees are separate in box.
- First use of removable snow to winterize buildings.

Church Of The Holy Light   59206

Dates	OSRP	VDTsv	Paid
2003^M - 2003	$75	$90 - $120	$_____

- Holiday 2003 Special Edition.
- Set of 6 includes the Church, "Christmas Eve Visit" accessory, birch tree, frosted pine tree, and snow.
- Adapter included to light star atop nativity scene.

Katie McCabe's Restaurant & Books   59208

Dates	OSRP	VDTsv	Paid
2003^M - 2004	$70	$70 - $98	$_____

- Fire escape (4 pieces) and sign are separate in box.

Empire State Building

59207

Dates	OSRP	VDTsv	Paid
2003^M - 2005	$185	$275	$_____

- Historical Landmark Series™.
- This is a replica of the Empire State Building in Manhattan.
- At 23 inches, this is the tallest building manufactured by Department 56.
- Features several holiday lighting effects, including different colors in detachable top section.
- Four American flags are separate in box.

Historic Chicago Water Tower

59209

Dates	OSRP	VDTsv	Paid
2003 - 2006	$65	$148	$_____

- Historical Landmark Series™.
- Set of 2 includes Tower and sign.
- This is a replica of the Chicago Water Tower, one of the few buildings to survive the great Chicago fire of 1871.

Blue Line Bus Depot

59210

Dates	OSRP	VDTsv	Paid
2003 - 2005	$75	$48 - $75	$_____

Harrison House

59211

Dates	OSRP	VDTsv	Paid
2003 - 2005	$70	$88	$_____

- Portions of the proceeds benefit ovarian cancer research.

5th Avenue Shoppes

59212

Dates	OSRP	VDTsv	Paid
2003 - 2006	$95	$98 - $105	$_____

- Includes delicatessen, art gallery, wine cellar, and flower shop. Archway is separate in box.
- 5th Avenue Series

East Harbor Ferry
59213

Dates	OSRP	VDTsv	Paid
2003 - 2004	**$85**	**$85 - $100**	$_____

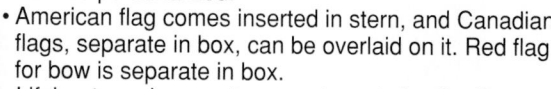

- Numbered limited edtion of 10,000.
- Set of 3 includes Ferry and "Ferry Ticket Sales" 2 piece accessory.
- Can be personalized.
- American flag comes inserted in stern, and Canadian flags, separate in box, can be overlaid on it. Red flag for bow is separate in box.
- Lifeboats and supports are extremely fragile. Do not hold vessel by them when removing it from box or locating it in a display.

Harley-Davidson® Detailing, Parts & Service
59214

Dates	OSRP	VDTsv	Paid
2003 - 2006	**$85**	**$85**	$_____

- Lantern is separate in box.
- Licensed by Harley-Davidson®.

Old Comiskey Park™
59215

Dates	OSRP	VDTsv	Paid
2003 - 2007	**$80**	**$138**	$_____

- Legendary Ballparks Series.
- Replica of the façade of Comiskey Park™ that once stood in Chicago.
- Licensed by Major League Baseball Properties, Inc.

Kelly's Irish Crafts
59216

Dates	OSRP	VDTsv	Paid
2003 - 2005	**$65**	**$118**	$_____

- Set of 2 includes building and "Tin Whistles - 25 Cents" accessory.
- Sign, Irish flag, lantern, and 2 baskets with hooks are all separate in box.

Crystal Gardens Conservatory 59219

Dates	OSRP	VDTsv	Paid
2004^M - 2004	$75	$75	$_____

• Limited to year of production.
• Set of 4 includes the building, "Christmas Topiaries" accessory, tree, and snow.

Royal Oil Company 59220

Dates	OSRP	VDTsv	Paid
2004^M - 2005	$75	$75	$_____

• Set of 2 includes the building and "Full Service Attendant" accessory.

Coca-Cola® Soda Fountain 59221

Dates	OSRP	VDTsv	Paid
2004^M - 2007	$85	$75 - $128	$_____

• Licensed by Coca-Cola®.

Art Institute Of Chicago 59222

Dates	OSRP	VDTsv	Paid
2004^M - 2005	$85	$168	$_____

• Lighted facade with historical facts on back.
• Licensed by Art Institute Of Chicago.

Souvenir Shops
See below

Dates	OSRP	VDTsv	Paid
2004ᴹ - 2005	$45	See below	

- The 4 Souvenir Shops are identical, other than the team names and colors.
- Legendary Ballparks Series.
- Licensed by Major League Baseball Properties, Inc.

Item #	Team	VDTsv	Paid
59224	New York Yankees™	$88	$_____
59227	Chicago Cubs™	$48	$_____
59229	Boston Red Sox™	$45	$_____
59231	Chicago White Sox™	$65	$_____

Taverns
See below

Dates	OSRP	VDTsv	Paid
2004ᴹ - 2005	$45	See below	

- The 4 Taverns are identical, other than the team names and colors.
- Legendary Ballparks Series.
- Licensed by Major League Baseball Properties, Inc.

Item #	Team	VDTsv	Paid
59225	New York Yankees™	$45	$_____
59228	Chicago Cubs™	$45	$_____
59230	Boston Red Sox™	$45	$_____
59232	Chicago White Sox™	$98	$_____

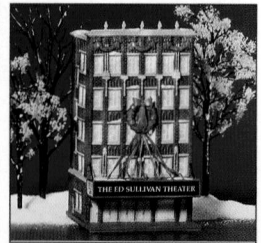

The Ed Sullivan Theater
59233

Dates	OSRP	VDTsv	Paid
2004 - 2005	$70	$98	$_____

- Licensed to year of production.
- Named for the theater on Broadway in New York City.
- Licensed by CBS, Inc.

Hensly Cadillac & Buick
59235

Dates	OSRP	VDTsv	Paid
2004 - 2006	$80	$80 - $97	$_____

- Licensed by General Motors.

Lowry Hill Apartments

59236

Dates	OSRP	VDTsv	Paid
2004 - 2007	$75	$110	$_____

Pier 56, East Harbor

59237

Dates	OSRP	VDTsv	Paid
2004 - 2008	$85	$98	$_____

• Includes adapter.

Milano Of Italy

59238

Dates	OSRP	VDTsv	Paid
2004 - 2007	$65	$65 - $70	$_____

Gardens Of Santorini

59239

Dates	OSRP	VDTsv	Paid
2004 - 2007	$65	$39 - $65	$_____

Christmas Treasures

59240

Dates	OSRP	VDTsv	Paid
2004 - 2006	$75	$98	$_____

• Decorating set of 4 includes building, tree, and 2 bushes.
• Long Life Cordless Lighting.

Golden Gate Bridge

59241

Dates	OSRP	VDTsv	Paid
2004 - 2006	$120	$120 - $240	$_____

• Historical Landmark Series™.
• Replica of the famous bridge in California.

Visiting Santa At Finestrom's

59243

Dates	OSRP	VDTsv	Paid
2005ᴹ - 2005	$75	$115	$_____

- Limited to year of production.
- Set of 5 includes "Look, It's Santa!" accessory, 2 street-lights, and snow.

Royal Flush Casino

59244

Dates	OSRP	VDTsv	Paid
2005ᴹ - 2008	$85	$85 - $125	$_____

- Long Life Cordless Lighting.

Russian Tea Room

59245

Dates	OSRP	VDTsv	Paid
2005ᴹ - 2006	$70	$98	$_____

- Long Life Cordless Lighting.

Baltimore Arts Tower

59246

Dates	OSRP	VDTsv	Paid
2005ᴹ - 2008	$65	-	$_____

- Historical Landmark Series™.

Brooklyn Bridge

59247

Dates	OSRP	VDTsv	Paid
2005ᴹ - 2006	$120	$225 - $250	$_____

- Historical Landmark Series™.
- Replica of the famous bridge in New York.

Cathedral Of St. Nicholas

59248

Dates	OSRP	VDTsv	Paid
2005 - 2006	$120	$120 - $265	$_____

• 30th Anniversary Series.
• Limited to year of production.

Woolworth's

59249

Dates	OSRP	VDTsv	Paid
2005 - 2008	$80	-	$_____

Caffé Tazio

59253

Dates	OSRP	VDTsv	Paid
2005 - 2008	$80	$48 - $86	$_____

• Long Life Cordless Lighting.

East Harbor Ferry Terminal

59254

Dates	OSRP	VDTsv	Paid
2005 - 2006	$100	$60 - $100	$_____

• Numbered limited edition of 15,000.

City Post & Telegraph Office

59255

Dates	OSRP	VDTsv	Paid
2005 - 2008	$65	$45 - $95	$_____

The Candy Counter

59256

Dates	OSRP	VDTsv	Paid
2006M - 2006	$85	$85	$_____

• Numbered Limited Edition of 8,000.
• 30th Anniversary Celebration Piece.

Victoria's Doll House 59257

Dates	OSRP	VDTsv	Paid
2006^M - 2006	$80	$80 - $98	$_____

- Includes: Accessory "Dolly's Dream House" and Tree.
- Interior Scenes With Rotating Doll Display!
- Limited to Year of Production.
- Set of 3.

Coca-Cola® Bottling Company 59258

Dates	OSRP	VDTsv	Paid
2006^M - 2007	$85	-	$_____

Downtown Radios & Phonographs 59259

Dates	OSRP	VDTsv	Paid
2006^M - 2007	$80	$64 - $80	$_____

- Numbered Limited Edition of 10,000.

Miss Shannon's School Of Dance 59251

Dates	OSRP	VDTsv	Paid
2006 - 2008	$75	$45 - $85	$_____

Flatiron Building 59260

Dates	OSRP	VDTsv	Paid
2006 -	$150	$120 - $150	$_____

- Includes: Removable wreaths and garland for holiday decorating.

Jamison Art Center, Collectors' Edition 59261

Dates	OSRP	VDTsv	Paid
2006 - 2007	$100	$100	$_____

• Lighted Interior.
• Limited Edition of 9,000.

Light Nouveau 59262

Dates	OSRP	VDTsv	Paid
2006 - 2007	$80	$80	$_____

• Christmas In The City 20th Anniversary.

Lenox China Shop 59263

Dates	OSRP	VDTsv	Paid
2006 - 2008	$80	$64 - $90	$_____.

• Lighted Interior Scene.
• Display Anywhere Lighting™.

Jambalaya Café 59265

Dates	OSRP	VDTsv	Paid
2006 - 2009	$80	$56 - $80	$_____

East Village Row Houses 59266

Dates	OSRP	VDTsv	Paid
2007ᴹ - 2007	$99	$99	$_____

• Limited To Year of Production.
• Set of 2.
• Holiday Value: "Walking The Dogs" accessory.

Christmas At Lakeside Park Pavilion 59267

Dates	OSRP	VDTsv	Paid
2007^M - 2007	$110	$110 - $195	$_____

- Collectors' Edition, Numbered Limited Edition 7,000.
- Skaters Circle The Ice Rink!
- Includes adapter cord.

Hammerstein Piano Co. 799941

Dates	OSRP	VDTsv	Paid
2007 - 2009	$90	$89 - $90	$_____

The Regal Ballroom 799942

Dates	OSRP	VDTsv	Paid
2007 - 2008	$130	$128 - $178	$_____

- Numbered Limited Edition 7,000.
- Couples dance around the balcony.
- Collectors' Edition.

American Diner 799939

Dates	OSRP	VDTsv	Paid
2007 -	$95	$76 - $95	$_____

Ferrara Bakery & Café 59272

Dates	OSRP	VDTsv	Paid
2007 - 2009	$85	$84 - $85	$_____

Topsy's Toys 799995

Dates	OSRP	VDTsv	Paid
2008^M - 2009	$85	$85	$_____

Miller & Sons Hardware & Garden Center

799994

Dates	OSRP	VDTsv	Paid
2008^M - 2008	$79	$79	$_____

• Celebrate Holiday Value Set. ($100 value)
• Includes Accessory "PickingThe Perfect Tree."
• Set of 3.

St. Mary's Church

799996

Dates	OSRP	VDTsv	Paid
2008^M - 2008	$100	$100 - $150	$_____

• Collectors' Edition.
• Limited Edition of 6,000.

Union Station

805532

Dates	OSRP	VDTsv	Paid
2008 - 2009	$140	$112 - $140	$_____

• Limited Edition of 7,000.
• Porter moves bags through terminal.

The Golden Ox Market

805533

Dates	OSRP	VDTsv	Paid
2008 -	$90	$72 - $90	$_____

Havana's Cigar Shop

805534

Dates	OSRP	VDTsv	Paid
2008 -	$90	$72	$_____

21 Club
805535

Dates	OSRP	VDTsv	Paid
2008 - 2009	$95	$76 - $95	$_____

• Famous New York restaurant, complete with miniature jockey statues.

The Prescott Hotel
805536

Dates	OSRP	VDTsv	Paid
2009^M - 2009	$79	$79	$_____

• Set of 3, includes "Welcome to the Prescott"
• Limited to year of production

Yankee Stadium 2009
805538

Dates	OSRP	VDTsv	Paid
2009^M -	$110	-	$_____

The Roxy
805537

Dates	OSRP	VDTsv	Paid
2010 -	$95	$76	$_____

Dayfield's Department Store
808795

Dates	OSRP	VDTsv	Paid
2010 -	$120	-	$_____

Jade Palace Chinese Restaurant   808798

Dates	OSRP	VDTsv	Paid
2010 -	$90	-	$____

64 City West Parkway   808805

Dates	OSRP	VDTsv	Paid
2010 -	$70	-	$____

Notes:

Looking
for the
Latest Releases?

Check our Village Resources section for reputable
retailers with brick-and-mortar stores and mail order
or online options. They will be happy to help you find
whatever new piece you happen to be looking for.

Contact these retailers and tell them you saw their ad in *Village D-tails*

Village Resources
Starts on page 583

Lighted Tree W/Children & Ladder

65102 - Set of 3

1986 - 1989

OSRP: $35

VDTsv: $110-
  $164

Paid: $_____

• Sleeves from the early shipments read "Christmas In the City" even though the village didn't make its debut for another year.
• Battery operated.
• Many have been sold on the secondary market as defective, but it's usually just a matter of crossed wires. Once they are switched, the unit works nicely.
• The boy on the ladder is often damaged from falling off.

Christmas In The City Sign

59609

1987 - 1993

OSRP: $6

VDTsv: $5-$16

Paid: $_____

Automobiles

59641 - Set of 3

1987 - 1996

OSRP: $15

VDTsv: $15

Paid: $_____

City People

59650 - Set of 5

1987 - 1990

OSRP: $27.50

VDTsv: $69-$75

Paid: $_____

City Newsstand

59714 - Set of 4

1988 - 1991

OSRP: $25

VDTsv: $27-$29

Paid: $_____

City Bus & Milk Truck

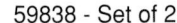
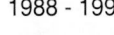

59838 - Set of 2

1988 - 1991

OSRP: $15

VDTsv: $46-$78

Paid: $_____

• Wording on sleeve reads "Transport."

Salvation Army Band

59854 - Set of 6

1988 - 1991

OSRP: $24

VDTsv: $70

Paid: $_____

• Conductor's baton is easily damaged.

Boulevard

55166 - Set of 14

1989 - 1992

OSRP: $25

VDTsv: $27-$48

Paid: $_____

• Includes 4 sections (2 straight/ 2 curved), 4 trees, 4 hitching posts, and 2 benches.

Mailbox & Fire Hydrant

55174 - Set of 2

1989 - 1990

OSRP: $5

VDTsv: $22

Paid: $_____

• Retired after one year due to unauthorized use of red and blue colors of U.S. Postal Service.

Organ Grinder

59579 - Set of 3

1989 - 1991

OSRP: $21

VDTsv: $16-$25

Paid: $_____

Popcorn Vendor

59587 - Set of 3

1989 - 1992

OSRP: $22

VDTsv: $12-$24

Paid: $_____

River Street Ice House Cart

59595

1989 - 1991

OSRP: $20

VDTsv: $59-$64

Paid: $_____

Central Park Carriage

59790

1989 -

OSRP: $30

VDTsv: $24-$30

Paid: $_____

• Designated as Christmas In The Park Series in 2002.

Mailbox & Fire Hydrant

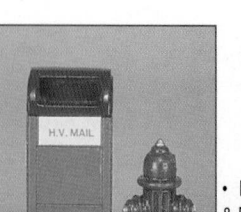

52140 - Set of 2

1990 - 1998

OSRP: $5

VDTsv: $13-$18

Paid: $_____

• Re-issue of Mailbox & Fire Hydrant (1989) after changing to red and green and putting "H.V. Mail" on front.

Busy Sidewalks

55352 - Set of 4

1990 - 1992

OSRP: $28

VDTsv: $62-$66

Paid: $_____

'Tis The Season

55395

1990 - 1994

OSRP: $12.50

VDTsv: $15-$20

Paid: $_____

• Separate metal kettle can easily be lost.

Rest Ye Merry Gentleman

55409

1990 - 2002

OSRP: $12.50

VDTsv: $10

Paid: $_____

• Bench is metal.

Utility Accessories

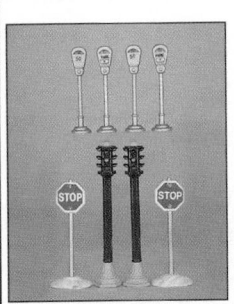

55123 - Set of 8

1991 - 1998

OSRP: $12.50

VDTsv: $10-$12

Paid: $_____

• It is not unusual for the stop signs to be discolored.
• Metal.

City Subway Entrance

55417

1991 - 1998

OSRP: $15

VDTsv: $25

Paid: $_____

• Metal.

All Around The Town

55450 - Set of 2

1991 - 1993

OSRP: $18

VDTsv: $10

Paid: $_____

The Fire Brigade

55468 - Set of 2

1991 - 1995

OSRP: $20

VDTsv: $18

Paid: $_____

• Includes plastic fire ladder separate in box.

"City Fire Dept." Fire Truck

55476

1991 - 1995

OSRP: $18

VDTsv: $88

Paid: $_____

• Includes plastic fire ladder separate in box.

Caroling Thru The City

55484- Set of 3

1991 - 1998

OSRP: $27.50

VDTsv: $25

Paid: $_____

Don't Drop The Presents!

55328 - Set of 2

1992 - 1995

OSRP: $25

VDTsv: $20-$40

Paid: $_____

Welcome Home

55336 - Set of 3

1992 - 1995

OSRP: $27.50

VDTsv: $13-$25

Paid: $_____

Village Express Van

58653

1992 - 1996

OSRP: $25

VDTsv: $8

Paid: $_____

• License plate is abbreviated address of Dept. 56 headquarters, 6435 City West Pkwy.
• See the Special Design section.

Playing In The Snow

55565 - Set of 3

1993 - 1996

OSRP: $25

VDTsv: $12-$20

Paid: $_____

• The branches are easily broken.

Street Musicians

55646 - Set of 3

1993 - 1997

OSRP: $25

VDTsv: $15-$20

Paid: $_____

• The violinist's bow is fragile.

Town Tree Trimmers

55662 - Set of 4

1993 - 2001

OSRP: $32.50

VDTsv: $68

Paid: $_____

Christmas At The Park

58661 - Set of 3

1993 - 2006

OSRP: $27.50

VDTsv: $25-$33

Paid: $_____

• Intended for use with the Town Tree.

Chamber Orchestra

58840 - Set of 4

1994 - 1998

OSRP: $37.50

VDTsv: $35-$42

Paid: $_____

• The conductor's baton and the musicians' bows and flute are fragile.

Holiday Field Trip

58858 - Set of 3
1994 - 1998
OSRP: $27.50
VDTsv: $39
Paid: $_____

Hot Dog Vendor

58866 - Set of 3
1994 - 1997
OSRP: $27.50
VDTsv: $35
Paid: $_____

• Porcelain and metal.

"Yes, Virginia..."

58890 - Set of 2
1995 - 2000
OSRP: $12.50
VDTsv: $6-$15
Paid: $_____

One-Man Band & The Dancing Dog

58891 - Set of 2
1995 - 1998
OSRP: $17.50
VDTsv: $16
Paid: $_____

Choirboys All-In-A-Row

58892
1995 - 1998
OSRP: $20
VDTsv: $42
Paid: $_____

A Key To The City CIC Sign

58893
1995 - 2001ᴹ
OSRP: $20
VDTsv: $24
Paid: $_____

• Porcelain and metal.

City Taxi

58894
1996 - 2001
OSRP: $12.50
VDTsv: $28
Paid: $_____

• Similar designs were produced for several retailers. See the Special Design section.

The Family Tree

58895
1996 - 2003
OSRP: $18
VDTsv: $22
Paid: $_____

Going Home For The Holidays

58896 - Set of 3

1996 - 1999

OSRP: $27.50

VDTsv: $28

Paid: $_____

Steppin' Out On The Town

58885 - Set of 5

1997^M - 1999

OSRP: $35

VDTsv: $35

Paid: $_____

• The gentleman's walking stick is fragile.

Johnson's Grocery Holiday Deliveries

58897

1997 - 2001

OSRP: $18

VDTsv: $34-$39

Paid: $_____

• Similar designs were produced for retailers. See the Special Design section.

Spirit Of The Season

58898

1997 - 1999

OSRP: $20

VDTsv: $10-$20

Paid: $_____

Let's Go Shopping In The City

58899 - Set of 3

1997 - 1999

OSRP: $35

VDTsv: $35-$48

Paid: $_____

Big Smile For The Camera

58900 - Set of 2

1997 - 1999

OSRP: $27.50

VDTsv: $18-$25

Paid: $_____

5¢ Pony Rides

58871 - Set of 3

1998^M - 1998

OSRP: *

VDTsv: *

* Accessory contained in the Scottie's Toy Shop Gift Set.

Heritage Village Utility Accessories

52776 - Set of 11

1998 - 2001

OSRP: $15

VDTsv: $18

Paid: $_____

• The sticker on the right side of the mailbox reads "S.V. Mail."

A Carriage Ride For The Bride

58901

1998 - 2004

OSRP: $40

VDTsv: $18

Paid: $_____

• The front wheels can separate from the rest of the carriage and cause damage.

To Protect And To Serve

58902 - Set of 3

1998 - 2005

OSRP: $32.50

VDTsv: $50

Paid: $_____

City Police Car

58903

1998 - 2001^M

OSRP: $16.50

VDTsv: $12

Paid: $_____

• Features a battery-operated beacon.

1919 Ford™ Model-T

58906

1998 - 2000

OSRP: $20

VDTsv: $48

Paid: $_____

• Licensed by Ford™ Motor Co.

Ready For The Road

58907

1998 - 2000

OSRP: $20

VDTsv: $12-$20

Paid: $_____

• Licensed by Harley-Davidson©.

The New Year's Kiss

55510

1999^M - 1999

OSRP: *

VDTsv: *

* Accessory contained in The Times Tower Gift Set.

Bringing Home The Baby

58909 - Set of 2

1999^M - 2000

OSRP: $27.50

VDTsv: $15

Paid: $_____

The City Ambulance

58910

1999^M - 2000

OSRP: $15

VDTsv: $12

Paid: $_____

Busy City Sidewalks

58955 - Set of 4

1999 -

OSRP: $32.50

VDTsv: $30-$68

Paid: $_____

Visiting The Nativity

58956 - Set of 3

1999 - 2006

OSRP: $37.50

VDTsv: $85

Paid: $_____

• Dream House Sweepstakes Deluxe Prize winner assisted in the design. Also see Nativity Creche in GVA.

Fresh Flowers For Sale

58957 - Set of 2

1999 - 2001

OSRP: $30

VDTsv: $17

Paid: $_____

• Dream House Sweepstakes Deluxe Prize winner assisted in the design.

Excellent Taste

58958 - Set of 2

1999 - 2002

OSRP: $22

VDTsv: $16

Paid: $_____

Picking Out The Christmas Tree

58959 - Set of 3

1999 - 2006

OSRP: $37.50

VDTsv: $98

Paid: $_____

All In Together Girls

58960

1999 - 2001^M

OSRP: $23.50

VDTsv: $15

Paid: $_____

Rockefeller Plaza Skating Rink

52504

2000^M - 2003

OSRP: $125

VDTsv: $90

Paid: $_____

Hailing A Cab

58961 - Set of 3

2000^M - 2002

OSRP: $27.50

VDTsv: $50

Paid: $_____

City Professions – Doctor & Nurse

58962 - Set of 2
2000^M - 2002
OSRP: $17.50
VDTsv: $22
Paid: $_____

A Treasured Book

58963 - Set of 3
2000^M - 2003
OSRP: $35
VDTsv: $24
Paid: $_____

1935 Duesenberg®

58964
2000^M - 2001
OSRP: $20
VDTsv: $68
Paid: $_____

City Professions - Postman & Dairy Delivery Man

58965 - Set of 2
2000^M - 2001^M
OSRP: $17.50
VDTsv: $32
Paid: $_____

City Professions - House Painter & Newspaper Boy

58966 - Set of 2
2000^M - 2001^M
OSRP: $17.50
VDTsv: $10
Paid: $_____

On To The Show

58967
2000 - 2003
OSRP: $20
VDTsv: $24
Paid: $_____

Fire Drill Practice

58968
2000 - 2004
OSRP: $25
VDTsv: $15-$25
Paid: $_____

1937 Pirsch Pumper Fire Truck

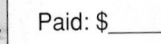

58969
2000 - 2003
OSRP: $25
VDTsv: $58
Paid: $_____

The Life Of The Party

58970 - Set of 2

2000 - 2002

OSRP: $30

VDTsv: $18-$19

Paid: $_____

• Mask in woman's hand and man's cane are easily broken.

Hot Chocolate For Sale

58971

2000 - 2003

OSRP: $27.50

VDTsv: $45

Paid: $_____

Russell Stover® Delivery Truck

58972

2000 - 2003

OSRP: $20

VDTsv: $35

Paid: $_____

• Licensed by Russell Stover® Candies, Inc.

Pretzel Cart

58973

2001^M - 2006

OSRP: $22

VDTsv: $65

Paid: $_____

Midtown News Stand

58974 - Set of 2

2001^M - 2006

OSRP: $32.50

VDTsv: $70

Paid: $_____

Planning A Winter Vacation

58975

2001^M - 2002

OSRP: $12.50

VDTsv: $11-$20

Paid: $_____

Full Count

58977 - Set of 2

2001^M - 2005

OSRP: $25

VDTsv: $15-$28

Paid: $_____

• Legendary Ballparks Series.
• Licensed by Major League Baseball Prop.

Look At All The Toys

58929

2001 - 2003

OSRP: *

VDTsv: *

* The accessory contained in Nicholas & Co. Toys Starter Set.

City Zoological Garden

58978 - Set of 7

2001 - 2003

OSRP: $95

VDTsv: $160

Paid: $_____

• Christmas In The Park Series.

Santa In The City

58979

2001 - 2009

OSRP: $25

VDTsv: -

Paid: $_____

• Christmas In The Park Series.
• Reindeer's antlers are very fragile.

City Shopping

58980

2001 - 2003

OSRP: $13

VDTsv: $15

Paid: $_____

Architectural Treasure

58981

2001 - 2002

OSRP: $12.50

VDTsv: $16

Paid: $_____

Hot Roasted Chestnuts

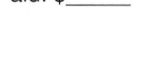

58983 - Set of 2

2001 - 2009

OSRP: $18

VDTsv: $18-$48

Paid: $_____

Raising The Flag In The City

58986

2001 - 2004

OSRP: $15

VDTsv: $35

Paid: $_____

Last String Of Lights

58937

2002ᴹ - 2002

OSRP: *

VDTsv: *

* The accessory contained in the Parkside Holiday Brownstone.

For Your Sweetheart

58987

2002ᴹ - 2004

OSRP: $22.50

VDTsv: $26

Paid: $_____

Serving Irish Ale

58988

2002^M - Current

OSRP: $20

VDTsv: $20

Paid: $_____

Peanuts, Pennants & Programs

58989

2002^M - 2005

OSRP: $15

VDTsv: $30

Paid: $_____

• Legendary Ballparks Series.

Choosing Rights

58990

2002^M - 2003

OSRP: $15

VDTsv: $30

Paid: $_____

• Legendary Ballparks Series.

The Radio City Rockettes

58991

2002^M - 2006

OSRP: $12.50

VDTsv: $50-145

Paid: $_____

• Originally designed with tall white hats.
• Licensed by Radio City Trademarks L.L.C.

Pizza Pick-Up

58949

2002 - 2004

OSRP: *

VDTsv: *

* The accessory contained in DeFazio's Pizzeria.

City Park Gateway

58992 - Set of 2

2002 - 2004

OSRP: $42.50

VDTsv: $25-$40

Paid: $_____

• Christmas In The Park Series.
• Working clock.

Asleep At The Bus Stop

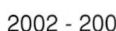

58993

2002 - 2005

OSRP: $12.50

VDTsv: $52

Paid: $_____

Presents For The Family

58994

2002 - 2004

OSRP: $12.50

VDTsv: $48

Paid: $_____

Family Out For A Walk

58995 - Set of 2

2002 - 2004

OSRP: $20

VDTsv: $40

Paid: $_____

Fresh Fish Today

58996 - Set of 2

2002 - 2005

OSRP: $27.50

VDTsv: $48

Paid: $_____

America's Finest

58998

2002 - 2006

OSRP: $20

VDTsv: $42

Paid: $_____

• Licensed by Harley-Davidson©.

For The Love Of Books

58999

2002 - 2004

OSRP: $18

VDTsv: $49-$65

Paid: $_____

Keep America Beautiful

59400

2002 - 2004

OSRP: $13

VDTsv: $28

Paid: $_____

Pumpkins In The Park

59402

2002 - 2004

OSRP: $40

VDTsv: $28-$48

Paid: $_____

Teaching The Torah

59403

2002 - 2003

OSRP: $15

VDTsv: $18

Paid: $_____

Can I Have Your Autograph?

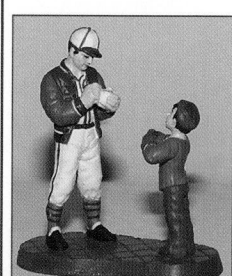

59405

2002 - 2006

OSRP: $16.50

VDTsv: -

Paid: $_____

• Legendary Ballparks Series.

Ebbets Field Scoreboard

59406

2002 - 2004

OSRP: $20

VDTsv: $20

Paid: $_____

• Legendary Ballparks Series.

How Tall Is It?

59407

2003^M - 2004

OSRP: $15

VDTsv: $15-$19

Paid: $_____

1930 Harley-Davidson® VL W/Sidecar

59409

2003^M - 2006

OSRP: $22.50

VDTsv: $38

Paid: $_____

• Licensed by Harley-Davidson©.

Milwaukee Or Bust

59410

2003^M - 2005

OSRP: $45

VDTsv: $72-$75

Paid: $_____

• Licensed by Harley-Davidson©.

Christmas Eve Visit

59206

2003^M - 2003

OSRP: *

VDTsv: *

• Adapter included
* The accessory contained in Church Of The Holy Light.

Ferry Ticket Sales

59213

2003 - 2004

OSRP: *

VDTsv: *

* The accessory contained in East Harbor Ferry.

Tin Whistles - 25 Cents

59216

2003 - 2005

OSRP: *

VDTsv: *

* The accessory contained in Kelly's Irish Crafts.

Blue Line Bus

59411

2003 - 2005

OSRP: $20

GBT357ru: $80

Paid: $_____

• Vintage Cars™ Series.

Off To College!

59413

2003 - 2005

OSRP: $17.50

VDTsv: $10-$28

Paid: $_____

Harley-Davidson® Motorcycle Truck

59414

2003 - 2006

OSRP: $20

VDTsv: $49-$58

Paid: $_____

• Licensed by Harley-Davidson®.

Hot Pretzels

59415

2003 - 2005

OSRP: $25

VDTsv: $44

Paid: $_____

• Christmas In The Park Series.
• Includes adapter.

1940 V16 Cadillac® Coupe

59416

2003 - 2006

OSRP: $20

VDTsv: $78

Paid: $_____

• Vintage Cars™ Series.
• Licensed by General Motors.

Taxi

59417

2003 - 2005

OSRP: $20

VDTsv: $20

Paid: $_____

• Vintage Cars™ Series.

Pier 87 Bait & Tackle

59419 - Set of 2

2003 - 2005

OSRP: $30

VDTsv: $30

Paid: $_____

• A simlar piece, "San Francisco Bait Shop" was sold at the D56 store in San Francisco.

Traffic Policeman

59421

2003 - 2005

OSRP: $15

VDTsv: $28

Paid: $_____

Sidewalk Games

59422 - Set of 3

2003 - 2005

OSRP: $20

VDTsv: $38

Paid: $_____

City Sledding

59423

2003 - 2006

OSRP: $45

VDTsv: $98

Paid: $_____

• Includes adapter.

Warming Up

59425 - Set of 2

2003 - 2006

OSRP: $16.50

VDTsv: -

Paid: $_____

• Legendary Ballparks Series.

Christmas Topiaries

59219

2004ᴹ - 2004

OSRP: *

VDTsv: *

* The accessory contained in Crystal Gardens Conservatory.

Full Service Attendant

59220

2004ᴹ - 2005

OSRP: *

VDTsv: *

* The accessory contained in Royal Oil Company.

Vintage Coca-Cola® Truck

59428

2004ᴹ - 2007

OSRP: $20

VDTsv: -

Paid: $_____

• Vintage Cars™ Series.
• Licensed by Coca-Cola®.

1939 Buick® Roadster™

59429

2004ᴹ - 2005

OSRP: $20

VDTsv: $65

Paid: $_____

• Vintage Cars™ Series.
• Licensed by General Motors.

A Coke® For You And Me!

59430

2004ᴹ - 2007

OSRP: $15

VDTsv: $26

Paid: $_____

• Licensed by Coca-Cola®.

Ballpark Bleachers

59436

2004ᴹ - 2006

OSRP: $45

VDTsv: $65

Paid: $_____

• Plays "Take Me Out To The Ball Game."
• Legendary Ballparks Series.

Refreshments Stands

Dates	OSRP	VDTsv	Paid
2004^M - 2005	$17.50	See below	

Item #	Team	VDTsv	Paid
59437	New York Yankees™	$18	$_____
59440	Chicago Cubs™	$18	$_____
59441	Chicago White Sox™	$35	$_____
59442	Boston Red Sox™	$18	$_____

• The 4 Stands are identical, other than the team names and colors.
• Legendary Ballpark Series.
• Licensed by Major League Baseball Properties, Inc.

A Day At The Ballpark

59443 - Set of 2

2004^M - 2006

OSRP: $18

VDTsv: -

Paid: $_____

• Legendary Ballparks Series

Baseball Diamond

59444

2004^M - 2006

OSRP: $10

VDTsv: -

Paid: $_____

• Legendary Ballparks Series.

A Shiny New Christmas Present

59445

2004 - 2006

OSRP: $17.50

VDTsv: $14

Paid: $_____

• Licensed by General Motors.

Erin Go Bragh

59446

2004 - 2006

OSRP: $15

VDTsv: -

Paid: $_____

Luigi's Gelato Treats

59448

2004 - 2008

OSRP: $20

VDTsv: $14-$25

Paid: $_____

A Night On The Town

59452

2004 - 2009

OSRP: $15

VDTsv: $42

Paid: $_____

Unloading Ice Blocks At The Dock

59453

2004 - 2006

OSRP: $17.50

VDTsv: $28

Paid: $_____

Delivery Truck

59454

2004 - 2006

OSRP: $20

VDTsv: $28

Paid: $_____

 • Vintage Cars™ Series.

Kid Gloves Moving

59456

2004 - 2006

OSRP: $17.50

VDTsv: $10-$40

Paid: $_____

Dressed For Success

59457

2004 - 2006

OSRP: $10

VDTsv: $25

Paid: $_____

Today's Specials

59458

2004 - 2006

OSRP: $12.50

VDTsv: $12-$17

Paid: $_____

Look, It's Santa!

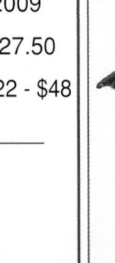

59243

2005ᴹ - 2005

OSRP: *

VDTsv: *

* The accessory contained in Visiting Santa At Finestrom's.

Handsome Cab

59459

2005ᴹ - 2009

OSRP: $27.50

VDTsv: $22 - $48

Paid: $_____

Tea, Darling?

59460

2005ᴹ - 2007

OSRP: $12.50

VDTsv: $26

Paid: $_____

1938 Police Car

59461

2005ᴹ - 2006

OSRP: $20

VDTsv: $75

Paid: $_____

• Vintage Cars™ Series.

Dockside Stevedore

59462

2005 - 2008

OSRP: $27.50

VDTsv: $14-40

Paid: $_____

Saltwater Taffy Boardwalk Booth

59465 - Set of 2

2005 - 2007

OSRP: $25

VDTsv: $12-$48

Paid: $_____

Christmas Pageant Dress Rehearsal

59466

2005 - 2006

OSRP: $18.50

VDTsv: $11-$48

Paid: $_____

• 30th Anniversary Series.
• Limited to year of production.

Guess Your Weight, 1 Cent

59467

2005 - 2007

OSRP: $18.50

VDTsv: $11-$22

Paid: $_____

Sidewalk Coffee Break

59470

2005 - 2008

OSRP: $18.50

VDTsv: $28

Paid: $_____

Your Telegram, Ma'am

59472

2005 - 2008

OSRP: $18.50

VDTsv: $12-$25

Paid: $_____

Windows Cleaned By Tom

59474

2005 - 2007

OSRP: $12.50

VDTsv: $12-$20

Paid: $_____

A Game Of Stickball

59475 - Set of 3
2005 - 2007
OSRP: $18.50
VDTsv: $48
Paid: $_____

A New Phonograph

59473
2006^M - 2007
OSRP: $17.50
VDTsv: $10-$25
Paid: $_____

A Coke® For Santa

59476
2006^M - 2007
OSRP: $25
VDTsv: -
Paid: $_____

Lobster Trap Boardwalk Booth

59464 Set of 2
2006 - 2008
OSRP: $35
VDTsv: $21-$48
Paid: $_____

Learning The Charleston

59468
2006 - 2008
OSRP: $15
VDTsv: $10-$25
Paid: $_____

Let's Get Out Of This Wind!

59477
2006 - 2008
OSRP: $15
VDTsv: $15-$20
Paid: $_____

The Caricature Artist

59478
2006 - 2008
OSRP: $18.50
VDTsv: $11-$32
Paid: $_____

A Bright New Purchase

59479
2006 - 2007
OSRP: $17.50
VDTsv: $17
Paid: $_____
• Christmas In
The City 20th
Anniversary

Window Shoppers

59481

2006 - 2007

OSRP: $17.50

VDTsv: -

Paid: $_____

• Set of Two.

Jazz At The Jambalaya

59482

2006 -

OSRP: $22.50

VDTsv: $22

Paid: $_____

Walking The Dogs

59266 Set of 2

2007^M - 2007

OSRP: $99

VDTsv: -

Paid: $_____

• Limited To Year Of Production.

Welcome To Christmas In The City

799987

2007 -

OSRP: $17.50

VDTsv: $17

Paid: $_____

Ferrara Bakery Cart

799983

2007 - 2009

OSRP: $25

VDTsv: $25

Paid: $_____

Bucket Lunch

799984

2007 - 2009

OSRP: $15

VDTsv: $15

Paid: $_____

A Shot For Your Fans, Please

799985 Set of 2

2007 - 2009

OSRP: $22.50

VDTsv: $18 - $22

Paid: $_____

Free Soda For You?

799986

2007 - 2009

OSRP: $17.50

VDTsv: $14 - $17

Paid: $_____

Praise In Perfect Harmony

804065

2008^M -

OSRP: $22

VDTsv: $16 - $20

Paid: $_____

Picking The Perfect Tree

799994 Set of 3

2008^M - 2008

OSRP: $79

VDTsv: $25

Paid: $_____

• Limited To Year Of Production.

Wind Him Up, Watch Him Go

804066

2008^M - 2009

OSRP: $15

VDTsv: $15

Paid: $_____

Read All About It

807252

2008 -

OSRP: $17.50

VDTsv: $17.50

Paid: $_____

Welcome To Chinatown

807253 Set of 2

2008 -

OSRP: $47.50

VDTsv: $47.50

Paid: $_____

• Includes 2 dog statues

Lanterns & Fireworks For Sale

807254

2008 -

OSRP: $28.50

VDTsv: $28.50

Paid: $_____

I'm A Daddy, Have A Cigar

807255

2008 -

OSRP: $18.50

VDTsv: $15 - $18

Paid: $_____

It's A Wrap

807256

2008 -

OSRP: $27.50

VDTsv: $27.50

Paid: $_____

Welcome To The Prescott

805536 Set of 3
2009^M - 2009
OSRP: $79
VDTsv: -
Paid: $_____

42nd St. Performance

807257
2010 -
OSRP: $25
VDTsv: -
Paid: $_____

An Early Start

808822
2010 -
OSRP: $20
VDTsv: $20
Paid: $_____

Eat In & Take Out

808824
2010 -
OSRP: $25
VDTsv: -
Paid: $_____

Keeping Sidewalks Clear

808830
2010 -
OSRP: $17.50
VDTsv: $17.50
Paid: $_____

Shoveling Fun

808837
2010 -
OSRP: $22.50
VDTsv: -
Paid: $_____

Notes:

North Pole Series™

"Yes, Virginia, there is a Santa Claus. He exists as certainly as love and generosity and devotion exist, and you know that they abound and give to your life its highest beauty and joy."*

And, so it was with this tiny village introduced in 1990. It consisted of "Santa's Workshop," the "Reindeer Barn" and the "Elf Bunkhouse." Period. These buildings most assuredly would make a wonderful vignette devoted to the jolly ol' man himself. After all, Santa Claus is such an important part of the holiday season for children of all ages.

At the time, the North Pole village provided many collectors with the opportunity to start their village collection from its inception. Other villages had already retired many of the original buildings. Many collectors thought this would remain a small village. The following year, the new introductions spelled out N-O-R-TH P-OL-E — seven buildings that gave a hint of thing to come. The North Pole Village became one of the most popular villages and the expansion was amazing. It currently has 127 lighted buildings.

A very busy community, Santa's campus includes the "Hall of Records," "Santa's Lookout Tower," and "Santa's Visiting Center." Other buildings are geared toward Mrs. Claus' talents. Tiny elves are active year around making dolls, teddy bears, trains, rocking horses, and other toys for good little boys and girls. And, there are schools to learn the trades. When they're off the clock, they have their own little residential subdivision known as Elf Land®. Spas, restaurants, ski resorts, and movie theaters — the elves not only work hard, but play hard, too!

Licensing agreements from major manufacturers such as LEGO® Blocks, Barbie®, Play-Doh®, Crayola® and Disney® have provided a touch of reality to this fantasy land. Because of its whimsical nature and strong use of color, the North Pole Village lends itself to be a creative favorite. Many of the newer pieces are animated, attracting attention to the various buildings, bringing delight and excitement to all who display it and view it.

"Yes, Virginia, there is a Santa Claus." He does exist — at least in the hearts and minds of North Pole Series™ collectors!

*Francis Pharcellus Church (22 February 1839 – 11 April 1906) was an American publisher and editor, most famous for his editorial reply to 8-year-old Virginia O'Hanlon, "Yes, Virginia, there is a Santa Claus." Originally published as "Is There a Santa Claus?" in *The New York Sun* (21 September 1897) Wikiquote

Santa's Workshop

56006

Dates	OSRP	VDTsv	Paid
1990 - 1993	**$72**	**$85 - $260**	$_____

• The original samples had a green roof.

NORTH POLE — Set of 2

56014

Dates	OSRP	VDTsv	Paid
1990 - 1996/2000	**$70**	**$14 - $70**	$_____

Reindeer Barn

56015

Dates	OSRP	VDTsv	Paid
1990 - 2000	**$35**	**$25 - $72**	$_____

• Variations exist with reindeer names duplicated and others omitted. The duplicated names vary.

Elf Bunkhouse

56016

Dates	OSRP	VDTsv	Paid
1990 - 1996	**$35**	**$12 - $40**	$_____

• The box and the bottomstamp both read "Elf Bunkhouse" while the sign above the door reads "Elves Bunkhouse."

NeeNee's Dolls And Toys

56200

Dates	OSRP	VDTsv	Paid
1991 - 1995	**$36**	**$30 - $75**	$_____

• The wreath on the front of the building contains the first letter spelling out "NORTH POLE."
• Early release to Showcase and GCC dealers.

NORTH POLE SHOPS — Set of 2

56219

Dates	OSRP	VDTsv	Paid
1991 - 1995	**$75**	**$90**	$_____

Orly's Bell & Harness Supply — 56219

Dates	OSRP	VDTsv	Paid
1991 - 1995	$37.50	$17 - $52	$_____

• The wreath on the front of the building contains the second letter spelling out "NORTH POLE."

Rimpy's Bakery — 56219

Dates	OSRP	VDTsv	Paid
1991 - 1995	$37.50	$45 - $62	$_____

• The wreath on the front of the building contains the third letter spelling out "NORTH POLE."

Tassy's Mittens & Hassel's Woolies — 56227

Dates	OSRP	VDTsv	Paid
1991 - 1995	$50	$45 - $200	$_____

• The wreaths on the front of the building contain the fourth and fifth letters spelling out "NORTH POLE."

Post Office — 56235

Dates	OSRP	VDTsv	Paid
1992 - 1999	$45	$40 - $88	$_____

• The wreath on the front of the building contains the sixth letter spelling out "NORTH POLE."
• Early release to Showcase Dealers.

Obbie's Books & Letrinka's Candy — 56243

Dates	OSRP	VDTsv	Paid
1992 - 1996	$70	$65 - $75	$_____

• The wreaths on the front of the building contain the seventh and eighth letters spelling out "NORTH POLE."
• The flag is fragile.

Elfie's Sleds & Skates — 56251

Dates	OSRP	VDTsv	Paid
1992 - 1996	$48	$45 - $50	$_____

• The wreath on the front of the building contains the last letter spelling out "NORTH POLE."

North Pole Chapel

56260

Dates	OSRP	VDTsv	Paid
1993 - 2000	**$45**	**$48 - $55**	**$_____**

• Early release to Showcase Dealers and select buying groups.
• There is a bell in the tower.

North Pole Express Depot

56278

Dates	OSRP	VDTsv	Paid
1993 - 1998	**$48**	**$21 - $41**	**$_____**

• The flags are fragile.

Santa's Woodworks

56286

Dates	OSRP	VDTsv	Paid
1993 - 1996	**$42**	**$35 - $45**	**$_____**

Santa's Lookout Tower

56294

Dates	OSRP	VDTsv	Paid
1993 - 2000	**$45**	**$34 - $50**	**$_____**

• Early samples have a completely red tower.
• Flags are easily damaged when removing from box.

Elfin Snow Cone Works

56332

Dates	OSRP	VDTsv	Paid
1994 - 1997	**$40**	**$40 - $48**	**$_____**

Beard Barber Shop

56340

Dates	OSRP	VDTsv	Paid
1994 - 1997	**$27.50**	**$20 - $34**	**$_____**

• A sign is separate in the box.

North Pole Dolls & Santa's Bear Works
56359

Dates	OSRP	VDTsv	Paid
1994 - 1997	$96	$75 - $98	$_____

• Set of 3 includes two lit towers and a non-lit center piece.

Tin Soldier Shop
56383

Dates	OSRP	VDTsv	Paid
1995ᴹ - 1997	$42	$22 - $58	$_____

• Metal sign attached to the front is easily broken.

Elfin Forge & Assembly Shop
56384

Dates	OSRP	VDTsv	Paid
1995 - 1998	$65	$48 - $65	$_____

Weather & Time Observatory
56385

Dates	OSRP	VDTsv	Paid
1995 - 1999	$50	$40 - $78	$_____

Santa's Rooming House
56386

Dates	OSRP	VDTsv	Paid
1995 - 1999	$50	$40 - $55	$_____

Elves' Trade School
56387

Dates	OSRP	VDTsv	Paid
1995 - 1998	$50	$35 - $55	$_____

• Early pieces have signs that read "Evles Trade School."

Popcorn & Cranberry House 56388

Dates	OSRP	VDTsv	Paid
1996ᴹ - 1997	$45	$80 - $101	$_____

• A lantern is separate in the box.

Santa's Bell Repair 56389

Dates	OSRP	VDTsv	Paid
1996ᴹ - 1998	$45	$35 - $60	$_____

North Pole Start A Tradition Set 56390

Dates	OSRP	VDTsv	Paid
1996ᴹ - 1996	$85	$45 - $55	$_____

• First available during the November 1996 Homes for the Holidays event. The price was reduced to $65 during the event.

• Set of 12 includes Candy Cane Lane set of 2 **Candy Cane & Peppermint Shop** (top) and **Gift Wrap & Ribbons** (bottom), a 2 piece accessory "Candy Cane Elves," 6 trees, Brick Road, and a bag of snow.

Route 1, North Pole, Home Of Mr. & Mrs. Claus 56391

Dates	OSRP	VDTsv	Paid
1996 - 2005	$110	$55 - $110	$_____

• Earliest shipments had the two green gates included in the box. Later ones have the gates already inserted into the fence. 3 flags are separate in the box.

Hall Of Records 56392

Dates	OSRP	VDTsv	Paid
1996 - 1999	$50	$35 - $55	$_____

Christmas Bread Bakers
56393

Dates	OSRP	VDTsv	Paid
1996 - 2000	**$55**	**$40 - $90**	$_____

• A directional sign is separate in the box.

The Glacier Gazette
56394

Dates	OSRP	VDTsv	Paid
1997ᴹ - 1999	**$48**	**$50 - $70**	$_____

Mrs. Claus' Greenhouse
56395

Dates	OSRP	VDTsv	Paid
1997 - 2001	**$68**	**$74 - $78**	$_____

• A sign is separate in the box.

Glass Ornament Works
56396

Dates	OSRP	VDTsv	Paid
1997 - 2003	**$60**	**$60 - $88**	$_____

• Glass ornaments and stands are extremely fragile.

Santa's Light Shop
56397

Dates	OSRP	VDTsv	Paid
1997 - 2000	**$52**	**$45 - $55**	$_____

Elsie's Gingerbread
56398

Dates	OSRP	VDTsv	Paid
1997 - 1998	**$65**	**$52 - $80**	$_____

• Limited to year of production.
• Uses Magic Smoke to create smoking effect rising from the chimney.

Custom Stitchers

56400

Dates	OSRP	VDTsv	Paid
1998 - 2000	$37.50	$27 - $40	$_____

• Elf Land™.
• 3 pieces of clothing and a bell are separate in the box.

Tillie's Tiny Cup Café

56401

Dates	OSRP	VDTsv	Paid
1998 - 2000	$37.50	$31 - $40	$_____

• Elf Land™.
• A bell is separate in the box.
• The sign on top of the building is easily snapped off.

The Elf Spa

56402

Dates	OSRP	VDTsv	Paid
1998 - 2001	$40	$40 - $59	$_____

• Elf Land™.
• A flag is separate in the box.

Real Plastic Snow Factory

56403

Dates	OSRP	VDTsv	Paid
1998 - 2001	$80	$69 - $85	$_____

• A bell is separate in the box.

Reindeer Flight School

56404

Dates	OSRP	VDTsv	Paid
1998 - 2002	$55	$65 - $88	$_____

• A weathervane and windsock are separate in the box.

Marie's Doll Museum

56408

Dates	OSRP	VDTsv	Paid
1999^M - 1999	$55	$49 - $85	$_____

• Inspired by Marie Osmond, the entertainer and avid doll designer and North Pole collector

Santa's Visiting Center

56407

Dates	OSRP	VDTsv	Paid
1999^M - 1999	$65	$60 - $80	$_____

- First available at the 1999 Discover Department 56 event.
- Set of 6 includes the Visiting Center, girl with dog, fence, tree, walkway, and bag of snow.
- Several national flags are separate in the box.

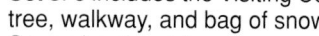
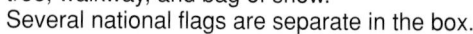

Elf Mountain Ski Resort

56700

Dates	OSRP	VDTsv	Paid
1999 - 2002	$70	$70 - $97	$_____

- 2 flags are separate in the box.

The Peanut Brittle Factory

56701

Dates	OSRP	VDTsv	Paid
1999 - 2002	$80	$85 - $135	$_____

- A sign is separate in the box.

Mini-Donut Shop

56702

Dates	OSRP	VDTsv	Paid
1999 - 2001	$42	$50 - $58	$_____

- Elf Land™.
- The umbrella is very fragile.

Cold Care Clinic

56703

Dates	OSRP	VDTsv	Paid
1999 - 2000	$42	$29.50 - $50	$_____

- Elf Land™.
- A sign and a bell are separate in the box.

Northern Lights Tinsel Mill 56704

Dates	OSRP	VDTsv	Paid
1999 - 2002	$55	$60 - $70	$_____

Jack In The Box Plant No. 2 56705

Dates	OSRP	VDTsv	Paid
1999 - 2000	$65	$55 - $65	$_____

• Limited to year of production.
• The smokestack is fragile.

Sweet Rock Candy Co. Gift Set 56725

Dates	OSRP	VDTsv	Paid
2000^M - 2000	$75	$80 - $128	$_____

• First available during the 2000 Discover Department 56 event.
• The silver bell honors Department 56's 25th anniversary.
• Set of 9 includes the building with silver bell, "Candy Mining" accessory, 3 peppermint trees, cobblestone walkway, 2 candy cane fences, and a bag of snow.
• The sign is easily broken.

Crayola® Polar Palette Art Center 56726

Dates	OSRP	VDTsv	Paid
2000^M - 2002	$65	$75 - $115	$_____

• 2 signs are separate in the box.
• Licensed by Binney & Smith.

Toot's Model Train Mfg. 56728

Dates	OSRP	VDTsv	Paid
2000 - 2001	$110	$225 - $300	$_____

• 25th Anniversary Limited Edition of 25,000.
• Includes animated model train that circles the smokestack.

ACME Toy Factory 56729

Dates	OSRP	VDTsv	Paid
2000 - 2002	$80	$80 - $98	$_____

- Set of 5 includes Factory and 4 Looney Tunes characters — Bugs Bunny, Daffy Duck, Sylvester, and Taz.
- Pennant is packaged separately in the box.
- Licensed by Warner Bros.

Northern Lights Fire Station 56730

Dates	OSRP	VDTsv	Paid
2000 - 2005	$64	$64 - $68	$_____

- Do not handle by candy cane pole.

Wedding Bells Chapel 56731

Dates	OSRP	VDTsv	Paid
2000 - 2001	$45	$48 - $60	$_____

- Elf Land™.

Ginny's Cookie Treats (Regular Issue) 56732

Dates	OSRP	VDTsv	Paid
2000 - 2004	$50	$50	$_____

- Elf Land™.
- This version includes only the building and 2 piece accessory "Gingerbread Corner."
- Sign is packaged separately in the box.

(Early Release) 56727

Dates	OSRP	VDTsv	Paid
2000^M - 2002	$50	$70	$_____

- This was an early release to the various May Co. department stores. It includes the building, accessory, 3 trees, and snow.

North Pole Beauty Shoppe 05733

Dates	OSRP	VDTsv	Paid
2001^M - 2001	$40	$65	$_____

- Elf Land™.
- Was available only through the Avon cosmetics catalog.
- Includes 2 trees and a bag of snow.

Design Works North Pole

56733

Dates	OSRP	VDTsv	Paid
2001ᴹ - 2001	$75	$585	$_____

- Each of the building's four sides depicts an aspect of the creative process.
- Only available at Dept. 56's silver anniversary event.
- Pennant and 4 signs separate in box.

Santa's Sleigh Launch

56734

Dates	OSRP	VDTsv	Paid
2001ᴹ - 2001	$75	$85 - $90	$_____

- First available during the 2001 Holiday Discover Department 56 event.
- Though box shows straight trees, this set includes curved trees.
- Set of 5 includes building, "All Clear For Take Off" accessory, 2 green glitter sisal trees, and a bag of snow.

LEGO® Building Creation Station

56735

Dates	OSRP	VDTsv	Paid
2001ᴹ - 2003	$90	$95	$_____

- Licensed by The LEGO® Group.

Caribou Coffee® Shop

56736

Dates	OSRP	VDTsv	Paid
2001ᴹ - 2003	$62	$65 - $120	$_____

- Set of 3 includes the Shop, a sign, and a reindeer.
- Licensed by Caribou Coffee® Co.

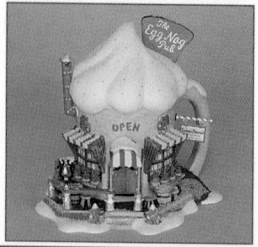

The Egg Nog Pub

56737

Dates	OSRP	VDTsv	Paid
2001ᴹ - 2003	$40	$45	$_____

- Elf Land™.
- Sign is separate in the box.

Twinkle Brite Glitter Factory — 56738

Dates	OSRP	VDTsv	Paid
2001 - 2003	$70	$40 - $75	$_____

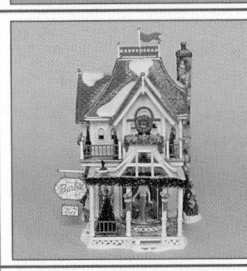

Barbie™ Boutique — 56739

Dates	OSRP	VDTsv	Paid
2001 - 2004	$80	$80 - $110	$_____

- Sign and flag are separate in the box.
- Licensed by Mattel, Inc®.

Beard Bros. Sleigh Wash — 56740

Dates	OSRP	VDTsv	Paid
2001 - 2003	$70	$70 - $70	$_____

Polar Palace Theater — 56741

Dates	OSRP	VDTsv	Paid
2001 - 2003	$40	$50 - $90	$_____

- Elf Land™.
- Bell is separate in the box.

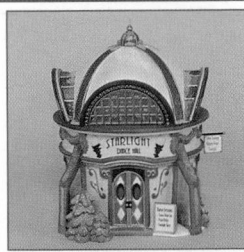

Starlight Dance Hall — 56742

Dates	OSRP	VDTsv	Paid
2001 - 2002	$75	$59 - $80	$_____

- Numbered limited edition of 25,000.
- Sign is separate in the box.

Grandma's Bakery — 05841

Dates	OSRP	VDTsv	Paid
2002ᴹ - 2002	$40	$85	$_____

- Elf Land™.
- Was available only through the Avon cosmetics catalog.
- Set of 3 includes the Bakery and 2 sisal trees.
- Sign is separate in the box.

The Antler Inn
56744

Dates	OSRP	VDTsv	Paid
2002ᴹ - 2004	$75	$75 - $118	$_____

• Two signs are separate in the box.

Glacier Park Pavilion
56745

Dates	OSRP	VDTsv	Paid
2002ᴹ - 2002	$110	$110 - $120	$_____

• Holiday 2002 Special Edition.
• Limited to year of production.
• Animated.
• Set of 9 includes Pavilion with skating rink, "Skating With Santa" accessory, 2 elf skaters, 2 winter birch trees, 2 frosted topiaries, and snow.
• Four flags and sign are separate in the box.

Play-Doh® Sculpting Studio
56746

Dates	OSRP	VDTsv	Paid
2002ᴹ - 2003	$80	$85 - $88	$_____

• Licensed by Hasbro Consumer Products.

Santa's Reindeer Rides
56748

Dates	OSRP	VDTsv	Paid
2002ᴹ - 2002	$50	$53 - $65	$_____

• Holiday 2002 Special Edition.
• Limited to year of production.
• Animated.
• Set of 6 includes the building, "Look At Him Go!" accessory, frosted topiary tree, 2 frosted topiary bushes, and snow.

Polar Power Company

56749

Dates	OSRP	VDTsv	Paid
2002 - 2003	$95	$95 - $140	$_____

• Limited to year of production.
• Animated with lighting effects.

Kringle Elfementary School

56750

Dates	OSRP	VDTsv	Paid
2002 - 2004	$45	$45 - $68	$_____

• Elf Land™.

Northwind Knitters

56751

Dates	OSRP	VDTsv	Paid
2002 - 2004	$65	$60 - $75	$_____

• Set of 2 includes building and "Drying The Wool" accessory.

Frosty Pines Outfitters

56752

Dates	OSRP	VDTsv	Paid
2002 - 2003	$60	$60 - $78	$_____

Hand Carved Nutcracker Factory

56753

Dates	OSRP	VDTsv	Paid
2002 - 2005	$65	$65 - $81	$_____

Coca-Cola® Fizz Factory 56754

Dates	OSRP	VDTsv	Paid
2002 - 2006	$85	$85 - $85	$_____

• Animated.
• If the bottle does not fizz, Dept. 56 suggests turning it over for 3 seconds, then upright before turning it on.
• Licensed by Coca-Cola®.

McElfin's Irish Restaurant & Gifts 56755

Dates	OSRP	VDTsv	Paid
2002 - 2004	$55	$55 -$85	$_____

Mitten Manor 56756

Dates	OSRP	VDTsv	Paid
2002 - 2004	$45	$45 - $54	$_____

• Elf Land™.
• Set of 2 includes Manor and "Newt & Emma" accessory.

Checking It Twice Wind-Up Toys 56757

Dates	OSRP	VDTsv	Paid
2003ᴹ - 2003	$75	$80 - $125	$_____

• Holiday 2003 Special Edition.
• Limited to year of production.
• Animated. Includes adapter.
• Set of 5 includes the building, "Everything Looks A-Okay" accessory, walkway, sparkle glitter birch tree, and snow.

Naughty Or Nice Detective Agency 56758

Dates	OSRP	VDTsv	Paid
2003ᴹ - 2003	$50	$55 - $65	$_____

- Holiday 2003 Special Edition.
- Limited to year of production.
- Animated. Includes adapter.
- Set of 6 includes the building, "Lots Of Good Children This Year" accessory, frosted pine tree, frosted pine shrubs, and snow.

Mickey's North Pole Holiday House 56759

Dates	OSRP	VDTsv	Paid
2003ᴹ - 2007	$85	$85	$_____

- Disney Showcase Collection.
- Licensed by Disney Theme Parks.

KOLD Radio 56761

Dates	OSRP	VDTsv	Paid
2003ᴹ - 2004	$60	$60 - $88	$_____

The Christmas Candy Mill 56762

Dates	OSRP	VDTsv	Paid
2003 - 2006	$75	$75	$_____

- Animated.

Flurry's Snowglobe Maker 56763

Dates	OSRP	VDTsv	Paid
2003 - 2006	$68	$68 - $80	$_____

Polar Roller Rink

56764

Dates	OSRP	VDTsv	Paid
2003 - 2005	**$65**	**$65 - $98**	$_____

• Animated.
• Includes "Elves On Wheels" accessory.

Red's Elf Land Diner

56765

Dates	OSRP	VDTsv	Paid
2003 - 2005	**$50**	**$50**	$_____

• Elf Land™.

Pointy Toed Shoemaker

56766

Dates	OSRP	VDTsv	Paid
2003 - 2007	**$35**	-	$_____

• Elf Land™.

North Pole Town Hall

56767

Dates	OSRP	VDTsv	Paid
2003 - 2005	**$65**	**$65 - $65**	$_____

• Plays *Jingle Bells*.

Santa's Castle

56768

Dates	OSRP	VDTsv	Paid
2003 - 2004	**$95**	**$66 - $95**	$_____

• Limited to year of production.
• Inspired by the Castle in the cartoon *Rudolph The Red-Nosed Reindeer*.
• Licensed by Good-Times Merchandising & Licensing.

Rudolph's Misfit Headquarters

56769

Dates	OSRP	VDTsv	Paid
2003 - 2004	**$70**	**$52 - $75**	$_____

• Limited to year of production.
• Inspired by the location in the cartoon *Rudolph The Red-Nosed Reindeer*.
• Licensed by Good-Times Merchandising & Licensing.

Yummy Gummy Gumdrop Factory 56771

Dates	OSRP	VDTsv	Paid
2004ᴹ -	$75	-	$_____

• Animated.

Christmas Critters Pet Store 56772

Dates	OSRP	VDTsv	Paid
2004ᴹ - 2009	$45	-	$_____

• Elf Land™.

North Pole M&M's® Candy Factory 56773

Dates	OSRP	VDTsv	Paid
2004ᴹ - 2006	$95	-	$_____

• Animated.
• Licensed by Mars, Inc.

Teddy Bear Training Center 56774

Dates	OSRP	VDTsv	Paid
2004ᴹ - 2004	$75	$75	$_____

• Limited to year of production.
• Set of 6 includes the building, "Plush Teddy Bear"
  accessory, flagpole, trees, and snow.

Bjorn Turoc Rocking Horse Maker 56775

Dates	OSRP	VDTsv	Paid
2004ᴹ - 2005	$70	$70	$_____

• Animated.

Lucky's Pony Rides 56776

Dates	OSRP	VDTsv	Paid
2004ᴹ - 2004	$65	$75	$_____

• Club 56 dealer exclusive. Limited edition of 5,000.

Santa's Toy Company (Early Release)   56892

Dates	OSRP	VDTsv	Paid
2004ᴹ - 2004	$75	$85	$_____

• 15th Anniversary Series; first of 5 buildings that spell Santa.
• Limited to 10,000 pieces.
• Early release, available through select Department 56 retailers.

Alfie's Toy School For Elves (Early Release)   56894

Dates	OSRP	VDTsv	Paid
2004ᴹ - 2004	$65	$85	$_____

• 15th Anniversary Series; second of 5 buildings that spell Santa.
• Limited to year of production.
• Available only on Department 56's web site.

Mrs. Claus' Hand Knit Christmas Stockings   56778

Dates	OSRP	VDTsv	Paid
2004 - 2006	$70	-	$_____

• Includes trees.
• Set of 3.

Arctic Game Station   56779

Dates	OSRP	VDTsv	Paid
2004 - 2006	$50	-	$_____

• Elf Land™.

Krinkles Christmas Ornament Design Studio 56780

Dates	OSRP	VDTsv	Paid
2004 - 2007	$75	-	$_____

• Includes tree.
• Set of 2.

Alfie's Toy School For Elves (Second Release) 56781

Dates	OSRP	VDTsv	Paid
2004 - 2005	$65	$65	$_____

• 15th Anniversary Series; second of 5 buildings that spell Santa.
• Limited to year of production.
• Has different color scheme from early release version.

Santa's Toy Company (Second Release)   56893

Dates	OSRP	VDTsv	Paid
2004 - 2005	$75	$75	$_____

- 15th Anniversary Series; first of 5 buildings that spell Santa.
- Limited to year of production.
- Has different color scheme from early release version.

Nettie's Mistletoe Manor   56895

Dates	OSRP	VDTsv	Paid
2004 - 2005	$55	$55	$_____

- 15th Anniversary Series; third of 5 buildings that spell Santa.
- Limited to year of production.

Tinker's Caboose Cafe   56896

Dates	OSRP	VDTsv	Paid
2004 - 2005	$65	$65	$_____

- 15th Anniversary Series; fourth of 5 buildings that spell Santa.
- Limited to year of production.

Art's Hobbies & Crafts   56897

Dates	OSRP	VDTsv	Paid
2004 - 2005	$60	$60	$_____

- 15th Anniversary Series; fifth of 5 buildings that spell Santa.
- Limited to year of production.

Scrooge McDuck & Marley's Counting House   56900

Dates	OSRP	VDTsv	Paid
2004 - 2006	$75	-	$_____

- Licensed by Disney.

Mickey's Cratchit's Cottage   56901

Dates	OSRP	VDTsv	Paid
2004 - 2006	$65	-	$_____

- Licensed by Disney.

Frosty's Sled's N' Saucers — 56449

Dates	OSRP	VDTsv	Paid
2005^M - 2005	$60	$60	$_____

- Limited to year of production.
- Licensed by Warner/Chappell Music, Inc.

North Star Commuter Train Station — 56782

Dates	OSRP	VDTsv	Paid
2005^M - 2005	$75	$75	$_____

- Limited to year of production.
- Set of 3 includes building, "I Hope The Train Comes Soon!" accessory, and snow.

Needle's Tree Farm — 56783

Dates	OSRP	VDTsv	Paid
2005^M - 2006	$65	-	$_____

Hot Wheel's Custom Car Shop — 56784

Dates	OSRP	VDTsv	Paid
2005^M - 2006	$80	-	$_____

- Available only in U.S.
- Licensed by Mattel, Inc®.

I.C. Dreams Igloo Construction Company — 56785

Dates	OSRP	VDTsv	Paid
2005^M - 2006	$70	-	$_____

- Includes tree.

Fretta's Fruit Cake Company 56786

Dates	OSRP	VDTsv	Paid
2005M - 2006	$45	-	$_____

• Elf Land™.

Frosty's Christmas Weather Station 56787

Dates	OSRP	VDTsv	Paid
2005M - 2005	$65	$65	$_____

• Limited to year of production.
• Set of 6 includes "Let Me Make You A White Christmas" accessory, 3 trees, and snow.
• Licensed by Warner/Chappell Music, Inc.

North Pole Porcelain Building Works 56788

Dates	OSRP	VDTsv	Paid
2005 - 2006	$85	-	$_____

• Limited to year of production.
• 30th Anniversary Series.
• Long Life Cordless Lighting.

North Pole Board Games Factory 56789

Dates	OSRP	VDTsv	Paid
2005 - 2007	$85	-	$_____

• Licensed by Hasbro Consumer Products.

Around The World In 24 Hours Flight Center 56790

Dates	OSRP	VDTsv	Paid
2005 - 2007	$70	-	$_____

Santa's Tailor Shop

56793

Dates	OSRP	VDTsv	Paid
2005 - 2007	$85	-	$_____

• Interior scenes in 2 front windows.

Reindeer Spa

56794

Dates	OSRP	VDTsv	Paid
2005 - 2008	$75	-	$_____

• Display Anywhere Cordless Lighting.

Santa's Hat Inn

56795

Dates	OSRP	VDTsv	Paid
2005 - 2008	$75	-	$_____

• Display Anywhere Cordless Lighting.

Poinsettia Palace

56796

Dates	OSRP	VDTsv	Paid
2005 - 2006	$100	-	$_____

• Numbered Limited Edition Of 15,000.
• Display Anywhere Cordless Lighting.

North Pole General Store

56797

Dates	OSRP	VDTsv	Paid
2005 - 2007	$60	-	$_____

• Elf Land™.

Christmas Sweet Shop

56791

Dates	OSRP	VDTsv	Paid
2006^M - 2006	$85	-	$_____

• Limited Edition of 10,000.
• 30th Anniversary Series.

Letters To Santa Sorting Station   56792

Dates	OSRP	VDTsv	Paid
2006^M - 2006	$80	-	$_____

- Set of 4 includes building and "Sorting Santa's Letter" accessory.
- Limited to year of production.

Countdown To Christmas Headquarters   56798

Dates	OSRP	VDTsv	Paid
2006^M - 2006	$95	-	$_____

- Limited Edition of 12,000.
- Gives official countdown for 12 days until Christmas by opening windows.

Sesame Street Building   56799

Dates	OSRP	VDTsv	Paid
2006^M - 2008	$75	-	$_____

- Licensed with Sesame Street™.

Santa's Sleigh Maker   56950

Dates	OSRP	VDTsv	Paid
2006 - 2007	$110	-	$_____

- Collectors' Edition.
- Set of 2. Includes accessory "Santa's New Sleigh."
- Limited Edition of 14,000.

Mickey Mouse Watch Factory

56951

Dates	OSRP	VDTsv	Paid
2006 - 2009	$85	-	$_____

Candy Cane Corner

56952

Dates	OSRP	VDTsv	Paid
2006 - 2009	$75	-	$_____

• Represents "C" (CLAUS), 5 Special Edition Buildings.

Light The Way — Santa's Beacon

56953

Dates	OSRP	VDTsv	Paid
2006 - 2009	$85	-	$_____

• Represents "L" (CLAUS), 5 Special Edition Buildings.
• Lighthouse beacon rotates.

Augie's Christmas Carols

56954

Dates	OSRP	VDTsv	Paid
2006 -	$75	-	$_____

• Represents "A" (CLAUS), 5 Special Edition Buildings.

Ulysses The Christmas Bell Maker

56955

Dates	OSRP	VDTsv	Paid
2006 - 2008	$75	-	$_____

• Represents "U" (CLAUS), 5 Special Edition Buildings.

Santa's Paper Snowflake Studio

56956

Dates	OSRP	VDTsv	Paid
2006 - 2008	$75	-	$_____

• Represents "S" (CLAUS), 5 Special Edition Buildings.

North Pole Snow Bank

56957

Dates	OSRP	VDTsv	Paid
2006 - 2008	$75	-	$_____

• Lighted interior scene.

North Pole Beard Trimmers

56958

Dates	OSRP	VDTsv	Paid
2007ᴹ - 2007	$85	-	$_____

• Limited Edition of 10,000.
• Includes interior scene

Elfin Toy Museum

56959

Dates	OSRP	VDTsv	Paid
2007ᴹ - 2007	$95	-	$_____

• Toy top on roof spins.
• Limited Edition of 10,000.
• Collectors' Edition

Christmasland Tree Toppers

56960

Dates	OSRP	VDTsv	Paid
2007ᴹ - 2007	$99	-	$_____

• Limited to year of production.
• Set of 2, Includes: "I Can Almost Reach It!" accessory.
• Tree Toppers Rotate On Display.

Sugar Hill Row Houses

56961

Dates	OSRP	VDTsv	Paid
2007ᴹ - 2009	$75	-	$_____

Dumpy's Toy Trucks

799915

Dates	OSRP	VDTsv	Paid
2007 -	**$90**	-	$_____

Jolly's Jigsaw Puzzle Workshop

799916

Dates	OSRP	VDTsv	Paid
2007 - 2009	**$70**	-	$_____

North Star Karaoke Club

799917

Dates	OSRP	VDTsv	Paid
2007 -	**$75**	-	$_____

• Interior scene of the DJ booth.

Polar Bear Palace

799918

Dates	OSRP	VDTsv	Paid
2007 - 2008	**$110**	-	$_____

• Collectors' Edition.
• Limited Edition of 12,000.
• Icy Polar Bears and sign have special lit effect.

Reindeer Flying Feed Store

799919

Dates	OSRP	VDTsv	Paid
2007 - 2009	**$75**	-	$_____

Rubber Duck Factory

799920

Dates	OSRP	VDTsv	Paid
2007 - 2009	**$125**	-	$_____

• Elf spins in rotating duck pool.

Twinkle Toes Ballet Academy — 799921

Dates	OSRP	VDTsv	Paid
2007 -	$95	-	$_____

• Elves dance inside the studio.

Robbie's Robot Factory — 799998

Dates	OSRP	VDTsv	Paid
2008ᴹ - 2008	$100	-	$_____

• Collectors' Edition.
• Limited Edition of 9,000.

Brite Lites Bulb Factory — 799997

Dates	OSRP	VDTsv	Paid
2008ᴹ - 2008	$79	-	$_____

• Set of 2, with accessory "All In A Tangle."
• Celebrate Holiday Value Set ($100).
• Nostalgic Christmas lights incorporated into design.

The Reindeer Stables, Dasher & Dancer — 799999

Dates	OSRP	VDTsv	Paid
2008ᴹ -	$85	-	$_____

• Dasher / Dancer Duplex

Hatly Hall — 804440

Dates	OSRP	VDTsv	Paid
2008ᴹ - 2009	$85	-	$_____

• Elf dorm, classic North Pole story.

Tinker Bell's Lighthouse

802825

Dates	OSRP	VDTsv	Paid
2008 -	$100	-	$_____

The North Pole Palace

805541

Dates	OSRP	VDTsv	Paid
2008 -	$150	-	$_____

• Palace is lit around North Pole, strung with LEDs.

The Reindeer Stables, Prancer & Vixen

805542

Dates	OSRP	VDTsv	Paid
2008 -	$85	-	$_____

The Lunch Box Café

805543

Dates	OSRP	VDTsv	Paid
2008 -	$75	-	$_____

Cocoa Chocolate Works

805545

Dates	OSRP	VDTsv	Paid
2008 -	$85	-	$_____

Nollie & Ollie's Custom Snowboards

805546

Dates	OSRP	VDTsv	Paid
2008 -	$95	-	$_____

North Pole Penguin Visitors' Center   805547

Dates	OSRP	VDTsv	Paid
2009^M - 2009	$79	-	$_____

• Set of 3, includes "Penguin Parade."
• Limited to year of production.

The Reindeer Stables, Comet & Cupid   805548

Dates	OSRP	VDTsv	Paid
2010 -	$85	-	$_____

Instant Snowman Kit Factory   808921

Dates	OSRP	VDTsv	Paid
2010 -	$65	-	$_____

Better Watch Out Coal Mine   808923

Dates	OSRP	VDTsv	Paid
2010 -	$85	-	$_____

Ice Breaker's Lounge   808924

Dates	OSRP	VDTsv	Paid
2010 -	$90	-	$_____

Baskets & Bows

808925

Dates	OSRP	VDTsv	Paid
2010 -	**$75**	-	$_____

Zenbolt's Handyman Shop

808926

Dates	OSRP	VDTsv	Paid
2010 -	**$80**	-	$_____

Notes:

Trimming The North Pole

56081

1990 - 1993

OSRP: $10

VDTsv: $15-$30

Paid: $_____

Santa & Mrs. Claus

56090 - Set of 2

1990 - 2007

OSRP: $15

VDTsv: -

Paid: $_____

• Early samples had books that read "Good Boys" instead of "Good Kids."

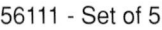

Santa's Little Helpers

56103 - Set of 3

1990 - 1993

OSRP: $28

VDTsv: $13-$42

Paid: $_____

• The reindeer's antlers are very fragile.

Sleigh & Eight Tiny Reindeer

56111 - Set of 5

1990 - 2007

OSRP: $40

VDTsv: -

Paid: $_____

• The reindeer's antlers are very fragile.

Toymaker Elves

56022 - Set of 3

1991 - 1995

OSRP: $27.50

VDTsv: $10-$26

Paid: $_____

Baker Elves

56030 - Set of 3

1991 - 1995

OSRP: $27.50

VDTsv: $6-$45

Paid: $_____

Letters For Santa

56049 - Set of 3

1992 - 1994

OSRP: $30

VDTsv: $18-$44

Paid: $_____

• The reindeer's antlers are very fragile.

Testing The Toys

56057 - Set of 2

1992 - 1999

OSRP: $16.50

VDTsv: $13-$18

Paid: $_____

Woodsmen Elves

56308 - Set of 3
1993 - 1995
OSRP: $30
VDTsv: $16-$46
Paid: $_____

Sing A Song For Santa

56316 - Set of 3
1993 - 1998
OSRP: $28
VDTsv: $20-$26
Paid: $_____

North Pole Gate

56324
1993 - 1998
OSRP: $32.50
VDTsv: $40-$55
Paid: $_____

• The flags are fragile.

Last Minute Delivery

56367
1994 - 1998
OSRP: $35
VDTsv: $13-$65
Paid: $_____

• Though introduced in 1994, shipments were delayed due to production problems.

Snow Cone Elves

56375 - Set of 4
1994 - 1997
OSRP: $30
VDTsv: $20-$30
Paid: $_____

• Features the first "elfette" in North Pole.
• Porcelain and metal.

Charting Santa's Course

56364 - Set of 2
1995 - 1997
OSRP: $25
VDTsv: $21-$28
Paid: $_____

I'll Need More Toys

56365 - Set of 2
1995 - 1998
OSRP: $25
VDTsv: $21-$25
Paid: $_____

• Porcelain and acrylic.

A Busy Elf North Pole Sign

56366
1995 - 1999
OSRP: $20
VDTsv: $21-$30
Paid: $_____

• Porcelain and acrylic.

North Pole Express

56368 - Set of 3

1996 - 1999

OSRP: $37.50

VDTsv: $40-$58

Paid: $_____

• Some samples read "N.E. Express" on the side of the tender.

Early Rising Elves

56369 - Set of 5

1996 - 1999

OSRP: $32.50

VDTsv: $20-$26

Paid: $_____

End Of The Line

56370 - Set of 2

1996 - 1999

OSRP: $28

VDTsv: $18-$20

Paid: $_____

• Includes sign and signal packaged separately in the box.

Holiday Deliveries

56371

1996 - 2001^M

OSRP: $16.50

VDTsv: $15-$18

Paid: $_____

Candy Cane Elves

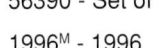

56390 - Set of 2

1996^M - 1996

OSRP: *

VDTsv: *

* Accessory contained in the North Pole Start A Tradition Set.

Don't Break The Ornaments

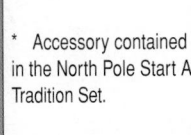

56372 - Set of 2

1997 - 2001

OSRP: $27.50

VDTsv: $30

Paid: $_____

• Ornaments are very fragile.

Delivering The Christmas Greens

56373 - Set of 2

1997 - 2001^M

OSRP: $27.50

VDTsv: $25-$26

Paid: $_____

Untangle The Christmas Lights

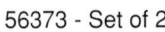

56374

1997 - 2000

OSRP: $35

VDTsv: $13-$50

Paid: $_____

• Lit by battery/ adapter.

Peppermint Skating Party

56363 - Set of 6
1998^M - 2000
OSRP: $64
VDTsv: $25-$72
Paid: $_____

Welcome To Elf Land Gateway Entrance

56431
1998 - 2005
OSRP: $35
VDTsv: $35
Paid: $_____

Loading The Sleigh

52732 - Set of 6
1998 - 2005
OSRP: $125
VDTsv: $125
Paid: $_____

• Animated — handcar runs back and forth along track. Lights on building flash.

Christmas Fun Run

56434 - Set of 6
1998 - 2000
OSRP: $35
VDTsv: $21-$33
Paid: $_____

Delivering Real Plastic Snow

56435
1998 - 2001^M
OSRP: $17
VDTsv: $17-$17
Paid: $_____

Reindeer Training Camp

56436 - Set of 2
1998 - 2002
OSRP: $27.50
VDTsv: $36-$75
Paid: $_____

• The reindeer's antlers are very fragile.

Have A Seat Elves

56437 - Set of 6
1998 - 2005
OSRP: $30
VDTsv: $30
Paid: $_____

Dash Away Delivery

56438
1998 - 2001^M
OSRP: $40
VDTsv: $13-$40
Paid: $_____

• The basket often comes unglued.
• Similar design made for Lord & Taylor. See Special Design section.

Tee Time Elves

56442 - Set of 2
1999^M - 2001^M
OSRP: $27.50
VDTsv: $21-$24
Paid: $_____

Happy New Year!

56443
1999^M - 2000
OSRP: $17.50
VDTsv: $14-$17
Paid: $_____

A Happy Harley Day

56706
1999 - 2001
OSRP: $17
VDTsv: $18
Paid: $_____

• Licensed by Harley-Davidson Motor Co.

Downhill Daredevils

56707 - Set of 2
1999 - 2001
OSRP: $16.50
VDTsv: $6-$27
Paid: $_____

Tangled In Tinsel

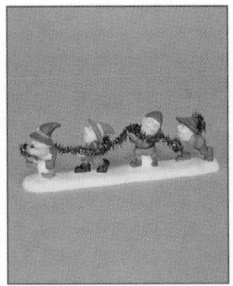

56708
1999 - 2006
OSRP: $25
VDTsv: -
Paid: $_____

Canine Courier

56709 - Set of 3
1999 - 2002
OSRP: $32.50
VDTsv: $13-$33
Paid: $_____

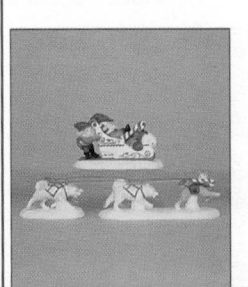

Ski Bums

56710
1999 - 2001
OSRP: $22.50
VDTsv: $25
Paid: $_____

Check This Out

56711

1999 - 2001

OSRP: $13.50

VDTsv: $14-$17

Paid: $_____

Marshmallows Around The Campfire

56712 - Set of 3

1999 - 2002

OSRP: $30

VDTsv: $32-$48

Paid: $_____

• The campfire is battery/adapter operated.

Open Wide!

56713

1999 - 2000

OSRP: $13

VDTsv: $14-$28

Paid: $_____

Elf Tree House

56446

1999 - 2000

OSRP: $42

VDTsv: $8

Paid: $_____

Candy Mining

56725

2000ᴹ - 2000

OSRP: *

VDTsv: *

* Accessory contained in the Sweet Rock Candy Co. Gift Set.

Cruisin' Crayola® Elves

56800 - Set of 2

2000ᴹ - 2002

OSRP: $16.50

VDTsv: $17-$20

Paid: $_____

• Licensed by Binney & Smith.

Leonardo & Vincent

56801

2000ᴹ - 2002

OSRP: $16.50

VDTsv: $16-$18

Paid: $_____

Party In The Hot Tub!

56802 - Set of 2

2000ᴹ - 2001

OSRP: $30

VDTsv: $32

Paid: $_____

Gingerbread Corner

56732 - Set of 2

2000 - 2004

OSRP: *

VDTsv: *

* Accessory contained in the Ginny's Cookie Treats Set.
• Elf Land™

All Aboard!

56803 - Set of 2

2000 - 2003

OSRP: $16.50

VDTsv: $22

Paid: $_____

Rescue Ready

56804

2000 - 2004

OSRP: $16.50

VDTsv: $18

Paid: $_____

Little Newlyweds

56805

2000 - 2001

OSRP: $13

VDTsv: $30-$40

Paid: $_____

Cutting The Trail

56806

2000 - 2003

OSRP: $14

VDTsv: $18

Paid: $_____

Catch The Wind

56807

2000 - 2002

OSRP: $17.50

VDTsv: $17-$17

Paid: $_____

Icy Delights

56808

2000 - 2003

OSRP: $17.50

VDTsv: $22

Paid: $_____

All Clear For Take Off

56734

2001^M - 2001

OSRP: *

VDTsv: *

* Accessory contained in the Santa's Sleigh Launch Gift Set.

Brick Lift

56809

2001^M - 2003

OSRP: $17.50

VDTsv: $20

Paid: $_____

• Licensed by the LEGO® Group.

Little Builders

56810

2001^M - 2003

OSRP: $16

VDTsv: $18

Paid: $_____

• Licensed by the LEGO® Group.

Just A Cup Of Joe

56811

2001^M - 2003

OSRP: $22.50

VDTsv: $23

Paid: $_____

• This was originally shipped in North Pole Woods sleeves.

Glitter Detail

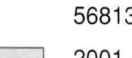

56812 - Set of 2

2001 - 2004

OSRP: $20

VDTsv: $22

Paid: $_____

Car Wash Cadets

56813

2001 - 2003

OSRP: $16.50

VDTsv: $18

Paid: $_____

Two For The Show

56814

2001 - 2003

OSRP: $16.50

VDTsv: $20

Paid: $_____

Kick Up Your Heels

56815

2001 - 2002

OSRP: $13.50

VDTsv: $14-$20

Paid: $_____

Peppermint Front Yard

56817

2001 - 2004

OSRP: $42.50

VDTsv: $48

Paid: $_____

Wrap And Roll

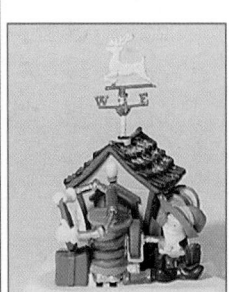

56818
2001 - 2003
OSRP: $20
VDTsv: $30
Paid: $_____

Raising The Flag At The North Pole

56820
2001 - 2004
OSRP: $15
VDTsv: $18
Paid: $_____

LEGO® Warehouse Forklift

56819 - Set of 5
2001 - 2003
OSRP: $140.00
VDTsv: $130
Paid: $_____

• Animated — forklift runs back and forth along track.
• Licensed by the LEGO® Group.

Skating With Santa

56745
2002ᴹ - 2002
OSRP: *
VDTsv: *

* The accessory contained in Glacier Park Pavilion.

Look At Him Go!

56748
2002ᴹ - 2002
OSRP: *
VDTsv: *

* The accessory contained in the Santa's Reindeer Rides.

More Play-Doh®, Please!

56822 - Set of 2
2002ᴹ - 2003
OSRP: $20
VDTsv: $22
Paid: $_____

• Licensed by Hasbro Consumer Products.

North Pole Petting Zoo

56823
2002ᴹ - 2004
OSRP: $35
VDTsv: $56
Paid: $_____

This Looks Like A Good Spot

56831 - Set of 2

2002^M - 2004

OSRP: $16.50

VDTsv: $20

Paid: $_____

Kringle Street Snowman

56833

2002^M - 2002

OSRP: $32.50

VDTsv: $34-$95

Paid: $_____

• Limited to year of production.
• Available only at Gold Key dealers.

Drying The Wool

56751

2002 - 2004

OSRP: *

VDTsv: *

* The accessory contained in the Northwind Knitters.

Newt & Emma

56756

2002 - 2004

OSRP: *

VDTsv: *

• Elf Land™.
* The accessory contained in Mitten Manor.

S'mores & Hot Chocolate Stand

56835

2002 - 2007

OSRP: $32.50

VDTsv: -

Paid: $_____

• Elf Land™.

Sparky The Plant Manager

56836

2002 - 2003

OSRP: $15

VDTsv: $20

Paid: $_____

School Sleigh Express

56837

2002 - 2005

OSRP: $25

VDTsv: $25

Paid: $_____

• Elf Land™.

Running The Loom

56838

2002 - 2004

OSRP: $12.50

VDTsv: $15

Paid: $_____

Ready For Adventure

56839

2002 - 2003

OSRP: $17.50

VDTsv: $20

Paid: $_____

Frozen Veggies

56840

2002 - 2004

OSRP: $15

VDTsv: $18

Paid: $_____

Coca-Cola® Taste Test

56841

2002 - 2006

OSRP: $17.50

VDTsv: -

Paid: $_____

• Licensed by Coca-Cola®.

Nutcracker Delivery

56842 - Set of 2

2002 - 2005

OSRP: $25

VDTsv: $25

Paid: $_____

Chimney Sweep For Hire!

56843

2002 - 2004

OSRP: $13.50

VDTsv: $17

Paid: $_____

Frostbite Tree House Day Care

56844

2002 - 2005

OSRP: $40

VDTsv: $40

Paid: $_____

• Elf Land™.

Frosty Playground

56846

2002 - 2005

OSRP: $32.50

VDTsv: $33

Paid: $_____

• Elf Land™.
• Animated.

Everything Looks A-Okay

56757

2003ᴹ - 2003

OSRP: *

VDTsv: *

* The accessory contained in Checking It Twice Wind-Up Toys.

Lots Of Good Children This Year

56758

2003^M - 2003

OSRP: *

VDTsv: *

* The accessory contained in Naughty Or Nice Detective Agency.

Kringle Street Town Tree

56847

2003^M - 2003

OSRP: $35

VDTsv: $42

Paid: $_____

• Includes adapter.
• Limited to year of production.

An Irish Cheer For Santa

56848 - Set of 2

2003^M - 2004

OSRP: $20

VDTsv: $22

Paid: $_____

Mickey Builds A Snowman

56849

2003^M - 2009

OSRP: $22.50

VDTsv: -

Paid: $_____

• Licensed by Disney Theme Parks.

Bustin' A Move

56850 - Set of 2

2003^M - 2004

OSRP: $15

VDTsv: $18

Paid: $_____

Coca-Cola® Sliding Hill

56851

2003^M - 2006

OSRP: $60

VDTsv: $60

Paid: $_____

• Licensed by Coca-Cola®.
• Includes adapter.

Reindeer Games

56853

2003 - 2004

OSRP: $45

VDTsv: $48

Paid: $_____

• Limited to year of production.
• Licensed by Good-Times M & L.

Don't Let Go!

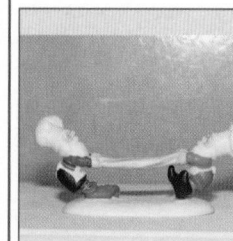

56854

2003 - 2006

OSRP: $10

VDTsv: -

Paid: $_____

Fillers & Flakers

56855
2003 - 2006
OSRP: $20
VDTsv: -
Paid: $_____

A Perfect Fit

56856
2003 - 2006
OSRP: $16.50
VDTsv: -
Paid: $_____

Elf Land™

The Key To The North Pole

56857
2003 - 2005
OSRP: $15
VDTsv: $15
Paid: $_____

Fly Through Elf

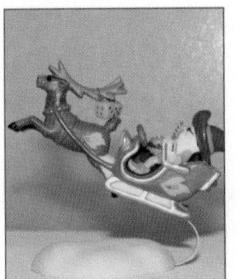

56858
2003 - 2006
OSRP: $15
VDTsv: -
Paid: $_____

• Elf Land™

Candy Cane Shack

56859
2003 - 2005
OSRP: $40
VDTsv: $40
Paid: $_____

• Working bubble lights.
• includes adapter.

The Misfits

56860
2003 - 2004
OSRP: $35
VDTsv: $30
Paid: $_____

• Limited to year of production.
• Licensed by Good-Times M & L.

Mrs. Claus' Cookies & Milk

56861
2003 - 2007
OSRP: $25
VDTsv: -
Paid: $_____

Proud Papa & Mama

56862
2003 - 2005
OSRP: $13.50
VDTsv: $14
Paid: $_____

• Elf Land™

New Year's At The North Pole

56863

2003 - 2005

OSRP: $20

VDTsv: $20

Paid: $_____

Ice & Snow Skating Pond

56867

2003 - 2006

OSRP: $50

VDTsv: -

Paid: $_____

• Animated.
• Includes adapter.

Can I Keep Them

56864

2004^M - 2009

OSRP: $10

VDTsv: -

Paid: $_____

• Elf Land™.

M&M's® Stamp Of Approval

56865

2004^M - 2006

OSRP: $18

VDTsv: -

Paid: $_____

• Licensed by Mars, Inc.

Swinging Disney Fab 5

56866

2004^M - 2007

OSRP: $65

VDTsv: -

Paid: $_____

• Animated, includes adapter.
• Licensed by Disney Theme Parks.

Do I Have A Deal For You!

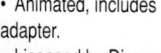

56868 - Set of 2

2004^M - 2005

OSRP: $20

VDTsv: $20

Paid: $_____

Kringle Street Town Santa

56869

2004^M - 2004

OSRP: $32.50

VDTsv: $36

Paid: $_____

• Limited to year of production.

Gumdrop Taste Test

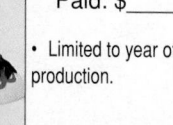

56870

2004^M - 2007

OSRP: $10

VDTsv: -

Paid: $_____

Christmas Around The World — Feliz Navidad

56871

2004 - 2006

OSRP: $30

VDTsv: -

Paid: $_____

• Christmas Around The World Series.

Hot Chocolate Tower

56872

2004 -

OSRP: $30

VDTsv: -

Paid: $_____

Ice Cold Coca-Cola®

56873

2004 - 2007

OSRP: $20

VDTsv: -

Paid: $_____

• Ice sculpture is lighted.
• Licensed by Coca-Cola®.

More Yarn For Your Stockings, Mrs. Claus!

56874

2004 - 2006

OSRP: $17.50

VDTsv: -

Paid: $_____

Testing Video Games Is The Perfect Job!

56875

2004 - 2006

OSRP: $12.50

VDTsv: -

Paid: $_____

• Elf Land™.

Krinkles For Sale

56876

2004 - 2006

OSRP: $18.50

VDTsv: -

Paid: $_____

Welcome To Nettie's B&B

56877

2004 - 2005

OSRP: $17.50

VDTsv: $18

Paid: $_____

• 15th Anniversary Series.
• Limited to year of production.

One Choo-Choo Burger Coming Up!

56889

2004 - 2005

OSRP: $10

VDTsv: $10

Paid: $_____

• 15th Anniversary Series.
• Limited to year of production.

Everybody's Been Good This Year!

56891

2004 - 2005

OSRP: $25

VDTsv: -

Paid: $_____

• 15th Anniversary Series.
• Limited to year of production.

Passing Inspection With Flying Colors

56898

2004 - 2006

OSRP: $17.50

VDTsv: -

Paid: $_____

• 15th Anniversary Series.
• Limited to year of production.

We Don't Need Instructions!

56899

2004 - 2005

OSRP: $15

VDTsv: $15

Paid: $_____

• 15th Anniversary Series.
• Limited to year of production.

Scrooge McDuck & The Ghosts Of Christmas

56940

2004 - 2006

OSRP: $50

VDTsv: -

Paid: $_____

• Adapter included.
• Licensed by Disney.

A Merry Mickey Christmas, Cratchits!

56941 - Set of 2

2004 - 2006

OSRP: $18.50

VDTsv: -

Paid: $_____

• Licensed by Disney.

Let's Give It A Spin

56441

2005^M - 2006

OSRP: $16.50

VDTsv: -

Paid: $_____

• Licensed by Mattel, Inc.™

I Hope The Train Comes Soon!

56782

2005^M - 2005

OSRP: *

VDTsv: *

* The accessory contained in North Star Commuter Train Station.

Let Me Make You A White Christmas

56787

2005^M - 2005

OSRP: *

VDTsv: *

* The accessory contained in Frosty's Christmas Weather Station.

An Igloo For Snowball

56878
2005^M - 2006
OSRP: $12
VDTsv: -
Paid: $_____

The Heavier The Better!

56879
2005^M - 2006
OSRP: $5
VDTsv: -
Paid: $_____
• Elf Land™.

Christmas Around The World — Germany

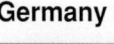

57200
2005 - 2007
OSRP: $25
VDTsv: -
Paid: $_____
• Christmas Around The World Series.

Polar Bear Taxi Service

57201
2005 - 2007
OSRP: $25
VDTsv: -
Paid: $_____

Holiday Photo Card Hut

57202
2005 - 2007
OSRP: $17.50
VDTsv: -
Paid: $_____

North Pole Maintenance

57203
2005 - 2007
OSRP: $70
VDTsv: -
Paid: $_____
• Lighted and animated.

Making Each House, Checking It Twice

57204
2005 - 2006
OSRP: $17.50
VDTsv: -
Paid: $_____
• 30th Anniversary Series.
• Limited to year of production.

Board Game Fun

57205
2005 - 2007
OSRP: $16.50
VDTsv: -
Paid: $_____

Santa's Flight Planning Team

57206

2005 - 2007

OSRP: $20

VDTsv: -

Paid: $_____

• Originally titled Santa's Weather Forecasting Team.

Just The Right Size, Santa!

57209

2005 - 2007

OSRP: $12.50

VDTsv: -

Paid: $_____

A Well Deserved Reindeer Massage

57210

2005 - 2008

OSRP: $18.50

VDTsv: -

Paid: $_____

Road Trip!

57211

2005 -2007

OSRP: $18.50

VDTsv: -

Paid: $_____

Mrs. Claus' Perfect Poinsettias

57212

2005 - 2007

OSRP: $15

VDTsv: -

Paid: $_____

Wee Deliver Groceries

57213

2005 - 2007

OSRP: $15

VDTsv: -

Paid: $_____

• Elf Land™.

Countdown To Christmas Mission Control

57214

2006M - 2007

OSRP: $17.50

VDTsv: -

Paid: $_____

Christmas Gifts From Elmo

57216

2006M - 2008

OSRP: $18.50

VDTsv: -

Paid: $_____

Ice Races Today!

57217

2006M - 2007

OSRP: $45

VDTsv: -

Paid: $_____

• Elves race cars around ice rink

Santa's New Sleigh

56950

2006 - 2007

OSRP: $110

VDTsv: -

Paid: $_____

•Set of 2.

Santa's New Sleigh — Design #56

57218

2006 - 2008

OSRP: $15

VDTsv: -

Paid: $_____

• Accessory Contained in "Santa's Sleigh Maker."

Mickey Approved!

57219

2006 -

OSRP: $22.50

VDTsv: -

Paid: $_____

• Licensed by Disney.

Earning Their Stripes

57220

2006 - 2009

OSRP: $22.50

VDTsv: -

Paid: $_____

Hope This Is The Correct Replacement Bulb

57221

2006 - 2008

OSRP: $12.50

VDTsv: -

Paid: $_____

Christmas Carol Rehearsal

57222

2006 - 2008

OSRP: $20

VDTsv: -

Paid: $_____

Christmas Bell Choir

57224

2006 - 2008

OSRP: $20

VDTsv: -

Paid: $_____

No Two Alike

57225

2006 - 2008

OSRP: $15

VDTsv: -

Paid: $_____

Breaking The Bank

57226

2006 - 2008

OSRP: $12.50

VDTsv: -

Paid: $_____

Christmas Around The World — Scandinavia

57227

2006 - 2008

OSRP: $25

VDTsv: -

Paid: $_____

Hide 'N Seek

57228

2006 -

OSRP: $18.50

VDTsv: -

Paid: $_____

I Can Almost Reach It

56960

2007M - 2007

OSRP: $99

VDTsv: -

Paid: $_____
• Set of 2.
• Limited To Year Of Production.
• Accessory Contained in "Christmasland Tree Toppers."

Teddy Bear's Truck Ride

57229

2007M - 2008

OSRP: $12.50

VDTsv: -

Paid: $_____

Moving Day

57230

2007M - 2008

OSRP: $15

VDTsv: -

Paid: $_____

Flight Training

57232

2007 -

OSRP: $55

VDTsv: -

Paid: $_____

Duck, Duck, Gray Duck

799906
2007 - 2009
OSRP: $12.50
VDTsv: -
Paid: $_____

A Puzzling Sign

799952
2007 - 2009
OSRP: $22.50
VDTsv: -
Paid: $_____

The Little Ballerina

799953
2007 -
OSRP: $17.50
VDTsv: -
Paid: $_____

Bringing Home The Tree

799954
2007 - 2009
OSRP: $17.50
VDTsv: -
Paid: $_____

Karaoke Night

799955
2007 - 2008
OSRP: $17.50
VDTsv: -
Paid: $_____

Motorcycle Test

799956
2007 - 2009
OSRP: $17.50
VDTsv: -
Paid: $_____

Polar Carving

799957
2007 - 2008
OSRP: $20
VDTsv: -
Paid: $_____

The Truck Works!

799958
2007 -
OSRP: $18.50
VDTsv: -
Paid: $_____

Welcome To The North Pole

799959

2007 -

OSRP: $17.50

VDTsv: -

Paid: $_____

Christmas Around The World — Hawaii

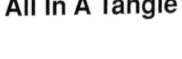

799960

2007 - 2009

OSRP: $25

VDTsv: -

Paid: $_____

Up North Outhouse

800009

2007 -

OSRP: $22.50

VDTsv: -

Paid: $_____

All In A Tangle

799997

2008M - 2008

OSRP: $79

VDTsv: -

Paid: $_____
• Set of 2
• Limited To Year Of Production.
• Accessory Contained in Brite Lites Bulb Factory."

Time For A Tune-Up!

804450

2008M - 2008

OSRP: $18.50

VDTsv: -

Paid: $_____
• Accessory Contained in "Robbie's Robot Factory."

Dasher

804451

2008M -

OSRP: $20

VDTsv: -

Paid: $_____
• Accessory for Reindeer Barn

Dancer

804452

2008M -

OSRP: $20

VDTsv: -

Paid: $_____

• Accessory for Reindeer Barn

Polar Pizza, Never Cold

804460

2008M - 2009

OSRP: $22.50

VDTsv: -

Paid: $_____

• Accessory Contained in "Hatly Hall."

Dressing Up With Tink

802826

2008 -

OSRP: $22.50

VDTsv: -

Paid: $_____

Gifts From Santa & Mrs. Clause

807235

2008 -

OSRP: $27.50

VDTsv: -

Paid: $_____

Prancer

807236

2008 -

OSRP: $20

VDTsv: -

Paid: $_____

Vixen

807237

2008 -

OSRP: $20

VDTsv: -

Paid: $_____

You Want Fries With That?

807238

2008 -

OSRP: $20

VDTsv: -

Paid: $_____

Too Good To Resist

807239

2008 -

OSRP: $30

VDTsv: -

Paid: $_____

The Snowboard Artist

807240

2008 -

OSRP: $20

VDTsv: -

Paid: $_____

The North Pole Curling Team

807241

2008 -

OSRP: $32.50

VDTsv: -

Paid: $_____

Hooked A Big One!

807242

2008 -

OSRP: $20

VDTsv: -

Paid: $_____

Christmas Around The World — China

807243

2008 - 2009

OSRP: $30

VDTsv: -

Paid: $_____

Packing The Gifts

807244

2008 -

OSRP: $25

VDTsv: -

Paid: $_____

Penguin Parade

805547

2009^M - 2009

OSRP: $79

VDTsv: -

Paid: $_____
• Set of 3. • Limited To Year Of Production.
• Accessory Contained in "North Pole Penguin's Visitor Center."

Best Dressed Snowman

808927

2010 -

OSRP: $27.50

VDTsv: -

Paid: $_____

Naughty Stocking Stuffers

808930

2010 -

OSRP: $25

VDTsv: -

Paid: $_____

Girls Night Out

808931

2010 -

OSRP: $20

VDTsv: -

Paid: $_____

Basket Weaving 101

808932

2010 -

OSRP: $22.50

VDTsv: -

Paid: $_____

Fixing Frozen Pipes

809460
2010 -
OSRP: $17.50
VDTsv: -
Paid: $_____

Comet

811777
2010 -
OSRP: $20
VDTsv: -
Paid: $_____

Cupid

811778
2010 -
OSRP: $20
VDTsv: -
Paid: $_____

Notes:

Notes:

Several buildings and accessories have been produced
within the North Pole Series.

These General Village pieces can be used by themselves
or in combination with those items.

Pole Pine Forest
$48   55271
1991 - 1998

Pole Pine Tree, Sm
$10   55280
1991 - 1998

Pole Pine Tree, Lg
$12.50   55298
1991 - 1998

Elves On Ice
$9   52298
1996 - 2000

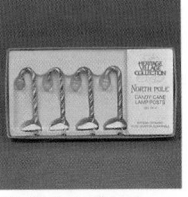
North Pole Candy
Cane Lampposts
$13   52621
1996 - 2001^M

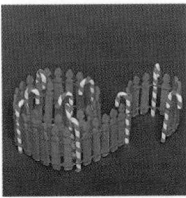
Candy Cane Fence
$8.50   52664
1997 -

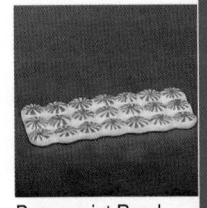
Peppermint Road
(Straight Section)
$5   52666
1997 -

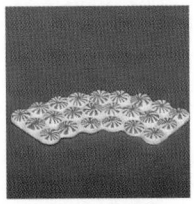
Peppermint Road
(Curved Section)
$5   52667
1997 -

Candy Cane Bench
$6   52669
1997 -

Downhill Elves
$9   56439
1998 - 2000

Holiday Cobblestone
Road
$10   56447
1999 - 2001

Peppermint Trees
$17.50   56721
1999 - 2003

Elves On Track
$10   56714
1999 - 2001

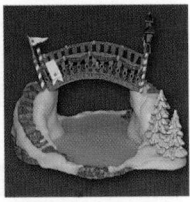
Bridge Over The Icy
Pond
$40   56720
1999 - 2002

Gumdrop Street
Lamps
$20   52871
2000 - 2001

Green Glitter Sisal Trees
$17.50   52902
2000 - 2001

North Pole Backdrop
$45   52962
2001 - 2002

Gumdrop Street Lamp, s/4
$18   52966
2001 - 2008

Gumdrop Tree w/LED Lights, 9 inch
$25   52967
2001 - 2007

Gumdrop Tree Non-Lit, 9"
$12   52968
2001 - 2004

Gumdrop Tree Non-Lit, 12"
$15   52969
2001 - 2003

Tinsel Ball Trees, s/5
$15   52971
2001 - 2004

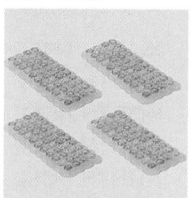
Village Gumdrop Road, s/4
$10   52978
2001 - 2006

Peppermint Landscape Set, s/7
$35   52991
2001 - 2003

Peppermint Trees s/2
$15   53011
2001 - 2003

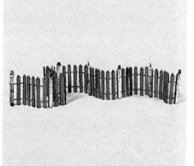
Faces Of The Season Picket Fence
$42.50   53029
2002^M -2004

North Pole Animated Train With Track, s/7
$42.50   53030
2002^M - 2003

Village Peppermint Sign
$7.50   53114
2003 - 2005

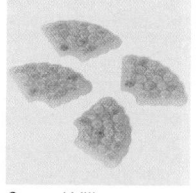
Curved Village Gumdrop Road, s/4
$10   53135
2003 - 2006

Gumdrop Topiaries, s/2
$12.50   53195
2004 - 2006

M&M'S Tree
$15   53196
2004 - 2006

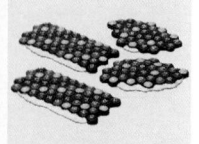
M&M'S Road, s/4
$12.50   53199
2004 - 2006

M&M'S Fun On Ice
$45   56440
2005^M - 2006

Gumdrop Pine Trees, s/2
$20   53614
2005 - 2008

Replacement 3 Volt Red & Green Bulbs
$5   804457
2008^M -

Small Collections

While most village collections seem to almost grow by leaps and bounds, there are a few that have followed a very different pattern. These small series were over almost as soon as they began, while two continuing collections are growing slowly.

Meadowland is a series of ceramic pieces that debuted — and retired — three years after Snow Village first appeared. It is the first instance of a village intended to be displayed other than during the winter.

Introduced in 1994, Disney Parks Village™ Series excited both village collectors and Disney fans with its reproductions of buildings from Orlando's Disney World and Anaheim's Disneyland. But within two years the relationship between the two companies abruptly ended.

Seasons Bay debuted in 1998 with six special first edition buildings and a series of seasonal accessories. The smaller pewter figures were created in scale to the buildings, a first for Department 56. A number of general accessories rounded out this Victorian village that retired after four years.

North Pole Woods™ began in 2000 and was produced for less than three years. It was treated by both Department 56 and collectors as a stepchild to the more popular North Pole Series™ and never seemed to acquire its own identity.

The two continuing series are the Historical Landmark Series® and Literary Classics®. Each had its roots within other Heritage Villages. The Literary Classics® pieces all include a building, accessory, and a copy of the book. Historical Landmarks® include several London structures as well as familiar American buildings.

New in this Second Edition, The Holy Land™ Collection has been moved to the Small Collections section. Since it was retired in 2006, we believe Small Collections is now a more appropriate location for the collection.

THE HISTORICAL LANDMARK SERIES™

Initial pieces were originally classified as part of Dickens' Village Series®. This varied series depicts some of the most well-known buildings in the world.

Tower Of London   58500

Dates	OSRP	VDTsv	Paid
1997ᴹ - 1997	$165	$100 - $345	$_____

- Limited to year of production.
- This, the White Tower, is one of the many towers that comprise the Tower of London, famous for housing a prison as well as the Crown Jewels. Legend says six ravens must be at the tower to preserve the monarchy.
- The actual Tower of London is located along the Thames River in London.
- Set of 5 includes the Tower, a gate with tower, the raven master, a sign, and a wall with ravens.

The Old Globe Theatre   58501

Dates	OSRP	VDTsv	Paid
1997 - 1998	$175	$138 - $139	$_____

- Limited to year of production.
- First samples of the building were made as two pieces. For production, it is one piece.
- Some early shipments have "The City Globe" stamped on the bottom.
- The Globe Theatre, located along the Thames River in London, was demolished in 1644 and was rebuilt in 1996 near the original site.

- Set of 4 includes the Theatre, two trumpeters, and a sign.

Independence Hall   55500

Dates	OSRP	VDTsv	Paid
1998 - 2000ᴹ	$110	$70 - $85	$_____

- This replica of Philadelphia's Independence Hall was first Historical Landmark not associated with England.
- First available during the 1999 July event.
- Set of 2 includes Hall and sign.

Big Ben
58341

Dates	OSRP	VDTsv	Paid
1998 - 2003	$95	$100 - $138	$_____

- It features a working clock on one of its faces. The other three read "5 of 6."
- It is a replica of London's Big Ben along the Thames River.
- Set of 2 includes Big Ben and sign.

The Old Royal Observatory Gold Dome Edition
58451

Dates	OSRP	VDTsv	Paid
1999 - 2000	Promo	$336	$_____

- Limited to 5,500, Department 56 sent one to its valued retailers as a thank you for their support.

The Old Royal Observatory
58453

Dates	OSRP	VDTsv	Paid
1999 - 2000	$95	$60	$_____

- Limited to 35,000.
- This is a replica of the Old Royal Observatory in Greenwich, England which keeps the world's time.
- Set of 2 includes Observatory and sign.

Cathedral Of St. Paul
58919

Dates	OSRP	VDTsv	Paid
2001ᴹ - 2001	$150	$529 - $535	$_____

- Replica of Cathedral of St. Paul in St. Paul, MN.
- Copper-colored roof.
- Only available at Dept. 56 25th Anniversary celebration.
- Christmas In The City bottomstamp. DV logo on box.

Cathedral Of St. Paul
58930

Dates	OSRP	VDTsv	Paid
2001 - 2005	$150	$529	$_____

- Re-issue of the copper colored roof version that was available at the Dept. 56 25th Anniversary celebration.
- Also designated as a Christmas In The City design.

Temple Bar
58564

Dates	OSRP	VDTsv	Paid
2002 - 2003	$60	$60 - $78	$_____

- This is a replica of a gate that once stood in London and is now on private property.
- Also designated as a Dickens' Village accessory.

Central Synagogue 59204

Dates	OSRP	VDTsv	Paid
2002 - 2003	**$110**	**$110 - $198**	$____

- Limited to year of production.
- This is a replica of Central Synagogue in New York City.
- Also designated as a Christmas In The City design.

Empire State Building 59207

Dates	OSRP	VDTsv	Paid
2003ᴹ - 2005	**$185**	**$185**	$____

- This is a replica of the Empire State Building in Manhattan.
- At 23 inches, this is the tallest building manufactured by Department 56.
- Features several holiday lighting effects, including different colors in detachable top section.
- Four American flags are separate in box.
- Also designated as a Christmas In The City design.

Tower Bridge Of London 58705

Dates	OSRP	VDTsv	Paid
2003 - 2004	**$165**	**$175**	$____

- Numbered limited edition of 20,000.
- Dickens' Village 20th Anniversary Series. Includes pin.
- It is a replica of London's Tower Bridge.
- Set of 4.

Historic Chicago Water Tower 59209

Dates	OSRP	VDTsv	Paid
2003 - 2006	**$65**	-	$____

- Set of 2 includes Tower and sign.
- This is a replica of the Chicago Water Tower, one of the few buildings to survive the great Chicago fire of 1871.
- Also designated as a Christmas In The City design.

Windsor Castle 58720

Dates	OSRP	VDTsv	Paid
2004 - 2007	**$95**	**$158**	$____

- This lighted facade is a replica of the world's largest occupied castle.
- Also designated as a Dickens' Village design.

Tower Bridge Of London

58721

Dates	OSRP	VDTsv	Paid
2004 - 2006	$135	-	$_____

- Re-issue of the limited edition that was issued in 2003.
- Also designated as a Dickens' Village design.

Guarding The Castle

58594

Dates	OSRP	VDTsv	Paid
2004 - 2006	$17.50	$33	$_____

- Also designated as a Dickens' Village design.

Golden Gate Bridge

59241

Dates	OSRP	VDTsv	Paid
2004 - 2006	$120	-	$_____

- Also designated as a Christmas In The City design.
- Replica of the famous bridge in California.

Notre Dame Cathedral, Paris

57601

Dates	OSRP	VDTsv	Paid
2005^M - 2005	-	-	$_____

- Collectors' Edition.

Brooklyn Bridge

59247

Dates	OSRP	VDTsv	Paid
2005^M - 2006	$120	-	$_____

- Also designated as a Christmas In The City design.
- Replica of the famous bridge in New York.

Baltimore Arts Tower

59246

Dates	OSRP	VDTsv	Paid
2005^M - 2008	$65	-	$_____

- Also designated as a Christmas In The City design.

Buckingham Palace

58736

Dates	OSRP	VDTsv	Paid
2005 - 2006	**$125**	-	**$____**

• Numbered Limited Edition of 12,000.
• Set of 4 includes the Palace, "Household Guards" set of 2 accessory, and front gate.
• Replica of Buckingham Palace in London.
• Also designated as a Dickens' Village design.

Victoria & Albert Museum

799992

Dates	OSRP	VDTsv	Paid
2008^M - 2008	**$125**	-	**$____**

• Collectors' Edition.
• Limited Edition of 9,000.
• Also designated as a Dickens' Village design.

Notes:

LITERARY CLASSICS® COLLECTION

These designs are Department 56's interpretation of the buildings and characters that come to life in some of the literary world's most cherished works. Each set includes a specially printed copy of the classic in addition to a lit building and accessories which help to bring the stories to life. Other literary works have also been recognized in several of the villages, but none have been as comprehensive or detailed as these versions. Notice that none of the buildings have snow on them.

Great Expectations Satis Manor   58310

Dates	OSRP	VDTsv	Paid
1998 - 2001	$110	$77 - $80	$_____

- Charles Dickens used Restoration House in Rochester, England as the model for his Satis Manor.
- Set of 4 plus book includes the Manor and a 3 piece accessory "Miss Havisham, Estella, and Pip."

Little Women — The March Residence   56606

Dates	OSRP	VDTsv	Paid
1999ᴹ - 2000	$90	$83 - $90	$_____

- Louisa May Alcott based the March Residence on the Orchard House in Concord, MA. where she grew up.
- Set of 4 plus book includes the Residence and a 3 piece accessory "A Letter From Papa" which includes Marmie, Jo, Amy, Beth, and Meg.
- The water pump's handle is very fragile.

The Great Gatsby West Egg Mansion   58939

Dates	OSRP	VDTsv	Paid
1999 - 2001	**$135**	**$85**	$_____

- This is Department 56's interpretation of the Long Island mansion that F. Scott Fitzgerald depicted in his novel.
- Some pieces were shipped with extra statues in anticipation of breakage.
- Set of 4 plus book includes the Mansion, Jay Gatsby, Daisy Buchanan, and the infamous car.
- Licensed through the Fitzgerald Estate, LTD.

The Adventures Of Tom Sawyer,   58600
Aunt Polly's House

Dates	OSRP	VDTsv	Paid
2000ᴹ - 2001	**$90**	**$175**	$_____

- Inspired by Mark Twain's first book, this is a depiction of the home and characters made famous in the book.
- Set of 5 plus book includes the House, and a 4 piece accessory "Painting The White Picket Fence" which includes Tom Sawyer, two friends, and the fence.

Sherlock Holmes – 221B Baker Street   58601

Dates	OSRP	VDTsv	Paid
2000 - 2003	**$90**	**$220 - $345**	$_____

- Inspired by Arthur Conan Doyle's famous works, this is Department 56's interpretation of the home of England's greatest fictional detective.
- Set of 3 plus book includes the house and 2 piece accessory "Elementary My Dear Watson."

DISNEY PARKS VILLAGE™ SERIES

Available for less than two years, this series reproduced familiar buildings at the Disney theme parks. First year releases were more plentiful, while scarcity of later buildings resulted in higher aftermarket values.

Mickey's Christmas Carol (10 Points)   53503

Dates	OSRP	VDTsv	Paid
1994 - 1996	$144	$158 - $199	$_____

- This version has gold spires at the lower corners and peaks of the dormers.
- Replica of Disney World building.
- Set of 2 includes main building and outbuilding.
- Holiday Collection stamped piece (#07420) sold by Disney Parks has: **VDTsv: $485** $_____

(6 Points)   53503

	VDTsv	Paid
	$58	$_____

- Has no spires at the lower corners of the dormers.
- Holiday Collection has: **VDTsv: $295** $_____

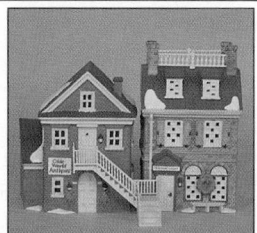

OLDE WORLD ANTIQUES SHOPS – Set of 2   53511

Dates	OSRP	VDTsv	Paid
1994 - 1996	$90	$98	$_____

- Holiday Collection stamped piece (#07429) sold by Disney Parks has: **VDTsv: $105** $_____

Olde World Antiques I   53511

Dates	OSRP	VDTsv	Paid
1994 - 1996	$45	$15 - $89	$_____

- A similar building is in Disney World's Liberty Square.
- Holiday Collection stamped piece (#07429) sold by Disney Parks has: **VDTsv: $105** $_____

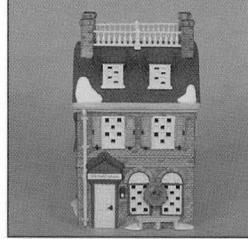

Olde World Antiques II   53511

Dates	OSRP	VDTsv	Paid
1994 - 1996	$45	$15 - $89	$_____

- A similar building is in Disney World's Liberty Square.
- Holiday Collection stamped piece (#07429) sold by Disney Parks has: **VDTsv: $105** $_____

Disneyland Fire Department #105 — 53520

Dates	OSRP	VDTsv	Paid
1994 - 1996	**$45**	**$69 - $150**	$_____

• Inspired by fire station on Main Street in Disneyland.
• Holiday Collection stamped piece (#07439) sold by Disney Parks has: **VDTsv: $150** $_____

Silversmith — 53521

Dates	OSRP	VDTsv	Paid
1995 - 1996	**$50**	**$98 - $236**	$_____

• Holiday Collection stamped piece (#07448) sold by Disney Parks has: **VDTsv: $108** $_____

Tinker Bell's Treasures — 53522

Dates	OSRP	VDTsv	Paid
1995 - 1996	**$60**	**$98 - $236**	$_____

• Holiday Collection stamped piece (#07449) sold by Disney Parks has: **VDTsv: $108** $_____

Mickey & Minnie

53538 - Set of 2
1994 - 1996
OSRP: $22.50
VDTsv: $18 - $39
Paid: $_____

Disney Parks Family

53546 - Set of 3
1994 - 1996
OSRP: $32.50
VDTsv: $10-$36
Paid: $_____

Olde World Antiques Gate

53554
1994 - 1996
OSRP: $15
VDTsv: $10 - $39
Paid: $_____

Balloon Seller

53539 - Set of 2
1995 - 1996
OSRP: $25
VDTsv: $23
Paid: $_____

NORTH POLE WOODS™ SERIES

Available for only three years, these life-in-a-forest pieces were incorporated by many collectors into their North Pole villages, while others treated it as a separate area. The accessories were more readily placed within the North Pole Series™ than the lighted trees.

Town Meeting Hall 56880

Dates	OSRP	VDTsv	Paid
2000ᴹ - 2002	$73	$50 - $83	$_____

• Adapter included.

Oakwood Post Office Branch 56881

Dates	OSRP	VDTsv	Paid
2000ᴹ - 2002	$70	$60	$_____

• Adapter included.
• Set of 2 includes Post Office and elf.

Reindeer Care & Repair 56882

Dates	OSRP	VDTsv	Paid
2000ᴹ - 2002	$65	$65 - $80	$_____

• Adapter included.

Trim-A-Tree Factory 56884

Dates	OSRP	VDTsv	Paid
2000ᴹ - 2001	$55	$50 - $65	$_____

• Adapter included.
• Set of 2 includes Factory and elf.

Santa's Retreat 56883

Dates	OSRP	VDTsv	Paid
2000 - 2002	$70	$68 - $70	$_____

• Early release to Parade of Gifts stores.
• Adapter included.
• Set of 2 includes tree and Mrs. Claus.

Rudolph's Condo

56885

Dates	OSRP	VDTsv	Paid
2000 - 2002	**$50**	**$52**	$_____

• Licensed by GTM&L.

Reindeer Condo

56886

Dates	OSRP	VDTsv	Paid
2000 - 2001	**$70**	**$70 - $80**	$_____

• Adapter included.
• Windsock separate in the box.

Chisel McTimber Art Studio

56887

Dates	OSRP	VDTsv	Paid
2001 - 2002	**$65**	**$130**	$_____

• Adapter included.
• Set of 2 includes tree and "Elf Sculpting" accessory.

Notes:

Welcome To North Pole Woods

Gateway Entrance

56920
2000^M - 2002
OSRP: $25
VDTsv: $18-$24
Paid: $_____

Tailored For You

56921 - Set of 2
2000^M - 2001
OSRP: $22.50
VDTsv: $23
Paid: $_____

• The snowman's arms are fragile.

Elves

56922 - Set of 4
2000^M - 2002
OSRP: $30
VDTsv: $30-$40
Paid: $_____

Scissors Wizards

56923 - Set of 2
2000^M - 2001
OSRP: $25
VDTsv: $25
Paid: $_____

• The reindeer's antlers are very fragile.

Nuts About Broomball

56926
2000^M - 2001^M
OSRP: $20
VDTsv: $20-$24
Paid: $_____

Birch Bench & Table

56927 - Set of 2
2000^M - 2001^M
OSRP: $9
VDTsv: $5
Paid: $_____

Pinecone Path

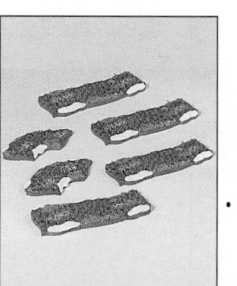

52874 - Set of 6
2000 - 2002
OSRP: $15
VDTsv: $22
Paid: $_____

• Straight and curved.

Acorn Street Lamps

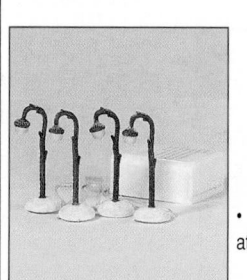

52875 - Set of 4
2000 - 2002
OSRP: $15
VDTsv: $12
Paid: $_____

• Battery / adapter operated.

Birch Bridge

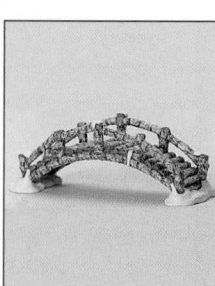

52876

2000 - 2002

OSRP: $13.50

VDTsv: $12

Paid: $_____

Birch Gazebo

52877

2000 - 2002

OSRP: $20

VDTsv: $18

Paid: $_____

• Weathervane is very fragile.

Birch Fence

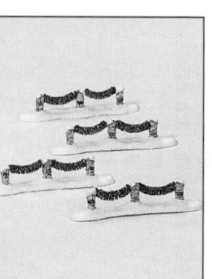

52878 - Set of 4

2000 - 2002

OSRP: $12

VDTsv: $10

Paid: $_____

Star Of The Show

56928

2000 - 2002

OSRP: $25

VDTsv: $20

Paid: $_____

• Licensed by Good-Times Merchandising & Licensing.

Polar Plowing Service

56929

2000 - 2002

OSRP: $30

VDTsv: $45

Paid: $_____

Gone Fishing

56930

2000 - 2002

OSRP: $35

VDTsv: $30

Paid: $_____

Ring Toss

56931 - Set of 2

2000 - 2002

OSRP: $17.50

VDTsv: $18

Paid: $_____

• Licensed by Good-Times Merchandising & Licensing.

Balancing Act

56932 - Set of 3

2000 - 2002

OSRP: $25

VDTsv: $25-$48

Paid: $_____

• The reindeer's antlers are very fragile.

SEASONS BAY® SERIES

For many years Department 56 was famed for creating winter villages. But many collectors wanted to display their pieces for more than just a few months each year, and Seasons Bay met that need. The buildings were exceptionally crafted, but what made them different was the fact that they all lacked snow.

It was not the buildings, though, that made this a truly unique village. It was the accessories. Set in the Victorian era, the collection featured people engaged in year-round activities. A variety of plants and trees reinforced the seasonal designs. Another unique feature was the diminutive size of the people. Accessories were created in pewter in order to present them in proportion to their residences. This is the only village in which this is true.

Grandview Shores Hotel (First Edition)   53300

Dates	OSRP	VDTsv	Paid
1998 - 1999	$150	$112	$_____

• This version is identified by its gold flags, weathervane, and First Edition decal on its bottom.

(Open Edition)   53400

Dates	OSRP	VDTsv	Paid
1998 - 2000	$150	$49 - $70	$_____

Bay Street Shops (First Edition)   53301

Dates	OSRP	VDTsv	Paid
1998 - 1999	$135	$101	$_____

• This version is identified by its gold flags and First Edition decal on its bottom.
• Set of 2 includes two buildings — Maggie's Millinery and Bayside Clothiers/Book Nook — that fit together.

(Open Edition)   53401

Dates	OSRP	VDTsv	Paid
1998 - 2002	$135	$62	$_____

• Set of 2 includes two buildings — Maggie's Millinery and Bayside Clothiers/Book Nook — that fit together.

Chapel On The Hill (First Edition)　　　　53302

Dates	OSRP	VDTsv	Paid
1998 - 1999	$72	$54	$_____

• This version is identified by its gold cross and First Edition decal on its bottom.

(Open Edition)　　　　53402

Dates	OSRP	VDTsv	Paid
1998 - 2001	$72	$46	$_____

Side Porch Café (First Edition)　　　　53303

Dates	OSRP	VDTsv	Paid
1998 - 1999	$50	$52	$_____

• This version is identified by the First Edition decal on its bottom.

(Open Edition)　　　　53403

Dates	OSRP	VDTsv	Paid
1998 - 2002	$50	$36	$_____

Inglenook Cottage #5 (First Edition)　　　　53304

Dates	OSRP	VDTsv	Paid
1998 - 1999	$60	$45	$_____

• This version is identified by the First Edition decal on its bottom.

(Open Edition)　　　　53404

Dates	OSRP	VDTsv	Paid
1998 - 2000	$60	$38	$_____

The Grand Creamery (First Edition)   53305

Dates	OSRP	VDTsv	Paid
1998 - 1999	$60	$45	$_____

• This version is identified by its gold flag and First Edition decal on its bottom.

(Open Edition)   53405

Dates	OSRP	VDTsv	Paid
1998 - 2001	$60	$32	$_____

Parkside Pavilion   53411

Dates	OSRP	VDTsv	Paid
1999 - 2002	$65	$50 - $88	$_____

• Set of 2 includes the Pavilion and fountain.

Parkside Pavilion Gift Set   53412

Dates	OSRP	VDTsv	Paid
1999 - 2000	$75	$56 - $58	$_____

• Available during the 2000 Spring Discover Department 56 event.
• Set of 9 includes the Pavilion, a 4 piece accessory "Art Classes At Morning's Light," and stick-on floral arrangements.

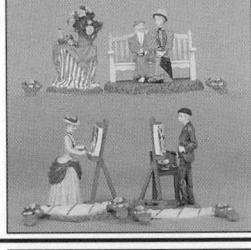

Springlake Station   53413

Dates	OSRP	VDTsv	Paid
1999 - 2002	$90	$165	$_____

• Early shipments had "filled-in" windows. Later shipments had the bottom half of the windows cut-out.
• Clock and 4 potted plants are separate in box.

Stillwaters Boathouse

53414

Dates	OSRP	VDTsv	Paid
1999 - 2002	$70	$137	$____

• Weathervane separate in box.

Mystic Ledge Lighthouse

53445

Dates	OSRP	VDTsv	Paid
2000ᴹ - 2000	$96	$168	$____

• Limited Edition – 5,600 pieces.

Garden Valley Vineyards

53446

Dates	OSRP	VDTsv	Paid
2000 - 2001	$125	$135	$____

• 25th Anniversary Limited Edition of 5,600.

Breezy Hill Stables

53447

Dates	OSRP	VDTsv	Paid
2000 - 2002	$68	$225	$____

• Weathervane and potted plant are separate in box.

East Cape Cottages

53448

Dates	OSRP	VDTsv	Paid
2000 - 2002	$95	$372	$____

• Set of 2.
• Do not handle by railings or columns.
• Ladders are very fragile.
• Boats are easily damaged.

Seaside Inn
53449

Dates	OSRP	VDTsv	Paid
2001^M - 2002	$68	$85	$_____

• Weathervane and potted plant are separate in box.

Bayport Souvenir And Kite Shop
53450

Dates	OSRP	VDTsv	Paid
2001 - 2002	$60	$175	$_____

• Pilings and fence are fragile.

SEASONS BAY ACCESSORIES

Relaxing In A Garden

53307 - Set of 3
1998 - 2001
OSRP: $25
VDTsv: $19
Paid: $_____

• Spring

A Stroll In The Park

53308 - Set of 5
1998 - 2002
OSRP: $25
VDTsv: $24
Paid: $_____

• Spring

I'm Wishing

53309
1998 - 2001^M
OSRP: $13
VDTsv: $10
Paid: $_____

• Spring

Sunday Morning At The Chapel

53311 - Set of 2
1998 - 2001
OSRP: $17
VDTsv: $17
Paid: $_____

• Spring

Fishing In The Bay

53313
1998 - 2002
OSRP: $13
VDTsv: $10
Paid: $_____
• Summer

Here Comes The Ice Cream Man

53314 - Set of 4
1998 - 2002
OSRP: $35
VDTsv: $26
Paid: $_____
• Summer

4th Of July Parade

53317 - Set of 5
1998 - 2002
OSRP: $32.50
VDTsv: $33
Paid: $_____
• Summer

Trick Or Treat

53319 - Set of 4
1998 - 2002
OSRP: $25
VDTsv: $19
Paid: $_____
• Fall

Back From The Orchard

53320
1998 - 2001
OSRP: $27.50
VDTsv: $21
Paid: $_____
• Fall

Afternoon Sleigh Ride

53322
1998 - 2001^M
OSRP: $27.50
VDTsv: $6
Paid: $_____
• Winter

Fun In The Snow

53323 - Set of 2
1998- 2001^M
OSRP: $15
VDTsv: $3
Paid: $_____
• Winter

Skating On The Pond

53324 - Set of 2
1998 - 2002
OSRP: $20
VDTsv: $18
Paid: $_____
• Winter

A Day At The Waterfront

53326 - Set of 2

1998 - 2002

OSRP: $20

VDTsv: $20

Paid: $_____

• Summer

The Garden Cart

53327

1998 - 2002

OSRP: $27.50

VDTsv: $21

Paid: $_____

• Spring

Art Classes At Morning's Light

53412 - Set of 4

1999 - 2000

OSRP: *

VDTsv: *

* Accessory contained in the 1999 Parkside Pavilion Gift Set.

The Garden Swing

53415

1999 - 2002

OSRP: $13

VDTsv: $10

Paid: $_____

• Spring

Arriving At The Station

53416 - Set of 5

1999 - 2002

OSRP: $32.50

VDTsv: $30

Paid: $_____

• Spring

The Perfect Wedding

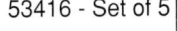

53417 - Set of 7

1999 - 2002

OSRP: $25

VDTsv: $25

Paid: $_____

• Summer
• Includes the book Wedding Customs And Keepsakes.

Gently Down The Stream

53418

1999 - 2002

OSRP: $25

VDTsv: $22

Paid: $_____

• Summer

A Grand Day Of Fishing

53419

1999 - 2002

OSRP: $25

VDTsv: $24

Paid: $_____

• Summer

An Afternoon Picnic

53420 - Set of 3

1999 - 2002

OSRP: $18

VDTsv: $18

Paid: $_____

• Fall

A Bicycle Built For Two

53421

1999 - 2002

OSRP: $17.50

VDTsv: $15

Paid: $_____

• Fall

Rocking Chair Readers

53422

1999 - 2002

OSRP: $15

VDTsv: $15

Paid: $_____

• Fall

Lifeguard On Duty

53423

1999 - 2002

OSRP: $20

VDTsv: $18

Paid: $_____

• Summer

A Day Of Holiday Shopping

53425 - Set of 3

1999 - 2002

OSRP: $25

VDTsv: $24

Paid: $_____

• Winter

The First Snow

53426

1999 - 2002

OSRP: $15

VDTsv: $15

Paid: $_____

• Winter

Singing Carols In Town

53427

1999 - 2002

OSRP: $22.50

VDTsv: $20

Paid: $_____

• Winter

Pull Together

53600

2000 - 2002

OSRP: $35

VDTsv: $34

Paid: $_____

• Summer

Evening Of Horseback Riding

53601 - Set of 2

2000 - 2002

OSRP: $30

VDTsv: $30

Paid: $_____

• Summer

Gathering Grapes

53602 - Set of 2

2000 - 2001

OSRP: $25

VDTsv: $25

Paid: $_____

• Fall

A Sleigh Ride With Santa

53603 - Set of 2

2000 - 2002

OSRP: $35

VDTsv: $35

Paid: $_____

• Winter

Fresh Seafood By The Shore

53604

2000 - 2002

OSRP: $27.50

VDTsv: $28

Paid: $_____

• Summer

The Kite of Spring

53608

2001 - 2002

OSRP: $12

VDTsv: $15

Paid: $_____

• Spring

Seasons Bay Flag Raising

53611

2001 - 2002

OSRP: $12.50

VDTsv: $15

Paid: $_____

• Spring

Notes:

Mini Sisal Evergreens
Set of 12
$13   52763
1998 - 2002

Garden Fountain
Set of 9
$40   53330
1998 - 2001

Potted Flowers8
Assorted
$12.50   53331
1998 - 2001^M

Flowering Potted Tree
- 2 Assorted
$20   53332
1998 - 2001

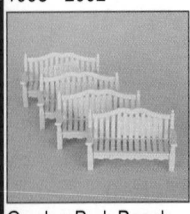

Garden Park Bench
Set of 4
$12   53333
1998 - 2001^M

Planter Box Topiaries
- Set of 4
$15   53334
1998 - 2001^M

Garden Gazebo
$15   53338
1998 - 2002

Seasons Bay Sign
$7   53343
1998 - 2001

Flowering Vine
2 Assorted
$20   53344
1998 - 2001

Geranium Window
Box
$12   53345
1998 - 2001

Beach Front
Set of 3
$15   53355
1998 - 2001

Park Street Lights
Set of 4
$15   53366
1998 - 2002

Potted Topiaries
Set of 4
$11   53370
1998 - 2001^M

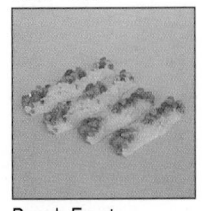

Beach Front
Extensions - Set of 4
$15   53374
1998 - 2001

Stone Footpath
Sections - Set of 12
$15   53375
1998 - 2002

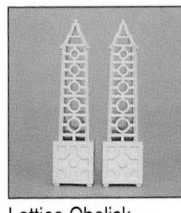

Lattice Obelisk
Set of 2
$6   53376
1998 - 2001^M

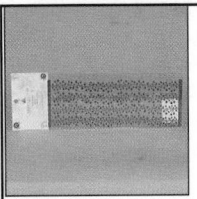

Ivy Vine
Set of 4
$7.50   53377
1998 - 2001^M

Spring/Summer Trees
- Set of 4
$24   53382
1998 - 2001

Autumn Trees
Set of 4
$24   53383
1998 - 2001

Winter Trees
Set of 4
$24   53384
1998 - 2001

Amusement Park
Carousel
$75   53410
1999 - 2002

Seasons Bay Park
Set of 8
$70   53428
1999 - 2002

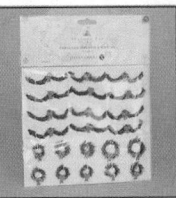

Christmas Garlands
& Wreaths - Set of 14
$10   53429
1999 - 2002

Sandy Beach
$6   53433
1999 - 2001

Adirondack Chairs
Set of 4
$10   53436
1999 - 2002

Harvest Decorations
Set of 12
$22.50   53431
2000^M - 2002

Patriotic Decorations
Set of 7
$12   53605
2000 - 2002

AMERICAN PRIDE™ COLLECTION

This collection was available to collectors through all D56 retailers. Strictly speaking, it was not considered a village, even though many collectors added the pieces to their village collections. According to D56, the original intent for the facades was to enable displays on shelving units.

The White House
57701

Dates	OSRP	VDTsv	Paid
2001 - 2005	$75	$275 - $279	$_____

The Lincoln Memorial
57702

Dates	OSRP	VDTsv	Paid
2001 - 2005	$65	$340 - $345	$_____

The Jefferson Memorial
57704

Dates	OSRP	VDTsv	Paid
2001 - 2005	$65	$228 - $239	$_____

American Pride Backdrop
57705

Dates	OSRP	VDTsv	Paid
2001 - 2004	$45	-	$_____

Ellis Island
57713

Dates	OSRP	VDTsv	Paid
2002 - 2005	$75	$75	$_____

Lady Liberty
57714

Dates	OSRP	VDTsv	Paid
2002 - 2003	$50	$90	$_____

Fireman's Memorial Monument
57707

Dates	OSRP	VDTsv	Paid
2002 - 2003	$50	$115	$_____

Statue of Liberty
57708

Dates	OSRP	VDTsv	Paid
2002 - 2005	$65	$65	$_____

9/11 Memorial
57712

Dates	OSRP	VDTsv	Paid
2002 - 2003	$75	$58	$_____

World Trade Center Memorial
91101

Dates	OSRP	VDTsv	Paid
2002 - 2002	$35	$50	$_____

Mount Rushmore
57715

Dates	OSRP	VDTsv	Paid
2003 - 2005	$65	$98	$_____

MEADOWLAND

This "non-winter" series was short-lived. Made of ceramic, it is considered by many collectors to be a companion series to the Original Snow Village®.

Thatched Cottage   50500

Dates	OSRP	VDTsv	Paid
1979 - 1980	$30	$400	$_____

Countryside Church   50518

Dates	OSRP	VDTsv	Paid
1979 - 1980	$25	$425	$_____

• This is a snowless version of the Snow Village 1979 Countryside Church.

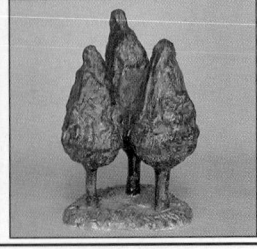

Aspen Trees   50526

Dates	OSRP	VDTsv	Paid
1979 - 1980	$16	$110	$_____

Sheep   50534

Dates	OSRP	VDTsv	Paid
1979 - 1980	$12	$60	$_____

• Set of 12 includes 9 white and 3 black sheep.

Notes:

WINTERS FROST

This is the most "winter" of all the villages and one of the most recent. Each of these buildings and its related trees and accessories is included on a single base. It's a "display in a box." Each box includes an adaptor.

Wooddale Church   809027

Dates	OSRP	VDTsv	Paid
2008 -	$99	–	$_____

Nicollet House   809028

Dates	OSRP	VDTsv	Paid
2008 -	$99	–	$_____

Calhoun House   809029

Dates	OSRP	VDTsv	Paid
2008 -	$99	–	$_____

Frosty Retreat   809458

Dates	OSRP	VDTsv	Paid
2009 -	$99	–	$_____

Winters Light   809459

Dates	OSRP	VDTsv	Paid
2009 -	$99	–	$_____

CARNIVAL

These Carnival pieces can be used by themselves or in combination with other villages.

The Red Ruby
Carousel
$85   53801
2004 - 2007

The Golden Vine
Ferris Wheel
$85   53802
2004 - 2007

Twirling Tea Cups
$75   53803
2004 - 2007

Ball Toss At The
Carnival
$20   53804
2004 - 2006

Family Day At The
Carnival, s/2
$18.50   53805
2004 - 2006

Flying High Space
Planes
$55   53806
2005^M - 2006

THE HOLY LAND™ COLLECTION

Originally a separate collection, Little Town of Bethlehem became one of the series within the Holy Land Collection. This umbrella collection also included the Easter series and the Parables From The Holy Land.

Department 56 originally created its version of the Nativity story in 1987. A self-contained set of 12, including three buildings and the primary characters, was released in porcelain and remained unchanged for a dozen years. In keeping with the tale and life of the time, the buildings were simple stone and brick structures.

In 1999 the set was retired, but within weeks new releases were announced. Collectors could purchase individual buildings and accessories that would complement the original set, or begin their Nativity scene using just the new pieces. The new accessories were crafted in resin, rather than porcelain, enabling the designs to be more detailed.

The new pieces not only augmented the original series with historical pieces such as Herod's Temple but have also added brilliantly crafted buildings like the Rug Merchant's Colonnade and accessories featuring people and animals in a desert camp and oasis, as well as in routine daily activities.

In 2006, the remaining pieces in this collection were retired.

Little Town Of Bethlehem Series

Little Town Of Bethlehem

59757

Dates	OSRP	VDTsv	Paid
1987 - 1999	$150	$119 - $225	$_____

- The early pieces have a small amount of snow on the manger's right wall. The later ones do not.
- Set of 12 includes manger with Jesus, inn, marketplace, Joseph, Mary, 3 wise men, shepherd with sheep, camel, cow and sheep, a donkey, and cypress trees.
- For the first four years of production, a sheep stood next to the cow. From 1991 through 1999, the sheep was not included.

Innkeeper's Caravansary

59795

Dates	OSRP	VDTsv	Paid
1999 - 2003	$70	$91 - $176	$_____

Gatekeeper's Dwelling

59797

Dates	OSRP	VDTsv	Paid
1999 - 2001	$55	$87 - $158	$_____

Nativity

59796

Dates	OSRP	VDTsv	Paid
1999 - 2006	**$55**	**$98 - $115**	$_____

- Set of 2 includes the building and Joseph, Mary, and Jesus accessory.
- This set is also included as part of the Gift Set, Holy Night Nativity, in 2002.

Herod's Temple

59799

Dates	OSRP	VDTsv	Paid
2000 - 2001	**$150**	**$169 - $225**	$_____

- 25th Anniversary Limited Edition of 5,600.
- Set of 5 includes Temple, 2 piece accessory "High Priests," gate, and vinyl ancient stone courtyard.

Carpenter's Shop

59801

Dates	OSRP	VDTsv	Paid
2000 - 2002	**$72**	**$395**	$_____

- Set of 3 includes Shop and 2 piece accessory "Carpenter & Son."

Rug Merchant's Colonnade

59802

Dates	OSRP	VDTsv	Paid
2000 - 2005	**$110**	**$148 - $189**	**$_____**

• Set of 4 includes Colonnade, 2 piece accessory "Rug Merchant & Wool Spinner," and ladder.

Small Collections

Caravansary Corner

59806

Dates	OSRP	VDTsv	Paid
2001 - 2003	**$75**	**$90 - $140**	**$_____**

• Set of 2 includes building and man.

Caravansary Rooms at the Inn

59807

Dates	OSRP	VDTsv	Paid
2001 - 2003	**$110**	**$295**	**$_____**

• Set of 3 includes building and two figurines.

Holy Night Nativity

05837

Dates	OSRP	VDTsv	Paid
2002^M - 2002	$85	$90	$_____

- Department store exclusive.
- Limited to year of production.
- Set of 6 is the combination of Nativity, "Wise Men From The East" accessory, and "Palm Trees."

Potter's Shop

59812

Dates	OSRP	VDTsv	Paid
2002 - 2005	$65	$75	$_____

- Set of 2 includes building and "Pottery Craftsman" accessory.

The Birth Of Christ Nativity Set

59816

Dates	OSRP	VDTsv	Paid
2003 - 2006	$75	$295	$_____

- Set of 11 includes the manger, the Holy Family, the wise men, and animals.

Notes:

The Easter Story Series

House Of The Last Supper Gift Set — 59809

Dates	OSRP	VDTsv	Paid
2001 - 2004	**$65**	$	$_____

- First available during the 2002 Spring Discover Dept. 56 event.
- Set of 2 includes building and "Palm Sunday" accessory.

Tower Of David — 59810

Dates	OSRP	VDTsv	Paid
2002ᴹ - 2004	**$75**	**$96**	$_____

- Set of 3 includes Tower and 2 piece accessory, "Tower Guard & Garden Archway" and scroll.

Church Of The Holy Sepulcher — 59814

Dates	OSRP	VDTsv	Paid
2003ᴹ - 2004	**$85**	**$295**	$_____

- Two crosses separate in box.

Heralding Angels

59759 - Set of 3

1999 - 2005

OSRP: $20

VDTsv: $28 - $39

Paid: $_____

Good Shepherd & His Animals

59791 - Set of 6

1999 - 2005

OSRP: $25

VDTsv:$167 - $168

Paid: $_____

Wise Men From The East

59792 - Set of 2

1999 - 2005

OSRP: $25

VDTsv: $68

Paid: $_____

• Also included as part of Holy Night Nativity Gift Set.

Town Well & Palm Trees

59793 - Set of 3

1999 - 2005

OSRP: $46

VDTsv: $149

Paid: $_____

Town Gate

59794 - Set of 2

1999 - 2001

OSRP: $25

VDTsv: $146

Paid: $_____

Palm Trees

52820 - Set of 2

1999 - 2005

OSRP: $45

VDTsv: $45

Paid: $_____

• Also included as part of Holy Night Nativity Gift Set.

Desert Oasis

59901 - Set of 5

2000 - 2003

OSRP: $60

VDTsv: $196

Paid: $_____

High Priests

59799 - Set of 2

2000 - 2001

OSRP: *

VDTsv: *

* Accessory contained in Herod's Temple.

Carpenter & Son

59801 - Set of 2

2000 - 2002

OSRP: *

VDTsv: *

* Accessory contained in Carpenter's Shop.

Rug Merchant & Wool Spinner

59802 - Set of 2

2000 - 2005

OSRP: *

VDTsv: *

* Accessory contained in Rug Merchant's Colonnade.

Merchant Cart

59902 - Set of 2

2000 - 2003

OSRP: $30

VDTsv: $88 - $102

Paid: $_____

Stonemason At Work

59903 - Set of 3

2000 - 2003

OSRP: $45

VDTsv: $198

Paid: $_____

Desert Camp

59904 - Set of 4

2000 - 2003

OSRP: $52

VDTsv: $55

Paid: $_____

Oil Lamps

59905 - Set of 2

2000 - 2002

OSRP: $25

VDTsv: $27

Paid: $_____

• Battery operated.

Star Of Wonder

59906

2000 - 2003

OSRP: $20

VDTsv: $119

Paid: $_____

• Battery/adapter operated.

Cypress Trees

59907 - Set of 3

2000 - 2005

OSRP: $20

VDTsv: $106f

Paid: $_____

• Originally released as "Cyprus" trees.

Town Wall Sections

59908 - Set of 2

2000 - 2005

OSRP: $16.50

VDTsv: $68

Paid: $_____

• Coordinates with Town Gate.

Desert Road

59909 - Set of 4

2000 - 2005

OSRP: $22.50

VDTsv: $26

Paid: $_____

Desert Rocks

59910 - Set of 5

2000 - 2003

OSRP: $25

VDTsv: $74 - $75

Paid: $_____

Limestone Outcropping

59911

2000 - 2003

OSRP: $40

VDTsv: $144

Paid: $_____

Olive Harvest

59912 - Set of 3

2000 - 2003

OSRP: $40

VDTsv: $138-$148

Paid: $_____

The Holy Land Backdrop

52965

2001 - 2003

OSRP: $45

VDTsv: $45

Paid: $_____

• 40" x 15

Palm Sunday

59809

2001 - 2004

OSRP: *

VDTsv: *

* The accessory contained in House Of The Last Supper.

Spice & Copper Vendors' Colonnade

59913 - Set of 3

2001 - 2005

OSRP: $75

VDTsv: $146

Paid: $_____

Desert Caravan

59914 - Set of 5

2001 - 2005

OSRP: $48

VDTsv: $218-$246

Paid: $_____

Caravansary Drinking Well

59915

2001 - 2003

OSRP: $27.50

VDTsv: $30

Paid: $_____

Caravansary Gate & Guard

59916 - Set of 2

2001 - 2003

OSRP: $42

VDTsv: $43

Paid: $_____

Caravansary Wall

59917 - 2 Asst'd

2001 - 2003

OSRP: $30

VDTsv: $98

Paid: $_____

Waterfall In The Wilderness

59918 - Set of 2

2001 - 2003

OSRP: $85

VDTsv: $289-$295

Paid: $_____

• Includes accessory "Man Drawing Water."

Tower Guard & Garden Archway

59810

2002^M - 2004

OSRP: *

VDTsv: *

* The accessory contained in the Tower Of David.

Sand Road

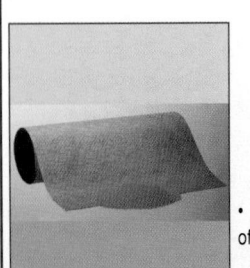

59921 - Set of 2

2002^M - 2005

OSRP: $15

VDTsv: $15

Paid: $_____

• Includes road and bag of sand.

Pottery Craftsman

59812

2002 - 2005

OSRP: *

VDTsv:$188-$210

* The accessory contained in Potter's Shop.

Revolving Nativity Scene

59813

2002 - 2004

OSRP: $130

VDTsv: $130

Paid: $_____

• Animated.

Holy Land Animals

59922 - Set of 3

2002 - 2005

OSRP: $35

VDTsv: $29

Paid: $_____

The Prodigal Son

59923 - Set of 3

2002 - 2004

OSRP: $35

VDTsv: $135

Paid: $_____

• Parables Series.

The Good Samaritan

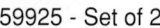

59924 - Set of 3

2002 - 2004

OSRP: $35

VDTsv: $110

Paid: $_____

• Parables Series.

The Sower And The Seed

59925 - Set of 2

2002 - 2004

OSRP: $35

VDTsv: $118

Paid: $_____

• Parables Series.

Holy Night Fiber Optic Backdrop

59815

2003 - 2005

OSRP: $150

VDTsv: $300

Paid: $_____

• Includes adapter.
• Both town and sky light up.

Notes:

Heritage Village® Collection

The term Heritage Village Collection® has sometimes confused collectors. It is not a separate village but an umbrella term that encompasses six porcelain villages — Dickens' Village Series®, New England Village® Series, Alpine Village Series®, Christmas in the City® Series, North Pole Series™, and Little Town of Bethlehem™ Series, as well as smaller series such as Disney Parks Village™ Series, Historical Landmark Series®, and Literary Classics® Collection.

Most of these pieces clearly belong to a specific village, and often can only be displayed in that series. This is true for most buildings and accessories. There is not too much flexibility when it comes to placing elves, taxicabs, or the angels and wise men. But there are some (usually) porcelain pieces that are more versatile and can equally well be placed in two or more of the villages. Many of those pieces are from the earlier years of the collection. Today, Department 56 "assigns" most pieces to a specific village or considers them as General Village Accessories. That was not always the case, as some accessories were seemingly designed with the intention of crossing village lines. Even today an occasional piece is actually designated for this category. There are a number of the ubiquitous Village Vans that have been created to celebrate holidays. The Crystal Ice Palace is the only lit building in this category.

The items in this section are more versatile than those in the individual village sections. That does not mean that each of them can go in every village, but none are restricted to a single location. Among the most versatile are a number of porcelain trees, porcelain fences, and several Event Pieces.

Sleighride (Version 1) (Version 2)

65110   1986 - 1990

OSRP: $19.50

VDTsv: $18-$30

Paid: $_____

• Early pieces have sleeves that read "Dickens' Sleighride," and the man has a narrow white scarf with red polka dots.

VDTsv: -

Paid: $_____

• Later pieces have a man with red polka dots on his scarf and lapels.

Porcelain Trees

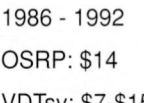

65374 - Set of 2

1986 - 1992

OSRP: $14

VDTsv: $7-$15

Paid: $_____

Skating Pond

65455

1987 - 1990

OSRP: $24

VDTsv: $14-$40

Paid: $_____

• Early shipments were made in Taiwan and had blue-streaked ice. Later shipments were made in the Philippines and had all blue ice.

Stone Bridge

65463

1987 - 1990

OSRP: $12

VDTsv: $34-$35

Paid: $_____

• Varies from light to dark color.

Snow Children

59382 - Set of 3

1988 - 1994

OSRP: $15

VDTsv: $11-$15

Paid: $_____

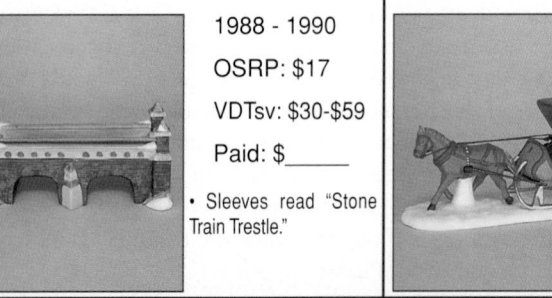

Village Train Trestle

59811

1988 - 1990

OSRP: $17

VDTsv: $30-$59

Paid: $_____

• Sleeves read "Stone Train Trestle."

One Horse Open Sleigh

59820

1988 - 1993

OSRP: $20

VDTsv: $18-$28

Paid: $_____

Village Sign With Snowman

55727

1989 - 1994

OSRP: $10

VDTsv: $7 - $10

Paid: $_____

Heritage Village Promotional Sign

99538

1989 - 1990

OSRP: $5

VDTsv: $6

Paid: $_____

• Variation features green lettering on green facade.

Porcelain Pine, Large

52183

1992 - 1997

OSRP: $12.50

VDTsv: $18

Paid: $_____

Porcelain Pine, Small

52191

1992 - 1997

OSRP: $10

VDTsv: $15

Paid: $_____

Churchyard Fence & Gate

55638 - Set of 3

1992 - 1992

OSRP: $15

VDTsv: $46

Paid: $_____

• Samples have gray stonework; production pieces have brown.
• Early release to GCC.

Churchyard Gate And Fence

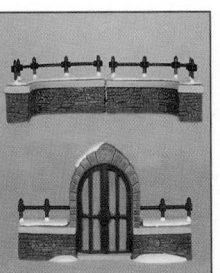

58068 - Set of 3

1992 - 1997

OSRP: $15

VDTsv: $24

Paid: $_____

Churchyard Fence Extensions

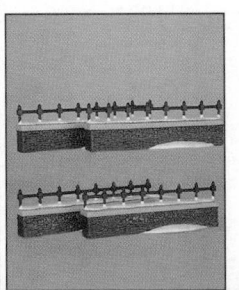

58076 - Set of 4

1992 - 1997

OSRP: $16

VDTsv: $12-$17

Paid: $_____

Porcelain Pine Trees

52515 - Set of 2

1994 - 1997

OSRP: $15

VDTsv: $20

Paid: $_____

Christmas Bells

98711

1996ᴹ - 1996

OSRP: $35

VDTsv: $27-$38

Paid: $_____

• 1996 Homes for the Holidays event piece.

Village Square Clock Tower

52591

1996 - 2000

OSRP: $32.50

VDTsv: $26

Paid: $_____

• Battery-operated.

The Holly & The Ivy

56100 - Set of 2

1997ᴹ - 1997

OSRP: $17.50

VDTsv: $12

Paid: $_____

• 1997 Homes for the Holidays event piece.

Poinsettia Delivery Truck

59000

1997 - 1999

OSRP: $32.50

VDTsv: $15

Paid: $_____

• Similar designs were produced for retailers. See the Special Design section.

Porcelain Pines

59001 - Set of 4

1997 - 2005

OSRP: $17.50

VDTsv: $18

Paid: $_____

Our Own Village Park Bench

02211

1997 - 1999

OSRP: $10

VDTsv: $10

Paid: $_____

• Sold plain or with retailer name on the back of the bench as a promotional piece.

Painting Our Own Village Sign

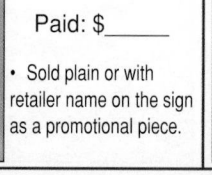

55501

1998 - 2000

OSRP: $12.50

VDTsv: $28

Paid: $_____

• Sold plain or with retailer name on the sign as a promotional piece.

Stars And Stripes Forever

55502

1998 - 1999

OSRP: $50

VDTsv: $30-$68

Paid: $_____

• July 1999 event piece.
• Plays *Stars and Stripes Forever.*
• Includes 3 flags.

Dorothy's Skate Rental

55515
1999 - 2002
OSRP: $35
VDTsv: $20
Paid: $_____

• Named after Olympic Gold Medal winner, Dorothy Hamill.
• Early release to only two stores.
• Lighted. Includes skates.

Hear Ye, Hear Ye

55523
1999 - 2001^M
OSRP: $13.50
VDTsv: $10-$13
Paid: $_____

• Includes stickers so the scroll can be personalized.

Village Monuments

55524 - Set of 3
1999 - 2001^M
OSRP: $25
VDTsv: $25-$35
Paid: $_____

Christmas Carolers

58631 - Set of 3
2000 - 2008
OSRP: $27.50
VDTsv: -
Paid: $_____

Crystal Ice Palace

58922 - Set of 9
2001^M - 2001
OSRP: $165
VDTsv: $132-$188
Paid: $_____

• Set of 9 includes Palace, 2 piece accessory "Palace Bears," 4 trees, snow crystals, and ice path. Pennant separate in box.
• Although this design is considered a Heritage village design, it was shipped with an Original Snow Village Collection hang tag.
• This was a 25th Anniversary celebration design and, therefore, should have been stamped as such. When Department 56 became aware that it had not been stamped, it supplied decals to retailers who in turn could provide them to collectors.

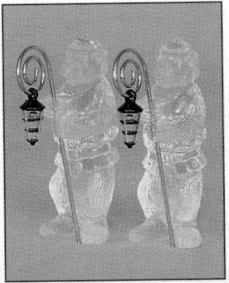

Crystal Ice King & Queen

58976 - Set of 2

2001^M-2001

OSRP: $20

VDTsv: $19-$38

Paid: $_____

• Limited edition of 25,000.
• 25th Anniversary celebration design.

Mountie

58632

2001 - 2003

OSRP: $24

VDTsv: $78

Paid: $_____

• Available only in Canada.

Village Memorial

53028

2002^M - 2003

OSRP: $35

VDTsv: $30-$35

Paid: $_____

• Be careful removing from box; the globe is separate.

Halloween Village Express

58634

2002^M - 2002

OSRP: $25

VDTsv: $20

Paid: $_____

• Club 56 and Gold Key dealer exclusive.

Christmas Village Express

58635

2002^M - 2002

OSRP: $25

VDTsv: $45

Paid: $_____

• Club 56 and Gold Key dealer exclusive.

Village Square Snowman

58638

2002^M - 2002

OSRP: $32.50

VDTsv: $42-$58

Paid: $_____

• Limited to year of production.
• Available only at Gold Key dealers.

Valentine Village Express

58639

2002 - 2003

OSRP: $25

VDTsv: $48

Paid: $_____

St. Patrick's Village Express

58640

2002 - 2003

OSRP: $25

VDTsv: $25

Paid: $_____

Easter Village Express

58641

2002 - 2003

OSRP: $25

VDTsv: $56

Paid: $_____

Happy Birthday Village Express

58642

2002 - 2003

OSRP: $25

VDTsv: $65

Paid: $_____

Walter's Hot Dog Stand

58643

2002 - N/A

OSRP: $45

VDTsv: N/A

Paid: $_____

No Photo Available

• This design was never produced.

Village Square Town Tree

58644

2002^{M} - 2003

OSRP: $35

VDTsv: $98

Paid: $_____

• Limited to year of production.

American Pride Village Express

58660

2002 - 2002

OSRP: $25

VDTsv: $40

Paid: $_____

• Limited to year of production.

Christmas Band

53310

2005 - 2007

OSRP: $18.50

VDTsv: $18-$35

Paid: $_____

Notes:

Special Designs

It could be argued that all designs are special ... and they are. In this case, the reference is to individual pieces or small groupings designed for specific organizations, businesses, or retailers. They are not available to collectors through traditional resources but must be acquired directly from a single source. Although they may be difficult to obtain, virtually every item in this section has been adopted into one or more villages by enthusiastic displayers.

The earliest pieces — the Bachman's Hometown Series — were produced for only a year. They have traits similar to Heritage Village® Collection pieces; in fact one piece served as the mold for a building in the Christmas In The City® Series.

The Profiles Department 56® pieces are manufactured by Department 56 for other corporations to distribute through their own marketing approaches, to stockholders, employees, or the general public.

The National Council of Clubs, an umbrella organization for collectors clubs, has released a number of pieces that have only been available at special events or through local collecting clubs that are affiliated with the national organization.

A large grouping involves contract arrangements with retailers or companies who have specially designed variations of regular village pieces. At times a single piece has been adapted for a number of retailers; other times only one variation has been created. These unique yet familiar pieces have often found their way into village displays where sometimes they are more appreciated than those they imitated. After all, something different always draws the attention of fellow collectors.

The largest portion of this section presents A Christmas Story Collection, based on the heartwarming Christmas classic. These pieces are available both through Sears and retail stores.

NATIONAL COUNCIL OF CLUBS (NCC)

The National Council of Clubs is an umbrella organization that dispenses information and advice to local Department 56 collectors' clubs.

Collectors Club House 54800

Dates	OSRP	VDTsv	Paid
1998 - 1998	**$56**	**$90 - $116**	**$_____**

- An exclusive for members of National Council of Clubs related collectors clubs, this set was available directly to clubs from Department 56.
- Collectors who purchased the Club House could have decals of their clubs' logos affixed to the signs.
- Set of 2 includes House and "Man & Woman" accessory.

Under The NCC Umbrella 02100 — 02104

Dates	OSRP	VDTsv	Paid
2000 - 2001	**$20**	**$65**	**$_____**

- Based on Dickens' Village Under The Bumbershoot, this accessory was sold by the NCC at Dept 56 events.
- Available in 5 colors—yellow (02100), green (02101), red (02102), blue (02103), and silver (02104).

Jack's Umbrella Shop 05826

Dates	OSRP	VDTsv	Paid
2001 - 2002	**$56**	**$56 - $148**	**$_____**

- An exclusive for members of National Council of Clubs related collectors clubs, this set was available through member clubs.
- Named after the Jack Skeels who envisioned the National Council of Clubs, an organization that would assist and support local clubs.
- Set of 2 includes Shop, "Is It Raining?" accessory, and pin.
- The umbrella stand is very fragile.

Ed, The NCC Snowman
06349

Dates	OSRP	VDTsv	Paid
2005 - 2005	$15	-	$_____

- An exclusive for members of National Council of Clubs related collectors clubs, this set was available through member clubs.

Snowflake, The NCC Snowgirl
06316

Dates	OSRP	VDTsv	Paid
2007ᴹ - 2007	$12.50	-	$_____

- The 9th exclusive, members-only piece of the National Council of 56 Clubs.
- Commemorates the 15th Anniversary of the NCC.

NCC Traders Pin Shop
804011

Dates	OSRP	VDTsv	Paid
2008ᴹ - 2008	$50	-	$_____

- 10th exclusive NCC member piece.
- Available only through Club Reps and at the 2008 NCC Convention.

NCC Lamplighter
804012

Dates	OSRP	VDTsv	Paid
2008ᴹ - 2008	$20	-	$_____

- One of three 2008 NCC Convention event pieces.
- Designed also as a Heritage Village accessory.

NCC Motorcycle Elves
804013

Dates	OSRP	VDTsv	Paid
2008ᴹ - 2008	$20	-	$_____

- One of three 2008 NCC Convention event pieces.
- Designed also as a North Pole accessory.

NCC Welcome Sign
804014

Dates	OSRP	VDTsv	Paid
2008ᴹ - 2008	$20	-	$_____

- One of three 2008 NCC Convention event pieces.
- Designed also as a Snow Village accessory.

PROFILES DEPARTMENT 56®

This is a series produced by Department 56 for use as promotional pieces by other companies. Many collectors, however, have adapted them into some of the Heritage Village Collections®.

Heinz® House — 07826

Dates	OSRP	VDTsv	Paid
1996ᴹ - 1996	$28	$90 - $125	$_____

• A replica of the home and first Heinz production building, this was given as a gift to Heinz vendors in late 1996 and sold by direct mail to its stockholders in 1997.

State Farm® — Main Street Memories — 56000

Dates	OSRP	VDTsv	Paid
1997 - 1997	$35.50	$48 - $89	$_____

• Made available to State Farm employees, this building depicts one similar to a Randy Souder painting.
• The gumball machine, broom, and awnings are fragile.
• Spire and sign are separate in box.

Heinz® Grocery Store — 05600

Dates	OSRP	VDTsv	Paid
1998 - 1998	$34	$95 - $129	$_____

• This corner grocery store was used by Heinz as a gift to Heinz vendors in late 1998 and sold by direct mail to its stockholders in 1999.
• Pickle sign is separate in the box.

Heinz® Hitch — 02291

Dates	OSRP	VDTsv	Paid
1999 - 1999	$31	$70	$_____

• Based on The Pumpkin Wagon, this was used by Heinz as a gift to Heinz vendors in late 1999 and sold by direct mail to its stockholders in 2000.

Heinz® Evaporated Horseradish Factory — 05710

Dates	OSRP	VDTsv	Paid
2000 - 2000	$40	$75	$_____

• This design was used by Heinz as a gift to Heinz vendors in late 2000 and sold by direct mail to its stockholders in 2001.

State Farm® – Main Street Fire Station No. 1   05709

Dates	OSRP	VDTsv	Paid
2000 - 2000	$37	$100	$_____

• Made available to its employees, this building depicts a similar one in Randy Souder's painting Main Street Memories that was commissioned by State Farm.
• Spire and lamppost are separate in the box.

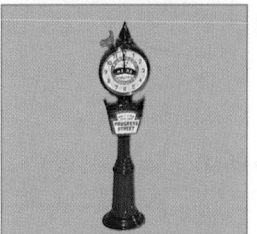

Heinz® Town Clock   05834

Dates	OSRP	VDTsv	Paid
2001^M - 2001	$15	$35	$_____

• This working Clock was used by Heinz as a gift to Heinz vendors in late 2001 and sold by direct mail to its stockholders in 2002.

Wells Fargo® Historic Office   05930

Dates	OSRP	VDTsv	Paid
2002^M - 2002	$42.50	$85	$_____

• This building was used by Wells Fargo as a promotional item to celebrate its 150th anniversary.

Spam® Museum   06956

Dates	OSRP	VDTsv	Paid
2003^M - 2003	$63.25	$130	$_____

• This building was used by Hormel's Spam division as a promotional item.
• It is a replica of the Spam Museum in Austin, MN.
• Licensed by Hormel Foods Corporation.

Applebee's® Neighborhood Grill & Bar   06230

Dates	OSRP	VDTsv	Paid
2004^M - 2004	$25	$165	$_____

• This building was produced exclusively for Applebee's in honor of its 25th anniversary.
• Limited to 4,000 pieces.

Cracker Barrel Restaurant

Dates	OSRP	VDTsv	Paid
2005 - 2006	$24.99	-	$_____

• This design was produced exclusively for Cracker Barrel Restaurant.

MISCELLANEOUS

Designs in this category include those that were made for one retailer or company or a select group of retailers. In almost all instances, they were based on existing pieces.

John Deere® Water Tower — 25104

Dates	OSRP	VDTsv	Paid
1988 - 1988	**$24**	**$610**	**$____**

• Produced exclusively for the John Deere catalog.
• The tower reads "Moline Home of John Deere."
• Licensed by Deere & Co.

Bachman's For Sale Sign — 05398

Dates	OSRP	VDTsv	Paid
1989 - 1989	**$4.50**	**$12**	**$____**

• This version of the For Sale Sign was produced exclusively for Bachman's of Minneapolis, MN. to sell during its 1990 Village Gathering.

To date 27 versions of the **VILLAGE EXPRESS VAN** have been produced. A green edition in Christmas in the City was one of the regular releases in 1992. That same year a black promotional edition was created, followed by the rarest, a gold version. Seventeen retailers' versions were produced in 1994 and 1995. A silver edition was created in 2001 to celebrate Department 56's 25th anniversary. Several holiday versions are recent additions.

Village Express Van — Black — 99511

Dates	OSRP	VDTsv	Paid
1992 - 1992	**Promotional**	**$58**	**$____**

• This van was originally given to Department 56 sales representatives as a gift at their National Sales conference in 1992. It was later used as a special event piece at the 1993 Bachman's Village Gathering.

Village Express Van — Gold — 99775

Dates	OSRP	VDTsv	Paid
1993 - 1993	**Promotional**	**$495**	**$____**

• Packed in a special gold box, this promotional "Road Show" edition was presented to potential investors before the company's initial public offering.

Village Express Van — Gatherings   See below

Dates	OSRP	VDTsv	Paid
1994 - 1994	**$25**	**See below**	

• The right side of each van features the Department 56 logo. The left side has the specific retailer's logo. 14 vans were produced—13 for Department 56 sponsored Village Gatherings and one for The Lemon Tree which sold it to its Collector's Club members.

Item #	Van	VDTsv	Paid
07293	Bachman's	$40	$_____
07374	Bronner's	$35	$_____
07307	Christmas Dove	$20	$_____
07390	European Imports	$20	$_____
07358	Fortunoff	$55	$_____
07323	Incredible Christmas	$40	$_____
07218	Lemon Tree	$18	$_____
07331	Limited Edition	$41	$_____
07315	Lock, Stock & Barrel	$54	$_____
07366	North Pole City	$37	$_____
07340	Robert's	$18	$_____
07412	Stat's	$15	$_____
07382	William Glen	$18	$_____
07404	Windsor Shoppe	$35	$_____

Village Express Van   See below

Dates	OSRP	VDTsv	Paid
1995 - 1995	**See below**	**See below**	

• The Parkwest van was a gift to retailers who were members of the Parkwest catalog group. It features the Department 56 logo on the right side, and Parkwest's logo on the left side.
• St. Nick's van features the Department 56 logo on the right side and its logo on the left.
• The Canadian van was produced for retailers in Canada. It features the Department 56 logo on the right side, and a red maple leaf on the left side.

Item #	Van	OSRP	VDTsv	Paid
07522	Parkwest	**Promo**	$300	$_____
07560	St. Nick's	$25	$35	$_____
21637	Canadian	$40	$44 - $65	$_____

Bachman's Squash Cart   07536

Dates	OSRP	VDTsv	Paid
1995ᴹ - 1995	**$50**	**$38 - $95**	$_____

• Produced exclusively for Bachman's of Minneapolis, MN, this commemorated the company's 110th anniversary and notes this with a bottomstamp. It was first sold at the 1995 Bachman's Village Gathering.

A Visit With Santa   See below

Dates	OSRP	VDTsv	Paid
1995 - 1995	**$25**	**See below**	

• Eight stores had this piece personalized with their names and choice of colors for the packages.

Item #	Store	VDTsv	Paid
07544	Bachman's	**$40**	$_____
07676	Fortunoff	**$40**	$_____
07684	Lemon Tree	**$30**	$_____
07641	Limited Edition	**$40**	$_____
07730	Pine Cone Christmas	**$35**	$_____
07650	Stat's	**$30**	$_____
07668	William Glen	**$35**	$_____
07692	Young's Ltd.	**$35**	$_____

Here Comes Santa   See below

Dates	OSRP	VDTsv	Paid
1996 - 1996	**$25**	**See below**	

• 24 stores had this piece personalized with their names on the banner. One store, Bachman's, had "Joy to the World" on the banner.

Item #	Store	VDTsv	Paid
07744	Bachman's	**$40**	$_____
07745	Bronner's	**$40**	$_____
07748	Broughton Christmas	**$30**	$_____
07752	Cabbage Rose	**$30**	$_____
07753	Calabash Nautical Gifts	**$35**	$_____
07751	Calico Butterfly	**$35**	$_____
07763	Carson Pirie Scott	**$35**	$_____
07755	Christmas Loft	**$35**	$_____
07750	Dickens' Gift Shoppe	**$40**	$_____
07762	European Imports	**$40**	$_____
07747	Fibber Magee's	**$35**	$_____
07741	Fortunoff	**$45**	$_____
07759	Gustaf's	**$35**	$_____
07754	Ingle's Nook	**$40**	$_____
07746	Limited Edition	**$40**	$_____
07742	North Pole City	**$40**	$_____
07740	Pine Cone Christmas	**$35**	$_____
07760	Royal Dutch Collectibles	**$30**	$_____
07756	Russ Country Gardens	**$30**	$_____
07757	St. Nick's	**$40**	$_____
07758	Seventh Avenue	**$35**	$_____
07749	Stat's	**$30**	$_____
07743	William Glen	**$40**	$_____
07761	Young's Ltd.	**$35**	$_____

St. Nick's Pick-up And Delivery 07821

Dates	OSRP	VDTsv	Paid
1996ᴹ - 1996	$10	$20	$_____

• Limited to 1,080 pieces, this personalized version of the Snow Village piece was produced exclusively for St. Nick's of Littleton, Co.

Bachman's Flower Shop 08802

Dates	OSRP	VDTsv	Paid
1997ᴹ - 1997	$50	$85	$_____

• A personalized version of the Snow Village Secret Garden Florist, this was produced exclusively for Bachman's of Minneapolis, MN and was first sold at its 1997 Village Gathering.

Bachman's Wilcox Truck 08803

Dates	OSRP	VDTsv	Paid
1997ᴹ - 1997	$30	$20 - $54	$_____

• A personalized version of the Heritage Village Poinsettia Truck, this replica of a Bachman's 1919 Wilcox was produced exclusively for Bachman's of Minneapolis, MN and was sold at its 1997 Gathering.

Lionel® Electric Train Shop 02202

Dates	OSRP	VDTsv	Paid
1998ᴹ - 1998	$55	$190	$_____

• Limited to 5,000, this personalized Snow Village design was produced exclusively for Allied Model Trains of Culver City, CA. 1946 is the year Allied opened, and 4411 is its actual street number. Licensed by Lionel.

Bachman's Greenhouse 02203

Dates	OSRP	VDTsv	Paid
1998ᴹ - 1998	$60	$80	$_____

• A personalized version of the Snow Village Secret Garden Greenhouse, this was produced exclusively for Bachman's of Minneapolis, MN and was first sold at its 1998 Village Gathering.

Say It With Flowers 02204

Dates	OSRP	VDTsv	Paid
1998ᴹ - 1998	$30	$34 - $48	$_____

• A personalized version of the Snow Village Christmas Visit To The Florist, this set was produced exclusively for Bachman's of Minneapolis, MN and was first sold at its 1998 Village Gathering.

Bachman's Tending The Cold Frame 02208

Dates	OSRP	VDTsv	Paid
1998ᴹ - 1998	$35	$22 - $35	$_____

• This personalized version of the Dickens' Village Tending The Cold Frame was produced exclusively for Bachman's of Minneapolis, MN and was first sold at its 1998 Village Gathering.

North Pole City's Father Christmas's Journey 02244

Dates	OSRP	VDTsv	Paid
1998ᴹ - 1998	$30	$35	$_____

• This personalized version of the Dickens' Village design was produced exclusively for North Pole City of Oklahoma City, OK to honor its 10th anniversary.

William Glen Delivery Truck 02300

Dates	OSRP	VDTsv	Paid
1998ᴹ - 1998	$37.50	$40	$_____

• This personalized version of the Heritage Village Poinsettia Delivery Truck was produced exclusively for William Glen of Sacramento, CA and was first sold at its 1998 Village Gathering.

Lord & Taylor Delivery Wagon 07880

Dates	OSRP	VDTsv	Paid
1998ᴹ - 1998	$32.50	$45	$_____

• This personalized version of the Dickens' Village Fezziwig Delivery Wagon was produced exclusively for Lord & Taylor department stores.

Lord & Taylor Flower Cart 02250

Dates	OSRP	VDTsv	Paid
1999ᴹ - 1999	$27.50	$40	$_____

• This personalized version of the Dickens' Village Chelsea Market Flower Monger & Cart was produced exclusively for Lord & Taylor department stores.

William Glen Grocery Delivery 02413

Dates	OSRP	VDTsv	Paid
1999 - 1999	$18	$30	$_____

• This personalized version of the Christmas In The City Johnson's Delivery Wagon was produced exclusively for William Glen of Sacramento, CA and was first sold at its 1999 Village Gathering.

Bachman's Original Homestead, 1885   02255

Dates	OSRP	VDTsv	Paid
1999^M - 1999	$75	$105	$_____

- Limited to 7,500, it is the first numbered limited edition Snow Village design. Inspired by a Bachman family home, it was sold as a commemorative piece during the 1999 Bachman's Village Gathering.

Lilac City Water Tower   02423

Dates	OSRP	VDTsv	Paid
1999 - 2000	$40	$70	$_____

- Limited to 500 pieces. Produced exclusively for Lock, Stock And Barrel of Rochester, NY.
- The tower reads "Lilac City… Rochester, New York, Incorporated 1834."

William Glen Taxi   02270

Dates	OSRP	VDTsv	Paid
2000^M - 2000	$12.50	$20	$_____

- This personalized version of the Christmas In The City City Taxi was produced exclusively for William Glen of Sacramento, CA and was first sold at its 2000 Village Gathering.

Feeney's Delivery Of Dreams   02272

Dates	OSRP	VDTsv	Paid
2000^M - 2000	$12.50	$20	$_____

- This personalized version of the Christmas In The City City Taxi was produced exclusively for Feeney's of Feasterville, PA.

Lord & Taylor Hot Air Balloon 2000   02440

Dates	OSRP	VDTsv	Paid
2000^M - 2000	$40	$45	$_____

- This personalized version of North Pole Dash Away Delivery was produced exclusively for Lord & Taylor department stores.
- The basket often comes unglued from the base.

Town Tree Carolers   05702

Dates	OSRP	VDTsv	Paid
2000^M - 2000	$65	$95	$_____

- Produced exclusively for NALED/Parkwest dealers.
- Set of 6 includes tree, set of 3 carolers, lampposts, and bench.
- Battery/adapter operated.

Village Express Van — Silver

52911

Dates	OSRP	VDTsv	Paid
2001ᴹ - 2001	$25	$75	$_____

- Special issue for Department 56's silver anniversary.
- Only available at that event.

25th Anniversary Village Footbridge

52910

Dates	OSRP	VDTsv	Paid
2001ᴹ - 2001	$15	$30	$_____

- Special issue for Department 56's silver anniversary.
- Only available at that event.

Toys For Tots

05746

Dates	OSRP	VDTsv	Paid
2001ᴹ - 2001	$50	$80	$_____

- Produced exclusively for the Carson Pirie Scott department stores.

Feeney's Our Sign For All Seasons

05832

Dates	OSRP	VDTsv	Paid
2001ᴹ - 2001	$15	$18	$_____

- This personalized version of the Village Sign And Bench was produced exclusively for Feeney's of Feasterville, PA.

Wegmans Delivery Wagon

05838

Dates	OSRP	VDTsv	Paid
2001ᴹ - 2001	$22.50	$35	$_____

- Based on Christmas In The City Johnson's Delivery Wagon, this piece was produced exclusively for Lock, Stock And Barrel of Rochester, NY. It features the name of a well known regional grocery chain.

Feeney's Anniversary Lamppost

06001

Dates	OSRP	VDTsv	Paid
2002ᴹ - 2002	$5	$12	$_____

- This personalized Lamppost was produced exclusively for Feeney's of Feasterville, PA.

Bronner's Custom Building

06227

Dates	OSRP	VDTsv	Paid
2004^M - 2004	$80	$125	$_____

• This personalized building was produced exclusively for Bronner's Christmas Wonderland in Frankenmuth, MI.

Frango Chocolate Shop

06300

Dates	OSRP	VDTsv	Paid
2004^M - 2004	$65	$75	$_____

• This building was produced exclusively for the Marshall Field's stores in honor of the chocolates that are sold only in its stores.

Frangos For You And I

06301

Dates	OSRP	VDTsv	Paid
2004^M - 2004	$15	$65	$_____

• This accessory was produced exclusively for the Marshall Field's stores in honor of the chocolates that are sold only in its stores.

Frango Factory

06302

Dates	OSRP	VDTsv	Paid
2005^M - 2005	$70	$70	$_____

• This building was produced exclusively for the Marshall Field's stores in honor of the chocolates that are sold only in its stores.

Frango Delivery Truck

06303

Dates	OSRP	VDTsv	Paid
2005^M - 2005	$20	$20	$_____

• This truck was produced exclusively for the Marshall Field's stores in honor of the chocolates that are sold only in its stores.

McHattie's Tea House

06229

Dates	OSRP	VDTsv	Paid
2006 - 2006	$20	-	$_____

• Collectors' Gallery, Woodbury, MN, 25th Anniversary Exclusive.

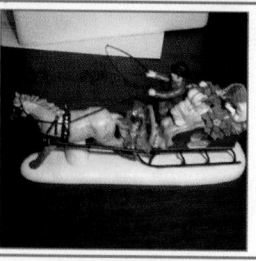

Sleighride On The Bay

06479

Dates	OSRP	VDTsv	Paid
2006 - 2006	**$30**	-	$_____

• Made Exclusively for PJ's and the 2006 Spirit of 56 on the Bay Gathering.
• Limited Edition of 1,000.

Bronner's Original Store Exclusive Dept. 56

06277

Dates	OSRP	VDTsv	Paid
2007 - 2007	**$99.99**	-	$_____

• Designed as a Snow Village piece.

ALLIED MODEL TRAINS DEPARTMENT 56 TRAINS

Allied Model Trains, one of the largest model train stores in the world, has produced a unique train set that has become highly collectible. Manufactured by Lionel Trains, each car features village-related artwork.

Snow Village Box Car

Dates	OSRP	VDTsv	Paid
1995 - 1995	**$45**	**$90**	$_____

• Limited Edition of 5,000.
• Produced by Lionel Trains.
• Licensed by Department 56.

Heritage Village Box Car

Dates	OSRP	VDTsv	Paid
1996 - 1996	**$50**	**$80**	$_____

• Limited Edition of 5,000.
• Produced by Lionel Trains.
• Licensed by Department 56.

Department 56 Caboose

Dates	OSRP	VDTsv	Paid
1997 - 1997	**$60**	**$105**	$_____

- Limited Edition of 3,000.
- Produced by Lionel Trains.
- Licensed by Department 56.

Holly Bros. Tank Car

Dates	OSRP	VDTsv	Paid
1998 - 1998	**$60**	**$90**	$_____

- Limited Edition of 3,000.
- Produced by Lionel Trains.
- Licensed by Department 56.

Department 56 Locomotive

Dates	OSRP	VDTsv	Paid
1999 - 1999	**$380**	**$625**	$_____

- Limited Edition of 1,717.
- Includes tender.
- Produced by Lionel Trains.
- Licensed by Department 56.

Real Plastic Snow Hopper

Dates	OSRP	VDTsv	Paid
2000 - 2000	**$60**	**$80**	$_____

- Limited Edition of 3,000.
- Produced by Lionel Trains.
- Licensed by Department 56.

Happy Holidays Gondola

Dates	OSRP	VDTsv	Paid
2001 - 2001	**$50**	**$70**	$_____

- Limited Edition of 3,000.
- Produced by Lionel Trains.
- Licensed by Department 56.

Notes:

BACHMAN'S HOMETOWN SERIES

This short-lived series was produced for Bachman's of Minneapolis, MN, the original parent company of Department 56. Three buildings were manufactured and distributed, but a fourth, a bookstore, never made it past the drawing board.

Boarding House · 06700

Dates	OSRP	VDTsv	Paid
1987 - 1988	**$34**	**$195**	$___

• Inspired by the Sprague House in Red Wing, MN.

Church · 06718

Dates	OSRP	VDTsv	Paid
1987 - 1988	**$40**	**$295**	$___

• Designed after a St. Paul, MN church.

Drugstore · 06726

Dates	OSRP	VDTsv	Paid
1988 - 1989	**$40**	**$685**	$___

• Same mold as the Christmas In The City 1988 Variety Store And Barber Shop. See the CIC section.
• Inspired by a store in Stillwater, MN.

A CHRISTMAS STORY

This collection is based on the heartwarming Christmas classic. Originally, pieces were sold exclusively through Sears. Beginning in 2008, there will be a select group offered through the gift & specialty stores, while Sears still carries part of the line.

* New item number/ Old Item Number are used with this listing. Numbers have changed due to new distribution numbering. The pieces and packaging will be the same. Any number that begins with "0" is an exclusive item — in this case for Sears.

Higbee's Department Store — 805027 / 06081

Dates	OSRP	VDTsv	Paid
2005 -	$39.99	$	$_____
D56 2008^M -	$50		

Ralphie's House — 805028 / 06082

Dates	OSRP	VDTsv	Paid
2005 -	$37.99	$	$_____
D56 2008^M -	$45		

Cleveland Elementary School — 805029 / 06083

Dates	OSRP	VDTsv	Paid
2005 -	$37.99	$	$_____
D56 2008^M -	$45		

The Fire House — 805666 / 06084

Dates	OSRP	VDTsv	Paid
2005 - 2005	$34.99	$	$_____
D56 2008 -	$50		

Chop Suey Palace

805030 / 06085

Dates	OSRP	VDTsv	Paid
2005 -	**$34.99**	$	$_____
D56 2008ᴹ **-**	**$45**		

Hammond Town Hall

06281

Dates	OSRP	VDTsv	Paid
2006 - 2006	**$39.99**	$	$_____

The Bumpus' House

805667 / 06282

Dates	OSRP	VDTsv	Paid
2006 -	**$37.99**	$	$_____
D56 2008 -	**$45**		

Schultz Optometry

06283

Dates	OSRP	VDTsv	Paid
2007 -	**$39.99**	$	$_____

The Uptown Theater

06284

Dates	OSRP	VDTsv	Paid
2007 -	**$39.99**	$	$_____

Pulaski's Candy Store

805668

Dates	OSRP	VDTsv	Paid
D56 2008 -	**$50**	$	$_____

The Police Station

809435

Dates	OSRP	VDTsv	Paid
D56 2010 -	$55	$	$_____

Notes:

Isn't It Beautiful?

805033 / 06093

2005 -

D56 2008^M -

OSRP: $12.99

D56 $15

VDTsv: $

Paid: $_____

It's Christmas Candy

805552 / 06096

2005 - 2005

D56 2008 -

OSRP: $7.99

D56 $13

VDTsv: $

Paid: $_____

Toys For Kids

805797 / 06094

2005 - 2005

D56 2008 -

OSRP: $7.99

D56 $13

VDTsv: $

Paid: $_____

Singing Carols

805034 / 06095

2005 - 2006

D56 2008^M -

OSRP: $7.99

D56 $11

VDTsv: $

Paid: $_____

Triple Dog Dare

805032 / 06091

2005 -

D56 2008^M -

OSRP: $12.99

D56 $15

VDTsv: $

Paid: $_____

The Perfect Tree

06097

2005 - 2005

OSRP: $14.99

VDTsv: $

Paid: $_____

• Lighted tree lot accessory.

Fire Truck

805669 / 06098

2005 - 2005

D56 2008 -

OSRP: $9.99

D56 $15

VDTsv: $

Paid: $_____

Bringing The Tree Home

805670 / 06099

2005 - 2007

D56 2008 - 2008

OSRP: $12.99

VDTsv: $

Paid: $_____

• Car with tree.

Department Store Elves

809453 / 06289

2006 - 2006

D56 2010 -

OSRP: $7.99

    D56 $11

VDTsv: $

Paid: $_____

Santa And Child

06290

2006 -

OSRP: $7.99

VDTsv: $

Paid: $_____

Town Tree

06291

2006 -

OSRP: $16.99

VDTsv: $

Paid: $_____

• Lit accessory.

Skut Farkus And His Toadie

805036 / 06292

2006 -

D56 2008 -

OSRP: $9.99

    D56 $13

VDTsv: $

Paid: $_____

• Lit accessory.

Ralphie To The Rescue

805037 / 06294

2006 -

D56 2008 -

OSRP: $9.99

    D56 $13

VDTsv: $

Paid: $_____

My Secret Decoder Arrived!

809443 / 805671 / 06296

2005 - 2006

D56 2008 -

D56 2010 -

OSRP: $7.99

    D56 $11

VDTsv: $

Paid: $_____

Higbee's Santa

805039 / 06299

2006 -

D56 2008^M -

OSRP: $16.99

    D56 $13

VDTsv: $

Paid: $_____

Turkey For The Bumpus Hounds!

809442 / 805672 / 06298

2006 -

D56 2008 - 2008

D56 2010 -

OSRP: $7.99

    D56 $11

VDTsv: $

Paid: $_____

Ralphie Glasses

06293
2007 -
OSRP: $7.99
VDTsv: $
Paid: $_____

Pink Nightmare

805038
2008^M -
OSRP: $15
VDTsv: $
Paid: $_____

Ralphie Visits Santa

801167
2008 -
OSRP: $30
VDTsv: $
Paid: $_____

Watching The Parade

801168
2008 -
OSRP: $15
VDTsv: $
Paid: $_____

Watch For Cars

809436
2010 -
OSRP: $14
VDTsv: $
Paid: $_____

Christmas Story Police Car

811266
2010 -
OSRP: $16.50
VDTsv: $
Paid: $_____

Notes:

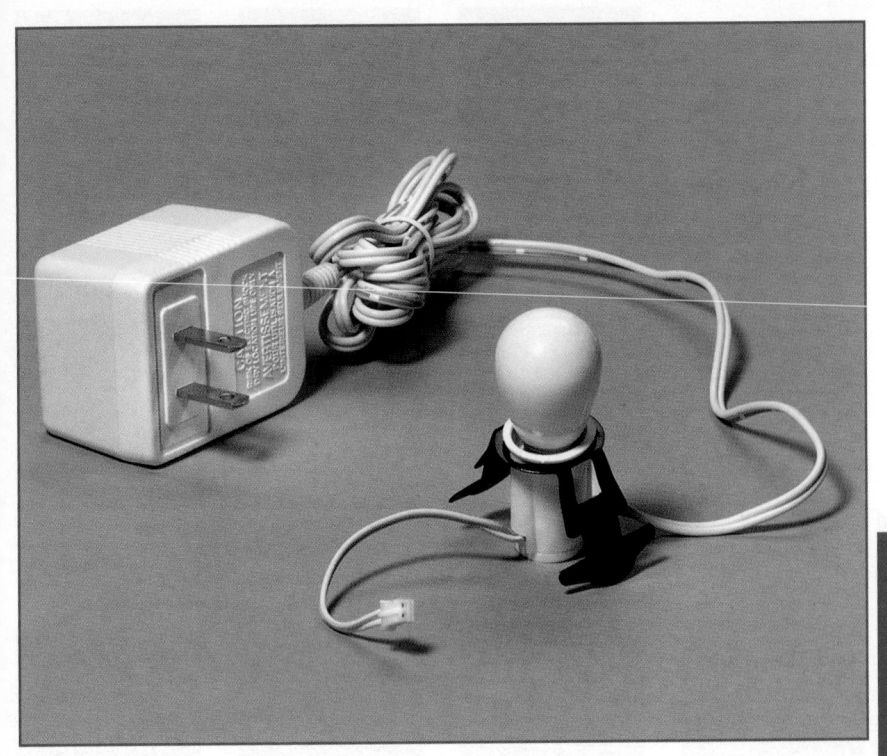

General Village Accessories

Items in this category are designed to accompany virtually any village. They are the final decorating touches that add character to a scene, or help to bring it to life. In this guide these accessories have been divided into five categories:

TREES: You can never have too many trees, and virtually all of them are here. A few, like Bethlehem's palm trees and the porcelain pieces can be found elsewhere, but all the other trees, shrubs, and hedges are in this section. If it's a tree — even if it lights — it's found in this category, not under the "Electrical" section.

ELECTRICAL: Both the pieces on display and the cords, bulbs, adapters, and multiple plugs that activate them are found under "Electrical." This includes all animated pieces, trains, Brite Lites, streetlights, and colored lights. The sole exception is trees with lights, which may be found in the "Trees" category.

FENCES, GATES, AND WALLS: With the exception of a few porcelain pieces, all the boundary markers and their entrances are located in this section.

SNOW AND ICE: The final finishing touches to every winter village are located in this frosty area.

MISCELLANEOUS: If it didn't appear in any of the above sections — and it's not made of porcelain or ceramic, this is the catchall category where you'll find roads, mountains, trim pieces, bridges, resin animals, and Mill Creek pieces.

Those General Village Accessories that have unique application to North Pole or Halloween displays are listed in separate color-coded pages at the conclusion of this section.

TREES
TREES
TREES
TREES
TREES
TREES
TREES
TREES
TREES

Spruce Forest
$90   65943
1987 - 1990

Spruce Tree With
Wooden Base, Sm
$3.50   65951
1987 - 1995

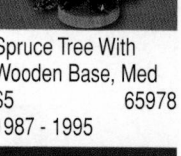

Spruce Tree With
Wooden Base, Med
$5   65978
1987 - 1995

Spruce Tree With
Wooden Base, Lg
$7   65986
1987 - 1995

Christmas Wreaths
$5   51110
1988 - 1991

Frosted Topiary
Village Garden
$16   51152
1988 - 1990

Sisal Topiary Garden
$50   51853
1988 - 1992

Frosted Cone Tree
w/Wood Base, Lg
$10   51934
1988 - 1989

Frosted Norway Pines
$12   51756
1989 - 1998

Winter Oak Tree With
2 Red Birds
$16   51845
1989 - 1990

Sisal Topiary, Lg
N/A   51861
1989 - 1989

Sisal Topiary, Med
N/A   51870
1989 - 1989

Sisal Topiary, Sm
N/A   51888
1989 - 1989

Sisal Topiary, Mini
N/A   51896
1989 - 1989

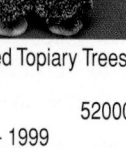

Potted Topiary Pair
$5   51926
1989 - 1994

Frosted Topiary Trees,
s/2
$12   52000
1989 - 1999

Frosted Topiary, s/4
$10   52019
1989 - 1999

Frosted Topiary, s/8,
Lg
$12   52027
1989 - 1999

Frosted Topiary, s/8,
Sm
$14   52035
1989 - 1999

Mini Spruce Forest
$50   65790
1989 - 1990

Winter Oak, Sm
$4.50   51810
1990 - 1994

Winter Oak, Lg
$8   51829
1990 - 1994

Sisal Trees, s/7
$16   51837
1990 - 1990

Frosted Evergreen
Papier-Maché, s/3
$16   65820
1990 - 1996

Evergreen Trees
$13   52051
1991 - 1997

Sisal Wreaths
$4   54194
1991 - 1998

Winter Birch Tree
$12.50   52167
1993 - 1996

Pine Cone Trees
$15   52213
1993 - 1995

Frosted Spruce Tree
15"
$12.50   52310
1994 - 1996

Frosted Spruce Tree
22"
$27.50   52329
1994 - 1996

Bare Branch Tree
With 25 Lights
$13.50   52434
1994 - 2001

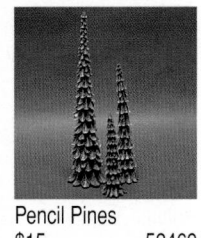

Pencil Pines
$15   52469
1994 - 1998

Autumn Maple Tree
$15   52540
1994 - 1997

Frosted Bare Branch
Tree, Sm
$6.50   52418
1995 - 1996

Frosted Bare Branch
Tree, Lg
$12.50   52426
1995 - 1996

Spruce Tree Forest
$25   52485
1995 - 1996

Frosted Zig–Zag Tree,
White
$10   52493
1995 - 1996

Frosted Zig–Zag Tree,
Green
$10   52507
1995 - 1996

Snowy White Pine
Tree, Sm
$15   52558
1995 - 1996

Snowy White Pine
Tree, Lg
$20   52566
1995 - 1996

Landscape
$16.50   52590
1995 -

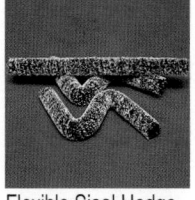

Flexible Sisal Hedge
$22   52596
1995 - 2001^M

Hybrid Landscape
$35   52600
1995 - 2006

Lighted Snowcapped
Revolving Tree
$35   52603
1995 - 1997

Lighted Snowcapped
Trees
$45   52604
1995 - 1997

Frosted Fir Trees
$15   52605
1995 - 1998

Cedar Pine Forest
$15   52606
1995 - 1998

Ponderosa Pines
$13   52607
1995 - 1998

Arctic Pines
$12   52608
1995 - 1998

Fallen Leaves
$5   52610
1995 -

Snowy Evergreen
Trees, Sm
$8.50   52612
1995 - 2000

Snowy Evergreen
Trees, Med
$25   52613
1995 - 2006

Snowy Evergreen
Trees, Lg
$32.50   52614
1995 - 2001

Snowy Scotch Pines
$15   52615
1995 - 2008

Autumn Trees
$13.50   52616
1995 - 1998

Wagon Wheel Pine
Grove
$22.50   52617
1995 - 1998

Pine Point Pond
$37.50   52618
1995 - 1999

Double Pine Trees
$13 - $25   52619
1995 - 1998

Jack Pines
$18   52622
1996 - 2006

Bare Branch Trees
$22.50   52623
1996 -

Holly Tree
$38   52630
1996 - 2000

Birch Tree Cluster
$20   52631
1996 - 2001

Towering Pines
$13.50   52632
1996 - 1999

Winter Birch
$22.50   52636
1996 -

Frosted Spruce
$25   52637
1996 - 2006

Frosted Hemlock
Trees
$32.50   52638
1996 - 1998

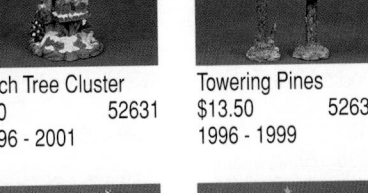

Town Tree
$35   52639
1996 - 1999

Autumn Birch/ Maple
Trees
$27.50   52655
1997 - 2006

Wintergreen Pines,
s/3
$7.50   52660
1997 - 2006

Wintergreen Pines,
s/2
$27   52661
1997 - 2003

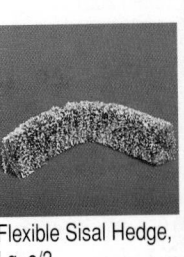

Flexible Sisal Hedge,
Lg, s/3
$10   52662
1997 -

Lighted Snowy Tree
$27.50   52683
1997 - 2000

Lighted Christmas
Tree
$48   52690
1997 - 1998

Flexible Autumn
Hedges
$10   52703
1998 - 2000

Decorated Sisal Trees
$12.50   52714
1998 - 2001

Craggy Oak Tree
$12.50   52748
1998 - 2001

Swinging Under The
Old Oak Tree
$22 - $40   52769
1998 - 2001^M

Pine Trees With Pine
Cones
$15   52771
1998 - 2001

Winter Pine Trees
With Pine Cones
$15   52772
1998 - 2001

Flocked Pine Trees,
s/3
$15   53367
1998 - 2000

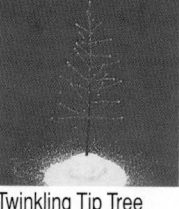

Twinkling Tip Tree
$24   52781
1999 - 2001

Pequot Pines
$50   52818
1999 - 2006

Pequot Pine, XLg
$32.50   52819
1999 - 2005

Twinkling Lit Town
Tree
$35   52837
1999 - 2001

Frosted Topiaries
$40   52842
1999 - 2001

Frosted Shrubbery
$20   52843
1999 - 2001

Frosty Light Trees
$20   52844
1999 - 2001

Up In The Apple Tree
$27 - $40   56640
1999 - 2000

Flocked Pine Trees,
s/2
$16   56715
1999 - 2001

Icicle Trees
$27.50   56722
1999 - 2001

Twinkling Lit Trees,
White
$32.50   56723
1999 - 2001[M]

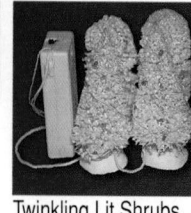

Twinkling Lit Shrubs,
White
$15   56724
1999 - 2001[M]

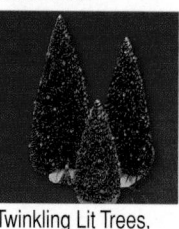

Twinkling Lit Trees,
Green
$32.50   52823
1999 -

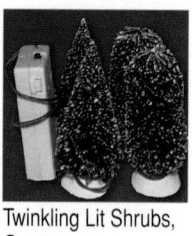

Twinkling Lit Shrubs,
Green
$15   52824
1999 - 2006

Celebration Tree
2000
$30   52850
2000[M] - 2001

Pinewood Trees, Lg
$26   56924
2000[M] - 2002

Pinewood Trees, Sm
$22   56925
2000[M] - 2002

Natural Evergreens,
s/8
$24   52885
2000 - 2006

Natural Evergreens,
s/16
$45   52886
2000 - 2003

Fiber Optic Trees
$17.50   52888
2000 - 2002

Icy Trees, Sm
$17.50   52889
2000 - 2003

Icy Trees, Med
$25   52890
2000 - 2003

Icy Tree, Lg
$27.50   52891
2000 - 2002

Winter Green Spruce
$17   52892
2000 - 2001

Landscape Starter
Set
$6.50   52898
2000 - 2006

Holly Topiaries
$12.50   52899
2000 - 2002

Holly Hedges
$15   52900
2000 - 2003

Holly Tree & Bush
$20   52901
2000 - 2001

Metal Bare Branch
Trees
$42   52931
2001^M - 2002

Village Twinkle Brite
Tree, Lg
$22.50   52301
2001 -

City Lit Bare Branch
Tree
$12.50   52973
2001 - 2006

Village Spring/
Summer Trees, s/4
$22.50   52974
2001 - 2007

Village Autumn Trees,
s/4
$22.50   52975
2001 - 2008

Village Winter Trees,
s/4
$22.50   52976
2001 - 2007

Village Twinkle Brite
Tree, Sm
$17.50   52983
2001 -

Fiber Optic Woods,
Green Trees
$48   52985
2001 - 2004

Fiber Optic Woods,
White Trees
$48   52986
2001 - 2003

Bag-O-Frosted
Topiaries, s/10
$8.50   52996
2001 -

Fiber Optic Woods
Grn Trees/Multi-lights
$94   53001
2001 - 2003

Tinsel Trees, s/4
$15   53012
2001 - 2006

Bag-O-Frosted
Topiaries, s/2
$6.50   53018
2001 -

Acrylic Green Glitter
Trees, s/3
$25   53032
2002ᴹ - 2005

Lighted Acrylic Trees,
s/2
$25   53033
2002ᴹ - 2003

Ice Crystal Pines, s/3
$50   53081
2002 - 2005

Lighted Crystal Pines,
s/3
$75   53083
2002 - 2004

Spring Oaks, s/2
$17.50   53084
2002 - 2006

Village Frosted
Spruce, Small, s/3
$20   53085
2002 -

Fall Oaks, s/2
$17.50   53086
2002 - 2006

Willow Trees, s/2
$17.50   53134
2003 - 2003

Lighted Street
Boulevard
$30   53137
2003 - 2006

Twisty Glitter Pines,
s/2
$22.50   53172
2004 - 2007

Christmas In The
Forest
$25   53178
2004 - 2006

Classic Tinsel Trees -
Red, Green, Silver
$10   53192
2004 - 2007

Lighted Christmas
Bare Branch Tree
$15   53193
2004 -

Lighted Peppermint
Tree, s/3
$30   53194
2004 - 2009

Urban Landscape, s/6
$35   53197
2004 - 2006

Classic Tinsel Trees
- White, s/3
$10   53207
2004 - 2006

Scotch Pines, s/3
$18 - $32   53612
2005 - 2008

Lighted Ornament
Trees, s/2
$30   53613
2005 - 2009

Lighted Holiday Hedges
$17   53615
2005 - 2007

Lighted Fresh Frost Trees
$32.50   53616
2006 - 2009

Lighted Christmas Gift Trees, S/2
$30   53617
2006 - 2008

Black Spruce Pines, S/3
$20   53618
2006 - 2008

Juniper Shrubs, S/6
$17.50   53619
2006-2008

Elegant Christmas Topiaries, S/6
$20   53620
2006 - 2008

Decorated Sisal Trees, S/7
$15   53621
2007^M - 2008

First Frost Trees, S/3
$17.50   800007
2007 -

Lit Tinsel Trees - White
$20   800008
2007 - 2009

Village Holiday Boughs, S/12
$12.50   800014
2007 -

Potted Spruce Tops, S/4
$10   800015
2007 - 2009

Classic Tinsel Trees - Bright Green, S/3
$12.50   800486
2007 - 2009

Classic Tinsel Trim - Bright Green, S/12
$12.50   800487
2007 - 2009

Wintergreen Trees, S/3
$25   800488
2007 - 2009

Frosted Sisal Tree, Tall
$42.50   802098
2007 - 2009

Frosted Sisal Trees, Large
$47.50   802099
2007 - 2009

Finial Trees, S/2
$30   802161
2007 - 2009

Potted Poinsettias, S/4
$10   802460
2007 -

Decorated Tree Set, S/5
$15   804459
2008^M - 2008

Snow Laden Sisal, S/3
$27.50   810836
2008 -

Twinkle Brite Frosted Topiary
$25   810837
2008 -

Twinkling Bare Branch Tree
$22.50   810839
2008 -

Garland And Bows
$10   810842
2008 -

Row-O-Frosted Topiaries, S/2
$12.50   810843
2008 -

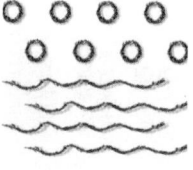

Village Jack Pines, Large, S/2
$50   810841
2008 -

Village Autumn Maple Trees, S/2
$22.50   810845
2008 -

Autumn Wreaths And Garland
$12.50   810847
2008 - 2009

Autumn Flexible Sisal Hedge
$12.50   810846
2008 -

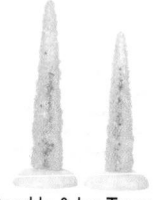

White Flexible Sisal Hedge
$12.50   810844
2008 -

Lit Crystal Tree
$25   809347
2010 -

Sparkle & Ice Trees, S/2
$35   809348
2010 -

Bejeweled Bare Branch Tree
$12.50   809349
2010 -

Lit Spiral Trees, S/2
$30   809350
2010 -

Heavy Snowed Pines, S/3
$20   809351
2010 -

Cypress Trees, S/4
$20   809352
2010 -

ELECTRICAL
ELECTRICAL
ELECTRICAL
ELECTRICAL
ELECTRICAL
ELECTRICAL
ELECTRICAL
ELECTRICAL
ELECTRICAL

Photo Not Available

Multi Color 10 Light Set
N/A   36323
1987 - 1989

Multi Colored 10 Light Set
N/A   36331
1987 - 1989

Photo Not Available

Amber 10 Light Set
N/A   36358
1987 - 1989

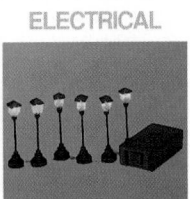

Street Lamps
$10   36366
1987 - 2000

Village Express Train - Black
$90   59978
1987 - 1988

Village Express Train - Red, Green
$95   59803
1988 - 1996

Streetlamp Wrapped In Garland
$10   59935
1988 - 1988

Streetlamp With Garland
$18   59943
1988 - 1988

Photo Not Available

Replacement Light Bulb
$2.50   99002
1988 - 1990

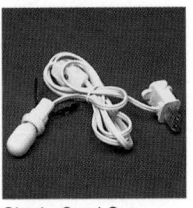

Single Cord Set
$3.50   99028
1988 -

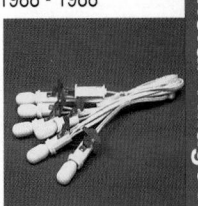

6 Socket Lite Set
$13   99279
1988 -

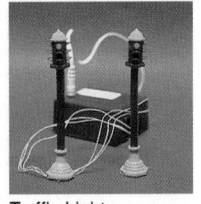

Traffic Light
$10   55000
1989 - 2001

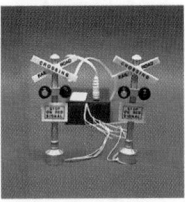

Railroad Crossing Sign
$10   55018
1989 - 2000

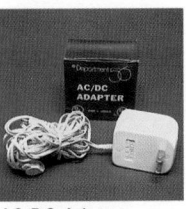

AC/DC Adapter
$10   55026
1989 -

Old World Streetlamp
$22   55034
1989 - 1991

Turn Of The Century Lamppost
$16   55042
1989 - 2006

Turn Of The Century Lamppost
$22   55050
1989 - 1991

Double Street Lamps
$13   59960
1989 -

Candles By The Doorstep
$7   52060
1990 - 1994

General Village Accessories

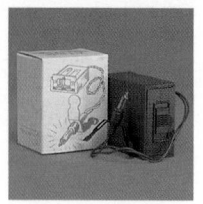

Battery Operated
Light
$2.50   99260
1990 - 1991

Lights Out Remote
Control
$25   52132
1991 - 1994

Mini Lights
$12.50   52159
1991 - 2000

Replacement Light
Bulbs
$2.50   99244
1991 -

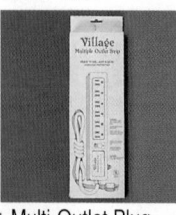

Multi-Outlet Plug
Strip, 6 Outlets
$10   99333
1991 - 2007

Yard Lights
$13   54160
1992 - 1994

I Love My Village
Brite Lites
$15   52221
1993 - 1997

Merry Christmas Brite
Lites
$13.50   52230
1993 - 2000

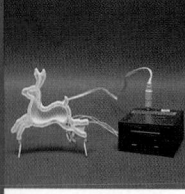

Reindeer Brite Lites
$10   52248
1993 - 1999

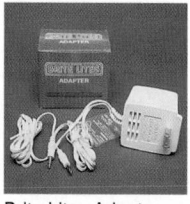

Brite Lites Adapter
$10   52256
1993 - 2006

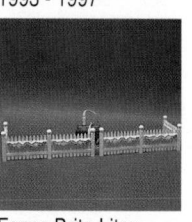

Fence Brite Lites
$19   52361
1993 - 1999

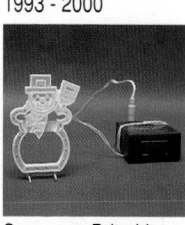

Snowman Brite Lites
$15   52370
1993 - 1999

Tree Brite Lites
$10   52388
1993 - 1999

Santa Brite Lites
$15   52396
1993 - 1999

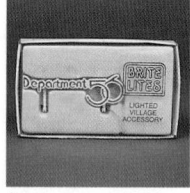

Department 56 Brite
Lites
$10   98469
1993 - 1997

Animated Skating
Pond
$60   52299
1994 - 2007

Streetcar
$65   52400
1994 - 1998

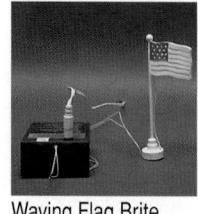

Waving Flag Brite
Lites
$15   52442
1994 - 1997

Set of 20 Red Lights
Brite Lites
$9   52450
1994 - 1997

Animated All Around
The Park
$95   52477
1994 - 1996

Coca-Cola Neon Sign
$10 - $18   54828
1994 - 1998

Let It Snow Machine
$85   52592
1995 - 1997

Up, Up & Away
$40   52593
1996 - 2001

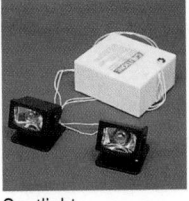

Spotlight
$7   52611
1996 - 2000

Mini Lights
$10   52626
1996 - 1998

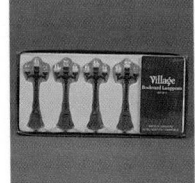

Boulevard Lampposts
$15   52627
1996 - 2006

Country Road
Lampposts, s/2
$12   52628
1996 - 1997

Revolving Turntable
$50   52640
1996 - 1999

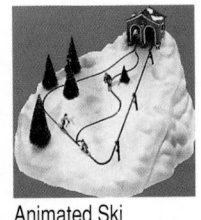

Animated Ski
Mountain
$75   52641
1996 - 1998

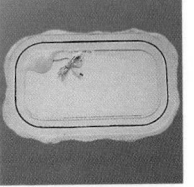

Animated Accessory
Track
$65   52642
1996 - 1999

Waterfall W/Electric
Pump
$65   52644
1996 - 1999

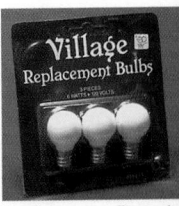

Replacement Round
Light Bulbs
$2   99245
1996 -

LED Light Bulb
$6.50   99247
1996 - 2000

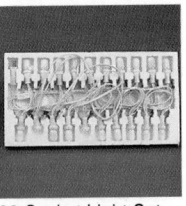

20 Socket Light Set
With Bulbs
$25   99278
1996 - 2006

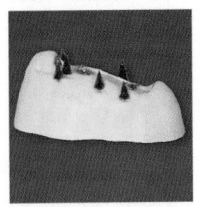

Animated Sledding
Hill
$65   52645
1997 - 2009

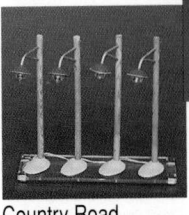

Country Road
Lampposts, s/4
$15   52663
1997 - 2001

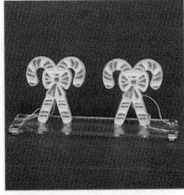

Candy Canes Brite
Lites
$18   52670
1997 - 1999

Angel Brite Lites
$15   52671
1997 - 1999

Snow Dragon Brite
Lites
$20   52672
1997 - 1999

Santa In Chimney
Brite Lites
$15   52673
1997 - 1999

Candles Brite Lites
$17   52674
1997 - 1999

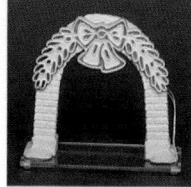

Holly Archway Brite
Lites
$25   52675
1997 - 1999

45 LED Light Strand
$22.50   52678
1997 -

Lighted Christmas
Pole
$32.50   52679
1997 - 2000

Road Construction
Sign
$12   52680
1997 - 2001ᴹ

Walkway Lights
$8   52681
1997 - 2000

Frosty Light Sprays
$12   52682
1997 - 1999

String Of Starry
Lights
$12.50   52684
1997 - 2000

Spotlight
Replacement Bulbs
$2.50   99246
1997 - 2000

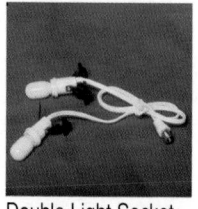

Double Light Socket
Adapter
$4   99280
1997 - 2006

Camden Park
Fountain
$84   52705
1998 - 2000

Carnival Carousel
LED Light Set
$20   52706
1998 - 2001

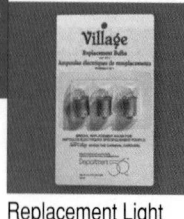

Replacement Light
Bulb, Clear
$3   52707
1998 - 2005

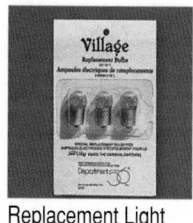

Replacement Light
Bulb, Yellow
$3   52708
1998 - 2005

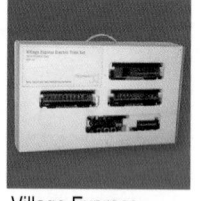

Village Express
Electric Train Set
$270   52710
1998 - 2006

Christmas Luminaries
$25   52715
1998 - 2002

Fireworks
$45   52727
1998 - 2004

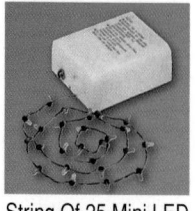

String Of 25 Mini LED
Lights
$10   52728
1998 - 2006

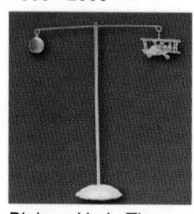

Biplane Up In The
Sky
$50   52731
1998 - 2000

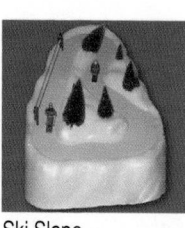

Ski Slope
$75   52733
1998 - 2009

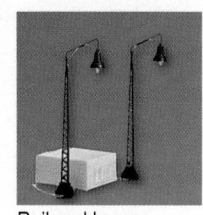

Railroad Lamps
$15   52760
1998 - 2001^M

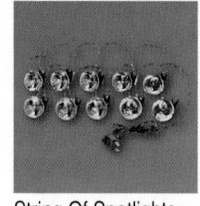

String Of Spotlights
$15   52779
1998 - 2002

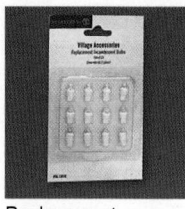

Replacement
Incandescent Bulbs
$4   13638
1999 - 2005

Animated Photo With
Santa
$90   52790
1999 - 2001^M

Through The Woods
Mountain Trail
$75   52791
1999 - 2003

Fireworks
Replacement Bulbs
$3.50   52800
1999 - 2004

Remote Switches,
Right & Left
$20   52807
1999 - 2005

Nativity Creche
$35   52822
1999 - 2007

Fieldstone Footbridge
$40   52827
1999 - 2006

Frosted Fountain
$58   52831
1999 - 2006

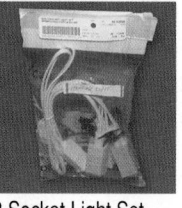

3 Socket Light Set
$7.50   52835
1999 -

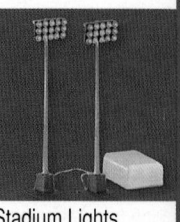

Stadium Lights
$22.50   52845
1999 - 2006

Bumper Fun Ride
$98   52500
2000^M - 2002

Look, It's The
Goodyear Blimp
$45   52501
2000^M - 2001

Santa's On His Way
$65   52502
2000^M - 2006

Replacement
Lightning Bulbs
$3   52846
2000^M -

Electric Foam Cutter
$25   52847
2000^M - 2007

Light Adapter for
NPW
$5   52852
2000^M - 2000

Light Adapter With 3
Jacks for NPW
$6   52853
2000^M - 2002

Mill Falls Working
Waterfall
$75   52503
2000 -2001

Holiday Singers
$75   52505
2000 - 2006

Festive Front Yard
$75 - $95   52506
2000 - 2006

Perfect Putt
$65   52508
2000 - 2001

Woodland Carousel
$75   52509
2000 - 2001

Village Junkyard
$98 - $99   52861
2000 - 2004

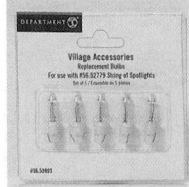

Repl Bulbs For 52779 String Of Spotlights
$15   52893
2000 - 2002

Repl Flickering Bulb For Creepy Creek Hs
$5   52904
2000 - 2005

Santa's Sleigh
$68   58630
2000 - 2007

Gondola Animated Scene
$85   52511
2001^M - 2009

Santa By The Light of The Moon
$37.50   52984
2001 - 2003

Hockey Practice, s/3
$37.50   52512
2001 - 2006

Valentine's Decorating Set, s/5
$34   53020
2002^M - 2004

Easter Decorating Set, s/5
$58   53021
2002^M - 2004

St. Patrick's Day Decorating Set, s/5
$22.50   53022
2002^M - 2004

4th Of July Decorating Set, s/5
$22.50   53024
2002^M - 2004

Sounds Of The North Woods
$85   53025
2002^M - 2006

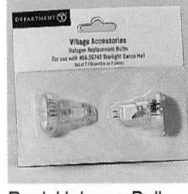

Repl. Halogen Bulb Starlight Dance Hall
$4   53027
2002^M - 2005

Packages Delivery
$31   53038
2002 - 2004

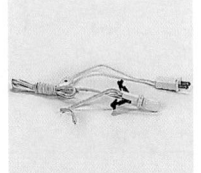

Replacement Aux. Cord With Light
$4.50   53039
2002 -

Snowflake Light Poles, s/4
$17.50   53049
2002 - 2006

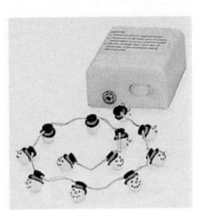

String Of 12
Snowman Lights
$10   53053
2002 - 2004

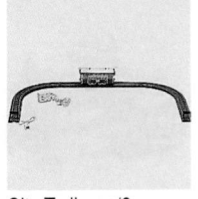

City Trolley, s/6
$75   53054
2002 - 2004

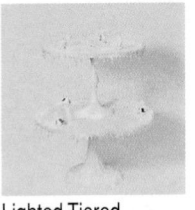

Lighted Tiered
Platform
$250   53089
2002 - 2004

Sounds Of The City
$52   53111
2003 - 2005

Replacement 3 Volt
Light Bulb, s/2
$4   53121
2003 -

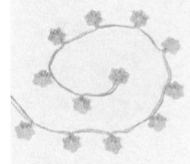

String Of 12
Snowflake Lights
$10   53122
2003 - 2006

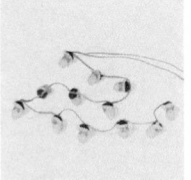

String Of 12 Santa
Lights
$10   53123
2003 - 2006

Year Round Lighted
Lawn Orns. , s/6
$30   53125
2003 - 2005

Village Twinkling
Snow Tree Skirt
$50   53152
2003 - 2004

Village Twinkling
Blanket Of Snow
$30   53153
2003 - 2005

Let's Swing!
$30   53154
2004^M - 2006

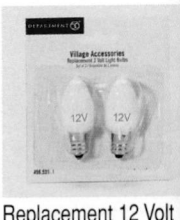

Replacement 12 Volt
Light Bulbs, s/2
$4   53161
2004 -

Clearing The
Driveway Again!
$60   53184
2004 - 2007

Figure Skater On Ice
$35   53185
2004 - 2009

Winter Sled Ride
$40   53186
2004 - 2008

String Of 12 Christmas
Candy Lights
$10   53187
2004 - 2006

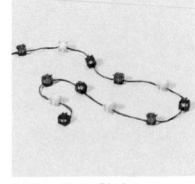

String of 12 Christmas
Presents Lights
$10   53188
2004 - 2006

Snowman Street
Lights, s/2
$17   53189
2004 -

Christmas Star Street
Lights, s/2
$15   53190
2004 - 2006

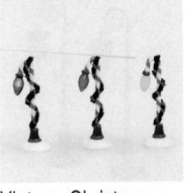

Vintage Christmas
Lights Street Lights
$15   53191
2004 - 2007

Multi-Building Lighting
System
$35   53204
2004 - 2005

Backyard Christmas
Greenhouse
$35   53306
2005 - 2007

Classic Village
Square
$118   53406
2005 - 2008

Go Fly A Kite
$40 - $68   53407
2005 - 2007

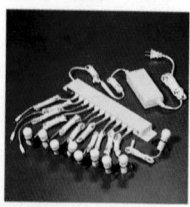

Buildings & Acc.
Lighting System
$50   53500
2005 -

Lighting Retrofit Unit
$17.50   53501
2005 -

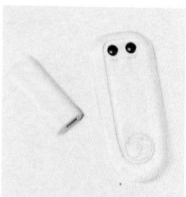

Lighting Remote
Control Starter Kit
$25   53502
2005 -

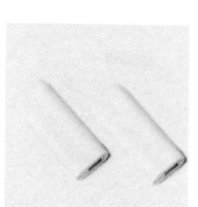

Lighting Remote
Control Receivers
$20   53504
2005 -

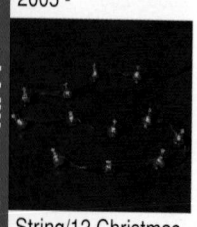

String/12 Christmas
Tree Lights
$12.50   53505
2005 - 2007

Classic Street Lights
$15   53506
2005 - 2007

Snowboard Hill
$80^M   53408
2006^M - 2009

Christmas Front Yard
$75   53318
2006 - 2008

Jingle Bells Sound
Scene, *Tune: Jingle Bells*
$60   53325
2006 - 2008

A New Bike For
Christmas
$70   53409
2006 - 2008

Skating Around The
Christmas Tree
$70   53424
2006 - 2009

Santa Land Train
Ride
$75   53430
2006 - 2008

Ornate Street Lamps,
S/2
$18.50   53507
2006 - 2009

Globe Street Lamps,
S/2
$15   53508
2006 - 2008

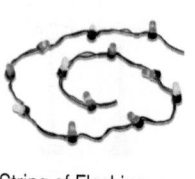

String of Flashing
LED Lights
$15   53509
2006 -

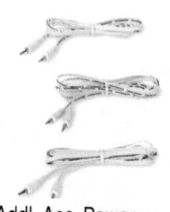

Addl. Acc. Power
Cords for Bldgs., S/3
$7.50   53597
2007^M -

516

Addl. Bldg. Light
Cords, S/3
$10   53598
2007ᴹ -

Display Anywhere
Lighting AC Adaptor
$7.50   53599
2007ᴹ -

Lit Acrylic Yard
Decorations, S/3
$22.50   800003
2007 - 2009

Holiday Street
Lamps, S/2
$20   800004
2007 -

Fifty-Six Street Lights,
S/2
$20   800006
2007 -

Santa Street Lights,
S/2
$20   800011
2007 - 2009

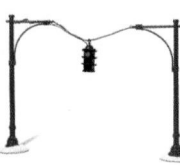

Village Main Street
Stoplights
$22.50   800020
2007 - 2009

New Animated
Skating Pond
$80   801130
2007 -

Village Corner
Stoplights, S/2
$20   802109
2007 -

Holly-Covered
Lampposts
$20   810827
2008 -

Small Town Street
Lamps
$20   810828
2008 -

Northern Lights
$50   810829
2008 -

Classic Luminaries
$15   810830
2008 -

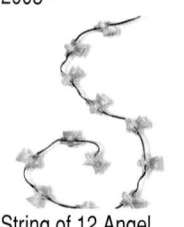

String of 12 Angel
Lights
$15   810832
2008 - 2009

String of 12 Bow
Lights
$15   810833
2008 - 2009

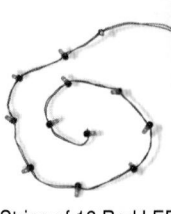

String of 12 Red LED
Lights
$12.50   810834
2008 -

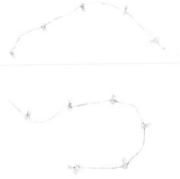

String of 12 Super-
Brite White Lights
$15   810835
2008 -

Fun At The Dog Park
$75   810809
2008 -

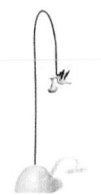

Up, Up & Away
Assortment
$65   810810
2008 -

Village MP3
Speakers
$50   810808
2008 -

Santa's Sleigh, Lit
Yard Decorations
$25   810812
2008 -

Building A Snowman
$60   809008
2010 -

Swan Pond
$45   809009
2010 -

Uptown Street Lights
$20   809331
2010 -

WALLS
FENCES
GATES
WALLS
FENCES
GATES
WALLS
FENCES
GATES

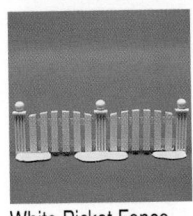

White Picket Fence
$3   51004
1987 - 2000

White Picket Fence
s/4
$12   51012
1987 - 1997

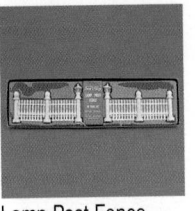

Lamp Post Fence
$13   55069
1989 - 1991

Photo Not Available

Lamp Post Fence
$13   55077
1989 - 1989

Lamp Post Fence
Extension
$3   55085
1989 - 1991

Photo Not Available

Lamp Post Extension
$10   55093
1989 - 1989

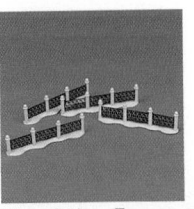

Wrought Iron Fence
$2.50 each   59986
1989 - 1998

Snow Fence
$7   52043
1991 - 1998

Frosty Tree-Lined
Picket Fence
$6.50   52078
1991 - 1997

Tree-Lined Courtyard
Fence
$4   52124
1990 - 1998

Wrought Iron Gate
And Fence
$15-$29   55140
1991 - 1998

Wrought Iron Fence
Extensions
$12.50   55158
1991 - 1998

Wrought Iron Fence
$10   59994
1991 - 1999

Courtyard Fence With
Steps
$4   52205
1992 - 1998

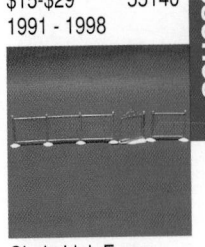

Chain Link Fence
With Gate
$16   52345
1993 - 1998

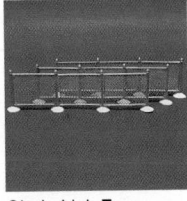

Chain Link Fence
Extensions
$20   52353
1993 - 1998

Victorian Wrought
Iron Fence w/Gate
$24 - $78   52523
1994 - 2001^M

Victorian Wrought
Iron Fence Extension
$15   52531
1994 - 2001^M

Split Rail Fence, With
Mailbox
$12.50   52597
1995 - 1997

General Village Accessories

519

Twig Snow Fence,
Wood
$6   52598
1995 - 2000

White Picket Fence
With Gate
$10   52624
1996 - 1998

White Picket Fence
Extensions
$10   52625
1996 - 1998

Stone Wall
$2.50   52629
1996 -

Stone Curved Wall/
Bench
$15   52650
1997 - 2001

Snow Fence
$7   52657
1997 -

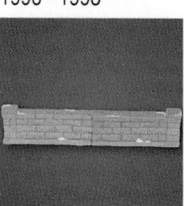

Camden Park Square
Stone Wall
$2.50   52689
1997 - 2000

Fieldstone Wall
$3.50   52717
1998 - 2007

Fieldstone Entry Gate
$11   52718
1998 - 2001M

Holly Split Rail Fence
$18   52722
1998 - 2001

Holly Split Rail Fence
w/Seated Children
$32   52723
1998 - 2001

Stone Wall With Sisal
Hedge
$5   52724
1998 - 2001

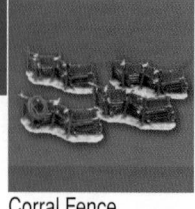

Corral Fence
$32   52746
1998 - 2001

Fieldstone Wall With
Apple Tree
$17 - $48   52768
1998 - 2001M

Tall Stone Walls
$20   52825
1999 - 2009

Fieldstone Curved
Wall/Bench, s/4
$15   53009
2001 - 2006

Brick Walls, s/4
$12.50   53312
2005 - 2009

Brick Edged Steps
$10   53315
2005 - 2009

Brick Edged
Sidewalk, s/4
$12.50   53701
2005 - 2009

Village Fence
$15   53328
2006 - 2008

Village Steps, S/2
$12.50   800016
2007 -

Village Straight Fence
S/4
$25   800021
2007 -

Split Rail Fence
$18.50   810823
2008 -

Limestone Wall
$12.50   810853
2008 -

City Fence
$17.50   809011
2010 -

SNOW & ICE
SNOW & ICE
SNOW & ICE
SNOW & ICE
SNOW & ICE
SNOW & ICE
SNOW & ICE
SNOW & ICE
SNOW & ICE

General Village Accessories

Real Plastic Snow
7 oz. Bag
$3　　　　　49981
1977 - 2006

Real Plastic Snow
2 lb. Box
$10　　　　49999
1977 - 2000

Acrylic Icicles
$4.50　　　52116
1990 - 2000

Blanket Of New
Fallen Snow
$7.50　　　49956
1991 -

**Photo Not
Available**

Let It Snow Crystals,
8 oz. Box
$6.50　　　49964
1991 - 1992

Fresh Fallen Snow 7
oz. Bag
$3.20　　　49979
1995 -

Fresh Fallen Snow 2
lb. Box
$12　　　　49980
1995 - 2000

Clear Ice
$6.50　　　52729
1998 - 2001ᴹ

Glistening Snow
$10　　　　53362
1998 - 2001

Ice Crystal Blanket Of
Snow
$6　　　　　52841
1999 -

Ice Crystal Gate &
Walls
$32.50　　56716
1999 - 2002

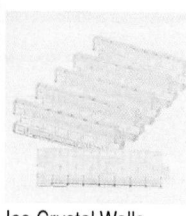

Ice Crystal Walls
$15　　　　56717
1999 - 2001

Pine Scented Fresh
Fallen Snow
$4.30　　　52848
2000 - 2004

First Frost Snow
Crystals
$3.50　　　52906
2000 - 2006

Crushed Ice
$5　　　　　52908
2000 - 2003

Acrylic Ice Block
Display Piece
$20　　　　53088
2002 - 2004

Real Acrylic Ice, mini,
bag of 12
$10　　　　44476
2003ᴹ -

Real Acrylic Ice,
small, bag of 6
$10　　　　44477
2003ᴹ -

Real Acrylic Ice,
medium, bag of 4
$12.50　　44478
2003ᴹ -

Real Removable
Snow, s/10
$5   53101
2003 - 2005

Village Real Acrylic
Ice, s/22
$10   53141
2003 - 2007

Real Acrylic Icicles
$5   53151
2003 - 2005

MISCELLANEOUS
MISCELLANEOUS
MISCELLANEOUS
MISCELLANEOUS
MISCELLANEOUS
MISCELLANEOUS
MISCELLANEOUS
MISCELLANEOUS
MISCELLANEOUS

General Village Accessories

Park Bench
$3.20   51098
1987 - 1993

Town Clock
$3   51101
1988 - 1998

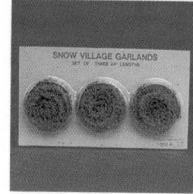

SV Garland Trim
$4.50   51128
1988 - 1991

Up On A Roof Top
$6.50   51390
1988 - 1999

Birds
$3.50   51802
1989 - 1994

Christmas Eave Trim
$3.50   55115
1989 - 2006

Town Square Gazebo
$13 - $34   55131
1989 - 1997

Mylar Skating Pond
$6   52086
1991 - 2000

Brick Road
$10   52108
1991 - 2009

"It's A Grand Old
Flag"
$4   54178
1991 - 1997

Greetings
$5   54186
1991 - 1994

Cobblestone Road
$10   59846
1991 - 2009

Tacky Wax
$2.50   52175
1992 -

"Village Sounds" Tape
With Speakers
$25   55247
1992 - 1994

"Village Sounds" Tape
$8   55255
1992 - 1994

Mountain, Sm
$31 - $57   52264
1992 - 2000

Mountain, Med
$94   52272
1992 - 2000

Mountain, Lg
$150   52280
1992 - 2004

Heritage Banners
$6   55263
1992 - 1995

Heritage Village
Promotional Banner
$0   09482
1992 - 1992

Wrought Iron Park
Bench
$5   52302
1993 -

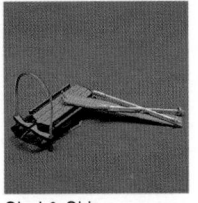

Sled & Skis
$22   52337
1993 - 2000

Mountain Backdrop
$65   52574
1994 - 2005

Mountain Tunnel
$37.50   52582
1994 - 2000

Let It Snow Snowman
Sign
$12.50   52594
1995 - 1998

Pink Flamingos
$7.50   52595
1995 - 2006

Election Yard Signs
$10   52599
1995 - 1997

Brick Town Square
$15   52601
1995 - 2007

Cobblestone Town
Square
$15   52602
1995 - 2007

Magic Smoke
$2.50   52620
1996 - 2000

Mill Creek
(Straight Section)
$36   52633
1996 - 2001

Mill Creek
(Curved Section)
$38   52634
1996 - 2001

Mill Creek Bridge
$72   52635
1996 - 2000

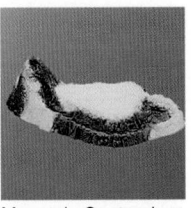

Mountain Centerpiece
$58   52643
1996 - 2000

Stone Footbridge
$16   52646
1997 - 2007

Stone Trestle Bridge
$37.50   52647
1997 - 2001[M]

Stone Holly Corner
Posts And Archway
$20   52648
1997 - 2007

Stone Holly Tree
Corner Posts
$12   52649
1997 - 2000

Mill Creek Pond
$55   52651
1997 - 2002

General Village Accessories

Village Gazebo
$26   52652
1997 - 2000

Mill Creek Wooden
Bridge
$32.50   52653
1997 - 2002

Mill Creek Park
Bench
$14   52654
1997 - 1999

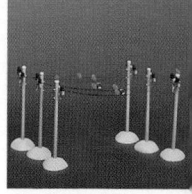

Telephone Poles
$18   52656
1997 - 2001

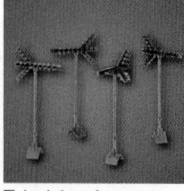

Television Antenna
$5   52658
1997 - 1999

Weather Vane
$6.50   52659
1997 - 1999

Log Pile
$6.50   52665
1997 -

Two Lane Paved
Road
$15   52668
1997 - 2006

Blue Skies Backdrop
$7.50   52685
1997 - 2000

Starry Night Sky
Backdrop
$7.50   52686
1997 - 2000

Camden Park Square
$58   52687
1997 - 2000

Camden Park
Cobblestone Road
$10   52691
1997 - 2001

Holiday Tinsel Trims
$8   52712
1998 - 2000

Tinsel Trims
$8   52713
1998 - 2007

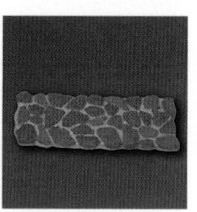

Slate Stone Path
Straight
$3   52719
1998 -

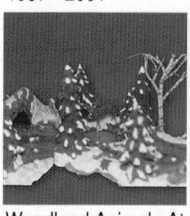

Woodland Animals At
Mill Creek
$32.50   52720
1998 - 2001

Stone Stairway
$13 - $23   52725
1998 - 2009

Green
$12.50   52739
1998 - 2007

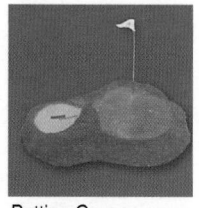

Putting Green
$48   52740
1998 - 2002

Moose In The Marsh
$25   52742
1998 - 1999

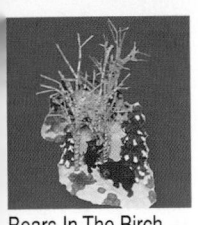

Bears In The Birch
$25   52743
1998 - 2003

Foxes In The Forest
$22.50   52744
1998 - 2000

Thoroughbreds
$29 - $60   52747
1998 - 2001

Gray Cobblestone Section
$7.50   52751
1998 - 2000

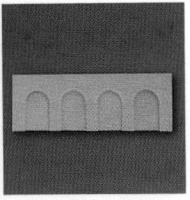

Gray Cobblestone Archway
$10   52752
1998 - 2000

Gray Cobblestone Tunnel
$6.50   52753
1998 - 2000

Real Gray Gravel
$5   52754
1998 - 2000

Gray Cobblestone Capstones
$6   52755
1998 - 2000

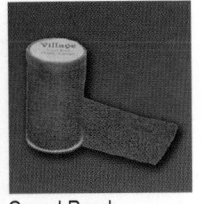

Gravel Road
$10   52756
1998 - 2000

Wolves In The Woods
$25   52765
1998 - 2001

Wooden Pier
$40   52766
1998 - 2005

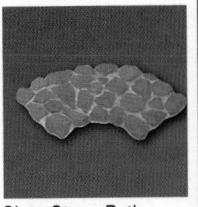

Slate Stone Path Curved
$3   52767
1998 - 2007

Grassy Ground Cover
$7.50   53347
1998 - 2006

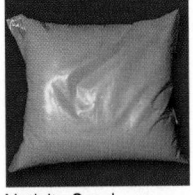

Nativity Sand
$6.50   41430
1999 - 2001ᴹ

Craggy Cliff Platform
$42   52794
1999 - 2003

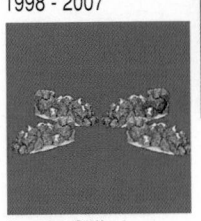

Craggy Cliff Extensions
$25   52795
1999 - 2003

Wooden Rowboats
$14 - $30   52797
1999 - 2002

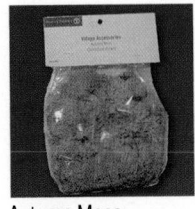

Autumn Moss
$7.50   52802
1999 - 2001

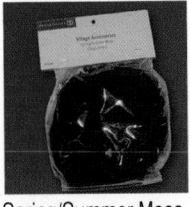

Spring/Summer Moss
$7   52803
1999 - 2001

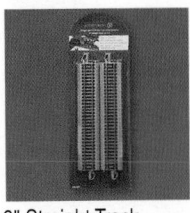

9" Straight Track
$12.50   52808
1999 - 2005

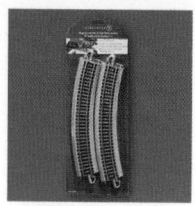

18" Radius Curved
Track
$12.50   52809
1999 - 2005

Personalize Your
Village Accessories
$9 - $16   52811
1999 - 2001

Woodland Wildlife
Animals, Lg
$32.50   52813
1999 - 2007

Majestic Woodland
Birds
$25   52814
1999 - 2002

Woodland Animals At
Cliff's Edge
$75   52816
1999 -2001

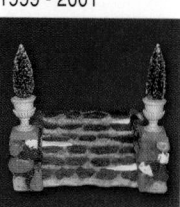

Fieldstone Stairway
$11 - $20   52826
1999 - 2001

Cats & Dogs
$15   52828
1999 - 2007

Lookout Tower
$18 - $50   52829
1999 - 2001

Wooden Canoes
$14 - $42   52830
1999 - 2003

The Trout Stream
$33 - $60   52834
1999 - 2005

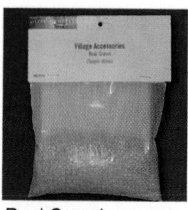

Real Gravel
$5   52839
1999 - 2001ᴹ

Ground Cover
$12.50 ea.   52840
1999 - 2006

Family Winter Outing
$16 - $28   55033
1999 - 2001

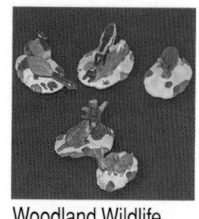

Woodland Wildlife
Animals, Sm
$27.50   55525
1999 - 2005

North Pole Photo
With Santa
$7.50   56444
1999 - 2000

Red Wrought Iron
Park Bench
$5   56445
1999 -

Park Bench
$7.50   52851
2000 - 2001

The Dockhouse
$40   52863
2000 - 2005

Mountain Lion's Den
$22.50   52864
2000 - 2001

Buffalo On The
Prairie
$22.50   52865
2000 - 2001

Birds Out Back
$30   52866
2000 - 2003

Smokehouse Incense
Burner
$15   52880
2000 - 2001

Balsam Fir Incense
$5   52881
2000 - 2001

Village Sign and
Bench
$20   52882
2000 - 2001

Fabric Cobblestone
Road
$10   52884
2000 - 2007

Light Hole Protectors
$7.50   52887
2000 - 2004

Mill Creek Campsite
$55   52894
2000 - 2005

The Woodshed &
Chopping Block
$50   52895
2000 - 2003

Personalize Pen
$5   52897
2000 - 2003

Mountain Stream
$150   52909
2000 - 2004

Good Fishing
$118s   56643
2000 - 2005

Winter Scene
Backdrop
$45   52930
2001 - 2003

Here Fishy Fishy Ice
House
$60   52937
2001 - 2004

Watching For Ducks,
s/2
$30   52938
2001 - 2004

Turkeys/Geese In The
Field, s/2
$27.50   52939
2001 - 2004

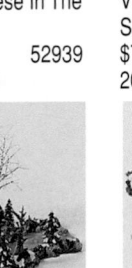

Village Lamppost And
Sign
$7.50   52940
2001 - 2002

American Flags, s/7
$12.50   52943
2001 - 2004

Village Flea Market,
s/38
$78   52945
2001 - 2003

Mountain Creek Y
Shape
$42.50   52946
2001 - 2005

Dog And Puppies,
Cat And Kittens, s/2
$50   52948
2001 - 2004

Village Bicycle And
Tricycle, s/2
$32   52950
2001 - 2004

Deer In The Woods
$22.50   52953
2001 - 2005

Bald Eagle Nesting
$18.50   52972
2001 - 2003

Village Mountain High
$75   52977
2001 - 2005

Village Moss 4 Asst'd
Colors
$7.50   52979
2001 - 2008

Woodland Landscape
Set, s/9
$35   52989
2001 - 2003

Snowy Landscape
Set, s/5
$48   52990
2001 - 2002

City Landscape Set,
s/13
$35   52993
2001 - 2004

Mallard And Wood
Duck, s/2
$12.50   53002
2001 - 2003

Mountain Creek
Waterfall
$88   53003
2001 - 2006

Mountain Creek
Curved Section
$17.50   53005
2001 - 2006

Mountain Creek
Straight Section, s/2
$48   53006
2001 - 2006

Fieldstone Fireplace
$12.50   53010
2001 - 2003

Mountain Creek Bear/
Moose, s/2
$22.50   53017
2001 - 2003

A Christmas Eve
Flight Backdrop
$45   53037
2002 - 2004

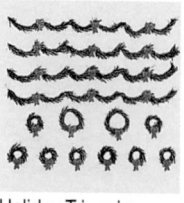
Holiday Trimmings,
s/14
$10   53042
2002 - 2006

Village Boats, s/2
$20   53043
2002 - 2005

A Harvest Feast
$93   53045
2002 - 2005

Rocky Mt. Wildlife-
Bears/Bobcat, s/2
$30   53047
2002 - 2005

Seasonal Lampposts,
s/4
$17.50   53048
2002 - 2004

Village Santa Sign
$7   53051
2002 - 2003

Village Roll Of Moss
$20   53052
2002 -

Spring/Summer
Landscape Set, s/10
$35   53076
2002 - 2004

Create A Scene
Village Platform
$32   53093
2003ᴹ - 2004

Snowy Platform, s/3
$20   53094
2003ᴹ - 2006

Summer Platform, s/3
$20   53095
2003ᴹ - 2005

Fall Platform, s/3
$20   53096
2003ᴹ - 2005

Potted Poinsettias,
s/4
$7.50   53105
2003 - 2007

Fresh Flower Cart
$20   53106
2003 - 2005

Winter Trimmings
$45   53107
2003 - 2005

Harvest Bounty
$65   53108
2003 - 2005

Spring Is Everywhere!
$88   53109
2003 - 2005

Fishing At Trout Lake
$50   53110
2003 - 2005

Brick Path, s/6
$15   53136
2003 - 2007

Autumn Landscape
Set, s/27
$35   53138
2003 - 2006

Winter Wonderland
Landscape Set, s/11
$35   53140
2003 - 2005

Holiday Streetlights,
s/2
$10   59427
2003 - 2005

Wiener Roast
$18.50   53179
2004 - 2006

The Ice Man Waiteth,
s/2
$25 - $45   53181
2004 - 2006

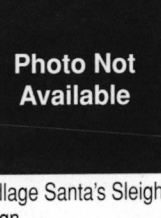

**Photo Not
Available**

Village Santa's Sleigh
Sign
$7   53183
2004 - 2006

General Village Accessories

531

Winter Display
Platforms, s/2
$15   53202
2004 - 2006

Formal Fountain
$17.50   53321
2006 - 2008

Clothes Line In The
Yard
$15   53329
2006 - 2008

Paws And Refresh
$7.50   800010
2007 -

Slate Stone Corners
$15   800012
2007 -

Snowman Watertower
$37.50   800013
2007 -

Village Mail Boxes,
S/4
$15   800017
2007 - 2009

Village Post Box
$5   800018
$2007 -

Village Stop Signs,
S/2
$7.50   800019
2007 - 2009

Village Parking
Meters, S/4
$7.50   802461
2007 -

City Park Bench
$5   810813
2008 -

Hung Out To Dry
$15   810814
2008 - 2009

English Phone Booth
$12.50   810815
2008 -

Village Drinking
Fountain
$8.50   810816
2008 -

Put Litter In Its Place
$8.50   810817
2008 -

Village Flamingos
$10   810818
2008 -

Stock Yard Sign
$3.50   810819
2008 - 2009

Village Scooters
$20   810820
2008 -

Christmas Eve
Caution Signs
$10   810821
2008 - 2009

Village Construction
Zone
$25   810822
2008 - 2009

Hay Bales
$7.50   810824
2008 -

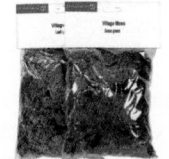

Village Spring Moss
$10   810850
2008 -

Village Autumn Moss
$10   810851
2008 -

Village Deep Blue
Sea
$20   810852
2008 - 2009

City Signs
$7.50   809012
2010 -

Fire Hydrant, Paper
Box
$7.50   809013
2010 -

Downtown Tinsel Trim
$12.50   809014
2010 -

Hanging Icicles
$7.50   809015
2010 -

She Shoots, She
Scores!
$20   809016
2010 -

Cobblestone Street
$9.50   809356
2010 -

Brick Street
$9.50   809357
2010 -

Limestone Topiaries
$10   809358
2010 -

Limestone Steps
$10   809359
2010 -

ITEM NUMBER INDEX

HOW DESIGNS ARE LISTED:

For years Department 56 used hyphens in its item numbers. For instance, a design's item number may have been 1234-5. However, several years ago, the company stopped using the hyphens. Therefore, all hyphens are omitted in both the index as well as in the content of the book. That same design's number would now appear as 12345.

Item Number Index

538

ALPHABETICAL INDEX

Village Resources

Examine the following pages to find...

...Information about the National Council of 56 Clubs (NCC).
Learn how you can attend and enjoy collector events, buy exclusive
club pieces and pins, get plugged into a local club, and expand your
knowledge base through online forums and club seminars. See how
NCC can enhance your enjoyment of your hobby!

**...Reputable retailers with brick-and-mortar stores and mail
order or online options.** They will be happy to help you find
whatever new piece you happen to be looking for.

**...Creative solutions to any display problems you might be
facing.** Whatever you're looking for — miniature accessories,
backgrounds, or resources to help you come up with new and
creative ideas — you'll find it all here.

...Dealers who both buy and sell secondary market pieces. You
can find that elusive piece you've been searching for, replace a
damaged piece, or downsize your current collection and make
room for more!

National Council of 56 Clubs

NCC Traders
Pin Shop

Why Join an NCC Club?

- ➤ Make friends with good people who understand your addiction.
- ➤ Learn the latest news about D56 products and your villages.
- ➤ Obtain the exclusive NCC pieces, when available, such as the "NCC Traders Pin Shop" and 2007's "Snowflake" accessory.
- ➤ Discuss the many techniques for making mountains and water.
- ➤ Discover the subtle nuances of lighting methods.
- ➤ Find out about special deals, closeouts and sales.
- ➤ Win door, game and contest prizes.

- ➤ Take excursions to gatherings, home tours and yard sales.
- ➤ Learn more about your village and display techniques from seasoned collectors.
- ➤ Contribute to a good cause. (Most NCC clubs support local charities.)
- ➤ Glean information and ideas from other clubs and collectors in the U.S. and Canada through the NCC Bulletin.
- ➤ Have others help you search for missing pieces.
- ➤ Meet new collector friends from outside your area in the NCC hospitality rooms at gatherings and conventions.

How to Find a Club

- ➤ Ask your local dealer.
- ➤ Visit the National Council of 56 Club's web site at www.ncc56.com
- ➤ Inquire at Internet chat sites
- ➤ Watch for special feature articles on collectors and check the events column in your local newspaper.
- ➤ Introduce yourself to fellow shoppers.
- ➤ Attend village conventions and collectable shows. (The NCC often provides informational tables.)
- ➤ Contact the NCC for help in starting your own club.

Snowflake

The National Council of 56 Clubs is an independent umbrella organization to help Department 56 collector clubs. The NCC is operated by volunteers dedicated to the goal of "clubs helping clubs help collectors."

NCC
30 Stag Mountain Road
New Hartford, CT 06057
860.482.7935
presidentncc@ncc56.com
www.ncc56.com

NEWS GAZETTE – page 2

House Fire Destroys Valuable Village Collection

Thousands of dollars worth of buildings and accessories were destroyed in a fierce blaze that ravaged a collector's home.

CHERRY HILL - The home of a well-known collectible village enthusiast was consumed by fire on Wednesday night, destroying a large, highly-detailed model village display. While there were no injuries, much of the collection was uninsured. "We assumed it was covered by our homeowners policy", said the stunned collectors. "We were sch~~ooked~~

Now is not the time to find out about exclusions in a homeowners policy.

You've spent years building your valuable collection. Don't let your investment vanish in a flash – protect it with a specialty policy from American Collectors Insurance. Find out the facts by contacting us for a quote today.

American Collectors Insurance

If it's worth collecting, it's worth protecting.™

Affordable Rates • Superior Service • Agreed Value • Industry Leader

Get an instant quote: www.AmericanCollectors.com/collect • 1-877-852-3484

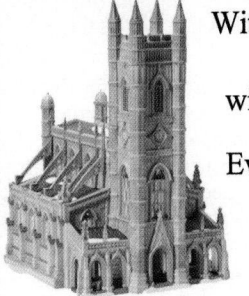

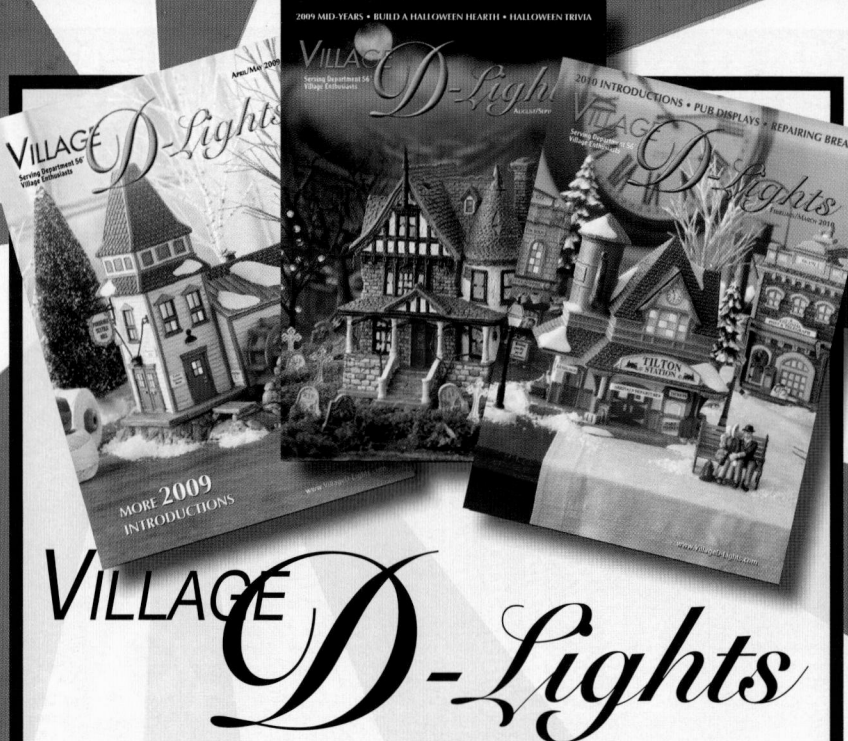

VILLAGE D-Lights

The "Village" Publication Serving Collectors
and Display Builders

Read Village D-Lights for

- How-to articles
- New releases from Deparment 56®
- Updates from Melinda Seegers
- Events Calendar
- Collector Displays
- Information on unique building variations
- News from the National Council of 56 Clubs

Subscriptions Only $26.95 • 1 Year • 6 Issues

Call 800.352.8039

Visit www.VillageD-Lights.com

Mention that you saw this ad in Village D-tails
and receive a free sample copy!

A Pioneer Communications, Inc. Publication

Village D-tails & Village Handbook

Ordering Information

For more copies,
order one of three ways:

1.) Internet

Purchase *Village D-tail* or *Village Handbook* online at the
Village D-Lights magazine website: **www.VillageD-Lights.com**

2.) Mail

Send check and mailing address to:
Village D-tails
P.O. Box 306
Grundy Center, IA 50638

U.S. Residents: $29.95 for Village D-tails ($24.95 + $5 shipping); $2.95 for
Village Handbook (add $1 for shipping if not ordering with Village D-tails)

Canadian Residents: $34.95 for Village D-tails ($24.95 + $10 shipping); $2.95 for
Village Handbook (add $1.50 for shipping if not ordering with Village D-tails)

All other international residents should call our office at 800.352.8039
to get shipping rates

3.) Phone

Call our office today to place your *Village D-tails* or
Village Handbook order: **800.352.8039**

A Closing Note of Thanks…

We would like to say thank you to our team of people who contributed to *Village D-tails* and the *Village Handbook* in numerous areas: production, editorial, typesetting, proofing, sales, graphic design, shipping, and simply generating ideas. Many thanks to: Brenda Abels, Alicia Fryslie, Heather Greiner, Ronda Jans, Linda Kruger, Sally Kueker, Deb Ringena, and the staff at Pioneer Graphics in Waterloo, Iowa, and our CEO Jim Slife.